Mike Alfr

Mike Alfreds was born in London and trained as a director at Carnegie Mellon University in Pittsburgh. He lived in the USA for eight years, during which time he worked for MGM Studios in Hollywood, was artistic director of Theatre West, Tucson, and then of the Cincinnati Playhouse-in-the-Park. For five years he worked in Israel where he became artistic director of the Jerusalem Khan Theatre. He has also worked in Australia, New Zealand, Canada, Germany, Norway, China and Mongolia. In the UK, he founded Shared Experience and ran it for thirteen years. He was artistic director of Cambridge Theatre Company, later renamed Method & Madness, and has directed for the Royal Shakespeare Company, Shakespeare's Globe, the Royal National Theatre, where he was an associate director, as well as for several regional repertory theatres. He has staged over two hundred productions, and won awards both abroad and in the UK. He has adapted novels and stories for the stage, devised performances and translated the texts of several of his productions. He maintains a parallel career as a teacher. He was a senior lecturer at Tel Aviv University and on the staff of LAMDA. He frequently gives courses on acting, directing, improvising and storytelling. His book, *Different Every Night*, also published by Nick Hern Books, describes his approach to theatre and some of his rehearsal processes when working on plays.

THEN WHAT HAPPENS?

Storytelling and Adapting for the Theatre

Mike Alfreds

NICK HERN BOOKS

London
www.nickhernbooks.co.uk

A Nick Hern Book

Then What Happens?
first published in Great Britain in 2013
by Nick Hern Books Limited
The Glasshouse, 49a Goldhawk Road, London W12 8QP

Copyright © 2013 Mike Alfreds

Reprinted 2015

Mike Alfreds has asserted his moral right
to be identified as the author of this work

Cover designed by Peter Bennett
Typeset by Nick Hern Books, London
Printed and bound in Great Britain
by Ashford Colour Press Ltd, Gosport, Hampshire

A CIP catalogue record for this book
is available from the British Library

ISBN 978 1 84842 270 4

MIX
Paper from
responsible sources
FSC
www.fsc.org   FSC® C011748

For
JANE ARNFIELD
without whom…

And in memory of
JENNY HARRIS
who did so much for so many

CONTENTS

PART ONE:
THOUGHTSHOPS FOR STORYTELLING

SECTION 1 THIS STORY OF MINE

SECTION 5   FROM NARRATIVE TO NARRATION

SECTION 6   FROM NARRATOR TO NARRATEE

SECTION 7 WHY ADAPT?

SECTION 8 WHY NOT?

SECTION 9 WORLDS

PART TWO:
WORKSHOPS FOR STORYTELLING

SET 1 INTRODUCTORY WORKSOPS 1–5

SET 2 WORKSHOPS FOR INDIVIDUAL
STORYTELLING SKILLS 6–8

SET 3 WORKSHOPS FOR THIRD-PERSON NARRATOR FROM OUTSIDE THE ACTION 9–12

SET 4 WORKSHOPS FOR MULTIPLE THIRD-PERSON NARRATOR FROM INSIDE THE ACTION 13–20

SET 5 WORKSHOPS FOR FIRST-PERSON NARRATION 21–23

SET 6 WORKSHOPS FOR BUILDING AN ENSEMBLE 24–36

SUBSET 1: PHYSICAL AWARENESS

SUBSET 2: SPATIAL AWARENESS

SUBSET 3: FOCAL AWARENESS

SET 7 WORKSHOPS FOR TRANSITIONS AND TRANSFORMATIONS 37–40

SUBSET 1: ACTIVITIES AND ENVIRONMENTS (WITHOUT TEXT)

SET 8 WORKSHOPS FOR CREATING
SOMETHING OUT OF NOTHING 41–42

SET 9 WORKSHOPS FOR USING ELEMENTS
43–47

SET 15 WORKSHOP FOR
SHORT-STORY STRUCTURES 60

HAPPILY EVER AFTER

ACKNOWLEDGEMENTS

The author and publisher gratefully acknowledge permission to quote extracts from the following:

The Alexandria Quarter by Lawrence Durrell. Published by and reprinted by permission of Faber and Faber Ltd.

Blood's a Rover by James Ellroy. Published by Century. Reprinted by permission of The Random House Group Limited.

The Bridge of San Luis Rey by Thornton Wilder. Copyright © 1927 by The Wilder Family LLC. Reprinted by permission of The Wilder Family LLC and The Barbara Hogenson Agency, Inc. All rights reserved.

Bright Lights, Big City by Jay McInerney. Copyright © 1984 by Jay McInerney. Published in the UK by Penguin Books and in the USA by Vintage, a division of Random House, Inc.

A Handful of Dust by Evelyn Waugh. Published by Chapman and Hall, 1934, and Penguin Classics, 2000. Copyright © 1934 by Evelyn Waugh. Reprinted by permission of Penguin Books Ltd.

Mr Scobie's Riddle by Elizabeth Jolley. Copyright © 1983 by Elizabeth Jolley. Published by Persea Books, New York. Reprinted by permission of Persea Books Inc., New York. All rights reserved.

The Nibelungenlied translated by A. T. Hatto. Copyright © 1965, 1969 by A. T. Hatto. Published by Penguin Classics, 1965, revised edition 1969. Reprinted by permission of Penguin Books Ltd.

Nights at the Circus by Angela Carter. Copyright © 1984 by Angela Carter. Reprinted by permission of the author c/o Rogers, Coleridge & White Ltd, 20 Powis Mews, London W11 1JN.

The Razor's Edge by W. Somerset Maugham. Published by Vintage Books. Reprinted by permission of United Agents on behalf of The Literary Fund.

The Roman Spring of Mrs Stone by Tennessee Williams. Copyright © 1950 by The University of the South. Reprinted by permission of Georges Borchardt, Inc., on behalf of the Tennessee Williams Estate.

William Blake wrote
'The Imagination is the Human Existence Itself'

A FEW NOTES AND A BRIEF GLOSSARY

Then What Happens? is the companion to *Different Every Night*, in which I describe some of my rehearsal processes when working on plays – that is, material written specifically to be performed. This book deals with the performance of narrative material intended to be read or told. With the former, the storytelling is implicit and the characters usually remain within the imaginary worlds of the plays they inhabit. With the latter, the storytelling is self-evident and the actor/characters function both within and without their imagined worlds. To perform this material, actors require additional techniques to those for performing in plays. These particular skills are what, for the most part, this book is about. Of course, the essential techniques of acting – actions, objectives, points of concentration – still apply and underpin all the storytelling techniques. I do refer to them in passing, but anyone interested in a more detailed account of my approach to those fundamentals of acting should take a look at the earlier book.

Plays are written to be performed. Without us, the live audience, their performance remains an impossible object. Their texts all share the same components that identify them as plays, the most obvious being dialogue, people interacting with each other and occasionally with us, supported at times by minimal descriptions of their behaviour and appearance. They are usually concerned with a limited number of characters in a limited number of locations over a limited period of time, for the most part chronological, and are conceived, with rare exceptions, to be performed over an average of say two-and-a-half hours, more or less non-stop, with the audience absorbing whatever it can as the action proceeds. The characters are rarely if ever explained. They reveal themselves through scenes of action that we, the observers, interpret. They are almost never seen from varying viewpoints, although the characters will, of course, talk about each other. Because of the consistency of these ingredients, true from the plays of Aeschylus to whatever contemporary plays are currently on offer, *Different Every Night* can describe a structured process of rehearsal applicable to any play.

Stories, however, apart from all being words on a page or in the mouths and memories of storytellers, have little in common with each other, let alone with plays. Stories that are written down are, unlike plays, intended to be read – and read at the pace of the reader who, unlike the audience at a play, has complete control over the experience, able to re-read, thumb back or flick forward, stop and start at will. Their length and their number of locations and characters are without limit. Their time spans, also without limit, can move freely between past, present and future.

They may exist with or without dialogue, description or commentary and can be told from any or many a point of view. A story may teem with physical action on an epic scale or contain its action within the depths of a character's psyche. Characters may remain enigmatic or be extensively analysed and described. This variation in the contents and structure of stories means that there's no one sequence of rehearsal work that could accommodate them all on their journey to the stage. Each story, whatever its source – novel, epic poem, myth – requires a unique treatment of its own. It is the particular needs of a particular story, the individual dramatic choices it demands, that will light the fuse of your imagination.

Consequently, this book can't and doesn't try to set out a structured sequence of work, but offers some ideas and workshops around the subject, the intention being to open up for consideration the rich possibilities of story-theatre.

In story-theatre four disciplines converge: storytelling, theatrical performance, the adaptation of material from non-dramatic sources, and the development of an ensemble with the necessary skills to fulfil its special demands.

Only actors give life to theatre. This is true whether they're performing plays or telling stories. That's why this book echoes the other in its insistence on the primacy of the actor. To that end, the reader should bear in mind that, as stressed in *Different Every Night*, all rehearsals and performances are kept alive by constant process. That's to say, the work aspires to constant development and never to predetermined results: to *allow* things to happen rather than to *make* them happen, to discover rather than to know, to become rather than to be.

The book is in two parts. Part One deals with the *What*, Part Two with the *How*.

Part One is in nine sections:

    Section One sets out my own experience of story-theatre.

    Section Two extols the virtues of storytelling and its difference from playacting.

    Section Three describes the optimal physical and spatial conditions for story-theatre.

    Section Four details the extensive skills that storytelling demands of performers.

    Section Five enumerates the component parts of narrative, together with some principles for transforming a narrative text for reading into a narrative text for performing.

    Section Six concentrates on the processes for transforming a narrative text for performing into an actual performance.

    Section Seven does some further extolling, this time of the virtues of adaptation.

Section Eight offers some techniques in the process of adaptation.

Section Nine discusses the creation of consistent worlds or realities.

Part Two contains sixty workshops to develop storytelling skills, grouped under fifteen topics.

Most of the workshops contain a considerable number of exercises. All exercises are in boxes.

Matters discussed in *Part One* are cross-referred with their appropriate workshops in *Part Two*. Workshops whose techniques may overlap are also cross-referred.

———

My experience of adapting and staging non-dramatic fiction is that the two functions form a synergy. At various stages in the process they can alternate, overlap or travel in parallel, but finally they're inseparable aspects of the same process. So whenever I use the word *Adaptation* or any of those *Trans*-words (*-pose, -late, -mogrify* and the like) I'm referring to the whole journey from page to stage. When I need to refer to them individually, the context should make it clear that I'm doing so.

Actor, Performer and *Storyteller* are all-embracing, interchangeable nomenclatures that apply whether an actor/performer/storyteller is narrating or playing a character or in any other way contributing to the performance; the *Storyteller* can act and the *Actor* can tell stories. *Narrator* refers specifically to whoever is actually delivering the narrative, that is to say, literally *telling* the story. When I need to distinguish between *Narrators* and the rest, especially when describing exercises, I refer to *Narrators* as such and the others as the *Group*. Both together I refer to variously as the *Company, Ensemble, Cast* or *Class*.

Story can refer to any sort of narrative, whether in prose or in verse, from a fable to a novella, from a biography to a devised piece; *Narrative* for the purpose of this book refers to all prose or verse with the exception of dialogue; *Scene* refers to any section of dialogue in a story.

Stage indicates any acting space; *Theatre*, any venue where a performance can take place.

Transition is any change from one state to another; *Transformation* is the nature of the change.

When I use *we*, I am at times identifying myself with the audience and the world at large; at others with the smaller world of theatre practitioners. Whenever I refer to *you*, I'm addressing whoever may be guiding a workshop or rehearsal. When I identify an individual, should I subsequently need to refer to them again, I'm adopting, as often as I can – at times, I acknowledge defeat – the grammatically incorrect 'they, them, their and theirs' (as I'm doing in this sentence). This is to preserve some euphony while avoiding the politically condemned 'he, him and his', the politically grovelling 'she, her and hers', and the acceptable but cumbersome 'he or she, she or he, her or him, his or hers'…

———

A Note for Devisers and Improvisers: To illustrate narrative devices, I'm inevitably taking examples from stories that already exist as texts. And this sort of material, mainly from novels, does predominate throughout the book. But the methods described can be intelligently put to use on devised and improvised storytelling. Devised work is usually spared many of the analytic procedures applied to existing texts since an improvised story and its interpretation usually arrive hand in hand; the what and the how tend to be created together. Of course, once a devised piece exists as a text, you can analyse it just like any other type of narrative or play. In fact, this is a useful way to find out with a cool head the subtextual themes and patterns underlying work that has been created in the heat of improvisation. It's also a useful way to ensure that the world that's been devised is coherent and consistent.

Part One

THOUGHTSHOPS FOR STORYTELLING

SECTION I

THIS STORY OF MINE
How I Came to Tell Stories

TO BEGIN AT THE BEGINNING...

HAVE I GOT NEWS FOR YOU!

Tell me! What?

I hardly know where to begin.

Oh, for God's sake! What??

Look, I've been sworn to secrecy. So...

Yes, yes, I promise!

Oh, maybe I shouldn't have –

Well, you did.

Forget I said anything.

Too late now. You've *got* to tell me!

Your words have triggered an instant reflex that arouses my need to know. And any delay increases it. The suspense might even kill me. You've tempted me with the promise of a story, a temptation that's hard to resist. If the offer's withdrawn, the story withheld, I'm left dangling: off-balance and incomplete. The need to tell and be told stories seems as essential to our existence as breathing. Stories transcend time and space, travelling down generations and across borders, cutting through the otherness of cultures and languages. Prehistory pieces together whatever evidence it can find to tell us possible stories about our earliest selves. Stories beckon us in pursuit of the unanswerable 'why', the relentless quest of that Holy Grail: to make sense of our lives and give them shape. But there are times when we want stories to take us in the opposite direction – out of ourselves. Is it possible to conceive of a world without stories? Without beginnings, middles and ends? Without manga, Man Booker and myths? Sagas and scandals and soaps? Stories nourish our imagination. Imagination nourishes our empathy.

How a story reaches us obviously affects its impact on us. Reading is an altogether private activity, done at our own speed and in circumstances of our own choosing. Nothing intrudes between the page and our imagination. But the process is totally one-way: from the story to us. We respond to it but we have no effect on it. More to the point, our response is to rewrite the story in our imaginations, but it remains unchanged on the page. But being told or read a story face to face creates the possibility of an exchange between teller and listener in which the listener's reactions may well affect the teller's telling. Inevitably, there must be some degree of interaction.

Storytelling in theatre lifts this interaction onto another level of possibilities entirely. Plays, of course, act out stories, but most often indirectly, at a slight remove. Story-telling refreshes theatre by restoring it to its roots: stories first, plays after.

Some people disapprove of the theatrical appropriation of texts not originally con-ceived for theatre. But theatre survives by a magpie existence, helping itself from other arts, crafts and disciplines to whatever seems useful for its own purposes. Its uniqueness and vitality reside not so much in the provenance of its materials as in the form of its expression: the phenomenon of performance. This is the domain of the actor. Only actors can bring life to the stage. They transform productions into performances. Actors *are* the performance. Acting is the *élan vital* of theatre, its breath, its pulse, its source of energy. And storytelling actors epitomise theatre at its purest and acting at its most multifaceted.

Actors exhibit our potential to transcend ourselves: to imagine what it's like to be someone else. Storytellers manifest our potential to transcend the moment we chance to live in: to imagine what it's like to be somewhere else in time and place, actual or speculative. Story's plot is theatre's action. Nothing offers a more invit-ing point of departure on an empathy-expanding journey of the imagination than a company of storytellers entering a space to greet the other company gathered there with the irresistibly seductive incantation:

ONCE UPON A TIME...

A Thousand and One Nights

I happened upon storytelling by chance. I came upon it in pursuit of an entirely different preoccupation: defining for myself precisely what I believed to be the essence of theatre. It was one of those rare and serendipitous occasions on which two seemingly separate paths of enquiry synthesise into one. Storytelling drew me into an entirely unexpected world where many of my questions about the nature of theatre were answered, and many of my instincts on the matter confirmed.

It happened through *A Thousand and One Nights*. I made the acquaintance of this cornucopia of stories while working in Israel. A friend suggested that they might be adaptable for the theatre. Reading a bunch of kids' stories didn't fill me with the greatest enthusiasm. To my surprise, the thirty or so I did read were far from the familiar tales of magic and adventure I'd expected. Since their first appearance in the West, many of them had been heavily expurgated and subsumed in that guise. These I read were altogether more sophisticated and revealed much of the life that would have been experienced in the cultures from which they'd evolved. What's more, they were flagrantly, joyfully carnal and their women, confounding some current burqa'd and niqab'd impressions of Islamic culture, clearly the more enterprising and dynamic of the sexes. These tales were immediately alluring: rich in plot, character and action, replete with city life, daily toil, landscapes, philosophical ruminations, religious proselytising, prayer, myth, magic, verse, romance, adventure, history, moral fables, shaggy-dog stories, dirty jokes and, as noted, celebratory eroticism; all human life was there. But they didn't seem to lend themselves to conventional adaptation into scenes of extended dialogue. Possibly because I was then living in the Levant, where there were still pockets of traditional public storytelling – not that I'd experienced this myself, but nonetheless romantically visualised it – it occurred to me that the ideal presentation of these stories might be to retain them in their natural form: as stories. The challenge was to find the dramatic means of doing so.

Initially, I was somewhat deterred by having seen too many dull adaptations with the undernourished narrator unimaginatively stuck in a corner of the stage making colourless links between scenes, a lazy way of conveying information that the dramatist had failed to resolve within the drama itself, one that offered the actor in question a thankless task in a boring role, remarkable only for its missed opportunities. From a practical standpoint, these stories roamed so frequently from one exotic location to another and involved such vast casts of characters that their adaptation as plays would have defeated the means of the most spiralling Defence Budget. What helped me to make a leap of imagination was that this challenge coincided with my own personal concern at that time with what exactly constituted an act of theatre. I was becoming more and more convinced this had to be the creative presence of the actor, the one ingredient in theatre that cannot be dispensed with; the only one necessary, together, of course, with an audience and their shared imaginations, for theatre to exist. The actor was the defining element of theatre. I began to visualise actors in an empty space, transforming themselves into concubines and caliphs, wise women and wazirs at the demands of a story and somehow, out of nothing, conjuring up to order souks and palaces, hammams and harems, fields of battle and the djinn-infested Upper Air. Looking back now, it all seems obvious, but then the solutions came slowly and piecemeal.

The eventual production, literally called *A Thousand and One Nights*, comprised some ten stories that most appealed to me. They had no thematic or dramatic connection. I linked them together in a rather obvious sequence of alternating long and short, dramatic and comic pieces, ending with the most elaborate. What held them together was the set, a large black box containing a sequence of smaller black boxes from which bolts of material were variously drawn, one for each story. In one, about a dyer who only knew of the colour blue, his moment of revelation came when, by the tug of a cord, the frieze of blue cloths festooning the black box was transformed into all the colours of the rainbow. But my moment of revelation was seeing the possibility of actors both playing their characters and telling us about their characters, moving to and fro between those two functions as the narrative required. From that discovery came the challenge to find unanticipated ways of rendering all types of narrative stage-worthy. The dramatic potential of narrative and narration opened up endless questions about attitude, viewpoint and role that eventually came to be explored in great detail when I returned to London and formed Shared Experience Theatre Company.

The Book of Esther

Before my return I created another piece of storytelling theatre based on the Old Testament *Book of Esther*, though, at the time, I didn't realise I was doing that. As part of my efforts to learn Hebrew, I'd acquired a bilingual Bible padded with footnotes quoting the conflicting, highly disputative interpretations of the text by very ancient rabbis (Here Rabbi Akiba says... But Ibn Ezra finds evidence... Less acceptable is Rashi's view...). *The Book of Esther*, one of the shortest in the canon, has considerably more than its fair share of such commentary. For these sages, it was also the most problematic. In the story, Esther, a nice Jewish girl, marries out of the faith (the King of Persia – to save her race from ethnic cleansing, it should be noted); but, more worrying than this, the name of God is never once invoked: two definite strikes against this story's right to belong amongst such scriptural company, one that needed a lot of explaining. I suddenly had the image of the characters in the story trying to get on with their lives, surrounded by a group of rabbis, draped in prayer shawls, constantly interrupting them with contradictory interpretations of their behaviour and demands for them to change their ways, all the while squabbling amongst themselves over some recondite point of scholarship. This image became the starting point for an eventual piece of theatre called *The Persian Protocols*. Researching the material, I found that, in keeping with the need for so many justificatory footnotes, there were more exegeses and versions of *Esther* than of any other book in the Old Testament. The final production was a retelling of the story five times, starting with the biblical version – complete with footnotes and rabbis – and moving through four variations (children's folk tale, agit-prop, ecstatic vision, and archetypal 'Everyman' legend), each written at a different period in the evolution of the Hebrew language, and manipulating the story to fit the prevailing needs and values of its community.

As my own footnote to this, I somewhat wistfully acknowledged to myself that whereas in Israel the entire population, religious and secular, could relate – and relate to – the story of Queen Esther, having studied it in school and celebrated it during Purim (the one playful holiday in the Jewish calendar), there was not now in our British culture a single narrative I could think of that would have the same communal, unifying familiarity, not Genesis, not the Gospels (despite their Christmas Story), nor the Arthurian legends, *Beowulf*, *The Canterbury Tales*, *Hamlet*, *David Copperfield*, *Pride and Prejudice* (coming pretty close), not World Wars One and Two, not even 7/7.

Sharing the Experience

I started Shared Experience Theatre Company to convince myself – and anyone else who cared – that all you needed to create theatre were actors with stories to tell and audiences to tell them to. What made theatre unique was one group of human beings transforming themselves into a second group of human beings in the actual – not virtual – presence of a third group of human beings who fulfilled – completed – this act of transformation by accepting and believing in that second group. This was the essence of pure theatre: *the shared imaginations of actors and audiences conjuring up characters who really weren't there: bringing the non-existent into existence.* Nothing and nobody else was necessary. Our boast was that we could perform any-where at any time for anyone.

But what were we to perform? Plays tell wonderful stories, but they carry a certain amount of predictable baggage that, to begin with at least, might have trapped us in old ways of working. I wanted to start fresh, free from received practice. I wanted the actors in neutral: clear, clean and uncluttered, ready to go in whichever direc-tion was required of them. I wanted them to come into their open acting space transparent, as themselves, greet the audience with a 'Hello'... and then what? Maybe 'There was once a wise woman... a fair princess... a fisherman... a mighty king... who...' The seemingly innumerable stories from the *Thousand and One Nights* were the ideal material for such a starting point to our travels.

I had no idea that from this point of departure we'd embark on what proved to be a ten-year voyage of discovery. Initially, storytelling was intended as a means to an end – a vessel to demonstrate the creative autonomy and dramatic sufficiency of actors in an empty space. It proved, in time, to be more than that and became part of the purpose. Storytelling revealed its vitality and completely refreshed my view of play-bound theatre. We made discoveries about stories and the nature of telling them. These led to discoveries about adaptation – the dramatic rendering of mate-rial from non-dramatic sources. This, in turn, led to the development of special techniques that enabled the actors to perform this new material. And finally, we dis-covered the many functions and identities, well beyond their traditional role as interpreters of character, that the actors had to acquire in their empty space. All of which is what this book deals with. Much of this new knowledge would eventually be applied to the performance of actual plays. At that time, I think, no play would have led us to any of these discoveries.

At first the company's name received a lot of sarcastic comment ('It sounds like a sanctimonious rock group'), but the name meant what it said. It defined theatre: the experience of actors and audiences together sharing in an act of imagination. And so it came to prove.

The principles on which I founded Shared Experience postulated that we should work without any of the usual theatrical reinforcements: no wings, no curtains, no scenery, no costumes, no props, no musical instruments, no blackouts, no dressing-rooms for the actors to escape to, no technology either ancient or modern, lighting only as an unvarying means of illuminating actors and audience together in the same space; nothing more. Accordingly, our first explorations were focused exclusively on how the actors could tell stories without resort to anything beyond themselves. We soon found that there was very little that they couldn't achieve on their own. I think that's worth repeating: there is nothing essential to a performance that actors cannot create by their own powers of suggestion.[1]

Theatre is embodied in the actors: in their relationship to their audience, to their material and to each other. They are the nucleus of theatre; everything flows through them. Storytelling created the possibility of pursuing in its purest form my conviction that the essence of theatre is the exercise of the imagination, our willingness to believe that something is happening that isn't happening at all. This is even more strongly stressed when actors work in an empty space, creating everything out of nothing other than their own infinite skills to tell stories. I am consequently unsympathetic, as you will gather, to theatre which employs dominating, frequently domineering – in fact, bullying – scenic means of communication that pre-empt the expressive power of the human being.

Much later on, the company did add scenic elements, but only when absolutely essential for the world of a story (its stylistic reality) to be realised in a particular way, and then only applied sparingly. Maximum economy for maximum expressiveness ensured that both actors' and audiences' imaginations would continue to breathe. The principle was to start with nothing and then, only after rigorously convincing ourselves of their necessity, to let other elements grow together with the actors from the core of the story. However, what I'll be describing is, by and large, a company of actors working in an empty space.

1. In June 1988, Michael Billington, the *Guardian*'s theatre critic, travelled to Tbilisi with Peter Hall's National Theatre productions of Shakespeare's last plays. The costumes and scenery were delayed en route and the first shows were of necessity played without them. He described the consequences:

> Touring is always hazardous. But the National Theatre's trip to Tbilisi in Georgia last weekend with *The Winter's Tale*, *Cymbeline* and *The Tempest* turned potential disaster into downright triumph. The company gave seven performances in three days without scenery or costumes (stuck in transit) and in hastily improvised lighting. The result was a staggering demonstration of what theatre is about: *the primacy of acting and language over spectacle and design.* [*My italics.*]

Some Storytellers

Roberto

The first professional storyteller I encountered was Roberto, who had a day job with the Post Office. As a way of launching the company's research into telling tales, we invited him to moonlight and share his skills with us. He sat us on the floor in the dark and told us Japanese ghost stories. He told them well and they were suitably spine-chilling.

Two things in keeping with my aims for the company struck me reassuringly. One was the strong impression he achieved with a minimum of means. By voice alone he drew us into a chilling atmosphere of fear and suspense. The other was that we were doing half the work ourselves. Because we were in the dark (we could only see him as a shadowy – haunting – presence), we were totally free to visualise these ghost stories, each one of us in our own way. He had promoted us from passive listeners to active participants. He had instantly established the principle of the shared imagination. He was doing precisely what reading and radio do: stimulating our individual, sensory imaginations. We were seeing what wasn't there; possibly hearing, tasting, smelling, feeling by touch, too, if a story so roused any other of our senses.

But as I far as I remember, he used only a portion of what a voice might do. He didn't, for example, characterise. I'm not even sure if there were any dialogues in his stories. He didn't make use of a particularly broad emotional range. He didn't use accents or dialects. He didn't use exclamatory sounds – or any sounds at all, come to that.

Emlyn Williams

Subsequently, thinking about Roberto, my memory was suddenly jolted. He was not the first storyteller I'd encountered. That role belonged to Emlyn Williams.[2] A quarter of a century earlier, when I was about fourteen, I had been to one of his recreations of Charles Dickens's public readings. His material, some of it chosen from the pieces that Dickens himself had performed on his own reading tours, covered a wide range of genres: the death of little Paul from *Dombey and Son*, the opening to *A Tale of Two Cities* ('It was the best of times, it was the worst of times'), the banquet given by the Veneerings in *Our Mutual Friend*... There it suddenly was; though I'd not consciously thought about that evening for more than twenty-five years, the entrancement of it came back to me in a rush. I remembered how I'd wanted to stay in that theatre for ever, listening to him tell

---

2. Emlyn Williams (1905–1987) was a successful and popular actor, playwright and memoirist. His best-known play, *Night Must Fall*, was made as a film by Karel Reisz in the 1960s and starred Albert Finney and Sheila Hancock.

those stories. And I also remembered, more likely realised at this moment of remembering – for I doubt that at the age of fourteen I'd have been conscious of how he achieved his effects – that it was what he did vocally that had made this impact on me. He was dressed and made up as Dickens and stood at a lectern as Dickens had done in his own performances. As far as I recall, his body language was of little interest other than to underline what he was doing with the language.[3] But with his voice he had used a whole battery of techniques: bold vocal characterisations and accents (with Dickens, what else?), huge variations in volume, tone, tempo and rhythm. His tessitura rivalled Yma Sumac's,[4] it seemed able to travel from basso profundo to the highest falsetto. He employed weeping and laughter, gasps and cries, pauses and silence… or so I seemed to remember; he was simpering, savage, plangent, soothing, pompous, incisive, sentimental… At this moment, I understood what an influential theatregoing experience that had been for me, though I hadn't thought about it in all those years! Yet there was the memory of it waiting for the appropriate moment to resurface and remind me of the power of the voice and the word.

Bruce Myers

This led to another recollection of a more recent vintage. While working in Israel for the five years prior to the start of Shared Experience, I was directing a production for Haifa City Theatre when Bruce Myers paid us a visit. Bruce, a superb actor, was one of the mainstays of Peter Brook's Paris-based International Centre for Theatre Research, of which he was to remain a stalwart member for many years. This was in its early days, not long after its first major project, *Orghast*, had been performed in Iran at Persepolis. Orghast was also the name of the project's language, devised for the company by Ted Hughes from several ancient languages. The emphasis was on the expressive sounds of the words at an instinctive, primal level,[5] rather than on their intellectual meaning. In addition to the formidable development of their physical skills, the actors had received intensive training in the creation of these sounds, many of which had initially been quite alien to them. We persuaded Bruce to demonstrate a few for us. We sat there, rapt and envious, as his voice seemed to range through his whole body, from bowels to occiput and back again, to places where an English-speaking voice is rarely asked to go, not even

3. Recently, online, I discovered some video clips of Emlyn Williams from what was no doubt a revival of one of his Dickens evenings during which, at one point, he performed little leaps and bounced up and down on his toes. So much for memory.

4. Yma Sumac was a singer, celebrated in the 1940s and '50s for a voice whose range of more than five octaves went from low contralto to A above High C. She was purportedly a Peruvian peasant descended from Inca kings. Some thought it was more likely she was Amy Camus from Brooklyn. The voice, though, was authentic.

5. Sounds identified by semiologists as iconic, indexical and symbolic. You look them up!

Emlyn Williams's. Some of these sounds were described in an account of the *Orghast* project as 'glissando shrieks, roars, hoarse whispers and harsh, explosive laughing sounds'.[6]

Telling stories was one thing; telling stories as theatre was another. As much as I wanted to distil the essence of theatre to actors, I didn't want to distil actors to just their voices. On the contrary. I wanted the whole of the actor to do everything that was needed to fulfil a complete theatre experience. Besides, theatre was about enacting events, embodying characters in action and in space. Theatre was about telling through doing.

Ruth Draper

Yet another solo performer, appositely one that exploited her entire presence, surfaced from my memory, someone else I'd seen when I was young – one of her performances was in fact a sixteenth-birthday present. Hard to know how to define Ruth Draper.[7] She wasn't a storyteller, though stories were inevitably relayed through her performances. She wasn't a monologist either. She created character studies. An austere-looking American woman in late middle-age, her particular brilliance was to fill the stage with people. Each character she played engaged with others that she imagined, people that you definitely saw and heard although she was the only one present. From the way she spoke to them, reacted to them, dealt with them, she could, like a juggler keeping several balls in the air, keep several of these invisible characters simultaneously alive in the space and in your imagination: for example, an actress of Slavic provenance receiving visitors in her Paris apartment, greeting them in several languages, fighting with her manager, handling her admirers and so forth. These sketches were really small dramas. In another, *Three Women and Mr Clifford*, she played, in sequence, a secretary, wife and mistress and, through each of them, created the man of the title, first at his desk, then in the back of a chauffeur-driven limousine and, finally, seated in a deep armchair, on an arm of which she lovingly perched to embrace her imagined lover. Her genius seemed to lie in her ability to wed an extraordinary precision of focus and use of space (aspects of mime) to an absolute conviction in the existence of the people she was conjuring up. Trying to describe the basis of her art, she wrote:

6. *Orghast at Persepolis* by A. C. H. Smith (Eyre Methuen, 1972).

7. Ruth Draper (1884–1956) was an American actress. She was described as a diseuse and her repertoire comprised thirty-six pieces of her own creation, embracing fifty-seven characters. She performed for American troops in France in 1918 and before George V at Windsor in 1926. She was awarded several doctorates and, in 1951, a CBE. She is credited as having being much admired by or highly influential on an impressive range of artists from Henry James and George Bernard Shaw to David Mamet and Simon Callow via, amongst others, Katherine Hepburn, Laurence Olivier and Maurice Chevalier. Joyce Grenfell, no mean performer herself in a similar mode, was a third cousin of hers.

I do nothing more than suggest… There, I believe, is where the whole thing has its greatest appeal. The people who come have to use their own imaginations to get the effect… There is no scenery, no person except myself on the stage. The others are the joint product of my own and the audience's imagination. You see, it appeals to the highest thing in the people who come. They… assist in creating an effect which I could never create alone.

She said it all! (You *could* stop reading this book right here.) Not only did she confirm for me the necessity of the audience's creative contribution to the performance; the fullness of what she achieved with such economy of means yet again reinforced my thoughts inspiringly about actors in empty spaces.

———

What connected these performers was their ability to create worlds and environments exclusively from their own presence with their own talents and powers of suggestion, and with only the most rudimentary scenic elements: Roberto in darkness; Emlyn Williams dressed as Dickens and provided with a lectern; Ruth Draper in elements of clothing that represented the character she herself was playing and the occasional piece of furniture; and Bruce Myers, whom I watched in Paris a couple of years later, doing wonders with a pair of old boots for a classroom full of children. Essentially, they all functioned in an empty space. From the postman to Persepolis, from Dombey to Draper, I'd been given plenty of food for thoughts about the company's work on storytelling. It was to nourish our explorations through the next decade. This book is about the discoveries we made and the techniques we developed to exploit them.

THE NEXT THING WAS...

Arabian Nights

When I returned to the UK from Israel, I set out to read the entire *Thousand and One Nights* canon, or as much of it as I could locate. Fortuitously, browsing in one of those specialist bookshops that cluster at the gates of the British Museum, I caught sight of a Victorian ten-volume set of the stories with an additional four volumes of Supplemental Tales, published privately – because unexpurgated – in the 1865 translation of Sir Richard Burton who, in addition, had annotated copious details of their cultural and anthropological provenance.[8] The volumes were large and slightly crumbling and entitled, in gold leaf on black, *Arabian Nights Entertainment* (*Arabian* on the front cover, *Nights* on the back, in full on the spine and on the first page: *Now Entitled the Book of The Thousand Nights and a Night* – the literal translation). I paid £80 for the lot, with an earlier three-volume expurgated translation thrown in for good measure. Over time, I read every story, creating an index card for each title, with a brief plot synopsis, a classification by genre, any noteworthy details and an indication as to whether I thought it stage-worthy.

This purchase was another occasion of serendipity. Up till then, the translations I'd read suffered either from censorship or bland language – or both – and created little atmosphere, little sense of time and place other than what you might get from a conventionally written fairytale. Burton's work was completely different. His translation is described as 'plain and literal'. I have no idea if this is so (though he was reputed to speak twenty-nine languages), but with my knowledge of its Semitic sibling, Hebrew, it indeed read to me as a commitment to the original Arabic, channelled through the sumptuousness of *The Song of Songs*. Plain it wasn't![9] With its eroticism intact, it evoked an extravagant culture, violent and voluptuous. It was language as much as plot that released my imagination. I began to visualise the possible direction an adaptation might take in conjuring up such an outrageously vibrant world. Stories ultimately are not defined by their plots, characters and themes, but by *how* they are told. Literature is language; the most individually expressed language creates a world uniquely its own. I can see that the writers I've subsequently adapted (Austen, Dickens, Waugh, Ellroy...) have claimed my imagination by their language's ability to summon up a particular

---

8. I also found an invaluable source of research in Manners and Customs of the Modern Egyptians by E.W. Lane, published in 1836. He describes in minute details, covering a wide range of topics (clothes, work, prayer...), the conduct of daily life, much of it – despite the vast time gap – corresponding to descriptions of life in the stories themselves.

9. Recently, in a radio interview about a new translation of the stories, I was abashed to hear his translation trashed as inaccurate, invented and plagiarised! But on comparing translations, I still incline to my initial enthusiasm.

vision of life. That's why I try to keep my adaptations as close as possible to their original texts, incorporating not only the dialogue but as much as I can of their narrative, precisely to retain the authorial voice. Paraphrasing dilutes, approximation distorts and free adaptation denies the individuality of a work. Many television versions of classic novels fall into a sort of uniformity because they've dispensed with the original voice. So those much-serialised works of Victorian novelists tend to blur into one generalised vision of nineteenth-century Britain, telling us more about British culture at the time of the adaptations than of the original writers' visions of their worlds. What you see and what you hear jar against each other: characters speaking an updated demotic language while wearing period clothes and moving within authentically recreated environments produce an unnatural hybrid, an artistic mule.

Shared Experience's first production, *An Arabian Night*, was a considerable development from my initial groping at storytelling with the Israeli *Thousand and One Nights*. This version was more firmly structured. Instead of a series of discrete stories, we used a framing story within which other stories with connection to the plot or the subject matter were integrated like blueberries in a muffin. We were encouraged in this by the extraordinary range of structures used in *A Thousand and One Nights* itself. There were anecdotes little longer than half a page, and sagas, the longest of which spanned three hundred pages. There were clusters of stories which debated a particular issue, presenting alternate sides of the argument. There were stories within stories within stories... [*Cross-refer Section 8: Short Stories; and Set 15, Workshop 60: Framing and Linking Stories*]

Our main story was called *The Loves of Kamar and Budur*, in which the eponymous would-be lovers, seeking each other throughout the world, become embroiled in a multiplicity of other liaisons en route. We had prepared a reservoir of relevant shorter stories that could be inserted at certain points in the performance. The actors responsible for initiating such stories on a particular night could, without forewarning the rest of the cast, announce which one they would have to take part in at that precise moment. The production was a huge success and encouraged us to redistribute some of the stories, add others and explore new structures, until this initial show had proliferated into three: *The First, Second and Third Arabian Night*: respectively a revised *Loves of Kamar and Budur*, *The Rogueries of Dalilah the Wily* and *The City of Brass*, each played in totally different conventions to best convey the particular themes and atmosphere – the World – of each specific *Night*. [*For our approach to the different conventions of this trilogy, cross-refer Section 8, Why Not?: Short Stories; Section 9, Worlds: From Analysis to Performance; and Set 9, Workshop 46: Something to Put On*] We toured these shows for about eighteen months, won a Fringe First at the Edinburgh Festival and were the company in residence at that year's National Student Drama Festival.

During this period we were invited by the London Borough of Barking to create a performance suitable for schools. I'd never planned a production specifically for children and was somewhat apprehensive until I was given the excellent advice to treat them like any other audience. (This, I'm now convinced, applies in all circumstances.) So we did just that and added a *Fourth Arabian Night: The Adventures of Hasan of Basra*, in a shorter and longer version for younger and older pupils. This proved to be an unexpectedly rewarding venture that completely reinforced my belief in storytelling. We would turn up at a school at nine o'clock in the morning (not the best time of day for an actor), and the company, wearing the clothes they'd come to work in, would perform in some shabby classroom in need of fresh paint and decent light, with the children seated on the floor in a semicircle around our 'empty space', totally transfixed. Later, we'd see them in the schoolyard, acting out variations on what they'd been watching. One teacher sent us what her class of eight-year-olds had drawn and crayoned, inspired by their early matinee. These pictures were filled with animals, characters, costumes, landscapes and incidents, all in the most brilliant colours and patterns; they had absorbed even the most casual, passing phrases and released them in this firework display of imagination. No design could have come anywhere near their riotous creations, in fact, might well have inhibited them. This was a gift and a vindication of the ability of storytelling to stimulate creative participation in its audience: one of those experiences that make you glad you work in theatre.

Eventually, we brought the three adult shows into London to the King's Head and with huge success played them in repertoire under the collective title, *Recitals of Mystery, Violence and Desire: Three Arabian Nights Entertainments.* The two years devoted to this *Arabian Nights* project was an exhilarating period of exhaustive, not to say exhausting, trial and error, steep learning curves, rewarding discoveries and the acquisition of new skills, all of which formed the basis of any subsequent storytelling work and flowed over into our productions of plays.

Bleak House

Shared Experience followed *The Arabian Nights* with Charles Dickens's *Bleak House*. I had been in Israel during the Yom Kippur War, left to kick my heels while the rest of the country slotted into its pre-assigned war duties. My tentative offers to be of use having been discouraged, I somewhat guiltily looked for something to take my mind off the situation. Work being on hold and socialising reduced to zero, I went to a Jerusalem bookshop and bought Penguin editions of half-a-dozen novels by Dickens whom, despite several attempts over the years, I'd never been able to read. Now I devoured him like comfort food, starting with *Martin Chuzzlewit* and making my way through *Little Dorrit, Our Mutual Friend, David Copperfield, Great Expectations* and, best of all, *Bleak House.* They were revelatory. I laughed out loud, cried uninhibitedly (no doubt already feeling somewhat shaky), held my breath, hung on to cliffs, gasped – even jumped – in surprise and kept my back firmly against the wall. They seemed to offer everything that makes good theatre.

But novels with exponentially proliferating casts of characters in multiple plots that take days to read do not. Or didn't until eventually we found ways of putting such abundance into a dramatic form. So for the moment *Bleak House* remained a shadowy project in a list of works I wanted somehow, some day, to direct.

Which happened a few years later. Around the time of *The Arabian Nights*, Robert Cushman, the then theatre critic for the *Observer*, reviewing Ken Campbell's nine-hour trilogy, *Illuminatus*, wrote to the effect that, given sufficient time, anything could be adapted.[10] This jolted me into reconsidering the possibility, long relegated to the back-burner, of a Dickens novel being rendered on stage *in toto*. The ambition – the challenge – was to create a form of performance that would retain as much as possible of Dickens in all his detailed variety of tone and scale. The '70s was a period of considerable optimism and innovation in the theatre. The fringe and alternative-theatre circuit had become the place for cutting-edge theatre and had usurped the traditional supremacy of London's West End, now regarded as – and indeed looking – tired and reactionary. These new venues and their audiences were open to experiment and willing to take risks. The idea of theatre as a special event was very much in vogue; rather than sitting in rows in a traditional, purpose-built structure for two hours, you might now be embussed to some mystery site far away from Theatreland,[11] maybe moved from location to location during a performance,[12] or made to mingle with the performers and the rest of the audience in theatres whose familiar arrangement of stage and auditorium had been radically reorganised to create the exciting disorientation of entering the unknown.[13]

In this mood of euphoria, the decision to adapt *Bleak House* in its entirety, taking as much time as we needed, seemed perfectly reasonable. I knew, of course, that some loss would have to occur, but that would be for reasons other than pressure of time. Eventually, we created a ten-hour show that was performed over four evenings, with six actors playing over a hundred characters. Members of Dickensian Societies expressed their amazed approval, convinced that we were presenting the entire

10. A few years later, this turned out to be a mere warm-up for Campbell's twenty-two-hour production of *The Warp*.

11. The London venue for Grotowski's 'Poor Theatre' was the crypt of a church in the depths of the East End.

12. The Living Theatre in a series of performances at the Round House, exhorted the audience, after some sort of love-in in the acting space, to march with them to stand vigil outside Wormwood Scrubs.

13. In performances by TOC (The Other Company), much admired at the time, the audience became the performers as, guided from one space to another, we were encouraged to observe and interact with each other.

novel. In actuality, we played one fifth of the text, subtly compressing the material rather than hacking out great chunks. One solitary tributary of a subplot and some half-dozen characters were all that hit the rehearsal-room floor. [*Cross-refer Section 8: Cutting v. Compressing*] This project covered the best part of a year. In the first three months, we created the first two evenings with which we began to tour. While touring, we created the third part. Then, while touring the three parts, we created the fourth. By this time, the actors had become virtually word-logged sponges, incapable of absorbing another syllable should they even try. But they tried and they did. Audiences, encouragingly, made no objection to seeing just one part of the whole, but better still, and quite unanticipated by us, would often travel from one part of the country to another to catch the episodes they'd missed. As with *The Arabian Nights*, we ended the project with a run in London, this time at the Royal Court, which included playing all four parts at weekends.

TO BE CONTINUED...

From *A Handful of Dust* to *The Tin Ring*

A Handful of Dust by Evelyn Waugh was the third adaptation for the company. It occurred five years later, after we'd reaped the benefits of our initial storytelling experiences by applying this fresh knowledge to the performance of proper plays by proper playwrights. The first of these was Shakespeare's *Cymbeline*. A play of his seemed the natural progression for developing the idea of theatre as the creation of something 'out of nothing', that is, relying exclusively on actors and the material they were performing. After *Cymbeline*, however, I felt that we'd painted ourselves into a corner: five actors, all in white, performing that entire text in an empty space seemed to have levitated us to a level of purity from which there was nowhere to go but up or – the only route available to us – back down to earth. In the intervening four years, between *Cymbeline* and *A Handful of Dust*, we continued to try out whatever skills and insights we'd gained from our narrative explorations on productions of plays in which we began to make slight gestures towards design.

For *A Handful of Dust*, we made the decision to create a storytelling production conceived exclusively for a proscenium stage, the space we'd found least sympathetic to telling stories and the least frequently used for our previous shows. We had favoured venues where we could be sure of a more intimate contact with the audience. But this type of stage seemed aesthetically right for this particular novel. Waugh displays his characters for our evaluation in a way that suggested we should observe them from a slight distance.

The novel was in many ways a gift for stage storytelling. It has a single, developing plot that builds on scenes of social gatherings. It is mainly executed through dialogue of great economy and wit, much of it over the phone. It has a containable range of some twenty characters viewed objectively with little attempt to get into their minds or describe their feelings; they reveal themselves by what they say and do, a requisite for most plays. And its length was manageable within a single performance.[14]

We twice revived *The First Arabian Night* for foreign touring, and later I recreated it with Norwegian actors for the Nationale Scene, formerly Ibsen's theatre in Bergen, where we introduced, as our single concession to design, a sort of magic carpet that started very small, folded as a cushion to sit on, and gradually opened up, episode by episode, until, in the final story, it spread out as a huge star-lit backcloth across the whole rear of the stage. I also adapted and directed for the Heidelberg Staatstheater a four-hour production of *King Omar and His Sons*, the longest story from the *Thousand and One Nights*, an epic saga about three dynasties of Moslems in their struggles against the wicked Christians. We played in a traditional theatre on a costly sand-coloured carpet that covered the entire stage floor, with a gauze canopy that shot out into the auditorium to link the actors and audience together. With the writer, Michelene Wandor, I indulged in yet another four-hour adaptation, this time for the Royal National Theatre, of *The Wandering Jew*, a sprawling, early-nineteenth-century French novel by Eugène Sue, an immensely popular writer in his time. He specialised in overwrought, operatically melodramatic political thrillers, multiplotted with inordinate complexity and fuelled by his loathing of all established institutions and their injustices. These last two productions were notable for finding fresh and flexible ways of presenting labyrinthine plots, multiple flashbacks, large casts of characters, huge crowd scenes and rapid movement between wildly various locations and events (battles, theatre spectacles, tavern brawls, a cholera epidemic...). Some of these were achieved by devising theatrical equivalents of certain cinematic techniques. [*Cross-refer Set 10, Workshop 49: Film Language*]

As artistic director of Cambridge Theatre Company, later reconceived as Method & Madness, I revived *A Handful of Dust*. After which, with David Glass, I adapted the screenplay of *Les Enfants du Paradis*, which largely involved reinventing the film's imagery. After this I made a series of adaptations which opened up new approaches to narrative. One was a Victorian terror story, *Uncle Silas*, by the Irish writer Joseph Sheridan Le Fanu, in which the first-person narrative, distilled through the unsuspecting eyes of the menaced heroine, made huge demands on the stamina of the performer playing the role. It required new solutions for the creation of the characters and events summoned up from her exclusive and subjective

---

14. In *Different Every Night*, I've described in some detail how we explored this material and discovered the form that brought this world to life, so I won't repeat that here.

vantage point. For the reader, as well as for the heroine, the novel is filled with moments of sudden terror and disorientation; we had to come up with the dramatic means of achieving much the same on an audience. This was in part achieved by creating a wall of hinged doorways that could rapidly shift the shape of the stage to reveal a sudden new character or location. Next came Jane Austen's *Emma*, in which I failed completely to locate in theatrical terms the writer's irony, but which was – an irony of a different sort – the most popular show the company ever did. The next project was Thomas Hardy's *Jude the Obscure*, in which four actors created the entire world of the novel. Then I adapted a group of short stories by Isaac Bashevis Singer under the title *Demons and Dybbuks*, in which I linked together material from several of his many collections which, though not ostensibly autobiographical, implicitly charted the journey of the author through the first-person narratives of various versions of himself – from an Orthodox Jewish upbringing in Poland to a penniless immigrant's initial deprivations in the United States and eventual fame and fortune. I did a revised version of this for the Cameri Theatre in Tel Aviv. Next came *The Black Dahlia* by James Ellroy, the fictional account of a notorious Hollywood murder in 1947, still unsolved in 2013.[15] I adapted this novel with the greatest degree of structural freedom I'd permitted myself up to then. [*Cross-refer Section 8, Why Not?: Changing the Structure*] This production was also recreated, slightly revised, in the States for Yale Repertory Theatre. And most recently, *The Tin Ring*, the memoirs of Zdenka Fantlova, a Holocaust survivor, in which a single performer tells her story through a variety of storytelling conventions.

All these projects have been consistently stimulating and engrossing. I should point out that I was always adapting material for myself to direct. I could only start an adaptation when I had some slight glimpse of how it might work onstage, not by any means a finished idea, but an image, a convention, a shape, a sense of flow... So the two processes went hand in hand, the adaptation continuing throughout the rehearsals and well into the period of performance.

15. For anyone curious, cyberspace can supply a vast range of speculations and theories as to the perpetrator, from the credible to the crackpot.

SECTION 2

WHAT STORYTELLING DOES

Storytelling Does Whatever Plays Do, Plus!

STORYTELLING v. PLAYACTING

All (well, most) plays tell stories. The fundamental difference between playacting and storytelling is the actor/character's ability, through narrative, to step outside the story being enacted in order to talk about it. This single, simple difference unleashes what seems an unstemable torrent of conventions, many of them highly sophisticated and in need of their own techniques. Of course, there are plays in which characters talk directly to the audience or interrupt the action to comment on it. These instances take the form of soliloquies and asides by characters sharing their thoughts and feelings with us because there's nobody else within the action to whom they dare to or care to unburden themselves. But most of such addresses to the audience function as confessions and confidences rather than narratives. Occasionally in a play – Brian Friel's *Dancing at Lughnasa* comes to mind – one of the characters will take on the function of a narrator. And in Conor McPherson's *The Weir*, the characters tell each other stories. But they stay firmly in character and within *their* story. In storytelling, the narrator is not necessarily a character involved in the action – or even a character at all – and can address the audience from on or beyond its periphery. But even talking to us *as* a character, a narrator's intention – tendency at very least – is to guide us, if at times unreliably, through the story rather than using us as an emotional dumping ground for such personal problems as whether to be or not.

NARRATIVE FLEXIBILITY

Once a narrator exists, there's the potential for unlimited flexibility in the way a story can be told. Storytelling can set up swiftly and clearly whatever needs to be known. A narrator, without assistance from any change of scenery or Ibsenite exposition, may override those methods of establishing the traditional unities of time, place and action simply by announcing a new scene, introducing a character or filling us in on events prior to those we're about to witness. In most plays, to avoid the falsity of characters telling each other information that they probably know already, the playwright is forced to considerable lengths of ingenuity to disguise such exposition and embed it as naturally as possible within the scene. Narration eliminates the need for what can be dross and presents the material in a direct and distilled state. In fact, narration makes it possible for transitions to occur with the same fluidity and rapidity as those in film, and can move the story around in any way it wants, back and forth across time and space in the split second it takes to utter one or two words. By comparison, scene changes, even those achieved digitally, can seem laborious. This immediacy is effected by language. In *Macbeth*, Duncan declares 'This castle hath a pleasant seat', and Bob's your uncle! – scene changed. Verbal stimulus replaces imagery on the stage with imagery in the mind's eye. The beginning of *Under Milk Wood*, Dylan Thomas's 'Play for Voices', invokes us to listen and, through listening, to see:

> You can hear the dew falling, and the hushed town breathing. Only your eyes are unclosed to see the black and folded town fast, and slow, asleep. And you alone can hear the invisible starfall...
> Listen...
> Listen...
> Look...
> Listen...
> Only you can hear the houses sleeping in the streets... Only you can see, in the blinded bedrooms, the coms and petticoats over the chairs, the jugs and basins, the glasses of teeth... Only you can hear and see, behind the eyes of the sleepers, the movements and countries... and big seas of their dreams.
> From where you are, you can hear their dreams.

With his repeated incantation of 'you alone', 'only your eyes' and 'only you', he declares his belief in the individual imagination of each and every reader or listener.

Narrators can indulge in a variety of relationships with us and encourage us to receive a story from a multiplicity of viewpoints. They can also function not just as guides to the story but also to the production. They can help us to recognise the conventions of the world being portrayed, to unpick the particular codes of a performance, indicating, for example, that where three or four actors are gathered together, they represent a crowd. In *Henry V* – once again, it's Shakespeare who sets the agenda – the Chorus establishes the way in which the audience should experience that play:

> On your imaginary forces work...
> Piece out our imperfections with your thoughts...
> Think when we talk of horses, that you see them
> Printing their proud hoofs i' th' receiving earth

Before theatre moved indoors with its consequent need to be seen by sources other than daylight, its conventions seem to have been much closer to those for telling stories: *reliance on the presence of the actor, the power of the word and the imagination of the audience.*

THE DUALITY OF THEATRE

Theatre is created with the expectation of an audience. Performances are defined by their effect on their audiences. But much theatre, despite the actors' awareness of the audience's restlessness or its held breath, its obliging titters or generous guffaws, is for the most part still conducted behind the conventional fourth wall. Storytelling breaks through that wall, in fact eliminates any idea of a wall, and openly declares the essential shared nature of theatre. Storytelling, by self-definition, deals with the actuality of theatre head-on in its deliberate contact with an audience. The audience is directly acknowledged throughout the performance. Storytelling means there's always narration – and therefore always narrators – framing the story, providing a continual point of reference for the hearers. The constant possibility of a return to the narrator is a reminder that while a story is compelling us to suspend our disbelief, we're still in the theatre watching a fiction. Existing simultaneously in two realities – here and now (audience with actors) and there and then (audience with characters) – the actors bridging them corporeally, audiences mentally, both imaginatively – is a phenomenon unique to theatre, an affirmation of our shared capacity for creative empathy. Storytelling is the preeminent exponent of this duality.

AUDIENCE PARTICIPATION

When I first saw Fellini's film, *La Dolce Vita*, every frame seemed perfection and the images lingered on my visual memory. I couldn't wait to see it again. I had to. Fifty years ago any further opportunity to see a film after its initial release was dependent on the vagaries of film-society programming. After a few months, however, I did manage to catch up with it elsewhere. But when the film was over, I was left utterly bereft by the absence of images from a sequence I'd been longing to re-experience. I assumed that the print must have been cut or in some way tampered with. Fast forward to modern technology: I've now seen the film several times on video, then on DVD, and they've never reappeared. So strong was my belief in the actuality of those images that it took me quite a while to grasp the likelihood that they were what my imagination had imposed on that part of the film, not in retrospect, but in the intense moment of watching it, so that they had been blended in my memory as part of the film itself. Now, looking at old movies, especially those of one's childhood when imagination hasn't yet been completely house-trained, I see this is a common phenomenon. It may well be that our richest, most lasting memories are entirely of our own invention. That's one reason, no doubt, why recalled details of events we've shared with others are so often contradictory. We see things through our own frames of reference, contributing our personal images to what we experience. I believe that this is what happens, or *should* happen, for every individual member of a theatre audience. In *La Dolce Vita*, I had been prompted to embellish imagery that already existed on screen. Theatregoers, with only an empty space, create their own images from scratch, without so much visual prompting. There's nothing to get in the way, nothing to intrude between the story and pure, personal imagination. *Theatre needs this creative involvement from the audience to express itself at its most essential. Audiences need this creative involvement to experience theatre at its fullest.*

AUDIENCE AUTONOMY

The greater the personal involvement of audiences, the deeper their sense of fulfilment and the fuller by far their pleasure. In conventionally conceived performances, audiences are usually shown what things look like and, more often than not, told what to think and think about. They are frequently and rather heavily prompted as to how they should react or feel (here comes a funny bit, nudge-wink; ah! this is a sad bit; sit up now, this is the *message*). They are essentially witnesses of other people's decisions, accepting what they approve of and rejecting what they don't. This shallower, less holistic engagement activates their tastes and judgement rather than their creativity, so that they become critics evaluating what they like and what they don't, consumers calculating whether or not they're getting their money's worth for a night out: theatre as retail therapy. With storytelling, however, matters can be much different: their senses, their memories and their imaginations are roused and put to work. That rich inner life that unknowingly we carry around with us has the opportunity to surface; and to surprise and delight us in just the same way that actors, playing with true spontaneity, will release something thrillingly unexpected and have 'no idea where it came from' or how it arrived.[1] This is a problem for actors: if

---

1. As I've grown older, I've become increasingly aware of this phenomenon. With more time and inclination for reflection, well, let's say, wool-gathering, I'm frequently overwhelmed by the extraordinary – not quite daydreams: I'm awake, very relaxed, but wide awake – movies, more like, of people, places and events that unroll before me on my mental screen, people and places of whom I haven't the least knowledge, of whom I haven't the slightest experience in my actual life, nor, consciously at least, from my reading or any other medium. At times, they turn and address me and on occasions I even answer back. Who on earth are these people? Where are these places? Where did they come from? And how do they come to be lurking in me? Buried in our unconscious, or so it seems, are entire worlds to which we have no direct access, nor even know exist. When these 'movies' occur, I have the thrilling sensation that deep within me is an immensely rich and limitless treasury of experiences that are just waiting for the right conditions to surface (in my case, I suppose, a relaxed and accessible state) and make themselves known. This treasury is the actor's true stock-in-trade.

they're always being asked for results and to work things out in advance, they're bypassing any chance of tapping into that deep reservoir of inner life. Good acting can only occur when they're permitted access to their true creativity.

This is true for audiences, too. Good audienceship can only occur if they're allowed space for their creativity. Instead of judging and shopping, each member of the audience participates actively in realising the performance and develops a more intimate relationship with it. Any moment in a performance can have a totally different meaning and be a totally different experience for each person. All members of the audience create their own story. *This is genuine audience participation.* Storytellers initiate, audiences complete. Storytellers suggest, audiences fulfil. This is precisely how Ruth Draper described the way her performances succeeded. After a performance of *Bleak House*, a woman thanked me 'for allowing us to see our own show'. I know that on those occasions when I'm totally caught up in a performance, my critical faculties become, for the moment, an irrelevance and cease to function. When I'm not engaged, there's nothing else to do but judge – or walk away. Appraisal, evaluation, appreciation can happen later, at leisure, at your own speed, once the event's had time to be absorbed. This must be the dilemma for critics, poor things: to give themselves up to the moment, pen in hand.

———

The *reductio ad absurdum* might be to conclude that all you need for perfect theatre is a single storyteller simply telling the story. But for theatre to exist, characters have to be seen in action. Actors have to transform themselves into other people. Conflicts have to be enacted. So storytelling in theatre is a judicious combination of enactment and narration, of images and words, and each text will suggest the form of narration most suitable for its particular story and the most appropriate ratio of narration to action. Story-theatre gives us the best of both worlds: words stirring our imaginations into action and actors reminding us what it means to be human.

Everything latent in theatre, everything particular to theatre, is more sharply present in storytelling: the immediacy, the spontaneity, the actor at centre, the actors' and audiences' mutual awareness, the appropriate interaction between the two, the invitation to imagine, the simultaneous here and now/there and then-ness, the bringing into existence of what actually doesn't exist. Storytelling allows us, performers and audiences, to go anywhere in space and time. No longer bound by the practical limitations imposed on plays by the actual space and duration of a performance, a human being who happens to be an actor can, in an instant, become a character, then another, another and another, travelling down the years and across the centuries, over lands and seas, up to the skies and into space as well as inwards to the depths of the psyche. By implying rather than imposing, actors evoke audiences' imaginations, *each of us democratically exercising our individual creativity whilst remaining part of a theatregoing community.*

SECTION 3

THE EMPTY SPACE

An Empty Space is the Starting Place for Telling a Story

THE EMPTY SPACE REVISITED

An experience not unfamiliar, I'm sure, to anyone who has chanced to enter an empty and darkened auditorium is suddenly to find yourself transfixed by the sight of a bare stage lit by a single safety lamp and containing, perhaps, a solitary chair. The empty space is filled with energy. Time seems on hold. The air vibrates with promise. And that solitary chair? It, too, seems to hover expectantly. Who will appear to sit in it… or lean on it… or push it to one side? Or transform it… into a throne, a steed, a shelter, a barrier, a travelling companion…? With its single chair, the space is far more beautiful empty than it could be filled by a set. A set by its very name sets limits on what might be ahead. An empty space releases the imagination to roam. A storyteller takes possession of the chair and we're off…

THE TEMPTATION OF TECHNOLOGY

Some of my most pleasurable moments as a director have been working with designers. Theatre's employment of other arts and crafts is, in all senses, a diversion. Music, clothes, film and the like are incredibly attractive, no doubt about it, so seductive in fact that they can easily become the end rather than the means. But as a piece of theatre tries to steer its course through the currents of dramatic action, their siren songs can lure its practitioners aground in the shallows of deceptive effects. When technical developments first made it possible to refocus lights and shuffle colours by remote control or to modify sound in any way you wished, I remember how utterly engrossing it was to play with these new sophisticated toys. They offered so many possibilities you were blinded by choice and often ended up selecting what was dazzling rather than desirable. Much theatre becomes prey to the alluring tyranny of increasingly rapid digital innovation. It's used because you can use it, rather than needing to use it. The obvious way in which many directors (think they can or have to) make their mark is by the dexterous use of such effects. How well actors perform is less obviously attributable to them.

Therefore empty spaces aren't too much in evidence. Productions seem cluttered with spurious attempts to fill a void rather than to embrace a space, attempts that come between me and any experience of real theatre. I feel I'm being fed the equivalent of junk food: artificial flavouring, artificial colouring, too much sugar, too much salt, too many trans-fats – about as authentic and nutritious as one of those hysterically hued cupcakes, all topping and not much nourishment underneath; that's to say, junk theatre: too much scenery, too much music, too much lighting, too many sound effects, circus acts, site-specific promenade installations – theatrical topping that's cloying and bloating rather than dramatically nourishing. A student's most thrilling moment from a production of *Richard III*, so she excitedly told me, was of soldiers descending on ropes from a helicopter. 'A helicopter! A helicopter! My kingdom for a helicopter!' Instead of additives, subtractions might produce a healthier theatrical diet. Storytelling cleanses the palate and detoxifies the system.

THE TYRANNY OF TECHNOLOGY

Essentially, theatre has nothing to do with technology, nor is it about sets and costumes. These are lifeless embellishments, often ornamental distractions from the core experience. These have their purposes, of course, they have their place, but they also have to know that place, earn it and keep to it: their place as supporting players. They can reinforce and enhance the life created by the actors (as they can do in our actual lives), and this they can do thrillingly and beautifully and meaningfully if rigorously integrated into the world of the production. Then they become one with the main event (the drama of the characters) and inseparable from it, superbly exemplified in the best work of, say, Ariane Mnouchkine, Peter Stein or Robert Lepage, where the smallest detail of design feels *meant* and *inevitable*. But design and technology cannot supplant life or be a substitute for it. Because the life of theatre comes from no one but actors, we have to start with them, and only then, gradually – selectively and rigorously – add solely what the actors absolutely *need* to wear, *need* to handle, *need* to inhabit to materialise the story in hand. The constant refrain should be: Is that really necessary? *Really* necessary? It might be nice to have, but what would be lost without it? Otherwise music, projections et al., effect by effect, will rob the actors of their autonomy, their immediacy, their power to evoke and, consequently, deprive theatre of its natural liveliness. Digital technology, even in 3D, is two dimensions being imposed on three-dimensional human beings. Human beings are not screens. True theatre exists in drama: the interrelationship of people struggling to make sense of life and their ways through it. And that means, first and last, three-dimensional actors.

MASSAGE OR WORKOUT

A thought experiment: Imagine the impact of most movies without music. Indeed, when I watch a film, I eagerly give in to the seduction of its sounds, its score, its vast moving images; I become willingly passive, I wallow in it, luxuriate in it, I allow myself to be manipulated into a dream state which I carry out of the cinema with me, so that the street becomes an extension of the film. When I watch theatre, however, I feel (and expect to feel) challenged to sit up and pay attention, to be active, to exercise my intelligence with my imagination, to look around for myself. When I leave good theatre, I feel more alive, more awake, more alert, present in the actual street which I see more sharply. *This is because I'm in the presence of live actors who demand my presence in exchange for theirs.* And this demand is inescapable in the immediacy of storytelling theatre. It's the difference between a massage and a workout. Two equally valid but totally different experiences.

LESS IS MORE

I can't believe that human beings have now become so much less interesting than things! Or that they have to be surrounded by things and labels to be made interesting. True, theatre is a visual medium. But what can be more beautiful than bodies moving in space? Nietzsche declared that all movement aspires to dance and all speech to song. Theatre offers you human beings aspiring to song and dance; what could be lovelier, more life-enhancing? Is it any wonder musicals are so popular? Actors are *present*: alive and flexible, imaginative and resourceful, able to think, able to improvise, to take advantage of the moment, to solve problems, to create, to play; technology rarely.[1] I want what is unique to theatre: human beings in action.

Storytelling in an empty space is when theatre is most itself, at its purest. If purity sounds like thin gruel, all I can say is that less is more, less is of the essence. If small is beautiful, less is even more so. With Shared Experience's first sortie into storytelling with the *Arabian Nights*, there was something perversely gratifying in using an empty space to portray such lavishness, such luxuriance. No design could compete with the

---

1. Two highlights of technological discomfiture that have invoked my *Schadenfreude* over the years: (i) the lighting board of the Lyric Hammersmith going berserk during a performance of *Little Eyolf* and running rapidly through its entire programme, turning Diana Rigg every colour of its lighting design; (ii) the tenement buildings on either side of the stage in *Les Misérables* managing to jam during their ponderously cumbersome descent to interlock as barricades, staggering like dinosaurs on their way to extinction.

vividness of an audience's imagination. (The children's drawings of an *Arabian Nights* performance of ours that I referred to earlier are evidence of that.)

A story invites our imaginations to take wing, so I really don't appreciate having mine grounded by an overwhelming bombardment of effects. The less encumbered the runway, the easier the take-off, the freer the flight. An empty space is the greatest stimulus to dramatic resourcefulness. Storytellers in an empty space can convince us utterly of the reality they're creating, then wipe that reality by reminding us of their presence together with us in the here and now – and in an instant, restore our belief in the there and then by resuming their commitment to what they're playing. The true theatrical event is the joyful human creation of something out of 'nothing'. Storytelling goes hand in hand with an empty space. *An empty space is the visual equivalent of 'Once upon a time'.*

HOW EMPTY IS AN EMPTY SPACE?

However, an empty space cannot be a vacuum, actors do need to breathe. Nor can it be an abyss; they also need some ground beneath their feet. And it can't extend beyond the range of human sight, into infinity. So already – even in an empty space – my much-vaunted purity is compromised. The world is still with us. There are decisions that have to be made about what sort of surroundings, what sort of ground – the air, of course, is preferably fresh. As most performances still take place in spaces designated as theatres with stages or performance areas, the floors and walls are a given. But even these can be modified. A text which is energetic, violent, rumbustious, slapstick, colloquial, fleshy, materialistic, improvisational might well be suited to work within whatever space it finds itself without adjustment, indeed taking spontaneous advantage of any features a particular venue offers. The lighting would make no attempt to disguise or hide or modify what exists; its purpose: to illuminate the proceedings. On the other hand, material considered more delicately nuanced, subtle, reflective, intimate, refined, formal, spiritual (whatever that means to you) might benefit from lighting that dematerialises any distracting surroundings, leaving the actors to perform in a pool of clear light. However, the floor will always remain visible and in fact becomes a background against which the actors play. Should it remain as it is, should it be rendered as neutral as possible, or covered or treated in some way? What particular colour or texture would best contribute to the world being created? And then, should other elements gradually prove themselves essential, more decisions have to be made. If there's to be that chair, what is its colour to be, its shape, texture, material, its structure? How is it to be used, moved, sat on? And shouldn't that chair resonate with associations, images and memories beyond its pure chair-ness, its sit-on-ness? Theatre (as opposed to more literal film) is a medium of visual synecdoche:

a single chair may represent a room, but each member of the audience will see a room of their own, of their own imagining. Each new element must contribute to the reality of the imaginary world and support the performers. The actor is not, like a catwalk model, there to display the costume, the costume is there to inform the character. How actors relate to their environment extends and enriches their revelation – and our understanding – of character and story.

SECTION 4

ACTORS AS STORYTELLERS
Storytelling Demands Skills and Responsibilities Beyond an Actor's Customary Parameters

THE CHILD IS PARENT
TO THE STORYTELLER

The most natural actors, the most truly instinctive, are those who seem able to retain in adulthood the imaginative openness of childhood, together with a child's spontaneity in play. Self-consciousness, the need to be grown-up and sensible, to be in one's head, hasn't totally crushed this imagination or displaced it with a head-bound knowingness. The requirement for storytelling in an empty space is exactly this, the ability to imagine: to imagine what isn't there *is* there or what is there – such, perhaps, as that chair again – *might* be something else. This ability reasserts this childhood capacity in the audience, too – really an upgrading of Doctors and Nurses. So storytelling at its purest touches something both profoundly playful and playfully profound in all of us. Imagining what it's like to be someone else and in their shoes means identifying with them.

When Shared Experience made their initial outing with *Arabian Nights*, we had cushions placed on the floor so that the audience would have to sit, loll or recline at the feet of the storytellers. We did this to break the audience's automatic expectation of how they should behave in a theatre, as well as trying to suggest some archetypal image of public storytelling, albeit not a particularly Anglo-Saxon one. During the show I kept one eye on the audience, and have the persistent picture of an elderly man and a very small boy seated side by side, cross-legged, their faces lifted, their mouths open, succumbing to the enchantment of being told a story.

THE MOST HUMAN ART

Theatre is the most human of the arts. Its fundamental element is that trio of human beings: actor, character and audience with their triangle of relationships: actor/character, character/audience, audience/actor; their tangle of relationships, too, if we add actor/actor, character/character, audience/audience. At its best, we experience this phenomenon first and foremost in the actor, the representative of our – the audience's – humanness, there in flesh and blood before us, acting out our lives for us. The actor creates us, becomes us, shows us each other, shows us ourselves. The actor evokes our empathy to imagine others, to feel like them, to feel for them. The actor awakens the actor in all of us. The actor is us. *The actor does noth-ing less than create life.*[1] And of all forms of theatre, storytelling is the essential expression of this humanness.

This may seems an excessively exalted claim for just one form of theatre. While I'm in hyperbolic mode, I'll make another: storytellers can reveal the *ne plus ultra* of human potential. We none of us really know – let alone realise – our innate capacities; but the women and men who choose to become actors are in a position to reach out far beyond the presumed limitations imposed on them by their profession. Their essential job of transforming themselves into other people implies the extraordinary ability to assume the bodies, pursue the thoughts and experience the feelings of any and every other person that's ever existed, in actuality and mythology; or at least playwrights' ideas of Greek tyrants, Southern belles, Russian doctors, Andalusian peasants, frustrated Nordic wives, Italians with identity problems, the bipolar, the autistic, the rich, the poor, abused and abusers, nuns and fops, heavy drinkers, saints and Satan, serial murderers, artists in garrets, mothers of ten, Nazis, Quakers, gays, wits, twits, twins, Henry VIIIs, Elizabeth Is and Jesus Christs… Every new role potentially expands the actor's capacity to think, move and feel. Acting is a vocation demanding ever-increasing insight and expressiveness. Theatre, however, is notoriously peopled by others deciding what actors can and can't do, should and shouldn't do and how they should or shouldn't do it; and, more perniciously, by actors themselves who, with their own self-doubts and fears, submit to the tyranny of typecasting and, worse still, obediently imprison themselves in pre-designated pigeonholes. The potential of any person is unknowable and therefore, for all practical purposes, open to discovery.

1. One hundred and fifty years ago, Benoît-Constant Coquelin, the renowned French actor, was lamenting in his *Art and the Actor* that actors were not taken seriously and considered little better than parrots. But he insists that actors are creative, as creative as any other artist, and brings to bear the declarations of many playwrights that actors had taken their characters and revealed aspects of them that *they had no idea existed*, transforming them into totally new creations. He also justifies the actor's creativity by explaining that, whereas the painter has his brush, canvas and paints, the sculptor his marble or bronze, the poet his words, the actor has his own material, himself.

ACTORS ARE DYING OUT

Actors demand the immediacy of our presence in response to theirs. But when actors don't fulfil their side of the bargain, the challenge dies, the desire to sit up and pay attention collapses; but, alas, we don't gently subside into cinematic reverie, we sink into the slow torture of auditorium torpor. At a conference held for directors in mid-career, the consensus view of the participants was that the theatre's future lay in working with 'real' people. Actors presumably were some sort of dying subspecies, artistic Neanderthals. But do we really want to see ex-tenants of the Big Brother House moving into Bernarda Alba's house? Such silliness aside, actors may have partially brought this view of them upon themselves by rarely digging any deeper than the same row they competently hoe, getting away with that strangely incurious slickness known to many as 'professionalism', well-wrought emotional clichés deputising for experience, the unexamined repetition of formulaic performances that are allowed to pass for Great British Acting. One Mark Rylance doesn't make a summer season. Actors, who are in fact the very life of theatre – its sine qua non – appear to have let themselves get, if not totally lost, seriously sidelined in the shuffle between technology, celebrity and 'real people' dragged off the streets.

But clearly, most of them have the ability to do so much better, confronting their resistance against going where (deep down they know) they ought to go and are capable of going: of letting go and going to that place within each of them that makes an actor an artist, an individual; the place that provides the possibility for each one of them to release those breathtaking moments of spontaneity, of imaginative insight, that are theirs alone; moments that, all of a sudden, make us, the audience, sit up, charged with an equivalent heart-pounding, pulse-racing, hair-raising, skin-prickling, sweat-inducing, utterly heightened sense of ourselves. Big stuff: shock and awe indeed, joy, revelation, grief, compassion… Total transparency – no protection, nowhere to hide. Totally present. Totally *there*.

THE MULTIFACETED STORYTELLER

When actors become storytellers, the dimensions of their work are extended far beyond that traditional function of playing characters in scenes. Their humanity is challenged to express itself more expansively, more variously, in a multiplicity of roles, relationships and functions needed to move a story forward. Because storytellers are usually providing the framework, the structure and environment as well as the content of a story, the demands become more evident, more specialised and more challenging.

The Storyteller's Many Roles

In plays, an actor usually performs a single role or, occasionally, two or three smaller ones. But because stories are not constrained by the limitations of time, space and budget within which most plays are written, their expansive plots can, more often than not, require the actors to play a broad gallery of characters for which the concept of casting becomes meaningless. They cannot rely, should they habitually do so, on certain patterns of performance that over time they've acquired (and now possibly, half-consciously, depend on) to see them through a series of roles in a sequence of plays. Storytelling forces them to break with these performing personae and search within themselves for many selves. Their virtuosity confirms that, latent within every one of us, there exists a universal connection, a protean understanding of others; we all possess something of everyone else, past, present and, at a reasonable guess, to come. Hardly surprising when we're all made of the same stuff. The storytelling actor exemplifies this capacity within us.

The Storyteller's Many Relationships

Storyteller to Audience

The actor's prime relationship is obviously to the audience. Their reception of the story is the reason for the telling. Consequently, an actor's awareness of the audience must exist at all times, not just while narrating to them directly. When storytellers play scenes, they are simply telling a story by other means, and they should sense that they're taking the audience with them into that scene rather than leaving them on hold until they return to their narrating persona. Storytellers have to ensure that the audience is travelling with them on every step of the story's way.

Their direct address must establish a genuine connection with the audience. They have to ensure that the entire audience is contacted, no punters left ignored and disgruntled in the upper circle, resentful of the people in the front stalls clearly having a far better time of it than they are. To talk *to* an audience is more easily said than done. It's not good enough to send lines sailing out into the dark, hoping that they'll land somewhere appropriate; actors have to make sure, simply, clearly, appropriately – neither self-effacingly nor self-promotingly – that their words reach their target. Consequently they need to remain open to possible responses from the audience (smiles, nods of agreement, concerned looks, furrowed brows, tear-filled eyes, even words) and ready, in turn, to respond to these, to allow these reactions to affect the subsequent course of their narrative, so that this give and take flows through the whole performance. Storytelling works in both directions. [*Cross-refer Set 12, Workshops 54-57: Developing Contact with the Audience*]

Telling the story to the audience underpins whatever else actors might be contributing to the performance, whether creating environments, providing music, even when watching their colleagues in action. [*Cross-refer Set 6, Subset 3, Workshop 36: Watching*] Everything that happens on stage should be there to serve this single purpose.

Storyteller to Story

In a play, it's perfectly possible (and probably quite common) for actors to keep their heads down and fulfil their part in the whole successfully enough without expending too much concern for the piece as an entirety, especially when, as is often the case, they're only called to rehearse the scenes they appear in and are not encouraged to participate in the creation of the piece as a whole. In performance, when they end a scene, they leave the stage to watch telly, chatter, and drink coffee in the green room, possibly conducting mini post-mortems on how they and tonight's audience are doing, or they retire to their dressing rooms to text, read a book, do a crossword, possibly check their script, change costume, repair their make-up and, if they have a sufficient gap, take a nap. Their connection with the performance is reduced to a rumbling obbligato on the tannoy, and their responsibility for it attenuates to such a degree that they have to rely on someone else (the stage management) to get them back on stage for their next appearance. Despite the best will in the world, they're yanked in and out of the reality of the performance, they lose contact with it, so that they can do little else but focus on their part in it.

But as narrators providing the framework for a story, they have to take on responsibility for the whole event. They must have a clear understanding of the world of the story, all the themes and motifs embedded in it, and their exact contribution to how these are placed and expressed. Consequently, they should remain on stage so that, watching from the sidelines, they have the opportunity – more objectively than when playing – to observe the energy and atmosphere existing between their partners and the audience on any particular night. When it's their turn to enter the action, the manner in which they do so can alert the others to any adjustments they feel necessary. Sometimes, for example, the collective mood of the company, quite unintentionally, may have become a little overconfident, causing a slight relaxation of energy. Those watching can rectify this when they re-enter the action by bringing with them a fresh impulse as a wake-up call to others. [*Cross-refer Set 6, Subset 3, Workshop 36: Watching*]

Storyteller to Character

Because the actor is functioning with this overview of the whole piece, character – though still the most important element of the actor's work – is no longer the sole one. Storytelling subsumes playacting. It may not be enough for actors to interpret their characters and play them subjectively from the characters' points of view as they'd usually (rightly) do in a play. The story could possibly require them to both represent *and* present them with different attitudes and from several viewpoints, according to the demands of the writer. Without the slightest loss of truth and commitment in playing a specific scene, storytellers must make sure they don't allow inappropriate choices to distort the character's function in the story, and disrupt the shape and flow of the story as a whole.

Storyteller as Narrator to Characters

This relationship can vary in kind and complexity. It depends on whether the narrator is also a character within the action; or someone who is privy to the action without participating in it; or is someone – usually unidentified – recounting the story from beyond its borders. It may depend on the discrepancy between the narrator's point of view and that of the characters. The narrator may support the characters, be in conflict with the characters or remain dispassionate towards them. The narrator may identify fully with a character.

Storyteller as Character to Narrator

The relationship in this direction is not automatically identical with that in the other. Usually, the characters (as opposed to the actors) are totally unaware of the narration surrounding their scenes. In this case, they function much more closely to characters in a play, subjectively 'accepting' how they have been set up by the narrator (who may or not be themselves). But it is conceivable that the characters might resist or even rebel against a narrator's portrayal of them. [*Cross-refer the above three paragraphs to Sets 3, 4, 5, Workshops 9-23 and Set 7, Subset 2, Workshops 39-40: all dealing with aspects of Narration*]

Storyteller to Space

Actors have to relate to the space and their use of it with the understanding of exactly how it supports and enhances the journey of a story. Spatial choices can define or reinforce two relationships: that of the actor to the audience – how near, how far, from a warm area or a cold one and so forth; and, similarly, that between the characters within the story. [*Cross-refer Set 3, Workshop 9: Areas of the Stage and Their Qualities; Workshop 10: Narration from Different Areas of the Stage; Set 6, Subset 2: Spatial Awareness, Workshops 29-31; Subset 3, Workshop 32: Spatial Focus; Set 12, Workshop 57: Spatial Relationship between Storyteller and Audience*]

Storyteller to Design

If there *is* to be any use of technological or scenic elements, actors must understand how these contribute to the telling of the story and be able to interact with them and exploit them, that is, be in creative control of them in the furtherance of that aim. Such elements imposed on performers inhibit their spontaneity and pre-empt their expressiveness; in other words, they do their work for them or in spite of them. Actors should have time to develop a relationship with any props, furniture, costumes, music, lighting and scenery, so that these become expressively integrated into their performance, in fact become *extensions* of themselves. The way in which an actor relates to an environment is part of the creation of character, world and what the story's about. [*Cross-refer Set 9: Workshops for Using Elements 43-47; and to relevant paragraphs below in The Storyteller's Many Functions: Storyteller as Set Designer, etc.*]

Storyteller to Storyteller (Actor to Actor)

And of course, just as in a play, the actors must at all times be good partners, working generously and openly with one another, responding spontaneously to each other's provocations and offering their own in return with the knowledge that their colleagues will respond in kind: healthy give and take. (By provocation I mean something entirely positive: any action or activity should be a source of stimulation between partners, an offer that cannot not be refused, that in fact should be accepted with enthusiasm, so that, playing off one another, actors may together create something totally fresh, surprising, but satisfyingly inevitable.) This applies whether between narrators and characters, between narrators sharing narration and, of course, between characters in scenes.

The Storyteller's Many Functions

Actors, when telling stories, may need to embrace a larger share of the performance than is normally asked of them, to turn their hands – their whole body in fact – to whatever helps move the story forward. This means assuming additional functions to that of playing characters in scenes: functions such as host, MC, public speaker, stand-up comedian, storyteller of course, narrator, guide, critic, commentator, analyst, designer, sculptor, painter, landscape artist, interior decorator, tailor, dressmaker, dresser, sound designer, lighting designer, choreographer, technician, stage manager, stage hand, dancer, mime, musician – magician even, inasmuch as they can, in an empty space, by means of their presence alone, conjure up what isn't there.

So storytellers create by other means what is usually provided by designers, musicians, and all the other traditional contributors to a performance. These are some of the necessary skills that actors need to acquire in the pursuit of total self-reliance during performance.

Storyteller as Athlete

Actors are athletes of a very particular kind. They're unlikely to win Grand Slams or scale Everest. Their physicality isn't designed to execute thirty-two fouettés on ice; that is, it's not intended to achieve the particular abilities of any one discipline. On the contrary, skilful actors need bodies capable of fulfilling an extraordinary range of skills in many areas.

Let's start with what is so obvious that it's probably taken for granted. The essential task of acting, the incarnation of character, means not only expressing the psychology of the character, but also, quite literally, embodying another person – which is, of course, an extension of that psychology. No two people move or relate to space identically or make the same shapes and gestures within it. So, to be capable of assuming a physicality quite different from their own, actors have first to understand how their own bodies work and, if necessary, to break physical patterns that have become so autonomically ingrained that they block the range of their expressiveness. They must consciously master muscles that most of us are probably unaware we possess. (I was once shown a Russian book on make-up that mainly concentrated on how to master control of the numerous muscles in the face – possibly some forty of them.) They must be able to change their habitual rhythms. Then, rather than resorting to a small repertoire of thoughtlessly applied gestural clichés (like old-fashioned opera singers), they can specifically create and inhabit someone else's skin.

Actors need to wed their physical abilities to their powers of observation and their empathic imagination. They have to spend time (more than I sense they do) studying other people. That's where they'll find the material to add to their store of behavioural knowledge. When recreating another person's way of movement, it's also necessary to discover the impulses and motives that cause that idiosyncratic use of the body. By committing themselves to the repetition of a particular gesture, employing a sort of reverse engineering, they are more than likely to engender the feelings that might have motivated such a gesture in the first place.

In addition to the creation of a basic physical characterisation, actors have to imagine and then execute a character's specific movement and behaviour in conditions that may be unusual for that character, for instance, people totally reliant on the service of others, suddenly having to fend for themselves. Actors will have to handle objects and wear clothing unfamiliar to them. Their characters may have occupations or circumstances that strongly influence their physical life – boxers maybe, miners, invalids, peasants, models… The actors may need to be convincingly pregnant or older, younger, lighter, heavier than they are (without padding!), possibly to play someone of the opposite gender. The status of characters will also create a particular set of physical patterns: how they wear their clothes, take up space, anticipate others' physical and spatial relationship to them. Beyond this, certain roles may demand specialised skills and techniques, such as dancing, wrestling, acrobatics, riding a horse, riding a motorbike, making strudel, erecting a marquee… Performers may have to acquire skills in different forms of mime, especially when working in an empty space; by their physicality they must be able to evoke environments and create images. They will need to develop strong proprioception – their sense of themselves in space and in their relationship to others.

Much of this, of course, is true for actors in plays. But many actors bring more or less the same body to every role they play. In storytelling, this simply won't work. The sheer profusion of roles and functions demands a protean flexibility and a rich physical imagination. In addition, storytellers will need all their movement skills to contribute to the ensemble's collective creation of physical images – frequently gymnastic – as well as fulfilling many of their other functions as designers, landscape artists, stage managers... [*Cross-refer Set 2, Workshop 8: Physical Work for Solo Performer; Set 6: Workshops for Building an Ensemble, Subset 1:Workshops 24-28 Physical Awareness; Set 9, Workshop 47: Shoes*]

Storyteller as Narrator

Actors need not only bodies with stamina, strength, flexibility and the ability to isolate muscles, but also voices with much the same attributes. The voice is a part of the body. Using the voice has as much to do with physical ability and athleticism as being able to swim or salsa. All those moving parts of the body that create voice and speech need to be at their command – the muscles of the ribcage that allow the lungs to expand, the jaw, the tongue and so forth... Imaginative vocal variety is rare from most performers. But narrators are likely to be confronted by unfamiliar, complex language, and their vocalism must be capable of dealing with such texts. Clarity of speech, expressive range of voice, sense of narrative logic, establishment of mood, ability with dialects, accents, even impersonations, are all part of a storyteller's toolkit. Narrators may need to encompass the roles of announcer and public speaker. They will need the ability to tell stories from different points of view: from themselves, from characters telling their story in the first person, from characters talking about themselves in the third. They may need to move nimbly from one characterisation to another. They have responsibility for firmly shaping a story's movement from event to event and giving each of those events its appropriate emphasis within the whole. *Furthermore, it's their job to ensure that what we listen to is as pleasurable as what we look at.* But, above all, to narrate well, the storyteller must be in true communion with the audience. [*Cross-refer Set 2, Workshop 7: Voice and Speech Work; Sets 3, 4, 5, Workshops 9-23; Set 7, Subset 2, Workshops 39-40: Exercises on multiple aspects of narration; Set 12, Workshops 54-57: To Develop Content with the Audience*]

Storyteller as Set Designer

By the way actors move within an empty space they're able to conjure images of specific places in the mind's eye of their audience. Audiences see what actors suggest. Not only through the literal miming of objects or surfaces are places evoked, but also by the distance on which the eyes focus, by expansion or contraction of the torso, by straightened or tilted spines, big strides or small steps, folded or loose arms and so on. Actors can create socially, psychologically and environmentally motivated behaviour that suggests whether their surroundings are congenial or unfriendly, dangerous or safe, public or private, familiar or strange, wretched or rich, indoors or out...

At a more deliberately stylised level, actors can establish environments by actually turning themselves into scenic objects, becoming waves, trees, doors, thrones – well, whatever's needed. This opens up a range of further possibilities, such as endowing such elements with personalities that react to what is going on around them or to how they're being treated. [*Cross-refer Set 8, Workshop 41: Bringing the Space Alive; Workshop 42: Individual Images*]

Storyteller as Costume Designer

Because storytelling is likely to contain a multiplicity of roles and changes of place and time, it's rarely practical for actors to be fully costumed in character – even if that were always desirable. But in keeping with the principle of working in an empty space devoid of design, what, then, should actors wear? Rather than costumes, think of clothes: everyday wear that doesn't draw attention to itself and certainly doesn't represent their characters; the sartorial equivalent of an empty space. Within such a convention, they should never relate to what they've actually got on their backs, but in the same way that actors may need to mime props, they may need to mime what their characters are wearing.

But in other circumstances they may find themselves performing in a range of conventions that clothes them in anything from an ensemble, all-purpose 'uniform' to single items like hats or scarves, from lengths of material they can drape themselves in to oddments grabbed as needed from a costume rack. But whatever the convention, each will require the actors to create an image or impression of appropriately garbed characters. In certain cases they may have to be skilful in manipulating – knotting or draping – pieces of material or in endowing elements of clothing with the sense of complete dress. If they do use full costumes, they may have to be adept at quick changes in front of an audience. They may at times function as each other's dressers. [*Cross-refer Section 9: From Analysis to Performance Worlds; Set 9, Workshop 47: Something to Put On*]

Storyteller as Lighting Designer

By the same token, in pure storytelling, there is no special lighting. The principle is to use whatever source is available to provide a single, constant state of white light to fulfil its primary purpose of illuminating actors and audience. *Lighting the audience is vital if the actors are to see to whom they're talking.* The actors create a sense of appropriate light and shade by the way they behave. In *Bleak House*, where the story demanded many sources of light – candlelight, chandeliers, street lamps, firelight – day and night-time were suggested by how freely or cautiously the characters moved, by the way they peered into shadows, adjusted their gaze to different eyelines, mimed carrying candles and related to imaginary firesides. Many audiences praised the lighting effects they were convinced we'd been using, despite the whole ten hours having been lit by the same single state of white light. Like the pupils who drew pictures of our school versions of *Arabian Nights*, they had been sufficiently stimulated by the actors' performances to see what actually wasn't there.

If lighting states *are* used, the actors should be given time to get out of the acting space in order to observe how they and the stage are being lit and what effects the lights create. They can then work with these qualities to enhance a particular moment: choosing to stay in shadow or cast shadows, to move between warm and cold, bright and dark areas, to be sculpted by sidelight, silhouetted by backlight and so forth… In this way, storytellers are in control of the technology. They might carry lights themselves to illuminate each other.

Storyteller as Musician

No sets, no costumes, no lighting effects. And no musical instruments. I believe that just as everyone is essentially an actor, everyone has some degree of innate musicality. So the actors have to provide any music that's needed by singing, humming and creating the sounds of musical instruments both vocally and percussively using their bodies and the floor. [*Cross-refer Set 11, Workshops 50-52: Developing Music*]

Storyteller as Sound Designer

And no sound technology. Apart from what it can do musically, the voice contains a potential treasury of sounds and, further, the rest of the body is an amazingly efficient sounding board for all sorts of aural effects. Patting, rubbing or slapping different parts of the body, both bare and clothed in a variety of materials, can create a gallery of sound effects. [*Cross-refer Set 11, Workshop 53: Creating Sound Effects*]

Storyteller as Stage Hand and Stage Manager

If there are to be any scenic elements on the stage, they have to be handled by the actors. Whenever we resorted to them, the actors functioned as their own stage hands, moving them as necessary. But the way in which they moved them was dictated by the aesthetics and form appropriate to the world of the play. We had to justify to our own satisfaction the sort of reality in which the characters could move objects or within what convention the actors could do so. The way in which actors move objects becomes another aspect of the world they're creating, part of its reality. One of the thematic threads in Hardy's *Jude the Obscure* is the characters' employment of doors and windows as barriers to relationships, obstacles that have to be forced open. So the set comprised doors and windows built on heavy trucks that had to be moved from place to place by the actors. The effort of pushing them physicalised the world of frustrated passions in which the characters struggled to relate to one another; the effort also helped the actors to reach the appropriate level of intensity they needed to enter a subsequent scene. Rigorously pursued, such movement can acquire – as it did in this case – the quality of dance.

Especially when narrating, storytellers may find themselves functioning as stage managers, setting up scenes – not only by words, but also by placing props and furniture, helping other actors to change costume and creating any sound effects needed for a scene; clearing the stage, too. [*Cross-refer Set 7, Workshop 40: Pitch and Tone for Third-Person Narrator Outside the Action Setting Up Scenes*]

Storyteller as Host and MC

In storytelling, the actors initiate the event. Nothing happens before they begin the story, whatever the manner of storytelling might be. This may mean welcoming the audience, possibly organising them, making them comfortable, putting them into a suitable mood or frame of mind to listen to the story they're about to tell. If they establish this role of host at the top of the show, they implicitly sustain it throughout the performance, ready to reassert it whenever necessary. If this function of organising the occasion continues steadily and deliberately throughout the storytelling, it may transform into the role of master of ceremonies as they announce and oversee the entire conduct of the evening. In these functions, the actors make very evident their presence outside the story.

Standing outside the story, they may need to act as guides, leading the audience through the labyrinth of the plot that the writer has constructed. They may become spokespersons for the director, clarifying certain stage conventions for us. They may be required to act as advisers to the audience, warning them of impending horrors (strobe lighting, loud bangs, nudity), even providing them with subsequent reassurance.

Storyteller as Critic and Commentator

Depending on the requirements of the writer, the narrators may well have to take on the role of commentators, satirists, judges, critics or defenders of characters, societies and their institutions. Actors in plays usually perform from the character's point of view, allowing other characters or the audience to form conflicting opinions of them. In storytelling, the actors themselves may have to deal with their own characters from several perspectives, even simultaneously. Often, critical observations are contained within the character's self-narration; then the actor has to become at once both character and critic of the character – a skill akin to patting your head while rubbing your stomach. They have to sustain the integrity of their characterisations while exposing them from varying perspectives to the audience's view. [*Cross-refer Set 4, Workshop 14: Narrators Embodying Their Characters while Commenting on Them*]

Storyteller as Athlete...

There may well be other functions lurking in a story waiting to make fresh demands on a storyteller that will only become apparent in the process of adapting different sorts of material. *Total availability to become or do whatever the story demands is the criterion for storytelling actors.* They need an extraordinary degree of flexibility and availability that we might call emotional and sensory athleticism, even athleticism of the spirit. They become not only athletes of the soma, but also of the psyche.

ACTORS IN CHARGE

Because storytelling demands that all the actors take responsibility, not only for their individual roles and text, but for the care and maintenance of the performance as a whole, it tends to take their minds off themselves and to release them from problems of ego that might, in conventional performances, become intractable. If actors have only one role to worry about, its failure or success can understandably become of such importance that it distracts them from the very thing they're anxious to achieve. But in storytelling, they have more than enough functions to override any preoccupation with just one. The show becomes more important than any one performer's contribution to it. This group endeavour endows each performer with equal ownership of the performance. The actors are not just cogs in the machine, but the machine itself. They make it and they run it. They own it. *The actors are in charge.* This proprietorial commitment to a production benefits the audience by the increased enthusiasm, care and consequent lift in energy with which the actors tell their stories.

SECTION 5

FROM NARRATIVE TO NARRATION

Transforming a Reading Text into a Performing Text

APPROACHING A TEXT

To tell stories onstage we transform narrative into narration. To put text into action, we have to discover performance equivalents for the literary devices of the fiction we're adapting. We are not attempting to turn a story into a play with the particular conventions that this would entail: extended scenes of dialogue in a limited number of locations. The intention is to create something more fluid and flexible, true as far as possible to both spirit and word of the story we're telling, closer to its original forms and structures. To make this transposition we have to know precisely what we're transforming – which means deconstructing a story, breaking it down into its component parts to study how each of them functions, so that we can reassemble them with a fuller understanding of how they interrelate. We're trying to learn how a writer, consciously or otherwise, has put a text together. In a sense, we're trying to enter the writer's creativity and become one with the material so that, to the best of our abilities, we recreate it in the performance language that we believe most closely fulfils what we've interpreted from our analysis of the text.

Of course, this process of analysis, interpretation and realisation doesn't always occur in a neat sequence of discrete procedures. These can overlap, get out of order or go into reverse – and it's not unusual to leap, or want to leap, straight from an initial reading of a story to an immediate idea of how to tell it. But before embarking on our analysis, let alone an interpretation, we should – and if not, why not? – have read the text several times in a relaxed and agenda-free state, allowing it, after our immediate first response, to soak into us more fully . If we're already somewhat familiar with the material, we should nonetheless try to meet it as though for the first time to prevent any preconceptions (which often prove to be misconceptions) blocking us from seeing what's *really* there.

If we've actually worked on the text before, we should still look at it afresh to search further and deeper. The material may be the same, but our circumstances will now be different. Apart from anything else, we've grown older; our perceptions and our experience, one hopes, will also have grown. Our collaborators with their own personal contributions to make are also likely to be different. To reuse the same ideas for the same material without reinvestigation is lazy, complacent; the end product may be perfectly correct, but it's almost certain be a pallid version of the original; not so much fresh revival as mere survival. Second-hand input: second-rate output. Without uncertainty, you'll never make discoveries. To know what you're doing, you must to some extent *not* know what you're doing.

Our instinct – which is nothing more mysterious than our innate abilities (nature) wedded to our learned abilities (nurture) – contains the greater and richer part of our creativity. But we need to check instinct against analysis. Early in our relationship with a text – before it's become a friendship and well before it's grown into a passion (but beware of love at first sight, aka blind infatuation) – we'll have glimpsed some initial ideas of how to realise particular sections of the material. Without them, it's unlikely we'd be stimulated to continue the work. These ideas may be perfectly good and right in themselves. But they may well be in ignorance of the full context and contents of the story. Initial responses may eventually need to be modified by a broadening and deepening knowledge of the whole. Analysis helps us to adjust or refine our initial impulses. Instinct confirmed by analysis should encourage us to proceed with confidence. If, however, there's conflict or contradiction between the two, we'll have to struggle to reconcile them, which in itself can be creatively purging or purgingly creative: at times we'll achieve a satisfyingly imaginative fusion, at others we may have completely to let go of some initial responses. Instant decisions about material can often be what we'd like the piece to be rather than what it is. This stage of the work can be painful (relinquishing our 'good ideas'). It demands that we relentlessly question our intentions and our honesty – which means not retreating into denial when confronted by textual evidence unsympathetic to what we want it to be.

So what sort of analysis can help us towards this understanding? First, the information we need is in the story. Research should remain a secondary source, useful, of course, to throw light on references in the text that may be obscure to us, but superfluous to requirements if it doesn't. Resist the temptation to insert intriguing but spurious details you've chanced upon in your searches; they will clutter rather than clarify.[1] We're rarely if ever going to understand the purpose or point of every word or thought that a writer has put on paper. Even the writer won't always know. But we can try to become as intimate as possible with a text by drilling down through its layers to excavate patterns of any sort – affinities, similarities, repetitions, mirror images, harmonies, counterpoints, parallels, shadows, contrasts, echoes, correspondences – that reveal thematic tendencies and emphases of structure, imagery and mood. If you dig deep enough, you may well find a fully formed interpretation awaiting you. The following is a brief glossary of the component parts of a story, to be dealt with in greater detail as we develop their application.

---

1. In a perfect world, we would first become expert on every aspect of the culture from which the story sprang. This would include learning the language. We would become knowledgable about the author's every word and life, capable of writing the definitive biography. We would wipe from our minds any knowledge we possessed that post-dated the publication of the story. We would then have become so steeped in the world that produced this story, that we could read it as a contemporary of its first readers, thinking like them and understanding like them. Our adaptation would make stringent use only of what research was absolutely pertinent to the story. But the story would still remain our first and last source of information. That is, in a perfect world!

DEFINITIONS

Story/Plot/Narrative

Story/Plot/Narrative are often somewhat hazily – lazily – treated as synonymous.

Story, of course, identifies a piece of fiction in its entirety – non-fiction, too, for that matter. But in a secondary sense story is the précis – a summing-up of the overall action – of that material. It answers the question: What's the story about? If you asked this about *Bleak House*, for example, I might reply that it's the story of Esther Summerson, an orphan (amongst several), who learns the truth of her origins as a great mystery linking many characters from vastly differing backgrounds, is uncovered against the slow-grinding, never-to-be-resolved proceedings of an iniquitous legal system.

Plot is the detailed scenario, event by event, which makes up the story, together with sufficient character motivation to link them logically. In *Bleak House*, Esther Summerson, a young woman who has no knowledge of her parentage, endures a repressive upbringing from a godmother who leads her to feel that it had been better had she never been born. At the death of this trustee, who proves to have been her aunt, Esther becomes the ward of John Jarndyce, a philanthropist, previously unknown to her, who arranges her education as a governess. At the age of twenty, Esther is assigned by the Court of Chancery to be companion to another orphan, Ada Clare. Ada, together with Richard Carstone (like her, a ward of court), will live under the guardianship of the same John Jarndyce at Bleak House. Here Esther experiences a happier existence. As she begins her new life, an unidentifiable man, a law-writer, is discovered dead in a sordid room above a junk shop… and so forth.

The essential elements of *Plot* are *Character* and *Event* (Who did What).

Character creates *Plot*. The ambitions and objectives of the characters drive the action forward and cause most of its obstacles and conflicts. Stories usually have a main character (Emma Woodhouse, David Copperfield, Esther Summerson, Tom Jones), not necessarily the most important or even the most interesting one, but the person with whom we have the most intimate relationship. In large novels with multiple plots, there may be several major characters. But even so, a single character usually acts as the pivot or lynchpin between the several strands of narrative. In *Bleak House*, there are many characters that Esther is unaware of, but their actions all move towards revealing the mystery at the centre of which she finds herself.

Event is any sort of incident, episode or occurrence – even the slightest, such as taking a walk or eating a meal. An event moves the plot forward by changing the situation in some way; and in doing so reveals some fresh aspect or development of characters. Most events are caused by the characters themselves, but the plot may be affected by events beyond their control, such as an outbreak of war, a delayed train or a natural disaster. These sorts of events usually become frames within which we observe how the characters behave in reaction to them.

Narrative is *the way* in which the *story* is told, *how* the *plot* is unrolled.

The particularity of a *Narrative* is defined by its *Viewpoint*, *Structure* and *Language*.

Viewpoint establishes through whose eyes and voice the story is being seen and told. *Bleak House*, for example, is told in two voices: through the *first* person of Esther Summerson in the *past* tense; and through an unidentified *third* person in the *present* tense. Esther's narrative is inevitably subjective, selective and obviously coloured by her values and feelings; the unattributed narrative is omniscient, satirical and objective (if satire can be said to be objective).

Structure is the means, usually in large blocks, by which the *plot* is organised and moves the story along: chronologically, maybe, or out of sequence; from multiple points of view between shifting time slots and locations. It is the way in which certain portions of plot are withheld or revealed; it may release the plot by indirection: incidental observations and unstressed details. It establishes the ratio between different elements of a story: scenes of dialogue, exposition, descriptive passages, philosophical disquisitions, and comments on, attitudes to, conjectures about and analyses of characters and events... Letters and diaries were once used extensively as part of a novel's structure; some novels, such as *Les Liaisons Dangereuses* and *Clarissa*, are in exclusively epistolary mode. Now writers are more likely to make use of emails, texting, tweets and other forms of social networking. These are essentially varying forms of *first-person viewpoint*. So if all or several of the characters in a story write letters or record diaries, these would be an example of multiple *first-person narratives*. In *Bleak House*, the story is told chronologically but in blocks of chapters with their alternating points of view: the first-person past tense of Esther and the third-person present tense of the unattributed voice. The juxtaposition of the two modes of narrative allows us to know much more about the circumstances surrounding Esther than she knows herself and therefore creates a subtextual irony for us while reading her portions of the story – an enrichment of her narrative that it wouldn't achieve on its own.

Language, the most individualising element of a story, is the particular choice of vocabulary, sentence structure, grammar and punctuation. Language expresses the unique vision and tone of the writer. A text may be rich in adjectives, imagery and metaphor. It might be succinct and undecorated. It may be conversational or structured with complex clauses. It may comment on its action or only present facts. It might be mostly in dialogue, such as Henry James's *The Awkward Age*, or entirely so as in Philip Roth's *Deception* – as opposed to his *Everyman*, which is almost without. The language may be demotic, as in DBC Pierre's *Vernon God Little*, or highly formal as the conversations in the novels of Ivy Compton-Burnett. It may be partially in dialect, like James Kelman's *How Late It Was, How Late*. There may be multiple voices, some as streams of consciousness, such as those in William

Faulkner's *As I Lay Dying*. A novel may be written in verse, like Pushkin's *Eugene Onegin* or Vikram Seth's *Golden Gate*. (Epic Poems, like *Sir Gawain and the Green Knight*, are stories.)

In *Bleak House*, the type of language used by each of the two narratives appropriately supports those two very different viewpoints: the third-person present employs a complex sentence structure and goes in for elaborate metaphor, rhetorical flourishes and a wide use of comic devices – irony, sarcasm, exaggeration and a sort of verbal slapstick – to achieve its satirical purposes:

> Jarndyce and Jarndyce drones on. This scarecrow of a suit has, in the course of time, become so complicated that no man alive knows what it means. The parties to it understand it least; but it has been observed that no two Chancery lawyers can talk about it for five minutes without coming to a total disagreement as to all its premises. Innumerable children have been born into it; innumerable young people have married into it; innumerable old people have died out if it. Scores of people have deliriously found themselves made party to Jarndyce and Jarndyce, without knowing why or how; whole families have inherited legendary hatreds with the suit. The little plaintiff or defendant, who was promised a new rocking-horse when Jarndyce and Jarndyce should be settled, has grown up, possessed himself of a real horse, and trotted away into the other world. Fair wards of court have faded into mothers and grandmothers; a long procession of Chancellors has come in and gone out; the legion of bills in the suit have been transformed into mere bills of mortality; there are not three Jarndyces left upon this earth perhaps, since old Tom Jarndyce in despair blew his brains out at a coffee-house in Chancery Lane; but Jarndyce and Jarndyce still drags its weary length before the Court, perennially hopeless. Jarndyce and Jarndyce has passed into a joke. That is the only good that has ever come of it.

Esther's language is simpler, more domestic in tone, spoken from the heart, and her occasional sorties into humour are in a much gentler and more sympathetic tone:

> Every part of the house was in such order, and every one was so attentive to me, that I had no trouble with my two bunches of keys: though what with trying to remember the contents of each little store-room drawer and cupboard; and what with making notes on a slate about jams, and pickles, and preserves, and bottles, and glass, and china, and a great many other things; and what with being a generally methodical, old-maidish sort of foolish little person; I was so busy that I could not believe it was break-fast-time when I heard the bell ring. Away I ran, however, and made tea, as I had already been installed into the responsibility of the tea-pot...

Theme/Topic (subject matter)

These can also be misread as synonymous.

Theme is the essential *idea* holding the many elements of a story in a coherent whole, a controlling vision that ensures every aspect of the narrative contributes to the story. Ideally it's expressible within a single sentence and usually conveys a broad idea. The theme of *Bleak House* might be: When institutions designed for the care of their dependents (government, philanthropy, law, family and the like) fail in their purpose, the only recourse is for individuals to take care of one another.

A theme is not necessarily something that's been consciously planned by the writer – who may, in fact, be unaware of – or indifferent to – its existence. But deep analysis of a text usually uncovers a unifying idea, a view of life implicit in what's written, deriving, no doubt, from the sub- or semi-conscious values and beliefs that the writer, like every other human being, inevitably holds and which, intended or not, must at some level pervade what's on the page. This may partially explain why many writers state that they've no idea what they've written until they read it. For readers or audiences, the theme exists much like a blueprint for a building, of which no one who uses the building is necessarily, or needs to be, (made) aware. It is, of course, far more interesting for them if they are. But whether so or not, from a sustained and consistent theme they'll experience a satisfying sense of cohesion. It is, of course, the interpreter/adapter's job to make every effort to discover the possible intellectual idea that underpins the edifice of a story in order to reconstruct it for the theatre.

Topic is the *subject matter* of a story, the vehicle or vehicles by which the *theme* is carried through the story. In *Bleak House*, the main *topic* is orphanhood; another is the law.

A *topic* is static (a word), a *theme* is active (a sentence). Syphilis, one of the topics of Ibsen's *Ghosts*, was initially treated by its critics as if it were his theme. But Ibsen's interest in venereal disease was as a vehicle for investigating social hypocrisy. More probably the actual theme of that play is: Those who live by lies will inevitably be destroyed by them.

A story in which the subject matter is erroneously treated as a theme usually becomes issue-based or documentary rather than fiction. It is likely either to promote a dogmatic agenda ('The Cure for Aids is Abstinence') or ramble inconclusively around the subject matter. Fiction, rarely prescriptive, uses topics (which may indeed happen to be of contemporary concern) as a means of penetrating into a wider and deeper view of life, one that it explores through open-ended action rather than closed statement. The urgency of contemporary issues fades over time, but the broader ideas implicit in a theme tend to remain valid and to reappear within new topics. When Ibsen wrote *Ghosts*, syphilis was inconceivable as a topic for public discussion and provided him with a daringly apposite vehicle to explore the effects of living dishonestly within an opaque, conformist society. Living now, he might have considered the topic of paedophilia more germane to his purposes.

World

World is the unique reality – the idiosyncratic mode, form or style – in which the story exists and is defined by the narrative's particular choice of *viewpoint*, *language* and *structure*, by the cultural setting of the story, and by the degree and manner in which the story departs from actuality (the reality in which we live). The particular components of a story (dialogue, action, diaries, newspaper clippings and so on) and the predominance of some over others also contribute to the definition of its *World*, its reality. The *World* of a story is an amalgam of all the elements that create a story. [*Cross-refer Section 9: Worlds; Set 10, Workshops 48-49: Worlds*]

———

Characters, events and *subject matter*, hence *plot*, are facts and therefore the *What* of the novel.

Viewpoint, structure and *language* are also *What* inasmuch as they exist on the printed page. But, more importantly, they are the *How*. They create the manner of the narrative by which the plot is told.

Theme is neither a *What* or a *How*, but a *Might Be*, because it's an interpretation, based on reasonable conjectures derived from the analysis of the *narrative*.

World, too, is a *Might Be*, similarly arrived at through the interpretation of the analysed elements.

THOUGHTS ABOUT PLOT

I'm a great believer in plot. From time to time it gets dismissed as some sort of middle-class aberration; but a story without a plot is an impossibility. Stories are about people. People do things. The things they do become plots. If, however, what they do makes no accumulative sense, if what they do is predictable and problem-free, if events are arbitrary, if anything can happen, if there are no rules in the world being presented, if the hero, for example, is a possessor of powers that can solve all problems and ensure escape from all dangers, then who can care when there is no outcome to be concerned about? Why go on reading? Unless something *happens*, unless there's *conflict*, the writing, whatever else it might be, isn't a story. You're left with a collection of causally unconnected incidents, reflections, character studies, mood pieces, meditations, examinations of a moment more akin to poetry. Lack of plot means lack of action: stasis. The plot of a story may be a single action or several actions intertwined or in parallel, within the same block of time or maybe travelling across separate time spans, moving forward chronologically or back and forth between different years, periods, even eras. The plot doesn't necessarily need to be presented in a linear fashion. Its incidents and episodes can be fragmented, told out of sequence or from conflicting viewpoints or relayed through stories within stories… But there should always be sufficient evidence and enough clues from which the reader or audience can make sense of a plot to their own satisfaction. So long as the audience has faith in the existence of a plot, you're free to do almost anything you wish with it. You can see story as a journey in which you pass by a sequence of milestones that sustain your direction of travel. If pertinent stones are missing, you lose your way. Plot is an aesthetic discipline. It holds the entire literary/dramatic structure of a story together. It provides a rigour without which there can be no real freedom, only caprice.

Plot Logic: Seven Questions

Seven questions (one more than Kipling's honest servingmen) need to be kept uppermost in the narrator's mind:

Who? did What? to Whom? Where? and When? possibly How? and Why?

If, in a portion of text, the answers to such questions are vague or absent, the listener or reader has no structure on which to attach any additions or elaborations; they are swamped by an inundation of words that fail to connect in a coherent flow of meaning. [*Cross-refer Set 2, Workshop 6: Logic; Set 14: Workshop 59: Logic and Dexterity in Handling Plots*]

This happens on a much more critical scale in relation to plot. If the audience isn't supplied with logical details of who is where, doing what and to whom, when and how, they are similarly vulnerable to a plethora of information that doesn't seem to connect. If audiences experience the carpet of plot being pulled from under their feet, as they usually do in detective fiction, they're entitled to have confidence that eventually they will be restored to terra firma or at least terra firma will be restored to them.

A lot of contemporary art has removed itself from narrative and linear logic. Partly, I suppose, because we no longer live in a world that appears to be structured and well ordered. We're all too well aware of existing within rapid and perpetual change with the accompanying sense of fragmentation and uncertainty. Half a century ago, you could still envisage the possible trajectory of your future with the same spouse in the same house in the same job in the same company for your entire life. Now that's inconceivable.

But without the form created by plot, theatre and storytelling merely echo our confusions and uncertainties rather than searching for a sense to them. Story, initially, is very naive. It says, 'This happened and then this happened'. Naivety, for me, means being open, enthusiastic and committed to experience in a childlike (but not childish) way. This is the level at which anyone in the audience can enter a story. Although the surface of a story can appear simple, there may be many levels of experience working in parallel, many resonances, many implications. Theatre, because it's lifelike, in fact a form of life itself, should offer all the complexities that life offers at any one moment. But for this to happen, the plot, the sequence of events, is vital because it provides the spine, the thread, on which we can build or from which we can suspend all else: character, theme, topic, atmosphere, culture, argument, conversation… It holds everything and everybody together (even though individual readers or spectators may be experiencing the story quite differently). If the narrative is removed or falters, then the thread snaps, the spine cracks, there is nothing to hang on to, nothing to support the accumulation of images, themes, meanings – and the story falls apart. A plot may be buried under layers of elaboration, but it must be there; it's your security, and with it there is nowhere you can't go, taking the audience with you.

Halfway through *The First Arabian Night*, we appeared to drop the main story and introduce entirely new characters in a story without any apparent link to what had gone before. But because of the way in which we'd set up the performance, the audience, though temporarily bemused, still trusted that we'd eventually lead them to something coherent. You could sense a definite rustling of 'What's this got to do with anything?' Considerably later in the performance, this story's purpose within the overall structure was suddenly revealed in a totally unexpected way, and the audience would release this pleasurable, audible reaction of 'Oh, yes!' The *way* in which this element of the plot was revealed seemed to give the audience as much pleasure as the new details of the plot itself.

As long as there is the *what* of plot, you don't always need the *why*. A plot doesn't necessarily require all the loose ends to be neatly tied by the denouement. But what has happened up to that point should provide the reader or audience with sufficient information to take away and complete their own scenario. Many of Pirandello's plays leave a central situation unexplained or unverified. In *The Collection*, an early one-act play by Pinter, its four characters are involved in an event which, partially or completely, may or may not have happened to them. The characters constantly change their stories or their conjectures but never provide a definitive version. Nonetheless, the audience leaves the performance – well, I did – with a perfectly satisfactory, self-deduced account of what had actually happened. However, in this play, the plot is not about what happened but about how the four characters use what *might* have happened as a means of gaining power in their various relationships.

Imagery and Symbols

Surrealist fiction and films, like *Un Chien Andalou*, are examples of creations, evocative as they are, that have no interest in telling stories; their images may be beautiful, disturbing, their juxtaposition piquant, but they don't create a narrative. Of course, in film, but less easily in theatre, a story *can* be told partly in images: the emptied glass, a child's hair ribbon lying on the grass... These are implications rather than incidents, clues to the plot, teasers rather than events, possibly McGuffins. (Is the glass empty because the contents in it were drunk? – and by whom? – or were the contents spilt? – and is it even the same glass? And have you actually seen that ribbon before?) Often an image is a brilliant short cut, an economical means of moving a story on. And images can work perfectly as part of a narrative if the conventions have clearly established the context in which – and the level at which – they should be read. They are steps along the plot – or, rather, steps that help the plot along – but in every case, the image has to have some connection with character. Without that connection, it has little dramatic interest.

Images, of course, may provide thematic or symbolic resonance, but interpreting symbols is a dubious exercise. Do all stampeding horses deputise for sexual arousal, does every shore-pounding wave proclaim female orgasm? What does a wild duck 'mean'? What or who does a seagull stand for? In the case of Chekhov's play, it is, more accurately, an ironic plot device that links three of its characters, and for each of whom it has different associations that disclose aspects of their psychology; two of them actually identify themselves with it. It is a specific object with multiple purposes threaded through the play. The eponymous *Cherry Orchard* is first and foremost a cherry orchard. It may also be a symbol, but it symbolises something quite different for every one of the characters. Good symbols are ambiguous motifs that add layers of resonance to a plot, that enrich its implications. But if images are deliberately established for their symbolic potential, but without any function in the plot – in fact, can be detached from the story without causing any loss – they are merely pretentious decoration. The cliché of rain at a funeral, for instance, all too self-consciously proclaims itself a symbol; but if that rain causes delays or accidents that have a bearing on the characters' actions, it becomes an altogether more satisfactory device. In *Emma*, by means of a light snowfall, Jane Austen wittily not only reveals and elaborates the selfish preoccupations of her characters, but convincingly and most naturally forces two of them into a circumstance that has serious consequences for the plot. Whether or not a reader chooses to see the snow as a symbol is entirely the business of that reader. What I'm suggesting here is that, when moving from narrative to narration, it's helpful to eliminate the inessential, decorative contributions to the writing, to distinguish the organically embedded from the superficially imposed.

Stories, whether told in books, on film or on a stage, must be about the people and the things they do. Then what they do and how they do them will inevitably reveal some sort of idea, reflect a view of life. Anything else – everything else! – works insofar as it supports plot, enhancing it, detailing it, colouring it, underpinning it with possible layers of irony, complexity, resonance and ambiguity. But on their own (without plot), design, direction, editing, imagery, language, lighting, movement, sound – all the ingredients of plays, productions, novels and films – fly apart and revert to their original disciplines, such as visual art, poetry, music, dance, technology, semantics and so on, all of which have their own laws and imperatives but lack the essential ingredient that makes a story a story.

NARRATIVE VIEWPOINTS

There are two basic points of view for telling a story: from the first person and from the third.

First Person

[*Cross-refer Set 5: Workshops for First-Person Narration*] The first-person narrative tells the reader that they are to receive the story through the perception and experience of one person, 'I', and that inevitably it will be subjective. The form of telling is initially straightforward, coming directly from 'me' recounting to you what happened to me and how I felt about it. Here is the beginning of Esther Summerson's narrative in Dickens's *Bleak House*:

> I have a great deal of difficulty in beginning to write my portion of these
> pages, for I know I am not clever. I always knew that. I can remember,
> when I was a very little girl indeed, I used to say to my doll, when we
> were alone together, 'Now, Dolly, I am not clever, you know very well,
> and you must be patient with me, like a dear!' And she used to sit
> propped up in a great arm-chair, with her beautiful complexion and rosy
> lips, staring at me – or not so much at me, I think, as at nothing – while I
> busily stitched away, and told her every one of my secrets.

Nonetheless there are possible variations and complications. For many reasons, the 'I' may be an unreliable narrator: from ignorance; from self-delusion; from the desire to present 'myself' in a certain light; from the deliberate intention to mislead; to protect someone; under the influence of someone who is dictating how 'I' view my story; or from any other private agenda. Readers or audiences may be alerted to the unreliability from the start or they may gradually discover it;

possibly they may never know for sure but be left to speculate. We might deduce from the above extract that Esther's low estimation of her own intelligence is not the whole truth, but throughout the story it's clearly what she believes to be true. So in that sense, she is probably a reasonably reliable though clearly self-deprecating narrator (an astutely observed aspect of her character).

———

Then, again, 'I' can recreate the events of my story with the vividness of the original experience. By narrating in the present tense, I can even recount them as if they're actually occurring to me as I speak and so, like you, have no idea of what will happen next. In *Justine*, the first part of Lawrence Durrell's *Alexandria Quartet*, a section of the novel describing an early morning shoot on a lake utilises this tense:

> There is hardly time to think now: for teal and widgeon like flung darts whistle over me and I begin to shoot slowly and methodically. Targets are so plentiful that it is difficult to choose one in the split second during which it presents itself to the gun. Once or twice I catch myself taking a snap shot into a formation. If hit squarely a bird staggers and spins, pauses for a moment, and then sinks gracefully like a handkerchief from a lady's hand. Reeds close over the brown bodies, but now the tireless Faraj is out poling about like mad to retrieve the birds. At times he leaps into the water with his galabeah tucked up to his midriff. His features blaze with excitement. From time to time he gives a shrill whoop. They are coming from everywhere now, at every conceivable angle and speed. The guns bark and jumble in one's ears as they drive the birds backwards and forwards across the lake.

In this example, the present tense seems to vivify the activity, conveying the spontaneity and a sense of several things happening at the same time. The sequence terminates in a possible murder.

———

Or, another possibility: the first-person narrator recalls past events tentatively, blurred as they are by the distance of time, as with Dickens again, on this occasion from *David Copperfield*:

> The light of my father's eyes had closed upon the light of this world six months, when mine opened on it. There is something strange to me, even now, in the reflexion that he never saw me…The first objects that

assume a distinct presence for me, as I look far back into the blank of my infancy, are my mother with her pretty hair and youthful shape, and Peggotty with no shape at all... I believe I can remember these two at a little distance apart, dwarfed to my sight by stooping down or kneeling on the floor... I have an impression on my mind which I cannot distinguish from actual remembrance, of the touch of Peggotty's forefinger as she used to hold it out to me. This may be fancy, though I think the memory of most of us can go further back into such times than many of us suppose... What else do I remember? Let me see...

I was crying all the time, but except that I was conscious of being cold and dejected, I am sure I never thought why I cried...

The effort of looking back becomes as important as the events it describes.

———

The first-person mode might seem to imply that 'I' am always at the centre of the story. But this isn't necessarily so. I may be recounting a story that is concerned with other people. I may be on the periphery of events, only occasionally participating in the story myself, piecing together my understanding of it from what I actually observed with what others have told me, adding my own – and possibly others' – speculations and conjectures to fill the gaps. These excerpts are from Somerset Maugham's *The Razor's Edge*:

This book consists of my recollections of a man with whom I was thrown into close contact only at long intervals, and I have little knowledge of what happened to him in between...

In 1919 I happened to be in Chicago on my way to the Far East, and for reasons that have nothing to do with this narrative I was staying there for two or three weeks...

I was not in Paris in the spring when, sooner than they had planned, Mrs Bradley and Isabel arrived to stay with Elliott; and again I have to eke out my knowledge of what passed during the few weeks they spent there by the exercise of my imagination...

I had come back from the East and was spending some time in London just then. It was perhaps a fortnight after the events I have just related that Elliott called me up one morning.

Here the narrator is setting out the limits of his knowledge of what you are about to read. He wants to interest you in people whose paths he intermittently crossed and is not writing about himself in any context but that. This viewpoint permits the writer quite justifiably to have gaps in his knowledge, to allow certain events to remain ambiguous, because this first-person narrator can't or doesn't always have to be present.

———

A first-person narrative can be highly prejudiced in favour of or against certain characters and events, and the narrator highly opinionated. In *Tom Jones*, Henry Fielding presents himself as such a narrator. He not merely observes the characters from the periphery of the action but intrudes whenever it suits him:

> I have told my reader... that Mr Allworthy inherited a large fortune; that he had a good heart, and no family. Hence, doubtless, it will be concluded by many, that he lived like an honest man, owed no one a shilling, took nothing but what was his own, kept a good house, entertained his neighbour with a hearty welcome at his table, and was charitable to the poor, i.e. to those who had rather beg than work, by giving them the offals from it; that he'd dy'd immensely rich, and built a hospital.

> And true it is, that he did many of these things; but, had he done nothing more, I should have left him to have recorded his own merit on some fair free-stone over the door of that hospital. Matters of a much more extraordinary kind are to be the subject of this history, or I should grossly misspend my time in writing so voluminous a work...

> Mr Allworthy had been absent a full quarter of a year in London, on some very particular business, tho' I know not what it was...

Here the narrator clearly identifies himself as the author, makes no attempt to hide the fact that he is writing and you are reading a long book, permits himself to comment, editorialise and decide what he can or can't be bothered to know. His very noisy voice provides an ironic commentary on the story he wishes to tell. If you remove Fielding from the proceedings, the novel is actually told in the third person.

———

First-person narrative can also occur in the plural, 'we', in which case the narrative voice speaks as a representative of a particular group of people. These excerpts are from William Faulkner's short story, *A Rose for Emily*:

When Miss Emily Grierson died, our whole town went to her funeral: the men through a sort of respectful affection for a fallen monument, the women mostly out of curiosity to see the inside of her house...

She was sick for a long time. When we saw her again, her hair was cut short... So the next day we all said, 'She will kill herself'; and we said it would be the best thing for her. When she had first begun to be seen with Homer Barron, we had said, 'She will marry him'. Then we said, 'She will persuade him yet'... Later we said, 'Poor Emily'...

This is narrated by an unidentified spokesperson for a community that over many years has had, mainly through gossip, only limited knowledge of the two people named and is now attempting to flesh out their story.

Third Person

[*Cross-refer Sets 3 & 4: Workshops 9-20 for Third-Person Narration from Without the Action and Within the Action respectively*] Probably the majority of stories is told in the voice of an anonymous third person, in which events are described and interpreted by means of an unidentified narrator (not at all the manner of Henry Fielding). At one end of the continuum of this particular mode of storytelling, the narrative is comprehensive, employing an omniscience able to describe and analyse the most intimate feelings and motives of all the characters, as well as establishing the wide social and historical details in which the story is set. Trollope applies this approach, say, to his *Barchester* novels. (He also intrudes his novelist's presence, not quite in the pushy manner of Fielding, but even choosing to give the plot away ahead of time – because he knows everything!)

This famous opening to Dickens's *A Tale of Two Cities* sardonically sets up the broad framework in which his story will take place:

It was the best of times, it was the worst of times, it was the age of wisdom, it was the age of foolishness, it was the epoch of belief, it was the epoch of incredulity, it was the season of Light, it was the season of Darkness, it was the spring of hope, it was the winter of despair...

There was a king with a large jaw and a queen with a plain face, on the throne of England; there was a king with a large jaw and a queen with a fair face, on the throne of France. In both countries it was clearer than crystal to the lords of the State preserves of loaves and fishes, that things in general were settled for ever.

...It was likely that in the woods of France and Norway, there were growing trees, already marked by the woodman, Fate, to come down and

be sawn into boards, to make a certain movable framework with a sack
and knife in it, terrible in history.

———

At the other end of the spectrum, the narrator doesn't attempt to speculate on
motives and feelings, causes and consequences, is almost devoid of opinion or
comment and observes events from the outside, describing only what's actually
happening at a particular moment, as exemplified in Evelyn Waugh's *Vile Bodies*:

> Everyone had finished dinner. They dined alone in a corner of the
> coffee-room, while the other waiters laid the tables for breakfast, looking
> at them resentfully. *It was the dreariest kind of English dinner. After dinner
> the lounge was awful*; there were some golfers in dinner-jackets playing
> bridge, and two old ladies. Adam and Nina went across the stable-yard to
> the tap-room of the townspeople. They sat hand-in-hand,
> unembarrassed; after the first minute no one noticed them. Just before
> closing time Adam stood a round of drinks. They said: 'Good health, sir.
> Best respects, madam,' and the barman said, 'Come along, please. Finish
> your drinks, please' in a peculiar sing-song tone.
>
> There was a clock chiming as they crossed the yard and a slightly
> drunken farmer trying to start up his car. Then they went up the oak
> staircase lined with blunderbusses and coaching prints to their room.
>
> They had no luggage (the chambermaid remarked on this next day to the
> young man who worked at the wireless shop, saying that was the worst of
> being in a main-road hotel. You got all sorts).
>
> Adam undressed very quickly and got into bed; Nina more slowly arranging
> her clothes on the chair and fingering the ornaments on the chimney-piece
> with less than her usual self-possession. At last she put out the light.
>
> 'Do you know,' she said, trembling slightly as she got into bed, 'this is the
> first time this has happened to me?'
>
> 'It's great fun,' said Adam, 'I promise you.'

The phrases I've italicised could be thought of more as personal opinion on the part
of the protagonists than observable fact, though Waugh might consider such comments as agreed taste amongst his readers and himself and therefore the next best
thing to fact. Otherwise, the passage is exclusively achieved through description
and dialogue. The characters are understood entirely through their behaviour.
There is no attempt to get inside their thoughts or feelings other than by what they
say and do.

On the continuum between these two extremes there's an infinitely nuanced scale of narrative variations.

———

The narrative can directly harangue the reader and the society of which the reader is part. In *Bleak House*, after the anonymous third-person present-tense narrative describes the death of Jo, the crossing sweeper – a death caused by public neglect and social indifference – it turns outwards, as it were, to accuse society directly in the person of the reader:

> Dead, your Majesty. Dead, my lords and gentlemen. Dead, Right Reverends and Wrong Reverends of every order. Dead, men and women, born with Heavenly compassion in your hearts. And dying thus around us every day.

———

Somewhere along this objective/subjective spectrum, the third-person voice can become almost at one with a character, not only able to interpret motives, but to talk or express the actual thoughts on behalf of the character, using what is called Free Indirect Speech. The authorial narrator and the character can become so blended together that the impact of the narrative is very close to that of first-person narrative. In this excerpt towards the end of Jane Austen's *Emma*, the heroine goes through a process of self-realisation, acknowledging that her unhappiness is entirely due to her own meddling in other people's lives:

> Mr Knightley and Harriet Smith! – Such an elevation on her side! Such a debasement on his! It was horrible to Emma to think how it must sink him in the general opinion… Could it be? No; it was impossible. And yet it was far, far from impossible. – Was it a new circumstance for a man of first-rate abilities to be captivated by very inferior powers? Was it new for one, perhaps too busy to seek, to be the prize of a girl who would seek him?…

> Oh! Had she never brought Harriet forward! Had she left her where she ought, and where he told her she ought! – Had she not, with a folly which no tongue could express, prevented her marrying the unexceptionable young man who would have made her happy and respectable in the line of life to which she ought to belong – all would have been safe; none of this dreadful sequence would have been.

How Harriet could ever have had the presumption to raise her thoughts to Mr Knightley! – How could she have dared to fancy herself the chosen of such a man till actually assured of it!... Alas! Was not that her own doing, too? Who had been at pains to give Harriet notions of self-consequence but herself?

This form allows narrators the best of both worlds: able to see and express events both from their characters' points of view and from their own. This discrepancy, depending on the size and quality of the gap between the two, can produce a sub-textual irony. They may apply this facility to one character in a story, to several or to all. [*Cross-refer Section 8: Changing the Narrative Viewpoint*]

And Second-Person Narrative?

On some occasions, narrators outside the action shift into personal address to the reader (as in the excerpt from *Bleak House,* when the narrator accuses us all of con-tributing to Jo's death, or in *Tom Jones*, where Fielding refers to 'my reader' – implicitly 'you'), a powerful device for storytellers who become so involved in the vicissitudes of their heroes and heroines that they need to engage the reader directly in their indig-nation, enthusiasm, joy or whatever particular intensity of feeling they're experiencing.

However, it's possible that the second person is directed not to the reader but can actually apostrophise the characters themselves. This occurs occasionally in some of *The Arabian Nights* stories when the narrator suddenly bursts out to the hero or heroine with an 'Oh, you were so brave!' or a 'How beautiful you are!'...

This is taken considerably further when a narrator commits totally to second-person narration and relates the characters' stories not to the reader at all, but exclu-sively to the characters themselves. It's a voice that's been used, albeit infrequently, by several writers. This is an excerpt from a short story, 'How to Be an Other Woman' by Lorrie Moore from one of her collections, *Self-Help*, which includes five other stories told in a similar mode:

At the movies he is tender, caressing your hand beneath the seat.

At concerts he is sweet and attentive, buying cocktails, locating the ladies' lounge when you can't find it.

At museums he is wise and loving, leading you slowly through the Etruscan cinerary urns with affectionate gestures and an art history minor from Columbia. He is kind; he laughs at your jokes.

After four movies, three concerts and two-and-a-half museums, you sleep with him. It seems the right number of cultural events. On the stereo you play your favourite harp and oboe music. He tells you his wife's name. It is Patricia. She is an intellectual property lawyer. He tells you he likes you a lot. You lie on your stomach, naked and still too warm. When he says, 'How do you feel about that?' don't say 'Ridiculous' or 'Get the hell out of my apartment.' Prop your head up with one hand and say: 'It depends. What is intellectual property law?'

He grins. 'Oh, you know. Where leisure is a suit.'

Give him a tight little smile.

'I just don't want you to feel uncomfortable about this,' he says.

Say: 'Hey, I am a very cool person. I am tough.' Show him your bicep.

Here the second person functions ambiguously: is she describing what is happening to her heroine or the sorts of things that can happen or might have happened to the heroine? Or is she instructing her on how to behave or advising any of 'you' women readers? Or, more likely, is the heroine talking to herself?

———

It feels more personally experienced than the following excerpt. Here, the imperative mood is more defined, reinforced by its title, 'How!', another story from the same collection:

Begin by meeting him in a class, in a bar, in a rummage sale. Maybe he teaches sixth grade. Manages a hardware store. Foreman at a carton factory. He will be a good dancer. He will have perfectly cut hair. He will laugh at your jokes.

A week, a month a year. Feel discovered, comforted, needed, loved and start sometimes, somehow, feeling bored. When sad or confused, walk uptown to the movies. Buy popcorn. These things come and go. A week, a month, a year.

In fact, all six stories have as part of their titles the words 'How To' or 'Notes' or 'Guide'.

———

Another example of the second person, this time sustained through an entire novel, is Jay McInerney's *Bright Lights, Big City*, in which the main character seems to be ironically observing himself in action:

You are not the kind of guy who would be at a place like this at this time of morning. But here you are, and you cannot say that the terrain is entirely unfamiliar, although the details are fuzzy. You are at a nightclub talking to a girl with a shaved head. The club is either Heartbreak or The Lizard Lounge. All might come clear if you could just slip into the bathroom and do a little more Bolivian Marching Powder. Then again, it might not. A small voice inside you insists that this epidemic lack of clarity is a result of too much of that already.

It's worth noting that the novel would have had an altogether different tone written in the past tense. Then there might be the sense of the narrator reviewing his life rather than watching it.

——

If any of the stories excerpted above were to be 'dramatised', the adapter's task would be to find theatrical conventions for their narration and performance that correspond to those of their narratives. This is the main work of adaptation and on which all other performance decisions depend. This is dealt with in the next section.

A NOTE ON NON-ATTRIBUTED STORIES

In the case of a story not based on a specific text but derived from our shared memory, such as folk tales or fairytales, fables or myths, we have the freedom that comes with devising and improvising, but we still have to find performance equivalents for the elements that give the story its identity. Clearly, some of the categories above will not be applicable. The actual language will be of your own invention. Probably the theme will very much depend on what slant you give the story. The received structure (pretty certain to be chronological) and viewpoint (very certain to be in third-person mode) are both open to your rearrangement or change. Even if you're working from a written version of the story with no ascribed authorship (collections of such material are plentiful), you'll be equally free to shape the story to your requirements. [*Cross-refer Section 8: Changing the Narrative Viewpoint, Changing the Tense, Changing the Structure*] If, however, you've selected a version credited to an author (Angela Carter and Italo Calvino are examples), it would seem self-defeating not to adhere to their take on the story.

SECTION 6

FROM NARRATOR TO NARRATEE

Transforming a Performing Text into Performance

ATTITUDES TO AUDIENCE

What is the Purpose of a Story?

This question doesn't imply that stories should preach sermons or send messages. Members of an audience have the right to make what they will of a story and to create their individual readings of a performance. They should never be told what the story means – if indeed it does 'mean' anything. On the other hand, there are, ultimately, some parameters within which a story has to stay if we, the adapters, want to remain in harmony with it; after all, adaptations of *Cranford* won't be aiming for raunchy sex romps any more than productions of *Lear* are likely to be going all-out for belly laughs (but, then, who knows!). Horror films should horrify, thrillers thrill, mysteries mystify. This, of course, has to do with acknowledging genres rather than hectoring audiences. But neither am I now suggesting that we should trap ourselves in formulas. The journey of every story on its way to performance merits an itinerary of its own; a good story, though it may conform to the specifications of a particular genre, is almost bound to possess elements that endow it with a measure of individuality.

But a performance should express what the writer appears to want the reader to experience. No piece of fiction is so loose that it can mean anything to anyone. This is where theme comes into its own; the purpose of a performance should be to offer the audience, to the best of our understanding and abilities, the most fully realised dramatisation of what we've interpreted as a story's underlying proposition. As we search for a way to retell a story in dramatic terms, the theme should point us in the appropriate direction of travel. This thematic route should make it more than likely that we'll arrive at an artistically coherent destination. The performance will then, of its own accord, do its work of delighting, enlightening or in any appropriate way affecting an audience. Take care of the theme and the purpose will take care of itself. Don't try to shock the audience or make them laugh or cry; tell them the story and leave them to take care of the reactions.

Nor is there any need to demonstrate the theme. The audience doesn't have to be told what (we think) it might be. They will experience a world, unique to itself and cohesive in all its parts, stemming from a central idea which, should they be so inclined, they can make sense of for themselves. The theme underpins the performance in just the same way that it subtextually informs the original material, implicit in every aspect of the production – the way it looks and moves and sounds in all its textures, tones and tempos. Dickens in *Bleak House* sustains the theme I've already suggested (the necessity for individuals to care for those around them in

the face of institutional dereliction of duty) as he presents us with a gallery of neg-
ligent parents and neglected children, responsible children and irresponsible adults,
youthful carers and mature egotists at every level of society – governmental, legal,
religious, philanthropic, even familial – with an occasional glimpse of happy home-
makers to remind us of other possibilities. For the actors, the knowledge of the
theme, their experience of it through rehearsals and their literal embodiment of it
in their performances contributes to their inhabiting and presenting a unified vision
of a world.

Who is a Story For?

Ideally, for anyone. But material is rare that has the breadth of appeal for everyone.
Most devotees of *Coronation Street* aren't likely to rush off to a performance of *The
Coronation of Poppea* or vice versa. Nevertheless, identifying a target audience
inevitably patronises that audience. Almost instinctively we censor what in our opinion they wouldn't understand and condescendingly insert what we decide they
would. This is the 'lowest common denominator' school of entertainment, giving
the punters what (we think we know) they want, which inevitably means giving
them only what they've been given before, what they already know. The other and
healthier approach is to involve ourselves in the sorts of stories that would excite
us to see in performance, fulfilling them to the best of our abilities in the hope that
enough people will be excited to see them, too. A story should be for anyone who
wants to experience it.

What is the Relationship Between
Storytellers and Audience?

This is a quite different question from whom a story is for. How do we talk to the
audience? How do we relate to them? As our friends? Our peers? Our children,
lovers, partners? The wise whose approval we seek? The uninformed in need of
enlightenment? The passive requiring exhortation to action? The anxious seeking
reassurance? The distracted in search of distraction? The complicit sharing in our
intrigues? In a piece on gender, do the men single out the men in the audience to
talk to, and the women, the women – or vice versa? Whatever identity we endow
the audience with should be influenced by the theme and is, of course, totally imagined. In the case of *Bleak House*, the actors playing orphans might at times identify
the audience as orphans like themselves, at others as parents or agents of the law.
Again, members of the audience needn't have this relationship spelled out for them.

They will experience – sense – a cohesion, a rightness, in what they're watching and interpret it in their own way. [*Cross-refer Set 12, Workshops to Develop Contact with the Audience: 54-57*]

THREE BASIC FORMS OF NARRATION

Having identified the type of narrative in a text, the most important decision is the appropriate choice of its narration – narrative being the tale, narration being the telling. On this decision, together with the theme, hangs the fate of the rest of the production: that is to say, all further decisions as to how the other elements of the performance are to be shaped, the sort of imagery, the level of characterisation and so forth...

Essentially, there are three basic forms of narration from which infinite variations can proliferate:

- Third-Person Narration from Outside the Action

- Third-Person Narration from Inside the Action

- First-Person Narration

Third-Person Narration from Outside the Action

Third-person narration from outside the action is usually delivered by an unidentified narrator (implicitly the self-effacing author), who has varying degrees of knowledge from ignorance to omniscience concerning events and characters and the worlds they inhabit. These anonymous narrators are usually reliable in terms of the information they provide for the simple reason that they are describers of, rather than participants in, the action. With no axe – or virtually none – to grind, they have no motives to deceive, though they may have to tease; and they may well narrate with attitude (irony, sympathy, disapproval...).

This mode was once the most common convention in adaptations and, as I've already indicated, was more often than not a flat and lazy device for getting across the exposition that the adapter had failed to incorporate into the body of the adaptation. And quite devoid of imagination. Burdened with this dull function of linking scenes, the poor actor would earnestly stand and deliver from a corner of the stage, possibly appearing to read from a leather-bound volume or a sheaf of letters, intoning the information with little more than a display of vocal competence. There are, however, much livelier possibilities for this mode. These may stem from the narrator's attitude towards the story, the narrator's attitude towards the audience and the narrator's purpose in telling it. (Be aware that the narrator's purpose in telling the story is not necessarily the same as the theme of the story or overall purpose of the production.) Is the narrator there in the place of the writer, deferentially conveying the authorial tone and attitude of the material? Or could the actor develop a personality suitable for imparting specific material, displaying any approach from, say, cool detachment to warm involvement? [*Cross-refer Set 1, Introductory Workshop 2 & Set 3, Workshops 9-12 for Third-Person Narrator Outside the Action; Set 7, Subset 2, Workshops 39-40: Transitions for Flow and Continuity*]

In this mode, there is usually only one narrator, the rest of the company conventionally playing the characters in scenes within the narrative. Of course, the narrative might suggest sufficient opportunities for the narration to be shared by more than one actor, even by the whole company. For example, one actor might narrate all descriptive passages, another all the action, a third any critical commentary on the characters; if the story moved between different passages of time, there might be individual narrators responsible for each period… At some moments, all those established as narrators might narrate chorally. But any such choices (and who knows how many others may be lying in wait to be discovered) will depend on the adapter's ability to visualise in what way they would enhance the telling of the story and reflect the form and tone of the original writing.

Omniscient third-person narrators may, by means of free indirect discourse, tell the story through the eyes of a single character (usually the protagonist) to whose thoughts and motives they are privy and able to interpret in such a way that narrator and character almost become one. [*Cross-refer Section 5, Narrative Viewpoints: Third Person; Section 8: Converting Free Indirect Speech into Direct Speech*]

Multiple Third-Person Narration from Inside the Action

Third-person narrative by characters functioning from inside the action allows them to describe themselves in the third person (as 'he' and 'she') as well as playing themselves in scenes in the first person (as 'I'), moving flexibly between the two states. This mode of narration offers *all* the actors/characters direct contact with the audience. And, of course, these multiple narrations with their variety of tone and attitude create the opportunity for conflicting accounts and doubtful reliability. It's particularly good for comedy or abundantly populated epics, and is probably the most flexible of the three modes, the one most open to imaginative variations in the way actors present their characters as they shift between narration and action. [*Cross-refer Set 1, Introductory Workshop 3: Group Storytelling Mode 2: Multiple Third-Person Narration from Inside the Action; Set 4, Workshops 13-20 for Third-Person Narrators Inside the Action; Set 7, Subset 2, Workshops 39-40: Transitions for Flow and Continuity*]

An Example of Text, *Our Mutual Friend*, Adapted for Third-Person Narration, from both Outside and Inside the Action

Both third-person modes of narration, that is either from inside or outside the action, can be applied to most stories written in the third person, which of course, can't distinguish between the two, these being entirely theatrical, rather than literary, conceits. Here are basic examples of both third-person modes of narration being applied to an excerpt from Dickens's *Our Mutual Friend*.

First, the excerpt as it is written (very lightly trimmed) in which the nouveau riche Veneerings greet their guests at a banquet:

> This evening the Veneerings give a banquet. Four pigeon-breasted retainers in plain clothes stand in a line in the hall. A fifth retainer, proceeding up the staircase with a mournful air – as who should say, 'here is another wretched creature come to dinner, such is life!' – announces 'Mis-ter Twemlow!' Mrs Veneering welcomes her sweet Mr Twemlow. Mr Veering welcomes his dear Mr Twemlow. Mrs Veneering does not expect that Mr Twemlow can in nature care much for such insipid things as babies, but so old a friend must please to look at baby. 'Ah! You will know the friend of your family, Tootleums,' says Mr Veneering, nodding emotionally at the new article, 'when you begin to take notice.'

> But now a fearful circumstance occurs.

> 'Mis-ter and Mis-sis Podsnap!'

> A too, too smiling large man, with a fatal freshness on him, appearing with his wife, instantly deserts his wife and darts to Twemlow with:

> 'How do you do? So glad to know you. Charming house you have here. I hope we are not too late. So glad of this opportunity, I'm sure!'

> When the first shock fell upon him, Twemlow twice skipped back in his neat little shoes and his neat little silk stockings of a bygone fashion, as if impelled to leap over a sofa behind him; but the large man closed with him and proved too strong.

'Let me', says the large man, 'have the pleasure of presenting Mrs Podsnap to her host. She will be', in his fatal freshness he seems to find perpetual verdure and eternal youth in the phrase, 'she will be so glad of the opportunity, I am sure!'

In the meantime, Mrs Podsnap, unable to originate a mistake of her own account, because Mrs Veneering is the only other woman there, does her best in the way of handsomely supporting her husband's, by looking towards Mr Twemlow with a plaintive countenance and remarking to Mrs Veneering in a feeling manner, firstly, that she fears he has been rather bilious of late, and, second, that the baby is already very like him.

Mr Veneering is not at all complimented by being supposed to be Twemlow, who is dry and weazen and some thirty years older. Mrs Veneering equally resents the imputation of being the wife of Twemlow. As to Twemlow, he is so sensible of being a much better bred man than Veneering, that he considers the large man an offensive ass.

———

Next, a version with the Third-Person Narration from Without the Action. Here, the actor/characters take only the direct speech (dialogue) ascribed to their characters and the actor/narrator takes everything else.

NARRATOR	This evening the Veneerings give a banquet. Four pigeon-breasted retainers in plain clothes stand in line in the hall. A fifth retainer, proceeding up the staircase with a mournful air – as who should say, 'Here is another wretched creature come to dinner, such is life!' – announces
5th RETAINER	'Mis-ter Twemlow!'
NARRATOR	Mrs Veneering welcomes her sweet Mr Twemlow. Mr Veneering welcomes his dear Mr Twemlow.[2] Mrs Veneering does not expect that Mr Twemlow can in nature care much for such insipid things as babies, but so old a friend must please to look at baby.
VENEERING	'Ah! You will know the friend of your family better, Tootleums,'
NARRATOR	says Mr Veneering, nodding emotionally at the new article,
VENEERING	'when you begin to take notice.'

NARRATOR   But now a fearful circumstance occurs.

5th RETAINER   'Mis-ter and Mis-sis Podsnap!'

NARRATOR   A too, too smiling large man, with a fatal freshness on
             him, appearing with his wife, instantly deserts his wife
             and darts to Twemlow with –

PODSNAP   'How do you do? So glad to know you. Charming
                  house you have here. I hope we are not too late.
                  So glad of this opportunity, I am sure!'

NARRATOR   When the first shock fell upon him, Twemlow twice
             skipped back in his neat little shoes and his neat little
             silk stockings of a bygone fashion, as if impelled to leap
             over a sofa behind him; but the large man closed with
             him and proved too strong.

PODSNAP   'Let me have the pleasure of presenting Mrs
                  Podsnap to her host. She will be – '

NARRATOR   in his fatal freshness he seems to find perpetual verdure
             and eternal youth in the phrase,

PODSNAP   'She will be so glad of the opportunity, I am
                  sure!'

NARRATOR   In the meantime, Mrs Podsnap, unable to originate a
             mistake on her own account, because Mrs Veneering is
             the only other lady there, does her best in handsomely
             supporting her husband's, by looking towards Mr
             Twemlow with a plaintive countenance and remarking
             to Mrs Veneering in a feeling manner,[6] firstly, that she
             fears he has been rather bilious of late, and, secondly,
             that the baby is already very like him. Mr Veneering is
             not at all complimented by being supposed to be
             Twemlow, who is dry and weazen and some thirty years
             older. Mrs Veneering equally resents the imputation of
             being the wife of Twemlow. As to Twemlow, he is so
             sensible of being a better bred man than Veneering, that
             he considers the large man an offensive ass.

See notes [2] and [6] after the second version below.

———

Now, a version with Multiple Third-Person Narration from Within the Action. Here the actor/characters take both their own narrative as well as dialogue.

MR & MRS V	This evening the Veneerings give a banquet.
4 RETAINERS	[1] Four pigeon-breasted retainers in plain clothes stand in line in the hall.
5th RETAINER	A fifth retainer, proceeding up the staircase with a mournful air – as who should say, 'Here is another wretched creature come to dinner, such is life' – [7] announces

'Mis-ter Twemlow!'

MRS V	Mrs Veneering welcomes her sweet Mr Twemlow.
VENEERING	Mr Veneering welcomes his good Twemlow
MRS V	[2] Mrs Veneering does not expect that Mr Twemlow can in nature care much for such insipid things as babies, but so old a friend must please to look at baby.
VENEERING	'Ah! You will know the friend of your family better, Tootleums,'

[3&7] says Mr Veneering, nodding emotionally at the new article,

'when you begin to take notice.'

TWEMLOW	[4] But now a fearful circumstance occurs.
5th RETAINER	'Mis-ter and Mis-sis Podsnap!'
PODSNAP	A too, too smiling large man, with a fatal freshness on him, appearing with his wife, instantly deserts his wife and darts to Twemlow [7] with;

'How do you do? So glad to know you. Charming house you have here. I hope we are not too late. So glad of this opportunity, I am sure!'

TWEMLOW	[9] When the first shock fell upon him, Mr Twemlow twice skipped back in his neat little shoes and his neat silk stockings of a bygone fashion, as if impelled to leap over the sofa behind him;
PODSNAP	but the large man closed with him and proved too strong.

[5] 'Let me',

says the large man,

'have the pleasure of presenting Mrs Podsnap to her host. She will be,'

in his fatal freshness he seems to find perpetual verdure and eternal youth in the phrase,

'she will be so glad of the opportunity, I am sure!'

MRS P   In the meantime, Mrs Podsnap, unable to originate a mistake on her own account,

MRS V   because Mrs Veneering is the only other lady there,

MRS P   does her best handsomely in supporting her husband's, by looking towards Mr Twemlow with a plaintive countenance and [7] remarking to Mrs Veneering in a feeling manner, [6] firstly, that she fears he has been rather bilious of late, and, secondly, that the baby is already very like him.

[8] VENEERING   Mr Veneering is not at all complimented by being supposed to be Twemlow,

[8] TWEMLOW   who is dry and weazen and some thirty years older.

MRS V   Mrs Veneering equally resents the imputation of being the wife of Twemlow.

TWEMLOW   As to Twemlow, he is so sensible of being better bred than Veneering, that he considers the large man an offensive ass.

———

Which option you choose will depend on the overall tone you're aspiring to – and will be more easily made if you've begun to establish a clear series of consistent conventions to guide the production. I would suggest, in this case, because of the satiric nature of the writing and the less than naturalistic portrayal of these characters, that the second option might give more irony and edge to the performance.

These two examples throw up all sorts of possible small adjustments to ease the flow of story. The following notes go into a lot of fine detail as an indication of the almost continuous need, throughout the process of adaptation, to make decisions, often from word to word, line to line.

Note: The numbers are not always in sequence through the scene.

1   For the second line assigned to the four retainers, it is unlikely that you would have four actors available, so it might be appropriate for this line to be added to the previous one spoken by the Veneerings. It does describe an aspect of their banquet and so can quite logically pertain to them.

2   This narrated indirect speech could be translated into direct speech. 'I don't suppose you can in nature care for such insipid things as babies, but so old a friend must please to look at baby.' This change is similarly applicable to the third-person narration mode outside the action.

3   The line of narration that cuts Veneering's sentence in half could be excised, or placed after the second half of the sentence: ' "Ah! You will know the friend of your family better, Tootleums, when you begin to take notice," says Mr Veneering, nodding emotionally at the new article.' (The actor could nod emotionally without needing to tell us he was doing so. But, once again, this is a question of stylistic choice.)

4   I assigned this line to Twemlow because I thought this social gaffe would be more embarrassing and upsetting for him – anyway, he's probably the only character who's aware that it actually is a gaffe. But, you might find it more appropriate for another of the characters.

5   These lines could be reorganised so that the direct speech is not so broken up: ' "Let me have the pleasure of presenting Mrs Podsnap to her host," says the large man. "She will be so glad of the opportunity, I am sure!" In his fatal freshness he seems to find perpetual verdure and eternal youth in the phrase'; or 'In his fatal freshness he seems to find perpetual verdure and eternal youth in the phrase "She will be so glad of the opportunity, I am sure!" ' But the original, though less easy to play, offers a more appropriate idea of a gauche attempt at a false idea of good manners.

6   As in note [2], Mrs Podsnap's reported speech could be rendered into direct dialogue with some minor adjustments: firstly, 'I fear Mr Veneering has been rather bilious of late', and, secondly, 'Baby is already very like him.'

7   Are you going to retain such words and phrases as: 'announces', 'says Mr Veneering', 'with', 'remarking to Mrs Veneering in a feeling manner' or any other of the 'he said', 'said she' variety of phrases that identify the speaker and assist the transition from narrative to speech? Retaining them creates a playfulness, a naivety, possibly a sense of irony; removing them shifts the tone slightly towards the more naturalistic. As this particular novel inhabits several stylistic shifts, it might be possible to vary their application dependent on where they seem more and less

effective. Remember that usually the 'he saids' and 'said shes' are narration directed to the audience, so it's important to visualise the effect that this might have.

8   *Important Note*: If you have difficulty in deciding on which character should be assigned a particular piece of text, the simple 'rule' is: The character who is the subject of the sentence or paragraph ('she' and 'he' rather than 'her' and 'him') should take it. Sometimes a sentence has to be shared as in this sentence shared between Veneering and Twemlow who in the first half is the object but in the second half becomes the subject of it:

VENEERING   Mr Veneering is not at all complimented by being
             supposed to be Twemlow,

TWEMLOW   who is dry and weazen and some thirty years older.

This 'rule' is necessary, if for no other reason than to avoid arguments. More to the point, it provides clarity and consistency. But, most important of all, it keeps the characters active, that is to say, in charge of their own actions.

9   Be aware of the brief change of tense from present to past. Here Dickens inserts Twemlow's reaction to Podsnap's greeting that logically would have occurred slightly earlier in parallel with Podsnap's initial speech; two things happen simultaneously, but can only be written about in sequence. If you wished, you could reorganise the text to avoid going into the past tense. Again a matter of stylistic choice.

———

Below, to clarify a couple of the above notes, is the extract with indirect speech converted to direct speech[1] and speeches interspersed with narrative comments set out with those comments removed to the end of the speech.[2]

MR & MRS V   This evening the Veneerings give a banquet.

4 RETAINERS   Four pigeon-breasted retainers in plain clothes stand in
              line in the hall.

5th RETAINER A fifth retainer, proceeding up the staircase with a
              mournful air – as who should say, 'Here is another
              wretched creature come to dinner, such is life'-
              announces

                     'Mis-ter Twemlow!'

MRS V	Mrs Veneering welcomes her sweet Mr Twemlow.
VENEERING	Mr Veneering welcomes his good Twemlow
MRS V	[1] 'I do not expect that you can in nature care much for such insipid things as babies, but so old a friend as Mr Twemlow must please to look at baby.'
VENEERING	[2] 'Ah! You will know the friend of your family better, Tootleums, when you begin to take notice.'
	[2] says Mr Veneering, nodding emotionally at the new article,
TWEMLOW	But now a fearful circumstance occurs.
5th RETAINER	'Mis–ter and Mis–sis Podsnap!'
PODSNAP	A too, too smiling large man, with a fatal freshness on him, appearing with his wife, instantly deserts his wife and darts to Twemlow with;
	'How do you do? So glad to know you. Charming house you have here. I hope we are not too late. So glad of this opportunity, I am sure!'
TWEMLOW	When the first shock fell upon him, Mr Twemlow twice skipped back in his neat little shoes and his neat silk stockings of a bygone fashion, as if impelled to leap over the sofa behind him;
PODSNAP	but the large man closed with him and proved too strong.
	[2] 'Let me have the pleasure of presenting Mrs Podsnap to her host. She will be – she will be so glad of the opportunity, I am sure!'
	[2] says the large man. In his fatal freshness he seems to find perpetual verdure and eternal youth in the phrase,
MRS P	In the meantime, Mrs Podsnap, unable to originate a mistake on her own account,
MRS V	because Mrs Veneering is the only other lady there,
MRS P	does her best handsomely in supporting her husband's, by looking towards Mr Twemlow with a plaintive countenance and remarking to Mrs Veneering in a feeling manner

[1] 'I fear he has been rather bilious of late. The
baby is already very like him.'

VENEERING   Mr Veneering is not at all complimented by being
supposed to be Twemlow,

TWEMLOW   who is dry and weazen and some thirty years older.

MRS V   Mrs Veneering equally resents the imputation of being
the wife of Twemlow.

TWEMLOW   As to Twemlow, he is so sensible of being better bred
than Veneering, that he considers the large man an
offensive ass.

———

It's entirely possible to create a convention in which you combine both third-person modes: characters narrating about themselves from inside the action *and* an unidentified narrator doing so from without. This might be useful if there were sections of narrative – for instance, some social observations or descriptions of place – that seemed inapplicable or unsuitable to any one character, either factually or metaphorically; nor appropriate to any one character more than another. It might also be useful to have an outside objective voice acting as a corrective to what might be a character's self-aggrandising or sympathy-seeking delivery. It's up to you to detect such possibilities, or even necessities, in a text.

———

As I hope you're beginning to see, once you start to explore a text in this way, the permutations of modes and conventions increase exponentially to the point where, so spoilt for choice – even bewildered by it – you might find it almost impossible to come to any decision. I stress again that this is exactly the importance of developing an increasingly firm idea of what stylistic world you want to offer to an audience. Certain options will then eliminate themselves and certain choices present themselves more persuasively. Whenever unsure, try all possible ways until one particular preference seems to select itself! The danger in this work is that, during the heat of rehearsal and because you are most of the time in uncharted territory, you can easily be seduced from moment to moment by ideas that are effective, clever, funny, charming, daring, shocking or surprising in themselves – yes, all those good things – but in the end add nothing to the scheme of the whole, in fact, confuse or blur it. By giving in to whims or unsubstantiated impulses, you will find yourself with a production of shreds and patches and an audience without a consistent code to sustain and guide it through the performance. It would be as though you initially led the audience to believe that the performance was to be delivered in received pronunciation (if such a thing still exists) and then, capriciously, started using a French accent, then contemporary street slang, then cod Jacobean, and all this because at various points in rehearsal somebody had thought that, at those moments, such choices were witty or significant without applying sufficient rigour to justify them within the overall coherence of the piece.

First-Person Narration

First-person narration is told from the perception of a single pair of eyes, and that person is most likely to be at the centre of the story. But whatever degree of propinquity the narrator has to the story, the narration is inevitably – and this is its strength and uniqueness – at the mercy of the teller's subjectivity. This makes it frequently unreliable. This mode best suits stories that are intimate, personal, in which states of inner experience (intense feeling, dream, reverie, introspection, stream of consciousness and the like) are dominant.

Similarly to the third-person narrator from outside the action, the first-person narrator is in charge of all the text apart from any dialogue of other characters.

First-person narrative has the interesting problem for narrators of deciding whether they are remembering events, not necessarily in serenity, but with the benefit of hindsight; or whether they're experiencing them exactly as they first experienced them. There is a spectrum to explore from recounting to recalling to reliving. The text rarely makes such distinctions, so this is very much a theatrical choice.

The way in which the first-person storyteller makes the transition from narration into a scene opens up possibilities: does the image or scene described by the narrator (and executed by the group) draw the narrator into it; or does the image surround the narrator. In other words, does the narrator go to the scene or does the scene come to the narrator?

Maybe the narrator watches his or her younger self, played by another actor. This might be applicable to material such as the excerpt from *David Copperfield* in *Section 5, Narrative Viewpoints, First Person*, in which David tries to look back at his early childhood.

Maybe the narrator is not the centre of the story and, though still a participant within its framework, closer to its periphery, functioning as a chronicler or observer of that story, possibly as its interpreter. Then where do such narrators place themselves in relation to the action? [*Cross-refer Set 3, Workshops 9 & 10: Areas of the Stage*]

There is the possibility of a narrator telling a story received from another narrator who has been told it in turn by yet another narrator… So there might be several first-person narrative frames existing simultaneously, creating the effect of receding mirrors yielding multiple reflections. [*Cross-refer Set 15, Workshop 60: Framing and Linking Stories*]

Narrators may use the first-person plural, 'we', which suggests that they belong to or represent a social group, neighbours, members of a community and so forth. This mode might be effected by a shared or choral narrative. [*Cross-refer Section 5, Narrative Viewpoints; the Excerpt from A Rose for Emily*]

Once more: many possibilities… [*Cross-refer Set 1, Introductory Workshop 4: Group Storytelling Mode 3: First-Person Narration; Set 5, Workshops 21-23 for First-Person Narrators*]

TENSE

The use of tense will strongly affect the way in which a story is communicated to its auditors. Most stories are, logically, told in the past tense; logical since, in order to be told, presumably they've already had to have happened.

The Present

Sometimes, however, the use of the present tense offers the possibility of the story being recounted as if it's occurring at the moment of telling and that the narrator has no more idea than the audience of what will happen next, intensifying the sense of something incomplete whose outcome we're all increasingly anxious to learn. Or the change into present tense might suggest that the narrator is literally reliving events. [*Cross-refer Section 5, Narrative Viewpoints, First Person: the Excerpt from Justine; Section 8: Changing the Tense*]

Sometimes the present tense can be employed to strengthen the idea of habitual patterns or routine behaviour repeated day after day.

> He gets up, washes, dresses, eats breakfast, takes the bus to work, works for eight hours, takes the bus home, eats dinner, undresses, washes, goes to bed…

The movement between tenses can be dramatically effective. The shift from past to present might raise the temperature, suggesting a sudden shift in energy, importance, surprise, danger... A switch in the opposite sequence might tend to soften or calm matters or offer an ironic anticlimax... Note the brief switch from the present to the past tense in the middle of the excerpt above from *Our Mutual Friend*, when Twemlow tries to escape from Podsnap (see note [9] above). It suggests a brief rewind to mention something missed out in the present-tense flow; or it might suggest Twemlow metaphorically wishing to escape from the vulgar present into the refined past. [*Cross-refer Section 5, Narrative Viewpoints, First Person: the Excerpt from* Justine*; Section 8: Changing the Tense*]

The Future

The future can be glimpsed by an all-knowing narrator looking ahead to fulfil the audience's need for some sort of resolution (Ian McEwan does this poignantly at the end of *On Chesil Beach*, though not actually using the future tense); or to effect some sort of irony, like the anonymous narrator of the German saga, *Das Nibelungenlied*, who bitterly foretells the future for his characters at various moments in the story:

> This Siegfried, you must know, lived with those lords in Gunther's land for a year on end without ever having seen the lovely maiden who was to bring him much joy and yet much sorrow, too.

> What terrible vengeance she took on her nearest kinsmen in days to come for slaying him. For his one life there died many a mother's child.

This device is also employed poignantly in Jennifer Egan's *A Visit to the Goon Squad*:

> 'Come on, Rolphus,' Charlie says. 'Dance with me.'

> She takes hold of his hands. As they move together Rolph feels his self-consciousness miraculously fade, as if he is growing up right there on the dance floor, a boy who dances with girls like his sister. Charlie feels it, too. In fact, this particular memory is one she'll return to again and again, for the rest of her life, long after Rolph has shot himself in the head in their father's house at twenty-eight: her brother as a boy, hair slicked flat, eyes sparkling, shyly learning to dance. But the woman who remembers won't be Charlie; after Rolph dies, she'll revert to her real name – Charlene – unlatching herself forever from the girl who danced with her brother in Africa. Charlene will cut her hair short and go to law-school. When she gives birth to a son she'll want to name him Rolph, but

her parents will still be too shattered. So she'll call him that privately, just in her mind, and years later, she'll stand with her mother among a crowd of cheering parents beside a field, watching him play, a dreamy look on his face as he glances at the sky.

You might find it justifiable, with certain stories, for the narrator to adjust the narrative to indicate future events.

SECTION 7

WHY ADAPT?
The Pleasures of Adaptation

THE PLAY IS NOT THE THING

What *is* the point of turning non-dramatic fiction into drama? Aren't there enough good plays around? Plays are plays and books are books... and so forth and so on. True, plays *are* specifically created for theatre, and therefore incomplete until they've been performed. Of course, all things being equal, there's nothing better in theatre than a Really Good Play. But one of the things that has to be equal is a Really Good Production. Plays have only a potential existence until they're performed and then they're only as good as the productions they get. Shakespeare wrote Really Good Plays – Great Plays – so did Euripides, so did Chekhov, so did... But their plays can barely survive, their potential brilliance dimmed, if not totally extinguished, by bad performances. In all honesty, how often have you, in all your theatregoing days and nights, come away from the performance of such plays truly life-enhanced? The usual response to such productions is that this actor's Hamlet is better than Sainsbury's but not quite as good as Tesco's, while this directorial concept (maybe the 'Denmark is a prison' one with hidden mikes and surveillance cameras) isn't quite up to the historic Waitrose production, while the ninety-minute Asda version for schools really did it for the kids (with fizzy drinks and crisps thrown in). *The Deep Blue Sea*, done well, is an infinitely more fulfilling experience than *The Three Sisters* done badly. How many times have you sat in a theatre being bored to death by a Really Great Play? You'll have been enduring the Deadly Theatre that Peter Brook anatomised so precisely in *The Empty Space*. Not only is it dead in itself, it's also likely to annihilate the audience. When you recklessly take yourself off to the theatre, you're risking an invasion of bodysnatchers: those actor/characters who appear so lifelike are actually zombies, the living dead, their deadly weapon, ennui, primed to sap you of the will to go on living. Which, I think, makes a reasonable point that theatre's existence is in the Doing of the Thing rather than the Thing itself. In fact, the Doing *is* the Thing. Plays are at the service of theatre, not the other way round. Which theoretically – potentially – opens theatre's doors to all sources of material. In simple words, a good play does not ensure good theatre; a great play does not ensure great theatre. Plays can't exist without theatre, but theatre *can* exist without plays.[1]

1. For many people, some of their most revelatory theatrical experiences have come from sources other than plays: productions by Joseph Chaikin's Open Theatre, Grotowski's Poor Theatre, Ariane Mnouchkine's Théâtre du Soleil, by Robert Lepage, Peter Brook in Paris, Joint Stock, The Living Theatre, the RSC's *Nicholas Nickleby*, and (I'll immodestly add) by Shared Experience under both its artistic directorships.

THE CHALLENGE OF NEW FORMS

I found that the adaptation of stories from non-dramatic material was a natural extension of storytelling. Konstantin in Chekhov's *Seagull* demands new forms for the
theatre. Without new forms, he cries, we're better off with nothing. The adaptation of
non-dramatic literature for theatre happens, I presume, because nothing within the
body of dramatic literature appears to offer similar possibilities latent in such material. Over two-and-a-half millennia, there have been surprisingly few great plays.
That's why the good ones keep getting used again and again until at times they appear
threadbare and, in desperate consequence, get crudely patched with concepts. A
friend of mine went to see a poor production of *The Cherry Orchard* and came back
declaring he'd never before realised what a bad play it was![2] I would hazard a guess
that within a considerably shorter period – say, two hundred and fifty years – there
have been far more fine novels, novellas and short stories. This isn't inexplicable. A
play insists that dramatists operate within daunting restraints not demanded of writers of other fiction: haiku rigour rather than epic spread. So, in search of good new
material, it's not unreasonable to look from time to time outside the canon.

The nature of theatre and theatregoing makes it almost inevitable that most plays conform to an unchanging model of drama, dictated by the practicalities of performance:
a limited number of characters and events, the containment of location and duration,
chronological flow, the dominance of dialogue – all of which are constraints or at least
guiding parameters for playwrights, even more tightly so when they're commissioned by
a specific theatre with its particular limitations of budget, space and time. If they want
to write for theatre, they're not likely to come up with novellas. They write plays because
they know that plays are what theatres perform. They also know by and large that a play
with a vast cast of characters will not find a production, nor one written in hundreds of
fifteen-second scenes, nor one lasting several days. From time to time, a Beckett or a
Handke will produce a piece that defies accepted conventions, just as, more recently,
Martin Crimp and Sarah Kane have created pieces that, on the page at least, bear more
resemblance to poetry; but, on the whole, plays are a series of scenes of dialogue (and
sometimes a bit of singing and dancing) between characters in some sort of conflict with
each other. It's almost impossible to write something deliberately for theatre that does-
n't have the conventions of a play. One of the most obvious ways to break moulds and
extend conventions then is to grapple with something *never intended for theatre*.

When I formed Shared Experience, it was more than a whim that decided me to work
with stories rather than plays. As I've said, I felt that plays might trap us in existing
patterns of work. With their structures – strictures – plays can be something of a
straitjacket. Some directors, out of sheer desperation, try to break out of those constraints by ignoring them, especially those of plays from the classic repertoire; after

2. It's a great play.

all, what is there possibly left to say about what will probably be the hundred-and-first *Hamlet* of the year unless you wildly deny what the writer has written. But the play is clearly set in a castle and Hamlet is clearly a student prince and people believe in ghosts and a ghost duly appears to those before whom he wishes to materialise. Shakespeare says so and he should know. Petruchio's domestic abuse of Katherine is seen as acceptable, even admirable by those around them, and at the end of the play she eulogises the role of a submissive wife for some forty-four lines without a trace of irony. Shylock is punished, leaving the rest of the characters free to sort out their happy ending. To find freedom in a play, you really don't solve the problem by breaking down the walls of its reality and escaping outwards into some totally different reality; your truer freedom comes from accepting those walls and being prepared to dig deeper into the world that Shakespeare and Co have taken the time and effort to establish for you. (So if you don't like what a play has to say, don't do it!) Depth rather than width may be a more rigorously demanding direction in which to explore, but ultimately the more rewarding one. Conceptual productions don't give you a performance of the actual play so much as a dissertation on it.

That's why turning to non-plays can be so liberating, so refreshing. Adaptations are inevitably reconstructions. You still dig deep within the story's reality. But at the same time, you *can* spread your wings. The walls of stories are more flexible, more porous; they let the air in and out more freely because there's so much more to play with. Because they were never designed for performance, they're open, as I've been suggesting, to many possible ways of rendering them dramatic, while still retaining their integrity. It's interesting to observe how many current attempts to broaden and enliven the nature of theatre (cabaret, burlesque, circus, installations, site-specific pieces, interactive events in which audience members are put through tests and challenges) end up being more about environments, atmospheres, stunts and turns rather than about what it means to be human. True theatre also provides environments and atmospheres (and, if necessary, stunts and turns), but as a context and partial explanation of what should be the focus of theatre: people and the way they live their lives. Adaptations and storytelling are possible ways out of the impasse of tired dramatic forms: new structures, new conventions, plenty of environment, plenty of atmosphere, but with human beings still firmly at the beating heart of the matter.

Of course, an adaptation can rarely recreate a story in its totality (although an American theatre company, The Elevator Repair Service, has, in fact, performed *The Great Gatsby*, entitled *Gatz*, in its entirety, every word of it). The change of medium can only make it a version of the original. But that resultant version can be true both to the spirit *and* a lot of the words of the original, as well as true to the nature of theatre. Adaptations need destroy neither theatre nor their source material. (The book is always there to be read, unlike the play which is there to be performed.)

With non-dramatic writing, the potential adapter is confronted with any amount of material, any number of characters, locations and events, with lengthy passages of narrative, indirect speech, flexible time-schemes and parallel plots. A story may offer the inner thoughts of many characters from differing viewpoints; maybe it offers a single all-knowing source of knowledge; maybe one with only limited understanding of events. All these devices challenge the adapter's skill to find their dramatic and theatrical equivalents. When I began adapting novels and short stories, I found that confronting these literary forms forced my imagination well beyond the stimulation it received from conventionally structured plays and led me to solutions which, at least to me, felt fresh. Lev Dodin, artistic director of the Maly Drama Theatre, St Petersburg, affirms that

> Adapting novels for the stage demands and creates a new theatrical language, a new form of theatre.

THE SURPRISE OF LANGUAGE

A most (if not the most) unexpected source of stimulation is a story's particular language, unexpected in the sense that it's probably a language not usually spoken or heard in a theatre, never having been conceived for performance. The dialogue of plays, of course, is often sparkling, evocative, poetic and, of course, speakable; the sainted Shakespeare aside, actors and audiences can be rewarded with such riches as the gift of poetic gab of almost any Irish playwright, including the brilliantly orchestrated argumentations of Shaw, as the pithy economies, in their different ways, of Coward, Pinter and Mamet, the lyrical cadences of Tennessee Williams and so on. But the dialogue in many novels is equal to – even superior to – much of the best in plays; conversations between the inhabitants of Jane Austen's world or those of Evelyn Waugh's are instances of dialogue as witty and active as any you're likely to find in the corpus of British High Comedy. But the language that actors are given to speak by playwrights is less likely to provide the sheer variety of forms, textures and tones that the language of fiction can offer as a portal into new worlds. Looking over my bookshelves, I find surprisingly few dramatists whose language creates a special world. That's understandable. Playwrights have only dialogue to work with; most of the time what they wish to communicate has to be embedded in reasonably recognisable conversation, frequently freighted with the subtle burden of subtext. They write well and their language serves its purpose. But stimulated by the language of narrative fiction, actors can find themselves exploring totally fresh territory. Here I'm not discussing just dialogue, but all types of prose (and verse), and the challenge of finding their theatrical, dramatic forms of expression. I'm definitely not encouraging actors to show off a writer's language any more than I would if they were playing Shakespeare, but to make active sense of it and allow it to affect the whole demeanour of their performance; spoken words must affect their physicality, behaviour, use of space and way of looking at life. Unique languages create unique worlds:

Men and women danced together, women danced together, men danced together. They danced, keeping a ferocious time that was like the gnashing of teeth in unison. At first, they were a storm of coarse red caps and coarse woollen rags; but, as they filled the place, some ghastly apparition of a dance-figure gone raving mad arose among them. They advanced, retreated, struck at one another's hands, clutched at one another's heads, spun round alone, caught one another and spun round in pairs, until many of them dropped. The rest linked hand in hand and all spun round together, until they all stopped at once, begun again, struck, clutched, and tore, and then reversed the spin... Suddenly they stopped again, paused, struck out the time afresh, formed into lines the width of the public way, and, with their heads low down and their hands high up, swooped screaming off. No fight could have been half so terrible as this dance. This was the Carmagnole.

Charles Dickens – A Tale of Two Cities

...they all saw it and shouted to look, look there it was and she leaned back ever so far to see the fireworks and something queer was flying about in the air, a soft thing to and fro, dark. And she saw a long Roman candle going up over the trees up, up, and, in the tense hush, they were all breathless with excitement as it went higher and higher and she had to lean back more and more to look up after it, high, high, almost out of sight, and her face was suffused with a divine, an entrancing blush from straining back and he could see other things too, nainsook knickers, the fabric that caresses the skin and she let him and she saw that he saw and then it went so high it went out of sight a moment and she was trembling in every limb from being bent so far back he had a full view high up above her knee no one ever not even on the swing or wading and she wasn't ashamed and he wasn't either to look in that immodest way like that because he couldn't resist the sight of the wondrous revealment half offered... and he kept on looking, looking... And then a rocket sprang and bang shot blind and O! then the Roman candle burst and it was like a sigh of O! and everyone cried O! in raptures and it gushed out of it a stream of rain gold hair threads and they shed and ah! they were all greeny dewy stars falling with golden, O so lovely! O so soft, sweet, soft!

Then all melted away dewily in the grey air: all was silent, Ah!

James Joyce – Ulysses

There would be not too much difficulty in imagining these excerpts on film, which would inevitably show you everything, but lose the specificity and resonance of the language. They would almost inevitably be cruder versions of their originals. How much more exciting to find a way to create these in live performances by means of the shared imagination of actors and audiences aroused by the language and in collaboration with it.

RELATING TO THE MATERIAL

People often ask what sort of material is good to adapt. The question is about as sensible as asking what weather is best. In theory, almost any piece of narrative writing is adaptable. The choice lies not so much with the material as with an individual's idea of theatre and its parameters. It depends on the would-be adapter's tastes, ambitions and ability to discern a viable adaptation within a particular text. It depends, too, on how far from the original the adapter is willing – or even eager – to depart. It's possible to make adjustments to characters and plot, change locations, shift time and to select one theme at the expense of others until the original piece is all but subsumed in its new guise. And in the cases of certain writers – Shakespeare and Brecht for example – their appropriations do become totally fresh pieces of work.

My enthusiasm to tell certain stories by dramatic means stems, I'm sure, from a desire to share with others the absolute pleasure I derived from reading them in their original form. I chose material because I was excited not just by the plots, characters and themes but, above all, by the language – the way in which the story was told. Because of that, my own attitude towards adaptation is to stay as true as possible to a story in its original state. In the consequent pursuit of that aim came the exploration, discovery and development of the techniques I'm describing in this book.

I've always chosen material that, to me at least, seems in no need of change. The radical process of translating from one medium to another with the practicalities that this involves is already shift enough. Rather than resisting, rejecting or reinventing, I'm convinced that collaborating with the text results in a deeper realisation in both senses of the word. There's a greater likelihood of coming into a more symbiotic relationship with its author and closer harmony with the material itself. I don't feel that my own creativity is in any way stifled; it's more than fully exercised in finding the appropriate dramatic correlations to bring its literary forms to life on stage, true both to the spirit and as much of the word as possible. Each work will demand its own treatment. The further a text recedes into the past, the less comprehensible or recognisable it becomes; inevitably an increasing amount of imaginative translation has to take place to render it viable for current audiences. It's always that delicate matter of degree. I'm convinced that struggling to maintain the principal of staying close to the original rather than eagerly rushing away from it will end up with something far more authentic, textured, resonant, essential and – maybe counter-intuitively – original.

Because I believe that what is essential to drama is the interaction of characters as they pursue their goals through life, with all the dilemmas and obstacles, the moral and practical challenges that these throw up, I always look for fiction that provides plenty of action (in both the Aristotelian and Stanislavskian senses). I tend to eschew writing that's too meditative or absorbed by the inner preoccupations of the characters at the expense of action. That's why, like so many others, I find myself drawn to nineteenth- and early twentieth-century novelists. There are many novelists whose work I relish, but can see no way – and therefore would find it pointless – to adapt.

When I was reading those Dickens novels, what struck me with such excitement, quite apart from the sheer range and virtuosity of the language, was the sense of performance in the writing, the juiciness of it: sumptuous in character, plot and incident, and, most wonderful to my taste, filled with great scenes of conflict conducted in dialogue of dazzling virtuosity and monologues of great energy and vivacity (*vide* Mrs Gamp), with comedy, drama, melodrama and farce, satire and diatribes lavishly on tap. (And having worked on one of his books, I'm here to insist that his characters, certainly in that one, are drawn with far greater psychological insight and credibility than he's usually given credit for.) This sense of theatre is heightened by Dickens's tendency to set a scene in great topographical detail, even writing stage directions ('Enter Mr Guppy'). Dickens's love of the theatre is well-known:

> Every writer of fiction, although he may not adopt the dramatic form,
> writes in effect for the stage.

Since the nineteenth-century theatre, devoted mainly to spectacle and bravura acting, wasn't remarkable for the quality of its drama, many novelists of that period may have been, or felt like, playwrights *manqué*. They expressed just such sentiments when referring to their own works in dramatic terms. Wilkie Collins, who had collaborated with Dickens on theatrical ventures, including a play, *The Frozen Deep*, expressed his hope that his writing would have the same effect on his readers as a play on an audience:

> ...the novel and play are twin-sisters in the family of fiction... the one is
> drama narrated... the other is drama acted; and... all the strong
> emotions which the playwriter (sic) is privileged to excite, the novel-
> writer is privileged to excite also.

William Harrison Ainsworth, another novelist of the period, wrote:

> The novelist is precisely in the position of the dramatist. He has, or
> should have, his stage, his machinery, his actors. His representation
> should address itself as vividly to the reader's mental retina, as the
> theatrical exhibition to the spectator... It is a drama, with descriptions to
> supply the place of scenery.

Certainly, of the world's literature, novels between the late eighteenth and early twentieth centuries are the ones that have most frequently been adapted to the stage (and,

with great popularity, for radio, television and film). The properties of these novels –
realism, psychology, strong plots and action climaxing in scenes of highly charged
conflict, intense emotion, vividly individualised characters expressing themselves in
rich, idiosyncratic language, a layered portrait of society, deeply embedded themes –
are all properties of good theatre. However, as I've noted, characters and plots exponentially proliferating over many locations and years are not.

Consequently, throughout the nineteenth and well into the twentieth century, the
many adaptations of such novels routinely squeezed them into the crippling corsets
of the prevailing theatrical structures of three- and four-act plays in which events were
squashed together in time and place, great swathes of material abandoned and dialogue invented to accommodate these adjustments. So the original voice of the novel
was diluted if not entirely lost in the process.

The challenge to us was to put these teeming works on stage in all their complexity,
without hacking them into manageable bits to fit an established structure. Syn-
chronicity struck in those heady days of the '70s when one felt free to take risks:
Shared Experience was recklessly devising its adaptation of Dickens's thousand-page
Bleak House, with over one hundred characters, that six actors would play for about
ten hours over four nights, at the same time as Robert Altman's groundbreaking film
Nashville, with its multiple plots and myriad characters, appeared in our cinemas. It
was inspiring and greatly reassuring. Now, of course, multiple plots and numerous
characters have become almost a commonplace both of film and theatre. We've found
ways of doing them! But thirty years ago, it seemed a monumental, nigh-impossible
task that would rupture the confines of theatrical possibilities.

As much as possible over the years I've tried to alternate between plays and stories.
I've found this to be a nourishing method of work. With plays, I've always felt secure
within their disciplined constraints; they are what they are, you honour what they are
and you find your creativity within what they are. With adaptations, I've felt uncertain, at risk and often out of control, but tremendously free to explore, as long as I
ultimately stayed true to the reality of the story. Moving from one to the other felt
like a healthy exercising of all my directorial muscles.

So, to sum up, what do adaptations give us? If we choose wisely, great stories, the likes
of which are unlikely to be found in the dramatic canon; characterisations more deeply
wrought, unconstrained time and space; idiosyncratic writing, unknown territory to
explore with the possibility of creating new worlds and extending the language of theatre; actors working at the peak of their multifaceted abilities to communicate richly
layered material; the evocation of the audience's imaginations; a genuine bond
between spectators and storytellers sharing the experience of a wonderful story.

SECTION 8

WHY NOT?
The Process of Adaptation

A DOUBLE PROCESS

Adapting non-dramatic fiction for the stage is two activities in one. It's not only the transformation of one sort of text into another – a text for reading into a text for performing – it's also the transformation of that text into flesh-and-blood performance. You might well say that the second activity is no different from turning a play into a performance. And that would be true, more or less, of any scenes of dialogue in a story or if a story were written entirely in scenes; their treatment would conform – roughly – to how one might work on scenes in a play.[1] But when you confront the rest of the story (those parts that are not in dialogue), you enter unfamiliar terrain, probably one of your reasons (certainly one of mine) for adapting the story in the first place: the lure of the unknown. The challenge comes in trying to visualise the possible dramatic forms for these narrative passages (description, exposition, commentary…). Once an adapter gets going, the two processes are constantly batting ideas back and forth between them, the words stimulating ideas, the ideas seeking confirmation from the words. This two-fold procedure has so many options that I find it hard to conceive of two separate individuals, a writer and a director, being involved in the process. The nature of this visualisation inevitably shapes the precise choice of what you retain of the text, be it a complete passage, a paragraph or just a word or two. Because you're travelling without a map, in fact trying to chart new territory, there are so many possible directions to head in that, for me, this has meant making most of those discoveries and decisions in rehearsal, practically, on my feet.

When I embarked on *Bleak House*, I made no attempt to prepare even a rough cut of this thousand-page novel. The actors and I started rehearsals with fat paperbacks in our hands, crossing out the odd sentence as we made our lengthy way. This was beneficial in that we explored the text in such detail that the actors ended up as authorities on the novel. Less beneficial, they also ended up with half of what they'd worked on having to be jettisoned when the first runthroughs took twice as long as intended, the first two parts taking ten hours instead of five. I learned that lesson.

---

1. In storytelling, the difference in playing scenes stems from the storytellers' responsibility for the entire story, an overarching concern to give to each part of the whole its appropriate weight and tone. This will, at any particular moment, determine their manner of playing. If, as an example, a passage of text contained the blurred memory of a incident or an incident from a half-remembered dream, the actors might represent this as something distant, in soft focus, incompletely heard. They would be trying to create the dramatic equivalent of the novelistic device – an impressionistic stream of consciousness, perhaps – which is not the sort of writing likely to occur in a play.

Nowadays I do make a rough cut in advance of rehearsals, removing what it's pretty indisputable won't be needed, eliminating repetitions and any material that wanders too far away from the main drive of the story. When unsure about something, I retain it to explore in rehearsal. The final script comprises whatever words remain from the original text. But those words, if read, should provide a reader with a complete, logically flowing story.

DECONSTRUCTION

If you're sufficiently attracted to a story at first reading, you'll probably be more than predisposed to believe it's adaptable. If so, you'll next need to come up with convincing evidence to support that belief. This you can only do sensibly by taking the text apart to find out exactly what it's made up of and how it's put together. Unless you make this effort, you won't be in a fit state to convert it into storytelling mode. Without this process to guide you to a convincing interpretation of a story, you'll find yourself floundering amongst innumerable possibilities, lurching from one arbitrary choice to the next as they contradict or cancel each other out. Either this or, carried away by enthusiasm for an initial concept that appears to be a complete solution for the adaptation, you'll allow a state of euphoria to become one of denial as you skim over whatever doesn't conform to this first interpretative impulse. It's not enough to have some good – even very good – ideas. What you're looking for should be beyond an 'idea'. Your increasing knowledge of the material – which in many respects you ought eventually to know better than the author[2] – should be drawing you towards a gradually cohering storytelling world that resonates with the world of the written story.

In *Different Every Night*, I've given a detailed description of some of the ways I deconstruct a play, taking the text apart to see what it contains and how it's structured. This includes making the Four Character Lists, in which every reference to a character is entered verbatim in an appropriate category.[3] In principle, this

---

2. Authors are often unaware of patterns and connections that have been instinctively released from their unconscious whilst they've been consciously focusing on other concerns, patterns that may be discerned by others. In this they're not dissimilar to actors or, I'm assuming, anyone in a creative state, whose best work, Zen-like, often happens to them rather than their making it happen. Refer back to note 1 in Section 4 in which the actor, Coquelin, describes the delighted surprise of playwrights at the unexpected interpretations of characters in their plays created by the actors. Evelyn Waugh is quoted as saying that only after completing a draft of *Put Out More Flags*, he realised that one of the characters was an alcoholic.

3. (i) The facts about the character; (ii) What the character says about her- or himself;

approach can be applied to non-dramatic texts and would work perfectly well as part of the analysis of a short story. But the difference between sifting the equivalent information from an eighty-page play and an eight-hundred-page novel would be a matter of months! In this circumstance, you might need to modify your approach to this process, for example, utilising only the first list for incontrovertible facts or applying the other three lists only to certain characters.

Apart from its greater length, a novel tends to a greater complexity of structural and narrative devices: the number of viewpoints from which the story is told, the nature of those viewpoints, the degree to which the story travels through space and time, whether there are sections providing historical or social background, whether there is the use or absence of metaphor, whether there is dialogue, whether that dialogue is direct or reported, whether action or atmosphere, stream of consciousness or commentary predominates, whether there are set pieces, dream sequences, flights of fancy... and what the ratio between such passages might be. In Section 5, I listed the component parts of a story that need to be disassembled and thought about. Each story demands its appropriate analytic filters.

Coaxing a text to yield up its secrets is always – for me, certainly – an exhilarating procedure. It occurs at a period when all the creative avenues towards your adaptation are still open; you have nothing to lose and everything to discover. You can continue to envisage – that is, sense rather than visualise – your ideal performance before reality sets in. You have yet to learn the parameters of the material, face the circumstances of the production (budget, space, time, collaborators) and, above all, accept the limits of your own imagination in relation to the text, all with their consequent demands for compromise. At some point, you'll have to set your initial instincts against your analysis.

To illustrate some approaches to adapting a text, I'm continuing to take most of my examples from *Bleak House*. It's a novel of huge scale, and offers a useful range of challenges and rewards. Having convinced myself that this was the story I wanted to experience in performance, I went through the book slowly, a chapter at a time, all sixty-seven of them, making detailed notes as to what happens in each, in terms of story, which characters appear, what themes, topics, events, locations, critical plot points, character observations, imagery... I made a note of which of the novel's many plot lines, however lightly referred to, passed through each of them. I broke a chapter down into sections (the equivalent of units in a play) and identified their particular forms: descriptive passages of environment or of character, scenes of dialogue, inner monologues, set pieces (a funeral, a banquet...), satirical commentary. In other novels, possible categories might be diary entries, phone conversations, all sorts of correspondence, emails, historical background, meditation, streams of consciousness

(iii) What other characters say about the character, (iv) What the character says about other characters. These should be written down verbatim. The facts should be free of any assumptions or conjectures.

and so on. The types of sections contained in a novel will tell you a lot about its structure and the sort of world its story inhabits. In Jane Austen's novels, for example, there is virtually no description of place, nor of what her characters look like, apart from those comments they make about each other (and so possibly unreliable); whereas in Dickens's writing, his characters and their environment are described in elaborate detail, physically, socially and metaphorically. Jane Austen deals with a relatively small and contained group of characters, more or less from the same upper-middle class and location. The number of characters in a Dickens novel usually runs to over a hundred and covers almost the entire range of society, from the destitute to the aristocratic, and moves between many places. Austen's language is factual, precise, detailed, devoid of imagery, metaphor or simile; his is elaborately filled with all three. Both writers provide lots of scenes and conversations. (Surprisingly, some of their characters could meet stylistically: *Little Dorrit*'s Flora Finching, if she moved out of London, could live next door to *Emma*'s Miss Bates.)

An Example of a Chapter Breakdown from *Bleak House*

CHAPTER 24: AN APPEAL CASE

(The last chapter of Esther's 5th narrative sequence)

STORY:

Richard, in debt and having given up his articles to a firm of solicitors, has joined the Horse Guards and is to be sent to Ireland. Therefore Jarndyce, as guardian to both Richard and Ada, urges them to relinquish their engagement vows. Trooper George comes to their lodgings in London to give Richard a lesson in swordsmanship. On first seeing Esther, George is disturbed that her appearance reminds him of someone.

On the day before his departure for Ireland, Richard persuades Esther to accompany him to the Chancery Law Courts to see how the suit of Jarndyce & Jarndyce (from which he has financial expectations) is faring. While there, Mr Guppy, a lawyer' clerk, introduces Esther to Mrs Chadband at the latter's request; formerly, as Mrs Rachael, she had been a domestic servant of Esther's first guardian. They also meet Trooper George, who has come looking for Miss Flite, another claimant regularly attending the court for the same unending suit.

Trooper George has been sheltering in his shooting gallery yet another frustrated claimant, Gridley. There is a warrant out for his arrest for disturbing the peace of the court. Gridley is on the point of dying and has asked to see Miss Flite. In their mutual situation, he wants her with him in his final hours. Miss Flite, together with Jarndyce, Esther, Richard – and Inspector Bucket who has come in disguise to arrest Gridley – visit Trooper George's shooting gallery and are present at Gridley's death.

CHARACTERS:

Esther, Ada, Richard, Jarndyce, Lord Chamberlain, Kenge, Trooper George, Miss Flite, Guppy, Mrs Chadband (Rachael), Phil Squod, Gridley, Bucket.

SECTIONS:

1. Richard's change of career is described. (Narrative)

2. Jarndyce encourages Richard and Ada to break off their engagement. (Scene)

3. Trooper George comes to give Richard a lesson in swordsmanship. (Scene)

4. Richard and Esther visit Chancery. (Narrative)

5. Guppy introduces Esther to Mrs Chadband, formerly Mrs Rachael. (Scene)

6. Trooper George comes in search of Miss Flite. (Scene)

7. Several of the characters attend Gridley's death. (Scene)

SCENES (DIALOGUE) WITH THEIR LOCATIONS:

1. Bleak House: Esther, Jarndyce, Richard and Ada (in section 2)

2. Lodgings in London: Esther, Jarndyce and Trooper George (in section 3)

3. The Law Courts: Fragmentary dialogue: Esther, Richard (i) Guppy, Mrs Chadband; (ii) Trooper George, Miss Flite (in sections 5 & 6)

4. The Shooting Gallery: Esther, Jarndyce, Richard, Miss Flite, Trooper George, Phil Squod, Gridley, Bucket (in section 7)

MAIN EVENTS:

A Visit to Chancery.

Gridley's death.

PLOT THREADS:

Chancery: The law suits of Richard and Ada, Gridley and Miss Flite.

Mlle Hortense's story.

Lady Dedlock's story.

Esther's childhood.

Mr Guppy's story.

PLOT POINTS:

Richard's developing resentment against Jarndyce.

A French woman is practising pistol shooting at Mr George's gallery.

Esther's appearance reminds Mr George of someone he once knew.

Esther begins to sense Richard's fate in the Flite–Gridley relationship.

Guppy reintroduces Mrs Chadband (formerly Mrs Rachael) to Esther.

The Chancery case of Jarndyce and Jarndyce continues to go nowhere.

Detective Bucket, in disguise, comes to arrest Gridley.

CHARACTER POINTS:

Richard's detachment from his 'family', his growing bitterness and irony.

A sympathetic side to Bucket.

Trooper George's awkwardness with women (Esther and Miss Flite).

Gridley is a shadow of his former self, a broken man.

THEMES:

The law destroys those who seek justice. 'The Law is a Ass.'

ESTABLISHMENT OF:

The next steps in Richard's career and a rift in the Jarndyce household.

A refocusing on the Chancery plots.

COMMENTS:

A complex and climactic chapter, linking many characters and plot-lines.

Gridley's death is a large set piece.

PROBLEMS:

Keeping all the plot strands alive.

Organising the fragmented Chancery sequence.

I used coloured pens to underline the different plot threads or character journeys – which helped to give me a quick visual idea of what was happening. Working my way through the book in this method gradually made the book's structure, dominant themes and multiple plot lines increasingly available to me.

ANALYSIS AND INTERPRETATION

You have chosen your story, analysed it and begun to think about the adaptation. The adaptation and the eventual form it will take on the stage should be indivisible (the double process referred to earlier). At very least, there must be a fluent journey from text to theatre. Possibly they proceed together.

With *Bleak House*, several possible approaches began to emerge. The sections dealing with Chancery and the never-ending, all-consuming, Byzantine case of Jarndyce and Jarndyce is treated satirically, at times grotesquely; the dispensers of justice with names like Tangle and Vholes veer towards caricature rather than character. These parts of the book qualified for the description of 'Kafkaesque', initially darkly comic but ultimately portraying a disturbing world devoid of either reason or compassion. This suggested an expressionistic production with representative types rather than rounded characters, heightened physicality, bold designs with distorted perspectives and strong contrasts of light. But the story is also the more layered and subtle story of a young girl's gradual discovery of her origins, filled with sentiment and feeling and multifaceted relationships. The book is also a detective story (a who-dun-what?), a rib-tickler, a tear-jerker, a cliffhanger; it is, too, a highly politicised critique of institutions and establishments. Focusing on or emphasising any one of these possible choices would have done a disservice to the others. The only appropriate way of playing the novel in a cohesive fashion was to incorporate all of them within an overall style which depended on totally truthful playing, with every scene given its full dramatic weight, but with a subtle shift of tone between the two contrasting narratives: realistic and for the most part gentler, and rounder, in Esther's first-person, past-tense narration; sharper and edgier in the third-person, present tense. In Esther's sections, Dickens invites you, more often than not, to care about the characters, to identify with them, empathise with them; in the other, to take a cool look at them, at times a derisive look, and, often, a furiously indignant one at the injustices they've wrought. Actors whose characters moved between the two modes made an adjustment of tone appropriate to whichever mode they found themselves in. A character who was essentially comic and not particularly complex still had to be able to play a scene with Esther in which both convincingly inhabited the same world. What this rewardingly achieved was to give more humanity and emotional life to those characters who might otherwise have ballooned into cartoons, and to give the more realistic characters a slightly bolder definition. The characters' mimed depictions of environments and handling of props was selective but realistically detailed. The outcome for the performance was that all hundred or more of the characters were played with a richness and complexity, never for laughs or easy effect. They each had an inner life. And most satisfyingly, once we started to dig into the characters, even those that seemed caricatured, we discovered that Dickens had provided them with the material for us to do so.

Apropos this matter, I would warn you against accepting received opinion or literary criticism uncritically. Much of what I read about the book, often by experts on Dickens, dismissed Esther Summerson as just another of Dickens's vapid virgins, one more in his line of sentimentalised goody-goody heroines. This proved not at all to be the case. Her behaviour made profound psychological sense: as an orphan without the least experience of being loved or needed, indeed believing it would have been better had she never come into the world, she spends her life trying to validate her existence by being of use to others and offering affection wherever she finds the slightest chink in the world's armour. The character was then perfectly playable without the slightest sentimentality; not the least trace of saccharine or schmaltz.

CUTTING v. COMPRESSING

By definition, all adapted material has to be shaped to the requirements of the stage. The obvious solution is to cut, which frequently results in large chunks of story that seem to present difficulties or irrelevancies being too readily hacked away, causing a lot of good, healthy baby to get thrown out with the bath water. On the other hand, adaptations with too many incidents crammed into too short a period can become ludicrously breathless and at the same time starved of colour. Too much plot, not enough detail. Too much detail, not enough flow. An astute balance has to be struck to retain in a different medium exactly what makes a story so very much itself and attractive to you, the adapter. The essential character of a story lies not in its plot and themes but in the way it is told: tone, attitude, viewpoint and, of course, its words. And these are precisely the elements that can be lost in transit.

What you remove depends on the purpose and nature of your adaptation: do you want to remain 'true' to what you believe the material to be? Or are you using the material as a basis for some purpose of your own that clearly diverges from the original, as a launching pad in a new direction? In all cases, adapters have to be very clear as to what they're about.

Personally, I've always aimed for the former approach, the material itself in all its aspects being what attracted me, rather than as a stepping stone to something else. Instead of cutting, I prefer a process of distilling, which in practice means starting with everything you believe you may need and then, through a rather slow and patient process of trial and error, squeezing out, literally by a phrase here, a word there, what becomes self-evidently superfluous to requirements or, at worst, the least necessary. With *Bleak House*, much material that early in the our work seemed impossible to do without proved, little by little, to be redundant or replaceable by other means. As we played the show – from one performance to the next – small cuts continued to reveal themselves all the way to the end of an eight-month tour. The actors' performances transformed a lot of description into action. When we found descriptions of character repeated throughout a story (writers of those serialised Victorian novels were frequently reminding their readership of characters they may not have heard from for a monthly instalment or two), we pasted all those passages together, filleted them for the most pertinent and vividly expressed characteristics and removed the repetitious rest. Sometimes, in conflating several passages into one, we quite fortuitously discovered that intervening material had now become unnecessary and could also be removed. So by a sequence of sensitive shrinkages, we retained a compressed – but authentic – version of the original (much in the way the reduction of a sauce retains and strengthens the richness of its essential flavours) with the unique voice of the writer secure and intact. Removing text, word by word or phrase by phrase, is a painstaking and, at times, painful process, but it does ensure that the true nature of the material remains.

Very few stories are perfect. Frequently there are digressions or elaborations of incidents that are engrossing in themselves but inessential to the story, not just to the plot but to its themes and imagery too. The big question for an adapter to keep asking is: 'What will be lost if I cut this?' I know, much to my woe and that of the actors I collaborated with, that trying to keep something just because you happen to like it or have a good idea for its staging or because it offers an actor a good scene are not always the best reasons for its retention.

Sometimes, complex language that a reader can comfortably absorb may be too dense for a listener to accommodate. We read at our own speed, pause to consider a phrase or a passage, re-read it as often and whenever we wish, turn pages back and forth to remind ourselves of past events or to peek into the future. We can even reach for a dictionary. We are totally in control of our reading, even its time and place. For where and when we choose to read may well influence how we react to the text. The power of the text to command our full attention may come into conflict with an adverse environment, in which case we can put the book down to pick up again at a more reader-friendly time and place. But when we watch a performance, our control over it is less than minimal. The performance carries relentlessly on at its own tempo whether we fail to keep up with it or have to wait for it to catch up with us.

So in adapting what by nature is word-heavy – made entirely of words – you have to consider how much language a representative audience can take in at any one time, neither patronising us as if we were rather slow children, funny foreigners or dumbed-down citizenry, nor ignoring the reality of our ability to listen, which has probably atrophied in this sound-bitten era of ours.

'REWRITING' THE TEXT

Fine writers compose in a language and structure unique to them that challenges us to find the best way of conveying to an audience what seems difficult to get both tongue and ear around. The extract from *Our Mutual Friend* is an example of this. Trying to solve this problem by updating the text with current references and phrases, simplifying it or demoticising it are reductive soft options. They're likely to remove precisely the quality of the story that made it so special and attractive to us in the first place. Inevitably, there are going to be pieces of text that simply have to be adjusted. But the problem has to be dealt with not so much through the process of cutting or rewriting but through helping the actors to find a way of coming to creative terms with language which isn't immediately or obviously speakable. Shakespeare presents exactly this problem for actors, certainly on first acquaintance, as do most period plays and the work of any playwrights with strongly idiosyncratic voices. This means that the actors have to work hard to link the vagaries of language to specific thought patterns until the text becomes their own, feeling totally natural to speak and sounding totally natural to hear (natural but not necessarily naturalistic), and convincing us that this is exactly the way – and the *only* way – in which the characters in this particular world would express themselves vocally and verbally. Referring to Shakespeare again, I'm sure everybody's familiar with actors who make his language absolutely clear and natural, and others (unfortunately the majority) who get trapped in monotonic rhythms and clichéd forms of delivery, rendering it incomprehensible. This is because they've failed to find any way to bond creatively with the text, to make it their own, so that what comes out of a character's mouth appears convincingly to be the result of how the character thinks. This is largely because their understanding of the text is generalised and approximate rather than specific, word for word, phrase for phrase, thought for thought.

CHANGING THE NARRATIVE VIEWPOINT

Sometimes, it may be useful, interesting, surprising, to try telling the story from a mode other than the one used in the text. In most cases, an adaptation will want or need to follow the narrative viewpoint established by the story. But there may be occasions when it might seem more effective for a character to shift from first-person narrative to third-person or from third to first. Again, it's hard to say when it might be appropriate, but if you feel the impulse to do this, try it both or several ways with the actors. Then compare what differences in impact these variations achieve until you're sufficiently convinced to make a decision one way or the other.

You might find some justification not only in changing the narrative viewpoint, but in changing the character from whose point of view the story is told (assuming the story is viewed through the eyes of a particular character). Changing both the view-point and the character with the narration is, of course, totally valid in devised or improvised work. In a version of *Cinderella*, you might explore the story, not, as is it usually viewed, through the eyes of Cinderella, but through those of the Ugly Sisters or the Fairy Godmother or Prince Charming. And with him, say, you could start either at the ball where he first sees Cinderella or, already happily married to her, recalling the events in which he's participated, possibly learning from her what he doesn't know or hasn't experienced himself. There may even be aspects of the story of which he will have no knowledge, and therefore nor will we. The possibil-ities are legion.

It's conceivable to convert a first-person narrative into third- or even second-person. What might happen? Let's try to adapt the beginning of Esther Summerson's first-person account of her life in *Bleak House*:

> I have a great deal of difficulty in beginning to write my portion of these pages, for I know I am not clever. I always knew that. I can remember, when I was a very little girl indeed, I used to say to my doll, when we were alone together, 'Now, Dolly, I am not clever, you know very well, and you must be patient with me, like a dear!' And she used to sit propped up in a great arm-chair, with her beautiful complexion and rosy lips, staring at me – or not so much at me, I think, as at nothing – while I busily stitched away, and told her every one of my secrets.

First, into third-person:

> She has a great deal of difficulty in beginning to write her portion of these pages, for she knows she is not clever. She always knew that. She can remember, when she was a very little girl indeed, she used to say to her doll, when they were alone together, 'Now, Dolly, I am not clever, you know very well, and you must be patient with me, like a dear!' And the doll used to sit propped up in a great arm-chair, with her beautiful

> complexion and rosy lips, staring at her – or not so much at her, she
> thinks, as at nothing – while she busily stitched away, and told her every
> one of her secrets.

This tends to distance her from us, so we observe her, more with curiosity or interest than emotional involvement.

Now let's try it in second-person narration:

> You have a great deal of difficulty in beginning to write your portion of
> these pages, for you know you are not clever. You always knew that. You
> can remember, when you were a very little girl indeed, you used to say to
> your doll, when you were alone together, 'Now, Dolly, I am not clever,
> you know very well, and you must be patient with me, like a dear!' And
> she used to sit propped up in a great arm-chair, with her beautiful
> complexion and rosy lips, staring at you – or not so much at you, you
> think, as at nothing – while you busily stitched away, and told her every
> one of your secrets.

This seems to be confronting Esther with her own conduct. The narrator could be an external voice reminding Esther of how she saw herself. The narrator could also be Esther reminding herself of how she once felt about herself. The narrator might even be the doll.

It's conceivable that Esther could narrate about herself, moving from third-person (she) to second-person (you) to first-person (I). The changes are marked by italics:

> *She* has a great deal of difficulty in beginning to write *her* portion of
> these pages, for *she* knows *she* is not clever. *She* has always known that.
> *You* can remember, when *you* were a very little girl indeed, *you* used to
> say to *your* doll, when *you* were alone together, 'Now, Dolly, I am not
> clever, you know very well, and you must be patient with me, like a dear!'
> And Dolly used to sit propped up in a great arm-chair, with her beautiful
> complexion and rosy lips, staring at *me* – or not so much at *me*, *I* think, as
> at nothing – while *I* busily stitched away, and told her every one of *my*
> secrets.

Such a change-of-person sequence might imply her gradually weakening attempt to remain at a distance from herself until she actually takes on her own experience fully. Moving from third to second might mean that she has become so engrossed in herself – or so inhibited – that she leaves the audience in order to come to terms with herself. Moving from second to first might intensify her self-involvement, but it also allows her to return to the audience more willing to share her experience with them.

A sequence of the three points of view needs not necessarily be in this or any other order, but can change with the way in which the narrative effects the narrator. This

CHANGING THE NARRATIVE VIEWPOINT

somewhat sophisticated approach would demand a great degree of discipline and sensitivity as well as accuracy of delivery from the actor. It might express something disturbing or surprising about the character, it might be moving or revelatory. It might also be merely fussy and confusing! The audience would have to feel secure at each transition and totally convinced of the dramatic validity for the constantly shifting viewpoints. The point I'm trying to make, yet again, is that narrative offers many options and that you should always be on the lookout for fresh possibilities.[4]

Now let's try putting the third-person excerpt from *Vile Bodies* [*on page 72*] into second-person narrative where it is used for more than one character. The narrator would be outside the action. The changes are marked by italics:

> Everyone had finished dinner. The *two of you* dined alone in a corner of the coffee-room, while the other waiters laid the tables for breakfast, looking at *you* resentfully. It was the dreariest kind of English dinner. After dinner the lounge was awful; there were some golfers in dinner-jackets playing bridge, and two old ladies. *You* went across the stable-yard to the tap-room and sat until closing time in a warm haze of tobacco smoke listening to the intermittent gossip of the townspeople. *You* sat hand-in-hand, unembarrassed; after the first minute no one noticed *you*. Just before closing time, *Adam, you* stood a round of drinks. They said: 'Good health, sir. Best respects, madam,' and the barman said, 'Come along, please. Finish you drinks, please' in a peculiar sing-song tone. There was a clock chiming as *you both* crossed the yard and a slightly drunken farmer trying to start up his car. Then *you* went up the oak staircase lined with blunderbusses and coaching prints to *your* room. *You* had no luggage (the chambermaid remarked on this next day to the young man who worked at the wireless shop, saying that was the worst of being in a main-road hotel. You got all sorts). *Adam, you* undressed very quickly and got into bed; *you, Nina,* more slowly arranging your clothes on the chair and fingering the ornaments on the chimney-piece with less than *your* usual self-possession. At last *you* put out the light. Trembling slightly as *you* got into bed, *you* said 'Do you know, this is the first time this has happened to me?'
>
> *Adam, you* said 'It's great fun, I promise you.'

This seems to confront characters with their behaviour, forcing them to acknowledge what they've done, how they've behaved.

---

4. Apropos moving from first to third person: in his autobiographical *Boyhood* and *Youth*, J. M. Coetzee writes about himself in the third person as though trying to objectify what were subjective experiences. The use of the third instead of the first person suggests he has been able to look back with a greater understanding of what he was experiencing than he was capable of at the time.

Or you could try this: Adam and Nina both share the narration in the first-person plural (we), but using the second-person towards each other (the changes are marked by italics).

ADAM	Everyone had finished dinner. *The two of us* dined alone in a corner of the coffee room, while the other waiters laid the tables for breakfast,
NINA	looking at *us* resentfully. It was the dreariest kind of English dinner.
ADAM	After dinner the lounge was awful; there were some golfers in dinner-jackets playing bridge
NINA	and two old ladies.
ADAM	*We* went across the stable-yard to the tap-room and sat until closing time in a warm haze of tobacco smoke
NINA	listening to the gossip of the townspeople.
ADAM	*We* sat hand-in-hand unembarrassed;
NINA	after the first minute no one noticed *us*. Just before closing time *you* stood a round of drinks. They said: 'Good health, sir.
ADAM	Best respects, madam,'
NINA	and the barman said, 'Come along, please. Finish your drinks, pleases' in a peculiar sing-song tone.
ADAM	There was a clock chiming as *we* crossed the yard
NINA	and a slightly drunken farmer trying to start up his car.
ADAM	Then *we* went up the oak staircase lined with blunderbusses and coaching prints to *our* room. *We* had no luggage
NINA	The chambermaid remarked on this the next day to the young man who worked at the wireless shop – she said that was the worst of being in a main-road hotel –
BOTH	you got all sorts!
NINA	*You* undressed very quickly and got into bed.
ADAM	*You* were more slowly arranging your clothes and fingering the ornaments on the chimney-piece with less than *your* usual self-possession. At last, *you* put out the light. Trembling slightly as *you* got into bed, *you* said 'Do you know, this is the first time this has happened to me?'

| NINA | *You* said 'It's great fun, I promise you.' |

This creates the impression that they are sharing, confirming and reminding each other of an intimate experience.

Another possibility for Adam or Nina: still using the shared first-person plural (we), but when referring to each other, instead of using the second-person (you), they revert to the original third-person (he and she). The changes are marked by italics:

ADAM	*We* sat hand-in-hand unembarrassed;
NINA	after the first minute no one noticed us. Just before closing time Adam stood a round of drinks. They said 'Good health, sir.'
ADAM	'Best respects, madam.'
NINA	and the barman said, 'Come along, please. Finish your drinks, pleases' in a peculiar sing-song tone.
ADAM	There was a clock chiming as *we* crossed the yard
NINA	and a slightly drunken farmer trying to start up his car.
ADAM	Then *we* went up the oak staircase lined with blunderbusses and coaching prints to *our* room. *We* had no luggage
NINA	The chambermaid remarked on this the next day to the young man who worked at the wireless shop – she said that was the worst of being in a main-road hotel –
BOTH	you got all sorts!
NINA	Adam undressed very quickly and got into bed.
ADAM	Nina was more slowly arranging her clothes and fingering the ornaments on the chimney-piece with less than her usual self-possession. At last, she put out the light. Trembling slightly as she got into bed, she said 'Do you know, this is the first time this has happened to me?'
NINA	Adam said 'It's great fun, I promise you.'

This might suggest that they are now sharing their experience with a third party (the audience).

Exploring the potential of variable viewpoints in this way allows you great flexibility of tone and nuance. These three variations and the original would have very different impacts in performance: the audience would see the characters through different filters and from different perspectives; the relationship between the couple would keep adjusting, the tone of the narrative would alter and all these possibilities would result in different stage life. Possibly, these choices would not be sustainable for a whole performance, but might be dramatically viable for parts of it. I'm not saying that any of these possibilities is an improvement on the original; merely illustrating a few of the many ways it might be possible – and in the cases of some other texts, desirable – to change viewpoints. Of course, it's more than likely, after all your explorations, that you'd find your preferred point of view is the one from which Waugh wrote the story!

As you see, minor changes to the text are inevitable if you alter the viewpoint. In second-person narration, what can be lost, or at least be difficult to maintain, is contact with the audience.

CHANGING THE TENSE

Similarly, it might be totally justifiable to keep shifting the tense to emphasise the drama of a story. Here is the passage from *Das Nibelungenlied*, describing the murder of Siegfried:

> Then Siegfried laid down his shield near the flowing water, and although he was very thirsty, he most courteously refrained from drinking until King Gunther had drunk.
>
> The stream was cool, sweet and clear. Gunther stooped to its running waters and after drinking stood up and stepped aside. Siegfried in turn would have liked to do the same, but he paid for his good manners. For now, Hagen carried Siegfried's sword and shield beyond his reach, ran back for his own spear and searched for the cross on the back of the brave man's tunic. Then, as Siegfried bent over the brook and drank, Hagen hurled the spear at the cross, so that the hero's heart's blood leapt from the wound and splashed against Hagen's clothes. No warrior will ever do a darker deed.
>
> Leaving the spear fixed in Siegfried's heart, he fled in wild desperation, as he had never fled before from any man.

This is how it would read if the second paragraph were changed into the present tense. The changes are marked by italics:

> Then Siegfried laid down his shield near the flowing water, and although he was very thirsty, he most courteously refrained from drinking until King Gunther had drunk.
>
> The stream *is* cool, sweet and clear. Gunther *stoops* to its running waters and after drinking *stands* up and *steps* aside. Siegfried in turn *would like* to

do the same, but he *will pay* for his good manners. For now, Hagen *carries* Siegfried's sword and shield beyond his reach, *runs* back for his own spear, and *searches* for the cross on the back of the brave man's tunic. Then, as Siegfried *bends* over the brook and *drinks*, Hagen *hurls* the spear at the cross, so that the hero's heart's blood *leaps* from the wound and *splashes* against Hagen's clothes. No warrior will ever do a darker deed.

Leaving the spear fixed in Siegfried's heart, he fled in wild desperation, as he had never fled before from any man.

In this case, the story moves from legendary to actual. In the present tense, the events seem to go into slow motion and close-up with a corresponding increase in tension. Then, reverting to the past tense, they seem to speed up again and go into long-shot.

CHANGING THE STRUCTURE

In some cases, probably stories with multiple plot lines and different batches of characters, you may find that, in the process of distilling the text, it may be necessary or advantageous to alter the order of certain events or to group them differently. Sometimes, through compression, such shifting might occur on its own. The way in which information is revealed may be made more effective if earlier parts of a story are placed later in the narrative.

It's difficult to provide an example of how this might work but, as pure speculation, it's just about conceivable, using *Bleak House* as a guinea pig, to put all of its third-person present-tense sections together into one continuous sequence (rather than in the original pattern of alternating blocks of chapters) and play them as the first half of the performance; then all the first-person past-tense blocks, grouped together by default, would constitute the second. For an audience, the first half of the story would probably seem more mystifying than it already is, leaving gaps in the flow of information but still sufficiently intriguing to encourage an audience to stick with it. Then in the second half, those gaps would gradually become filled and the whole story come together. But, as I say, this is entirely speculative and whether it would offer any advantages over its original structure – greater ironies, bigger surprises – I'm not prepared to guess.

When I adapted James Elroy's *The Black Dahlia*, I changed the structure of the opening chapters. The novel has a very dense backstory culminating in a boxing match which brings the narrative and its two main protagonists up to its actual starting point. The performance started with the fight, and the backstory was inserted, incident by incident, between each of the ten rounds.

SIMULTANEITY

One of the opportunities denied to written fiction that theatre *can* offer is to present more than one thing at a time. Simultaneous events that can only be written about sequentially can be shown happening at the same time. Past and present events can also occur in visual simultaneity. Scenes and events can overlap. And it's entirely possible for the same character or characters to be playing in two or more scenes at one and the same moment. (It's even possible for an actor to be playing two different characters in separate scenes simultaneously.) Such counterpoint is a useful vehicle for irony and narrative compression.

This is a slightly condensed sequence from Evelyn Waugh's *A Handful of Dust* in which Jock, a friend of her husband, has to break the news to Brenda (who is in London conducting an affair with John Beaver) that her little boy, John Andrew, has been killed in a hunting accident on their country estate, Hetton. There are three concurrent events happening in three different rooms: Jock waiting to tell Brenda the news in one, Brenda's society friends in a second, gossiping and awaiting their turns to have their fortunes told by Mrs Northcote, who is reading the soles of their feet in a third. These could be played simultaneously, overlapping and intercutting, with the characters in each keeping their situations alive throughout the entire sequence. Mrs Beaver is not present in any of the scenes but sets up the situation:

MRS BEAVER Mrs Beaver had discovered a new fortune-teller called Mrs Northcote and for every five guineas she earned at her introduction Mrs Beaver took a commission of two pounds twelve and sixpence.

ROOM 3

MRS N Mrs Northcote told fortunes by reading the soles of the feet.

ROOM 2

POLLY There was a little party at Polly's to consult her.

BRENDA   What a time she is taking over Daisy.

POLLY   She is very thorough, and it tickles rather.

DAISY Presently Daisy emerged.

BRENDA   What was she like?

DAISY   I mustn't tell or it spoils it all.

ROOM 3

BRENDA	It was Brenda's turn now.
MRS N	Mrs Northcote began tracing the small creases of the sole with the point of a silver pencil case.

ROOM 2

DAISY	Where's Mr Beaver to-day?
POLLY	He's flown over to France with his mother to see some new wallpapers. She's been worrying all day, thinking he's had an accident.
DAISY	It's all very touching, isn't it? Though I can't see his point myself…

ROOM 3

MRS N	You must never do anything on Thursdays.
BRENDA	Nothing?
MRS N	Nothing important. You are intellectual, imaginative, impulsive, sympathetic, affectionate. You are highly artistic and are not giving full scope to your capabilities.
BRENDA	Isn't there anything about love?
MRS N	I am coming to love.

ROOM 2

JENNY	Princess Abdul Akbar was announced.
	Where's Brenda? I thought she'd be here.
DAISY	Mrs Northcote's doing her.
JENNY	Jock Grant-Menzies wants to see her. He's downstairs.
POLLY	Darling Jock. Why on earth didn't you bring him up?
JENNY	He's got to see Brenda alone.
DAISY	My dear, how mysterious.
JENNY	Jenny told them the news.

ROOM 3

MRS N	Four men dominate your fate, one is loyal and tender, one is passionate and overpowering.
BRENDA	How very exciting. Who *can* they be?
MRS N	One bodes no good for you; he is steely-hearted and rapacious.
BRENDA	I bet that's my Mr Beaver, bless him.

ROOM 1

JOCK	Downstairs Jock was waiting. It was five past six.

ROOM 2

BRENDA	That was most enjoyable. Why, how odd you all look.
POLLY	Jock Grant-Menzies wants to see you downstairs.
BRENDA	Jock? How very extraordinary. It isn't anything awful, is it?
POLLY	You'd better go and see him.

ROOM 1

BRENDA	What is it, Jock? I'm scared. It's nothing awful, is it?
JOCK	I'm afraid it is. There's been a very serious accident.
BRENDA	John?
JOCK	Yes.
BRENDA	Dead? Why do you know about it first?
JOCK	I've been down at Hetton since the week-end.
BRENDA	Hetton?
JOCK	Don't you remember. John was going hunting to-day.
BRENDA	John... John Andrew... I... Oh, thank God..

ROOM 3

MRS N	Upstairs, Mrs Northcote had Souki Foucauld-Esterhazy by the foot.
	There are four men dominating your fate. One is loyal and tender...

DOUBLING THE INFORMATION

Often part of a narrative can be acted out, eliminating the need for the narration describing that particular behaviour or activity. If you simultaneously apply both the acting out and the telling, this usually results in one of two main effects: a strong underlining of the activity in question, giving it emphatic reinforcement – which might be entirely appropriate for critical or climactic moments; or a deliberate simplicity, which can usefully support comic stories or those with an apparent naivety or innocence. Applied without purpose or point, it creates a heavy-handed literalness. When narrating the description of some activity, you can layer and enrich the occasion and broaden its resonance by giving the narrator some activity to fulfil other than the one being described. As a simple example, when Ester Summerson describes how she used to talk to her dolly, she might indeed have the doll with her, but instead of literally talking to it, she might be in the process of dressing it or simply cradling it – or she might be carrying out some domestic activity, such as embroidering a cushion, without the doll there at all. There is also the possibility of describing an activity without enacting it but with a physicalised attitude to it that could be effected in two ways: one in which the physicalisation deliberately conveys the character's feelings about the matter; the other in which the character's physicality inadvertently reveals or discloses a subtextual, subconscious attitude to it. [*Cross-refer Set 2, Workshop 8: Gesture*] The actor could also carry out the activity while narrating a different section of the story. So you have several options:

i.   Narrating the activity without any activity.

ii. Narrating the activity and at the same time carrying it out literally – in effect, illustrating or doubling the information you're describing.

iii. Narrating the activity while performing some other – possibly analogous – activity, i.e. layering the experience.

iv. Narrating the activity and in some way physicalising your attitude to it, without actually enacting it.

v.   Carrying out the activity whilst narrating something else.

As an example, here are the five possible ways of dealing with the following extract from *Bleak House*. It is Esther's birthday, and she has just been told by her godmother that her mother was her disgrace and she is her mother's, that she is different from other children and set apart.

> I went up to my room, and crept to bed, and laid my doll's cheek
> against mine wet with tears; and holding that solitary friend upon my
> bosom, cried myself to sleep. I knew that I had brought no joy, at any
> time, to anybody's heart, and that I was to no one upon earth what
> Dolly was to me.

i.   Esther simply sits or stands and tells us this without any sort of
     physicalisation.

ii. Esther tells us this while acting out as much as is practical of what she
     describes; certainly lying down and pressing the doll's cheek against hers.

iii. Esther tells us this while trying to dry her tears with a handkerchief or,
     possibly, making sure that her hair and her clothes are tidy and not
     dishevelled by the emotional scene she has just been through with her
     godmother; but *not* acting out the actions she describes.

iv. Esther tell us this while spreading her arms apart in a gesture of futility;
     or maybe collapsing onto a chair barely able to sit upright; or possibly she
     could hug herself in an attempt to control the shuddering caused by the
     shock of what she has heard; or perhaps… Well, who knows what
     physical expression the actor might find?

v.   Esther physically fulfils as much as she can of the first sentence while
     narrating *only* the second sentence to us. If she cuddles her doll and is
     crying, it's really not necessary to know that she went up to her room and
     crept into bed and cried herself to sleep. The second sentence – which
     can't be acted out – contains the important information: that she is
     totally alone in the world. This sort of technique helps to compress the
     text without losing details.

As with so much of the work on storytelling, these choices frequently require a great
subtlety and precision of execution. And, I reiterate, the options are virtually without limit and can only be contained by a disciplined commitment to the chosen
conventions of the performance and, of course, to the interpretation of character. In
the above extract, is Esther recalling these events from the present and reacting to
them in hindsight; is she reliving and literally re-enacting events as if they are happening for the first time; or is she showing us what she did and how she felt at the
time – something between the two? I repeat: when in doubt, try out all the possibilities that occur to you. [*Cross-refer Set 4, Workshop 19: Physical Life
Accompanying Narration*]

CONVERTING FREE INDIRECT DISCOURSE INTO DIRECT SPEECH

This form of narrative in which the third-person narrator almost becomes one with a character could be adjusted. This section from *Emma* (slightly trimmed) could be played in two basic ways:

1. Exactly as written, in its combination of free indirect discourse, indirect and direct speech, with the interesting challenge to the actor of playing all these in character but allowing her to convey an ironic judgement on herself while subjectively experiencing the pain of the situation: [*Cross-refer Set 4, Workshop14: Narrators Embodying their Characters while Commenting on Them*]

> Mr Knightley and Harriet Smith! – Such an elevation on her side! Such a debasement on his! It was horrible to Emma to think how it must sink him in the general opinion... Could it be? No; it was impossible. And yet it was far, far from impossible. – Was it a new circumstance for a man of first-rate abilities to be captivated by very inferior powers? Was it new for one, perhaps too busy to seek, to be the prize of a girl who would seek him?...

> Oh! Had she never brought Harriet forward! Had she left her where she ought, and where he told her she ought! – Had she not, with a folly which no tongue could express, prevented her marrying the unexceptionable young man who would have made her happy and respectable in the line of life to which she ought to belong – all would have been safe; none of this dreadful sequence would have been.

> How Harriet could ever have had the presumption to raise her thoughts to Mr Knightley! – How could she have dared to fancy herself the chosen of such a man till actually assured of it!... Alas! Was not that her own doing, too? Who had been at pains to give Harriet notions of self-consequence but herself?

2. By converting the whole section into direct speech, a naturalistic stream of consciousness, changing some verbs from the past to the present and from the conditional to the indicative, it becomes the equivalent of a soliloquy, easier to play, less challenging, less complex and, possibly, less interesting. Any textual changes are indicated by italics:

> Mr Knightley and Harriet Smith! – Such an elevation on her side! Such a debasement on his! *It's* horrible to think how it must sink him in the general opinion... *Can* it be? No; *it's* impossible. And yet *it's* far, far from impossible. – *Is* it a new circumstance for a man of first-rate abilities to be captivated by very inferior powers? *Is* it new for one, perhaps too busy to seek, to be the prize of a girl who would seek him?...

Oh, had *I* never brought Harriet forward. Had *I* left her where she ought, and where he told *me* she ought! *Have I* not, with a folly no tongue can express, prevented her marrying the unexceptional young man who would have made her happy… [*…and on to the end*] Alas! *Isn't this my* own doing, too? Who *has* been at pains to give Harriet notions of self-consequence but myself?

———

A Reminder: There can be no hard-and-fast rules applying to all stories. Each story has its own demands and each production its own conditions and requirements, possibilities and limitations. The point of all this is, of course, to try, under whatever circumstances you're working, to remain true both in spirit and word to the story you're transforming into a piece of theatre.

SHORT STORIES

Possibly a selection of short stories may attract you as the basis for a production rather than one sustained narrative. (Of course, it's entirely possible that a single short story will more than suffice for an evening.) A challenging aspect of working with several stories is discovering in what way they're connected in terms of content (theme, plot, character…) or context (author, genre, location…) and then the best way in which to structure their movement through the performance. Groups of stories in *A Thousand and One Nights* are linked in a variety of structures that are well worth a look. [*Cross-refer Set 15, Workshop 60: Framing and Linking Stories*]

The stories we selected for each of our three *Arabian Nights* productions were put together in different ways to create the appropriate worlds they seemed to demand. *The First Arabian Night* was a story concerning separated lovers searching the world for each other. The plot bifurcated into two alternating narratives concerning each of the pair which, at their reunion, of course blended into one. Their narratives also contained other stories, as adjuncts to the main plot, inserted as exemplars or moral tales to enlighten or influence the lovers as they pursued their mutual search. *The Second Arabian Night* was a picaresque series of shaggy-dog stories, always linked to the main character, moving in chronological sequence as episodes in a simple plot – Dalilah, wily widow of royal pigeon-keeper, plays clever tricks on Baghdad citizenry to persuade Caliph to let her inherit her late husband's job – and achieving an accumulative effect as the performance proceeded. *The Third Arabian Night* was constructed within the framework of a journey through the desert to a mythical city during which individual travellers explained what had brought them on this pilgrimage. Each story was discrete and only connected to the others by the shared hope of redemption when they reached their destination.

The Book of Esther that I described earlier is an example of telling the same story more than once, in this case five times, each variation putting the story through a fresh interpretive wringer. The impact of this repetition gave the story increasing resonance. Each new telling was enriched by what had preceded it.

Demons and Dybbuks was constructed from the many stories in Isaac Bashevis Singer's vast output that have a strong autobiographical basis, albeit imaginatively transmuted into fiction. Raised in a poor ultra-orthodox Polish-Jewish community, he emigrated, after a somewhat feckless youth, to the United States where initially he led the demeaning life of a penniless writer, eventually becoming a successful novelist and storyteller, first within the American Jewish Diaspora – he always wrote in Yiddish – then in translation with the wider public, eventually winning the Nobel Prize for Literature. This journey was our guiding principle. So the stories we selected, all in the first person, began with anecdotes of a superstitiously devout childhood, followed by accounts of teenage promiscuity, penniless immigrant life in Brooklyn, success and fame as a writer and, finally, a spiritual return to his roots, in a sense creating a circular narrative. In this way, these stories, though discrete and complete in themselves and ranging from the farcical to the mystical, contained resonances and themes, grappling mainly with sex, religion and storytelling, that linked them together. We didn't think it necessary to explain this structure to the audience but hoped that they would sense a cohesiveness in the overall work. It was essentially a blueprint for ourselves.

SECTION 9

WORLDS

The How of the What:
Form and Content,
Style and Substance,
Manner and Matter

DEFINING WORLDS

The content, the substance, the matter are what. The plot is what. The characters with their actions are what. The given circumstances of the story are what. The subject matter is what. The writer's how – the choice of language, structure and narrative viewpoint – becomes the adapter's what. All these whats are facts. They're facts because the writer has established them as such. These irrefutable facts are what we have to analyse, interpret and then translate into the language of theatre, into the how of performance.

The form, the style, the manner are how. There are two levels of how: the way in which the author has chosen to tell the story and the way in which the story is adapted and performed. The how of the performance should reflect the how of the writing. The way the actors act is how. The way the language is spoken is how. The way the story moves in the space is how. The way it looks is how. The way it sounds is how. How is the performance of the interpreted facts, the translation of a literary world into a dramatic world.

A world is the how of the what, a seamless blending of form and content. A world is the expression of a particular reality. That reality is a version of the actuality we inhabit (the life we experience) seen through the unique lens of its author. I prefer the word *world* to the more commonly used *style*, which to me always suggests a veneer, a high gloss imposed on the material rather than an organic form emerging from it.

Evolving the performance world of a story is the process of exploring how best to enact and relate that story in a way most congenial to the original, a way that brings to life most fully its moods and meanings, structures and forms. (This is the essential job – the craft and purpose – of directing.) Different media affect us differently, and in adapting from one medium to another, there are – as in translating from one language to another – no neat one-to-one equivalents. Nevertheless, we have to devise a particular theatrical language that will recreate something close to the impact of the particular literary language, the chosen devices and techniques of the writer. Ideally, the how should be inevitable, fused to the what so that content and form become an indivisible totality. A world is a unique reality, constantly self-reinforcing, true to its own rules and conventions.

DISCOVERING WORLDS

We have two worlds to deal with: the world of the written story and the world of its performance. In what kind of performance world can this or that story best exist? What is its reality? There are no pre-existing worlds (or styles or forms or manners) awaiting your adoption. Beware of being ensnared by clichés such as Dickensian, Pinteresque, Restoration, à la Coward, in the manner of Jane Austen... which are somewhat lazy generalisations, interpretive short cuts which may be useful to point you in broadly the right direction so long as you're aware that many received ideas are likely to be inaccurate, if not downright wrong. Every story demands its own analysis. Beyond a certain point – the facts having been analysed – interpretation becomes subjective, a matter of personal taste and insight. No two people, given the same information, will interpret it in exactly the same way. This, of course, is precisely how artists reveal their individuality. It goes without saying – I'll say it nonetheless – that the more rigorous the analysis of the content, the greater the possibility of discovering a form for the original material that feels organic and inevitable and penetrates more deeply. With sufficient rigour, every production could (would and should) be a completely unique event, unlike any previous pro-duction: a world of its own that only these particular artists could have created from this particular material at this particular time. A play, because of its purpose (to be performed), will come with certain indications of how it might be staged implicit in the text. A story, because it's been conceived without any such intention, seems open to an embarrassment of choices and consequently places stringent demands on the interpretive discipline of its adapters.

Each time we embark on new material, we have to learn the rules of the particular game we are playing. And each and every game, that's to say, each and every story-telling, will have its own set of rules. And that is precisely what rehearsals are for: to discover, learn, absorb and make tangible those specific rules and conventions. Just as you cannot play tennis with the rules for cricket, you cannot play Shakespeare like Chekhov, or Dickens like George Eliot. But even that sort of thinking is a mis-taken generalisation; there are no overall rules for playing the works of a particular writer. Each of a writer's stories is unique. If you move from *The Pickwick Papers* to *Hard Times*, from *Hay Fever* to *'Peace in Our Time'*, *Romola* to *Silas Marner*, you will have to start from scratch each time you set out on your road to discovery, even if you do pass through a certain amount of familiar terrain en route.

We have to put the flesh of dramatic action onto the bones of literary structures. In crude categories, we have to consider whether the physical realisation of a text should be fast or slow, colourful or monochromatic, noisy or quiet, flowing or erratic, multilevelled or single-planed, light or dark, hot or cold, relaxed or intense, moving in straight lines or on curves, naturalistic or heightened, elaborate or aus-tere, playful or formal, fantastic or slice-of-life... or anywhere along the spectra between the extremes of these or any other contrasted qualities. Does a world favour the physical over the verbal, the intellectual over the emotional, extroversion over introversion...? Or vice versa? Only after detailed analysis of the facts – those dealing with structure and those dealing with content – and then interpreting that analysis can we begin to test such choices in action. By proceeding with sufficient diligence, by digging sufficiently deep, we may even reward ourselves by excavating a completely conceived world. The elements of story that need such archaeological delving are language, structure, plot, narrative, character, themes, topics, culture and reality. Many of their qualities and values will overlap and cross-relate; all but the last two are identical with the component parts of a story that I listed in *Section 5: Definitions*.

Language (words, grammar, punctuation)

The main what of a text-based story is its language. As I've noted, the uniqueness of a story lies not necessarily in its plot or characterisations but in the way – how – it's written. (After all, we're told often enough that there are only seven basic plots.) In realising a performance, all the other elements must be developed from the way in which, first and foremost, we interpret the actual words of the text, the way they're organised on the page and the way they sound when we read them aloud. Is the language formal, demotic or archaic, does it use jargon, slang or dialect? Does it employ metaphor and simile or limit itself to statements of fact? Is it elaborate and luxuriant or precise and contained? Does it stick to the point or digress? Does it resonate with ironic subtext or strive to tell it as it is? Is the tone hot, loud and emphatic or cool, quiet and restrained? Does it contain dialogue – and to what extent? Is the dialogue direct or indirect? What sort of vocabulary dominates: plain Anglo-Saxon or fancy Latinisms? What are the dominant forms of its sentence structure? Does the punctuation – full of hyphens, brackets, dashes, semi- and full colons – generate long and complex sentences proliferating meticulously detailed clauses within clauses? Or is it reduced to full stops and the occasional comma, simple and terse? Does it at times dispense with verbs? Does it allow for ambiguities of meaning? The layout of the text is also worth noting: how the words are set out on the page – brief paragraphs or solid page-long blocks, short sentences or long, jagged or flowing – may suggest particular patterns of energy and rhythm for performance. Having identified all of this, the critical question is: what is the behaviour and physicality, what the environment and values, of characters whose mouths issue such-and-such a form of language?

Here are two translations from the opening of *Das Nibelungenlied*:

1. We have been told in ancient tales many marvels of famous heroes, of mighty toil, joys and high festivities, of weeping and wailing, and the fighting of bold warriors – of such things you can now hear wonders unending.

    In the land of the Burgundians there grew up a maiden of high lineage, so fair that none in any land could be fairer. Her name was Kriemhild. She came to be a beautiful woman, causing many knights to lose their lives. This charming girl was as if made for love's caresses: she was desired by brave fighting men and none was her enemy, for her person was beyond all measure lovely. Such graces did the young lady possess that she was the adornment of her sex.

2. The old stories tell us of great heroes, joy and misery, feast and lament, and the clash of brave warriors. All this you may hear now, if you will.

    There lived in Burgundy a young girl of great nobility, and beauty unparalleled in any country, and her name was Kriemhilde. Later she grew into a beautiful woman, and caused the death of many a knight. She seemed made for loving; many a brave knight would have had her if he could, and no one was her enemy. She was unbelievably beautiful, and her qualities were such as any woman could desire.

At first glance, there seems no essential difference between them that would lead a dramatiser to chose one over the other. But in fact, both have a distinct individuality. The first piece seems to have set out to recreate an archaic tradition of storytelling, more elaborate ('This charming girl was as if made for love's caresses'; as opposed to 'She seemed made for loving'; 'beyond all measure lovely' as opposed to 'unbelievably beautiful'), given to wider hyperbole ('so fair that none in any land could be fairer' as opposed to 'beauty unparalleled in any country'), adjectives following the nouns they qualify (wonders unending) and a richer choice of vocabulary, especially of synonyms ('maiden, beautiful woman, charming girl, her person, young lady' as opposed to 'young girl, beautiful woman').

The second choice seems to be trying to bridge the gap between ancient and modern ('There lived in Burgundy a young girl of great nobility', as opposed to 'In the land of the Burgundians there grew up a maiden of high lineage'), and to elide phrases that seem repetitious ('She was unbelievably beautiful, and her qualities were such that any woman could desire' as opposed to 'for her person was beyond all measure lovely. Such graces did the young lady possess that she was the adornment of her sex'). Both translations, of course, have their purposes and integrity. The first piece is shaped closer to the original.[1]

1. The original in High Middle German is written in short verse lines with an A-B-A-B rhyming scheme. This knowledge might possibly suggest a surface naivety in delivering the text.

My own reaction to the first piece draws me into a distant and unfamiliar past, more mysterious, mythical, archetypical. It suggests to me a heightened performance: characters with a sense of their mythic destiny and their unique status, their gestures bold, their use of space dynamic, their emotions intense, their landscapes, their possessions strongly defined and essential, conveying their primordial existence.

The second piece seems brisker, more efficient (it's almost two lines briefer than the first piece), slightly coloured by more modern attitudes ('many a knight would have had her if he could'), less distant – more of an adventure story – which in part it certainly is. It evokes a sharper, lither, edgier, more excitable, possible more playful world, one less weightily driven.

My observations of the two translations and my visualisation of their theatrical possibilities, I think, can be considered reasonable initial conjectures while still being my personal response; my preference for the first over the second is, of course, totally subjective.

Structure (organisation)

The frame that supports a story will suggest a specific world; whether its structure, for example, is episodic or linear, chronologically sustained, or shifting back and forth between blocks of time; the way its several threads of plot interweave. The organisation of different sequences and the ratio between such components as exposition, stream of consciousness, conversation, philosophical meditation, action, analysis, diaries, letters, emails, and so forth may throw light on where narrative and dramatic emphasis should be placed. A story with a lot of dialogue and little commentary will materialise on stage very differently from one with lots of action and little speech. A structure will affect the energy, movement and rhythm of the performance. Here are some examples of books whose structures would have to be reconceived dramatically.

Samuel Richardson's vast novel, *Clarissa* (the longest in English literature), is constructed exclusively in letters. But those letters often enclose other letters and contain intercepted and undelivered letters, at times causing the chronology to lose its linearity.

In Cormac McCarthy's *No Country for Old Men*, the anonymous, omniscient third-person narrative that places two or three different characters at the centre of the developing action is interspersed with italicised chapters in which one of those characters, in the first person, muses on his life and values.

The Blind Assassin by Margaret Atwood is built on the first-person narrative of a very old woman remembering the past but also experiencing her present life, interwoven with a novel in the third-person, purportedly written by her dead sister, which contains yet another novel. These are also interspersed with old newspapers cuttings.

The Pulitzer Prize-winning novel by Jennifer Egan, *A Visit from the Goon Squad*, comprises thirteen discrete chapters, resembling short stories, in which some of the characters re-appear at different ages in changing relationships and combinations, not necessarily chronologically. One chapter is presented in graphics like a Power-Point demonstration.

These four differently structured novels clearly demand their own individual treatment. You could, of course, extrapolate from each of them a chronologically shaped narrative in third-person mode, and you would certainly retain the plot. But almost everything that makes these stories what they are would be lost.

For instance, it would be entirely possible to create a straightforward, linear, anonymously narrated story from *Clarissa*, but that would seem to defeat the particular quality of how the story has been put together. What would be lost? Well, the multiple first-person narratives that are of necessity the nature of letter-writing and inevitably subjective and self-interested, the tension in waiting to find out how a letter has been received by its addressee or whether it even reached its destination, and the curiosity as to how the recipient will respond. Then there is the option, not possible in the book itself, of having a letter read by either the sender or the recipient or by both. There is also the theatrical option of reliving the events rather than recalling them. There is also the effect on the correspondents – the strain on hand and eyesight (writing by candlelight), together with the stress of the contents – in a society whose only means of communication over distance requires so much more time than ours and far more physical effort in the scribatious use of quill, ink and pounce.[2]

In dealing with the Cormac McCarthy novel, how would one shift from a third-person observation of events to first-person introspection raised by these events? Again, the actual plot could remain intact without those first-person chapters, with any necessary content from them possibly subsumed into the third-person narrative.[3] But this would lose the story's depth of purpose and, in fact, the justification for its Yeatsian title. Of course, it would theatrically be easy enough for the character who owns the first-person narrative to step out of the action to talk to us directly about himself. But somehow this seems a banal, somewhat weak solution for

---

2. I can conceive of a stage full of desks at which characters are seated, quills in hand, inkwells, pounce pots, sealing wax and tapers at the ready, energetically corresponding under various degrees of urgency, constraint or caution; characters reading letters as they are being acted out, all accompanied to the constant scratching of quills applied with varying intensities… and so forth.

3. This, of course, is how the screen adaptation dealt with it.

material that has a huge change of energy and tone, and is, in fact, the filter through which we absorb the story. It would need a form and weight to equate with its impact in the novel.

As for *The Blind Assassin*, its elaborate and complex structure would need an ingenious convention of equal bravura to contain and shift between its many levels of reality and allow a gradually developing connection between these initially unconnected forms. And much the same goes for *A Visit from the Goon Squad*: and what might be the theatrical equivalent of its chapter carried out with its text entirely within diagrammatic shapes?

Plot (events)

The way the plot negotiates its journey through the narrative and the sorts of events of which it's comprised (social, domestic, erotic, dramatic…) will suggest how it might be realised, the particular tone and energy that seems appropriate. A single-stranded linear plot with a limited number of characters might imply a sustained atmosphere to be explored in nuanced detail at a steady pace. A multistranded plot that twists and turns into subsidiary plots and moves a large cast of characters around in time and space will probably need many changes of mood, sharp delineations of character and location: less depth and nuance, more litheness and attack. Does a plot slide its events towards you or chuck them at you? Does it present them at a steady rhythm, occasionally making one or two of them leap out at you? Does it beckon you to take brief peeps at some of its events through very limited gaps in time? Or does it race along, event after event, expecting you to sprint along with it? These examples are, of course, metaphorical ideas of how a plot might be shaped, but this sort of thinking might help you part of the way towards a visualisation of its concrete, tangible physicalisation on a stage.

James Elroy's *American Tabloid* has three main protagonists constantly on the move, each with his complicated plot line, overlapping with the others, teeming with events that Ellroy describes with a startling economy, so that you really have to sit up and take notice to avoid losing vital information. Any adaptation would have to find an equivalent sharp, witty compression.

Narrative (point of view)

The point of view from which a story is narrated, as we have already discussed in some detail, will have a huge bearing on the form and tone of performance, depending on where along the spectrum between objective and subjective the narrative falls, and in which tense it is told. The viewpoint will control the expressive range of the material, defining what may be seen and blocking out anything that doesn't comply with that vision.

Henry James's *What Maisie Knew*, for instance, sets an interesting challenge from the point of view of its point of view. Although it's written in a basic linear third-person narrative with the occasional intrusion of the novelist's awareness of the reader, James brilliantly manages to convey much of the story through the mind of his child-heroine and to chart her growing awareness as she moves from initial incomprehension to eventual understanding of the events around her (the divorce, remarriages and extra-marital affairs of her parents), which is, of course, the point and purpose of the novel, embedded in the title. James is able to describe, with the utmost subtlety and precision, Maisie's almost imperceptible flashes of insight, the nuances of which might be well nigh impossible to express in theatre. This would be the challenge for someone choosing to adapt the novel: to discover an equivalent dramatic delicacy of revelation. Here, the act of reading in which you, the reader, can take all the time you need to absorb the elaborately detailed description of a perception lasting barely a second, confronts that split-second it would take to occur in actuality – in performance. Discovering how to perform sustained descriptions of inner perceptions would go a long way to defining the performance world of this story: the way the language is expressed, its physical–spatial correlation, the possible slowing-down of time. (In terms of expansion of time, opera expresses a similar reality when the thoughts and words that are sung repeat themselves over a far longer duration than their actual (non-musical) delivery would take.[4]) So this would be your job: to create a world in which it is truthful and natural (but not naturalistic) for people with lengthy, complex, nuanced thoughts to exist, behave and express themselves.

In a story where the thoughts or points of view of all the characters are given expression, as in the novels of Anthony Trollope, the space would have to be mobilised to accommodate the shifting perspectives from which the audience should watch the action.

---

4. Opera is a very good general example of a specific world; one in which the natural condition for its characters – their reality – is to communicate by singing; sometimes also by recitative and occasionally by the spoken word. And everything else about such a world would have to be shaped around that major fact. Of course, within that broad category, every opera has its own particularities of form and content.

Character (action)

The level and degree of actuality in which the characters exist must strongly affect their creation. Are they presented three-dimensionally, fully rounded with complex emotional, intellectual and social lives? Or are they sketched to emphasise certain idiosyncrasies? Are they described or analysed or simply presented by their actions?

You don't need too much imagination to recognise a different level of existence for the characters in *Gormenghast* from those in *Middlemarch*, or those in Malory's *Morte d'Arthur* from those in P. G. Wodehouse's *Jeeves* series. Not only a matter of cultural differences, but altogether different realities: in rough terms, Eliot's people being the most naturalistic and Mervyn Peake's, the least. Wodehouse's characters are a species of upper-class ninnies that inhabit a between-the-wars world that never quite existed; Malory's are national myths, magical, doomed by tragic destinies, living anachronistically according to a medieval code of chivalry. Each of these needs the actors to speak, move, behave, use space, think, express themselves in totally different ways, most of them not realistic, but for whose characters they have to find a particular truth. The actors' job is to make us accept totally that these Armoured Knights or Flannelled Fools would behave in such-and-such a manner, utterly believable despite the fact that we would never come across such a form of existence in actuality.

Novels are peopled with rich characterisations, often of a complexity and detail for which a play rarely has the space or time. Here are two samples of succinct and vivid character drawing, informed by the very specific use and sound of the language, above and beyond the actual meaning of the individual words.

> When anyone asked Beaver why he stayed there instead of setting up on his own, he sometimes said he thought his mother liked having him there, sometimes that it saved him at least five pounds a week.

> He was twenty-five years old. From leaving Oxford until the beginning of the slump he had worked in an advertising agency. Since them no one had been able to find anything for him to do. So he got up late and sat near his telephone most of the day, hoping to be rung up.

> Most of Beaver's invitations came to him at the last moment, occasionally even later, when he had already begun to eat a solitary meal on a tray... 'John, darling, there's been a muddle and Sonia has arrived without Reggie. Could you be an angel and help me out? Only be quick, because we're going in now'... Then he would go headlong for a taxi and arrive, with apologies, after the first course...

> *A Handful of Dust* – Evelyn Waugh

Meg Bishop was a woman-journalist who had written a series of books under the basic title of *Meg Sees*, all dealing with cataclysmic events in the modern world and ranging historically from the civil war in Spain to the present guerrilla fighting in Greece. Ten years of association with brass hats and political bigwigs had effaced any lingering traits of effeminacy in her voice and manner. Unfortunately she did not choose to wear the tailored clothes that would be congruous with her booming, incisive voice and her alert, military bearing. The queenly mink coat that she wore, the pearls and the taffeta dinner gown underneath, gave her a rather shockingly transvestite appearance, almost as though the burly commander of a gunboat had presented himself in the disguise of a wealthy clubwoman.

The Roman Spring of Mrs Stone –
Tennessee Williams

In the first excerpt, Waugh brilliantly nails his character's parasitical passivity by the simple grammatical construct of making him the object of most of his sentences. He waits for things to be done to him. He only displays initiative when he goes 'headlong for a taxi' on the chance of a free meal. The choice of words encourages a slight drawl in their pronunciation, probably because of a predominance of long vowels with a minimum of percussive consonants. It almost sounds as if Beaver is delivering his own description.

For his character, Williams uses strong, assertive words with closed endings, consonant-heavy and short-vowelled, that demand a tighter attack and more effort to enunciate.

Though they are both presented realistically, their worlds are very different.

Themes and Topics (subject matter)

In terms of attitudes, behaviour and actions, the characters are more than likely (in good writing) to share similarities, to mirror or echo or counterpoint each other. The accumulated super-objectives of all the characters should collectively reveal a strong idea of the story's super-objective, that is, what the story's intention may be – in fact, its theme. The characters' objectives and actions are what create the plot and move it forward. So it's only logical that these should convey the underlying purpose of the whole. This must make sense: what the characters are trying to achieve in their lives and circumstances must be what the story is about.

Therefore, the theme holding the different elements of a story together is likely to be close to, if not synonymous with, the super-objective of the story. It would be a strange story in which the actions and needs of the characters went in one direction, while the theme went in another. In *Bleak House*, the objectives of the mainly neglected children – and the poverty-stricken members of society – are, in varying degrees, to cope with life, supporting each other wherever possible, abandoned as they are by parents (and parental institutions) whose own objectives are to absolve themselves of any obligations or responsibilities to follow their own selfish interests. The story is the conflict between these two groups as they pursue their opposing needs; its theme (yet again!): when institutions designed for the care of its citizens (government, philanthropy, law, family and the like) fail in their purpose, the only recourse for individuals is to take responsibility for the care of each other. Ideally, every detail of a world should in some way manifest its theme.

The subject matter – the topics – of a story will also influence the nature of the world. The subject of high finance, say, will exist in a very different world from that dealing with the nature of memory. Or, in *Bleak House*, with the legal system. The actors who portray the characters representing its practice have to become embodiments of its Byzantine incompetence, its corruption, its jargon, rituals, self-serving bureaucracy and absence of compassion. Every aspect of how they talk, behave, interrelate, wear their clothes, move in their space should be expressive of this subject matter. With a couple of important exceptions, they influence the action from the fringes of the story, often as unseen presences exerting pressures that decide the fate of the 'victims'. In the novel, their client/victims are the characters whose stories we follow most closely. The challenge of creating these two groups is to develop them in such a way that they can both exist together in the same world.

As you can see, theme, topics, characters and plot interrelate. By looking at each of them in turn, you should discover a gradually accumulating reinforcement of details, qualities, atmospheres and energies that goes to make up a consistent world.

Culture (society)

The place and period in which a story is set will demand a knowledge and understanding of the beliefs, values, and accepted conduct of that society. The urge to move stories out of their original ambience is understandable. Overexposure to dull renditions of classic dramatic texts makes them (and us) scream out for fresh treatment. But this is a superficial solution – changing the externals – when it's the inner life of a story that needs to be more deeply expressed. Updating or changing periods in the belief that only by stressing contemporary parallels, while removing anything else that doesn't fit that scheme, will the work be comprehensible patronises an audience quite capable of discerning the pertinence of a text for themselves. For the most part, it is pretentiousness posing as (that dreaded word) relevance. In fact, changing periods is a tired device that's been around for a long while.

Our relatively recent non-smoking, smart-phoning, blogging, tweeting world of instant communication presents real problems for the updater. The danger of moving the content of material out of its own frame of reference into another is to end up with something broken-backed, neither one thing or the other, not true to its original world nor true to its transposed reality. Falling between two stools, throwing the baby out with the bath water – all those clichés rise up against this process. It is true, of course, that there are no absolutes (another one). Stories are inextricably connected to their time and place; how characters think and behave and what they value are psychologically enmeshed in their culture. Why would one even consider updating Dickens, for instance? We now know things that one hundred and fifty years ago his characters would have had no way of knowing; similarly, they knew or believed things that are no longer part of our received knowledge or value systems. Little Nell really can't listen to Stockhausen any more than *Kick-Ass*'s Hit-Girl is likely to have 'Pale Hands I Loved' on her MP3 player. People separated by time and place are not identical. There are no conveniently neat equivalents. Our bodies, our emotional capacity, our psychological potential may be the same, but the patterns of our daily lives, how we express our feelings – all these are selectively tied to the period in which we live. When Ibsen wrote *A Doll's House*, he didn't know any people who live in the twenty-first century. The Three Sisters are *not* Irish.

Despite immense difference in the manner and milieux of the following random examples, their common denominator is that they all fall within a realistic reality: *Love in a Cold Climate* (Nancy Mitford – upper-class English in their 1930s country houses), *Tobacco Road* (Erskine Caldwell – poor white Georgia sharecroppers in their shacks during the Depression), *A Dream of Red Mansions* (Cao Xueqin – a wealthy and influential eighteenth-century Chinese clan living in their enclosed family compounds), *Père Goriot* (Honoré de Balzac – a social mix of residents in a Parisian boarding house during the Bourbon Restoration).

This area of work, the cultural framework, is essentially realistic, even if the text in question as a whole is not. So if you were working on novels like *Cold Comfort Farm* or Fielding's *The Life and Death of Jonathan Wild*, both of which are satirical pastiches, you would nevertheless need to familiarise yourself with the cultures and societies from which they were derived before you began to explore the distorting mirrors through which they're reflected.

Reality (relationship to actuality)

Which brings us to the reality of a text. A story, as already noted, is not necessarily realistic: that is, it's not attempting to replicate a reality recognisable as the reality we perceive ourselves to be living in. If we call our experience of life, as we live it from day to day, actuality, we have to find out by how much and in what way – with which elements included and which excluded, which emphasised and which minimised, to what degree heightened or distorted – a story departs from or approaches that actuality. What is its specific reality? In very crude terms, does it belong within a general classification like Romanticism, Expressionism, Naturalism and so on? Possibly it fits into a genre such as Victorian Melodrama, American Noir or RomCom. But such taxonomies are merely flags of convenience to link together works of art bearing approximate similarities. They suggest that certain elements of actuality have been selected and possibly stressed at the expense of others. For example, in melodrama, complex psychology usually takes a back seat and the characters veer towards types with preordained functions, such as hero and villain, while elaborate plotting and high emotion are very much to the fore. But again, no two melodramatic pieces will be identical and won't always conform to those qualifications I've suggested. There are worlds of difference between *Murder in the Red Barn* and *The Little Foxes*.

Every good story has a truth of its own, is a reality in itself, worthy of fresh, unprejudiced examination and never to be slipped lazily into some formulaic envelope. How does a story represent life? As a piece of slapstick or a vale of tears? Is it focused on the internal life of its characters at the expense of their external existence? Does it present a reality totally informed by ideas of social conduct or by derring-do across oceans and continents? Does it portray characters as animals or spiritual beings? Does it convey life as a frenetic, urban rat race or bathe it in a bucolic sunset glow? Is life a grotesque exaggeration or a delicate gauze of filters and shadows? Start with broad categories by all means – that's a way in – but then you have to keep asking questions, increasingly specific and detailed, to discover the unique reality of a particular story.

Worlds

The world of a story is the accumulation of all the elements of the story (language, structure, culture, degree of relationship to actuality, etc.), and therefore also the sum of our analyses of these components. As noted, the nature of these categories overlap and seep into each other, strengthening our vision of how this world might be realised in action.

The results of these investigations then become the basis for a whole other batch of questions. How would people behave in a world, say, of diary entries written in short, undecorated sentences, from a single viewpoint, with episodic events and

rituals spread throughout a year, few locations, indirect speech and aristocratic characters with heightened behaviour patterns, concern for status and social decorum,
absence of psychological penetration but plenty of ironic comment, all set in tenth-
century Japan? How would such a world look; how would it sound; how would it
move; what might be its dominant elements – colour, energy, temperature, rhythm,
tempo; what aspects of our actuality would be eliminated, which selected and in
what way intensified – if at all; what would be the values and attitudes with which
its characters saw one another and looked at life?

The technical and physical solutions to the performance of a story also become part
of the conventions of that world: whether props are mimed and in what manner,
whether the actors remain present throughout a performance, whether there is
music and of what kind and produced by what means, and so forth and so on... *The
world encompasses everything.*

The following are the opening passages of several novels. I'm not suggesting that
all or any of them would finally be suitable material for adaptation, but their structure and language invite us to enter very particular worlds that would be challenging
to realise on stage. All of them lead us to a reality that moves away from or exag-
gerates or selectively closes in on aspects of our own actuality. See what images are
spontaneously conjured up in your imaginations on a first reading. Do they suggest, if any, colours, types of movement, degrees of energy, shapes, sounds, ways of
speaking, types of people, sorts of space, visions of life, the need for lighting,
props...?

ONE

On Friday noon, July the twentieth, 1714, the finest bridge in all Peru
broke and precipitated five travellers into the gulf below. This bridge was
on the high road between Lima and Cuzco, and hundreds of persons
passed over it every day. It had been woven of osier by the Incas more
than a century before, and visitors to the city were always led out to see
it. It was a mere ladder of thin slats swung out over the gorge, with
handrails of dried vine. Horses and coaches and chairs had to go down
hundreds of feet below and pass over the narrow torrent on rafts, but no
one, not even the Viceroy, not even the Archbishop of Lima, had
descended with the baggage rather than cross by the famous bridge of
San Luis Rey. St Louis of France himself protected it, by his name and
by the little mud church on the farther side. The bridge seemed to be
among the things that last for ever; it was unthinkable that it should
break. The moment a Peruvian heard of the accident he signed himself
and made a mental calculation as to how recently he had crossed by it
and how soon he had intended crossing by it again. People wandered
about in a trance-like state, muttering: they had the hallucination of
seeing themselves falling into the gulf.

TWO

Suddenly:

The milk truck cut a sharp right turn and grazed the curb. The driver lost the wheel. He panic-popped the brakes. He induced a rear-end skid. A Wells Fargo armoured car clipped the milk truck side/head-on.

Mark it now:

7.16 a.m. South L. A., 84th and Budlong. Residential darktown. Shit shacks with dirt front yards.

The jolt stalled out both vehicles. The milk truck driver hit the dash. The driver's side door blew wide. The driver keeled and hit the sidewalk. He was a fortyish male Negro.

The armoured car notched some dents. Three guards got out and scoped the damage. They were white men in tight khakis. They wore Sam Browne belts with buttoned pistol flaps.

They knelt beside the milk truck driver. The guy twitched and gasped. The dashboard bounce gouged his forehead. Blood dripped into his eyes.

Mark it now:

7.17 a.m. Winter overcast. This quiet street. No foot traffic. No car-crash hubbub yet.

The milk truck heaved. The radiator blew. Steam hissed and spread wide. The guards coughed and wiped their eyes. Three men got out of a '62 Ford parked two curbs length back.

They wore masks. They wore gloves and crepe-soled shoes. They wore utility belts with gas bombs in pouches. They were long-sleeved and buttoned up. Their skin colour was obscured.

Steam covered them. They walked up and pulled silencered pieces. The guards coughed. It provided sound cover. The milk truck driver pulled a silencered piece and shot the nearest guard in the face.

The noise was a thud. The guard's forehead exploded. The two other guards fumble-grabbed at their holsters. The masked men shot them in the back. They buckled and pitched forward. The masked men shot them in the head point-blank. The thuds and skull crack muffle-echoed.

7.19 a.m. It's still quiet. There's no foot traffic and no car-crash hubbub yet.

THREE

'Lor' love you, sir!' Fevers rang out in a voice that clanged like dustbin lids. 'As to my place of birth, why, I first saw the light of day right here in smoky old London, didn't I! Not billed the "Cockney Venus" for nothing, sir, though they could just as well 'ave called me "Helen of the High Wire", due to the unusual circumstances in which I come ashore – for I never docked via what you might call *normal channels*, sir, oh, dear me, no; but, just like Helen of Troy, was *hatched*.'

'Hatched out of a bloody great egg while Bow Bells rang, as ever is!'

The blonde guffawed uproariously, slapped the marbly thigh on which her wrap fell open and flashed a pair of vast, blue, indecorous eyes at the young reporter with his open notebook and his poised pencil, as if to dare him: 'Believe it or not!'...

Fevers, the most famous *aerialiste* of the day; her slogan, 'Is she fact or is she fiction?' And she didn't let you forget it for a minute; this query, in the French language, in foot-high letters, blazed forth from a wall-size poster, souvenir of her Paris triumphs, dominating her London dressing-room. Something hectic, something fittingly impetuous and dashing about that poster, the preposterous depiction of a young woman shooting up like a rocket, whee! in a burst of agitated sawdust towards an unseen trapeze somewhere above in the wooden heavens of the Cirque d'Hiver. The artist had chosen to depict her ascent from behind – bums aloft, you might say; up she goes, in a steatopygous perspective, shaking out about her those tremendous red and purple pinions, pinions large enough, powerful enough to bear up such a big girl as she. And she was a *big* girl.

Evidently this Helen took after her putative father, the swan, around the shoulder parts.

But these notorious and much-debated wings, the source of her fame, were stowed away for the night under the soiled quilting of her baby-blue satin dressing-gown, where they made an uncomfortable looking pair of bulges, shuddering the surface of the taut fabric from time to time as if desirous of breaking loose. ('How does she do that?' pondered the reporter.)

FOUR

NOTICE

Do Not use my Good Blankets And
Pillows in Room Three
                                        Signed Matron H Price

---

NOVEMBER 1 NIGHT SISTER'S REPORT
ROOM 3 Mother vioded 4 a.m. Nothing abnormal to report.
                                        Signed Night Sister M. Shady

NOVEMBER 2 NIGHT SISTER'S REPORT
ROOM 3 Mother vioded also Mrs Murphy, Mrs Renfrew and Mrs
Tomkins. Nothing abnormal to report.
                                        Signed Night Sister M. Shady

NOVEMBER 3 NIGHT SISTER'S REPORT
ROOM 3 Mother vioded also Mrs Murphy Mrs Renfrew Mrs Tomkins
Miss Hailey and Miss Nunne, Nothing abnormal to report
                                        Signed Night Sister M. Shady

*Night Sister Shady: Please will you report more fully. Please report on the
other patients. You are supposed to wash the kitchen floor too you seem to have
forgotten this. I seem to have to remind you too often that if a patient upsets her
tea in bed you are to boil up some water and pour on at once. All my sheets are
getting ruined. Also my brother lt col. (retired) I. Rice has something to add.*

TO ALL NIGHT STAFF TO WHOM IT MAY
CONCERN IT HAS COME TO MY NOTICE
THAT STAFF ARE USING THE FOR THEIR
OWN PERSONAL LIFE THIS MUST CEASE
IMMEDIATELY
                    SIGNED I. PRICE (LT COL. RETIRED

And Night Sister Shady please note spelling of void. V.O.I.D
                                        Signed Matron H. Price.

NOVEMBER 4 NIGHT SISTER'S REPORT
ROOM 3 Mother vioded voided room three sponged slept well 4 a.m. kitchen
floor washed as request sweet potatoes prepared also pumpkin please matron
can I have a knife for the veggies. Nothing abnormal to report.
                                        Signed Night Sister M. Shady

Night Sister Shady: it is unfortunate that one of the patients is you mother please will you refer to her in this book as Mrs Morgan which is her correct name. Please bring your own knife; it is not practical for me to provide knives as all previous night nurses have left and taken them. Please report more fully and why always 4 a.m. Is this the only time you know? Please boil the beetroots.

                                                    Signed Matron H. Price.

FIVE

A small, rather smart, well-sprung four-wheeled carriage with a folding top drove through the gates of an inn in the provincial town of N.; it was the sort of carriage bachelors drive in: retired lieutenant-colonel, majors, and landowners with about a hundred serfs – in short, all those who are described as gentlemen of the 'middling' station in life. The gentleman in the carriage was not handsome, but neither was he particularly bad-looking; he was neither too fat, nor too thin; he could not be said to be old, but he was not too young, ether. His arrival in the town did not create any great stir, nor was it marked by anything out of the ordinary; only two Russian peasants standing at the door of the public house opposite the inn made certain remarks, referring, however, more to the carriage than to the gentleman in it. 'Lord', said one of them to the other, 'what a wheel! What do you say? Would a wheel like that, if put to it, ever get to Moscow or wouldn't it?' 'It would all right,' replied the other. 'But it wouldn't get to Kazan, would it?' 'No, it wouldn't get to Kazan,' replied the other. That was the end of the conversation.

ONE: Thornton Wilder – *The Bridge of San Luis Rey*

TWO: James Ellroy – *Blood's a Rover*

THREE: Angela Carter – *Nights at the Circus*

FOUR: Elizabeth Jolley – *Mr Scobie's Riddle*

FIVE: Nikolai Gogol – *Dead Souls*

FROM ANALYSIS TO PERFORMANCE WORLDS: SOME EXAMPLES

Having analysed and interpreted the text, and having some imaginative glimpses of what its performance world might be, the exciting but challenging job is to evolve the precise forms which will reveal it to an audience. [*Cross-refer Set 10, Workshops for Worlds 48-49*]

When we created our *First Arabian Night: The Loves of Kamar and Budur*, we used, as I've mentioned, the Richard Burton translation as a basis. He uses very idiosyncratic language, archaic in flavour and considerably heightened, close to the original Arabic and redolent of the *Song of Solomon*:

> With every day that passed over him, Kamar-al-Zeman increased in loveliness. Every breeze bore the tidings of his gracious favour. His eyelids were languorous like those of a gazelle; his eyebrows were arched like drawn bows.

> Her hair is as dark as the separation of friends; it falleth in rivers to her feet like a night without moon. Here complexion is as white as the day when lost friends meet; when she gazes towards the moon, two moons shine in one moment.

> When she walketh away, her hind parts are like unto mighty waves smiting one against the other in a stormy sea.

The challenge for a production is to find a suitable physical, visual and aural three-dimensional world that will bring to life most appropriately the world of the language. In the above examples, the language is clearly elaborate, ornate, voluptuous, hyperbolic, connecting humans metaphorically with elemental nature. Our response was to find a form of physical life that reinforced this language. Since the language takes its time to make its point, it seemed right that no character's movement should take the shortest distance between two points. Rather it should avoid straight lines and favour curves and circles, different parts of the body often moving in different directions at the same time, intertwining, writhing, rotating, gyrating... As both the language and the stories are uninhibitedly sexual, we did our homework on Eastern erotic art, including highly serious research into the *Kama Sutra*, the *Ananga Ranga* and *The Perfumed Garden*, all also obligingly translated by Sir Richard Burton. Their meticulous instructions for the gratification of all five senses preparatory to the athletic, not to say acrobatic, sexual encounters depicted in such extraordinary detail encouraged us to develop an overall movement style of virtuosic voluptuousness. Because of the frequent references to nature, we decided that the actors should, when required, transform their bodies, singly or in groups, into scenic elements. They became oceans, mountains, trees, thrones. These images were decorative, sensuous and curlicued. The actors did a lot of training in carrying, lifting and generally moving together in various combinations. As the culture of the stories was predominantly floor-based, the company explored ways of using the ground as a (literally) fundamental expression of the characters' lives, moving along the floor as well as getting on and off it in the most flowing, natural ways possible. At some point in rehearsals, we did consider deliberately counteracting the elaborate nature of the language with a precise cut-and-dried style of movement. But after some attempts at this approach, we found we were subverting, if not totally undermining, the world of the text rather than loving it and living it.

Our decisions in response to the language were reinforced by the structure of the plot itself, which was about separated lovers who wander the world in search of each other. The plot was consequently sprouting erotic tributary stories which contained other stories within them, rather on the principle of Chinese Boxes or Russian Dolls. So the structure, like the language, was also ornate, elaborate and indulgent.

The indulgence of the structure and language, reinforced by the overheated self-dramatisation of the characters, found them constantly in the throes of intense emotions of one sort or another (passion, grief, stubborn determination, ecstasy... you name it). The narrative was in the third person from within the action, so that the actors both described and played their characters with extreme intensity of feeling, taking themselves and their portrayals with total seriousness and remaining in character at all times – except for brief snatches of narration when they reverted to their own (actor) identities to calm down moments that had become a little too overwrought. They wore loose, flowing clothes in rich colours, paralleling the glowing colours of Persian and Indian miniatures (this was the period when tie-dyed shirts, Indian scarves and harem pants were in fashion) and worked barefoot. They used the space freely and expansively. We studied Middle-Eastern music and mastered some of its intricate rhythms and cadences, recreating the sounds vocally and by percussive use of the stage floor and the actors' own bodies – that is, totally without instruments. (*Cross-refer Set 11, Workshop 52: Becoming Instruments*)

The performance evolved into a highly eroticised, romantic, melodramatic world. For the audience it became charming, sexy, very funny and finally – rather wonderfully – moving; this because of the actors' *total* belief in their characters' existences.

By contrast, *The Second Arabian Night: The Rogueries of Dalilah the Wily*, a long, shaggy dog of a story, was told in a very different manner. It concerned the eponymous heroine, the widow of the Caliph's chief pigeon-handler, who is thrown out of the palace after her husband's death. She is determined to be instated in her late husband's job by proving to the Caliph that she is the cleverest person in his city. So she makes her way through the streets and alleys of the city, playing tricks, some considerably brutal, on a collection of victims and dupes from all classes of

Baghdad citizenry, in order to force his attention on her abilities. The situations escalate and proliferate in extremity and complexity until she gains his grudging admiration – and the job.

We felt that, in contrast to the previous piece, this rough, violent, comic, urban story would benefit from being improvised. So it was narrated in direct, contemporary language and played as a sort of broad farce. The actors developed their own individual styles of stand-up comedy to accommodate their third-person narrations from within the action, and played it as themselves in their stand-up personae on behalf, as it were, of the characters whom they played fully in their scenes. They employed the present tense for the sense of immediacy. The text was open to nightly change by each actor and went something along these lines:

> So this old woman, Dalilah, thinks, Right! I'll show that arsehole of a Caliph he made a mighty big mistake when he kicked me out of the palace. So she goes into the streets looking for opportunities to show off her cunning stunts and prove she's the cleverest woman in Baghdad – oops, I'll correct that! – the cleverest person in Baghdad.

> Just at this moment, along comes a donkey boy, leading his donkey and looking for work. Now this donkey boy is good-hearted but not what you'd call bright, and so far he hasn't had much luck today to earn himself a decent meal. So he's only too available.

> When Dalilah sets eyes on him, she can tell he's the perfect dupe to start on. A nice easy warm-up, if you're with me. So she goes into her 'feeble old woman' act and hobbles up to said donkey boy, weeping and holding out a very shaky hand…

The scenes between the sections of narrative were also improvised nightly. Because there was a complicated plot to follow, each of the scenes had a fixed starting and ending point, but how the actors got from alpha to omega was entirely up to them The effect we wanted was sketch-like, fast and funny, the physical life Tom-and-Jerry-ish. So, someone opening a door would crudely extend an arm and twist a wrist, while making the sound of creaking hinges in their throat. Because the proliferating incidents created proliferating characters, the actors each played more and more characters, sometimes several within the same scene, the logical outcome of which was that they sometimes ended up playing scenes with themselves. They wore jeans and T-shirts of their choice in a range of sand colours. The characterisations were strongly delineated. But, even if the reality was cartoon-like, the storytellers always played their characters with total conviction as though their lives depended on their actions which, in some cases, they did. This commitment to playing with utmost truth in a very heightened manner made their predicaments at times surprisingly and satisfyingly involving. The piece was performed with the actors playing virtually on the spot, in a tight, straight line not much wider than the five of them. This choice, in fact, reinforced the 'stand-up' idea we had started with. And the spatial restriction strengthened the slapstick reality we were aiming for. The actors constantly leaping from one character to another and then another within a tight space created a sense of profusion, of crowded alleyways and souks. The actors never became elements of scenery but occasionally allowed a part of their body to become a sketchily mimed prop, a closed fist becoming a doorknob or an open hand palm-up serving as a dish.

The Third Arabian Night: The City of Brass was a series of first-person narratives by ill-fated characters who recounted to each other the circumstances that had brought them on a shared pilgrimage to the mythical City of Brass in the Maghreb in the hope of finding relief from their sorrows and answers to the prayers. We used a somewhat literary language, totally free of the ornate flourishes of the Burton translation:

> In Damascus, the Khalifah, Abd al-Malik bin Mirwan, being interested
> in the history of past peoples in order to improve the conduct of his own
> rule, equipped and dispatched two thousand men of differing crafts and
> trades to pay homage to the ruler of the great City of Brass, which lay
> some one and a half years distant across the vast deserts of the Maghreb.
> According to the records of the Ancients, the city was the seat of great
> wealth and learning and was considered by many to be a place of spiritual
> fulfilment. The approximate location was known only from the records of
> past wanderers who had survived the rigours of this inhospitable region.
> Accordingly from the four corners of the Empire, the travellers
> assembled and in the month of Al-Maharram they set out, each man
> fired by the hope of his own salvation. To while away the darkness that
> nightly halted their progress, some of them recounted the events that
> had brought them on this pilgrimage. The first to speak was a man who
> was never seen to smile but spent his days in weeping and lamentation:

> One day as I sat beneath a wall where I would daily offer myself for hire,
> an old man dressed in black approached me....

The tone of the text was somewhat formal despite a certain economy. It suggested stories of an epic nature. The performance tried to echo these qualities visually by strong but minimal movement. The actors, dressed in loose-fitting black, formed images of people, but never turned themselves into scenery or objects. They created group images of travellers on camel-back, arduously making their way through desert, and shared between them a sort of choral narration for the sections of third-person narrative from outside the action that linked the individual stories. They made transitions into the first person for their personal stories. As each one described the circumstances that had brought them on this journey, the rest of the company would, at climactic moments, form themselves into images of other characters in that story as though conjured into existence by the passionate re-experiencing of the storyteller. Either they would surround the narrator or the narrator would be drawn into the image they created, as though sucked into a phys-ical recreation of the story by the intensity of the moment. So a narrator moved between recalling and reliving.

But the simplest account I can give of creating a world is when, years ago in rep, I had two weeks to rehearse *Lady, Be Good*, a Gershwin musical from the early '20s. The characters were two-dimensional, the dialogue sharp, silly and snappy. The music was rhythmically tricky and very syncopated. The ideal feminine form was flat and angular. All this led me, almost without thinking, to say to the company on the first day of rehearsal: move in straight lines, never on curves or diagonals, and whenever you turn, make it a full ninety degrees. That simple instruction succeeded way beyond anything I could have anticipated. The restricted movement affected the way the actors thought and felt, turning them into airheads who leaped before they looked, abrupt, reactive, rather frantic and very, very fast: a complete and con-sistent world. Oh, that it were always that simple! (But this was a simple world.)[5]

————

It's not easy to visualise productions from written descriptions, I know, but I hope that in some way the above summarised accounts of very different productions may suggest possible routes to take from text to performance in the creation of an appro-priate world. The numerous and varying translations and versions of the *Arabian Nights* allowed us to create what we felt was appropriate language for the very dif-ferent worlds of the three groups of stories we had chosen. This process would apply to any fairy stories, myths and legends that have entered the popular consciousness.[6]

5. See Note 3 in *Workshop 5, Voice and Speech Work: Tempo* for the description of Steven Berkoff's production of *Salome*, in which he created a total, self-referential world from what appears to have been a single strong decision.

6. In *Different Every Night*, I've given very detailed accounts of the highly elaborate worlds of two other productions, one of an adaptation (Evelyn Waugh's *A Handful of Dust*), the other of a play (Nikolai Gogol's *Marriage*).

Part Two

WORKSHOPS
FOR STORYTELLING

Telling stories and adapting stories for the theatre is an activity without limit. Assuming that you could tell every story that's ever existed, there will always be those you might create yourself. The what and how of storytelling are infinite. The workshops that follow cover a wide range of subjects and techniques; some of the more technical exercises are set out in great detail and often accompanied by lots of questions rather than answers; others are briefer and more loosely structured as suggestions and encouragement for your own inventions. They represent the approaches that I've found useful for my own work, but in all cases they are not so much instructions as ways of thinking about telling stories. Whenever I've been confronted with a problem, I've always found it a useful rule of thumb to exercise the problem. And more often than not, that's been a successful way of breaking through a block. All I know is that with each new idea or technique we developed, I had the sense that we were only scraping the surface, that there were layers of possibilities awaiting someone's imagination to release to the light of day.

These workshops don't have to be followed in any sequence, apart from the introductory set that establish some fundamentals of storytelling. They are modules to be moved around and used as you see fit. Some of them do overlap and bleed into each other. I've noted whenever exercises can be usefully cross-referred. Many of them, of course, are perfectly applicable for work on plays. They vary in complexity, particularly those dealing with third-person narration when the narrator is also a character – and these, too, like the introductory set, may just possibly benefit from being tackled in the order in which they've been set out, building the necessary skills as you proceed

Our Shared Experience explorations began in the simplest way possible: one actor telling a story in an empty space. This somewhat obvious starting point seemed essential as a way of introducing the actors to some of the basic skills they'd need to master before moving on to more elaborate forms of storytelling; to acquire abilities as solo storytellers before developing the sophisticated work of an ensemble. They had to practise their scales before attempting sonatas and well before embarking on duets, quartets and full ensemble pieces. In the beginning was the Word, so language seemed the logical launching pad for our endeavours. Over time, of course, the Word became Flesh as we moved on to the physical and dramatic aspects of storytelling, that is, to the duets, quartets and ensemble pieces. The more skills we developed, the more we realised that storytelling demanded specialised techniques of a refinement and complexity not usually required of actors playing characters in plays. These workshops are the outcome and a distillation of those explorations.

Most of the exercises can be used for classwork as well as rehearsals. If you decide to use any of them, you will have to judge for yourself which particular workshops – and how much from them – you can reasonably deal with in the time at your disposal. In my own work, I've been able to shape them to accommodate anything from half-day, weekend and week-long classes (in which cases I've usually selected a particular theme or area of work to focus on) to as much as three-month rehearsal periods.

Pre-view

To visualise as accurately as possible the way in which these workshops and exercises work best, I suggest that you imagine an entirely open space, evenly and unchangingly lit, empty but for the constant presence of actors, visible and able to make relaxed contact with an audience. Dressed in unobtrusive daily clothing, loose enough to permit easy movement and, when necessary, strenuous physicality, they'll probably be seated on the floor upstage, along the rear perimeter of the space, from where they're able to watch the action – and the audience – and, when called upon, to move smoothly back and forth, downstage into the action and back upstage out of it. These basic features provide the conditions for actors to tell stories, free of technology and design, dependent totally on their own skills and abilities. On the occasions when props or other elements are involved in an exercise, simply include them in your visualisation of the open space.

Note: I refer to an audience even during rehearsals or workshops. There should be a few people other than just whoever is running the session, to whom the actors can tell their stories. Under no circumstance should actors be allowed to narrate 'out front' to thin air; to do so would be as ludicrous as rehearsing a scene without its other participants. They must develop the practice of genuinely talking to people, not pretending to do so. Storytelling is a two-way process.

Note: I've supplied excerpts from several stories to apply to some of the exercises ahead. But before you begin, it might be a good idea to gather a selection of your own from stories you're interested to explore or planning to work on, so you have a useful range of material at your disposal.

SET 1

INTRODUCTORY WORKSHOPS
1–5

This first set of five workshops is an introduction to the three basic modes of narrative. Unlike later sets, its individual workshops are devised in a progressive sequence, each one growing out of its predecessor. So I would recommend, initially at least, employing them in this way. Of course, it's perfectly possible to insert any of them as a module into other structures.

WORKSHOP 1: ONE STORYTELLER TELLS A STORY

In advance of the first session, ask each of the participants to be prepared to tell a story. It can be from any source, invented or extant. Ideally, it should contain several characters and locations and possibly a journey. It should not last more than ten minutes. For this initiation into storytelling, fables, folk and fairytales, myths and legends can usefully serve the purpose. It's perfectly acceptable to use familiar material. Originality is not the point here. At this stage, storytellers should avoid using first-person narratives. The opening workshop is to introduce the participants to some fundamental requirements for a storyteller/narrator, and also to generate material for the following workshops in this set. These initial workshops deal with both the story and the way it is told.

A Single Actor Tells a Story

For these early sessions, everyone should be seated on the floor with the listeners at a comfortable distance in a semicircle around the storyteller.

1. An actor tells a story.

2. The group comments on (a) how the story was told, and (b) the nature of the story itself. These are some of the areas that might be discussed:

a.   Did the storyteller make genuine contact with the audience?
     [*Cross-refer Set 12, Workshops 54-56: Contact with the Audience*]

     Did the storyteller tell the story confidently or apologetically?

Did the storyteller exhibit excessive self-consciousness?

Did the storyteller, in respect of this, seem more concerned with personal effectiveness than with the impact of the story?

Did the storyteller maintain a reasonable fluency and logic? [*Cross-refer Set 2, Workshop 6: Logic; Set 14, Workshop 59: Logic and Dexterity in Handling Plots*]

What means did the storyteller use to convey the story?

Did the storyteller use direct speech (dialogue) or reported speech or no speech at all? [*Cross-refer Set 4: Workshop 20: Indirect Speech to Direct Speech*]

Did the storyteller attempt to characterise? And if so, by what means? And to what degree?

What physical means, if any, did the storyteller use to reinforce the telling of the story? [*Cross-refer Set 2, Workshop 8, Physical Work: Gestures*]

Did the storyteller use any variations of voice and speech (volume, tempo, dialect…)? [*Cross-refer Set 2, Workshop 7: Voice and Speech*]

What sort of language did the storyteller use (colloquial, literary, archaic…)?

What happened when or if the storyteller tried to remember a part of the story?

Did the storyteller give the story a point of view or want us to receive the story in a particular way, i.e. what sort of impression did the teller want the story to make on the listeners?

Did the storyteller have an attitude to the audience, i.e. why this particular story was being told to this particular audience?

b. What is the purpose of the story (to raise laughter, to rouse indignation, to induce tears, to scare the pants off you…)?

What is the world of the story (magical, realistic, romantic, noir, political…)?

Is the story didactic, i.e. does it have an explicit moral or lesson?

Is the story character-led, plot-led, mood-led or theme-led?

How important is atmosphere and environment?

a & b. Was the storyteller's way of telling the story appropriate to the nature of the story?

Once the discussion is underway, storytellers can, should they wish, describe what they thought they were doing, what they thought they achieved and what they found difficult.

Note: Many of the above points are usually far too advanced to have even occurred to a first-time storyteller, let alone put into practice. But even so, it's useful – right from the start – to mention them so that the actors can get a glimpse of the multilayered work that's ahead of them.

Note: Of course, you can add or substitute questions of your own, should they seem more pertinent to your purposes.

Note: It's not unusual, in these early sessions, for the observing actors, out of sympathy for their colleagues and in the knowledge that their turn may come, to be overly generous in their remarks, encouraging them with generalised praise rather than describing precisely what they experienced. With every new story we tell, we're stepping into an unknown world with fresh dilemmas needing to be resolved, unfamiliar knots needing to be untied. Consequently there's likely to be a large amount of exploration, trial and – inevitably – error. So, from the outset, it's important to establish that comments should never be taken as personal criticism but rather as straightforward observations attempting to deal as objectively and as rigorously as possible with matters of technique. You should, if you find it necessary, help to steer and shape the group's comments. But never dismiss anyone's opinions unless they are blatantly irrelevant or irresponsibly destructive.

3. Invite another participant to tell the *same* story but in their *own* way and their *own* words.

4. Raise the same points as in 2.

5. Ask the group to compare and evaluate the variations in the two ways of telling. These are some additional points that might be raised:

How much had the second storyteller benefited from observations about the first storyteller's rendition?

Which elements, vocal or physical, seemed more appropriate for the story?

Was there a difference in the sort of language used? And if so, which seemed more suited to the story?

Was there a difference in tone or attack?

Did the second storyteller introduce more details?

6. Depending on the time available, you might ask several more people to retell this story in their own words. Again, ask the questions and compare the variations. In short, repeat 3, 4 and 5.

7. You may want someone to tell a different story in order to observe the demands and provocations of different material. (Also, an additional story or two will provide the group with more choice of material in the follow-on workshops.)

8. Compare the stories and their possibly different requirements in being told. These are some points that might be raised in discussing another story:

In what ways were the stories similar or dissimilar (structure, narrative viewpoint, world)?

Which elements, vocal or physical, were more appropriate for the telling of each story?

Did or would the stories benefit from different energies, tempos and tone in their telling?

What aspects of each story demanded particular techniques?

Things to note throughout Workshop 1:

Storytellers must have the courage to make genuine contact with their audience, not to pretend to do so by a generalised facing in their direction. The listeners/observers should feel that they have been contacted, really spoken to.

Storytellers, in their turn, must be open to audience response and allow it to affect their storytelling; that means that the contact works in *both* directions.

Storytellers must try to carry through with some consistency the way in which they'd intended to tell the story.

Any extraneous gesturing, fidgeting, humming and hawing blurs a story.

The sequence and flow of the story must make sense.

The storytellers' own involuntary reactions to any parts of the story that spontaneously affect them as they tell it can enhance the telling, so they should never censor themselves – for instance, genuinely finding something funny or unexpectedly moving. This, of course, implies an extremely strong commitment to the story and the telling of it.

Variations and Elaborations

These are more demanding and time-consuming exercises, possibly more useful when embarking on longer-term projects.

A

1a. An actor who has not already done so, tells one of the same stories, with everyone seated on the floor as already described. Except that for this starting point, the listeners either close their eyes or turn their backs.

2a. The listeners then comment on the vocal and verbal clarity, logic and expressiveness of the telling. Some areas for comment might be:

Was the storytelling agreeable to listen to?

Was there vocal variety?

Did the story make sense?

Did the storytelling arouse images in the listeners' imaginations?

3a. The same storyteller tells the story a second time, now with the audience watching, as in 1 above.

4a. The group then discusses in what way the physical life of the storyteller added to or subtracted from the impact of the story when it was only heard. They can use some of the questions listed in 2 above.

5a. After this or any of these sequences, the storyteller could be asked to tell their story again, taking on board as many as possible of the observations; or, more usefully, concentrating on one particular element at a time.

B

1b. An actor tells a story creating musical and/or sound effects using only voice and body, such as humming, singing, droning, clicking the tongue, smacking the lips; tapping, hitting, slapping the body, clothes or floor. [*Cross-refer Set 11, Workshops 50-53: Musical and Sound Scores; Set 2, Workshop 7: Expressive Sounds*]

2b. The group discuss in what way this enhanced or detracted from the story: Some areas for comment might be:

Did the sounds/music slow down or break up the flow of the story?

Did the telling and the creation of sounds occur simultaneously?

Did the sounds/music dominate the story?

In what way did the sounds/music further the story?

Did the sounds/music create strong atmospheres?

Did the sounds/music provide information that would not have existed without them?

c

1c. An actor tells a story very deliberately using gestures. [*Cross-refer Set 2, Workshop 8, Physical Work: Gestures*]

2c. The group discuss what they have observed in much the same way as 2b above.

Note: You should feel free to repeat, vary, elaborate or shift the exercises in any way the circumstances of a session suggest might be most useful.

WORKSHOP 2: GROUP STORYTELLING MODE 1: THIRD-PERSON NARRATION FROM OUTSIDE THE ACTION

This second workshop should follow immediately from the first or be the start of a second session. Divide the group into two, so that there's always one half available to observe those who are performing. Periodically change the participants within the halves.

Several Actors Tell a Story

1. Using the story – or a story – from the first session (*Workshop 1*), ask one of the actors who has not yet done so to narrate it in their own words. Ask the others in the performing half of the group to support the narrator and contribute in any way they can whatever they believe will enhance the telling of the story. Make clear that this is an improvisation, nothing may be planned or discussed in advance. They must take their cues spontaneously from the narrative as it proceeds. The other half of the group observes. Now it's

probably more helpful if the audience shifts from a semicircle to watching straight-on.

I would recommend giving no further instructions. This will allow you the opportunity to see whether any of the actors have experience of similar work, how imaginatively they respond to the material, how enterprising they are in the execution of their choices, and how generously they react to each other's initiatives and provocations.

The result is, of course, unpredictable. The fewer your instructions, the more the group have to work out for themselves what does or doesn't help the story. The outcome may be an inventive romp, it may be a chaotic mess, but no matter. Whatever the result, it will yield plenty of material to discuss and build on.

2. Discuss what happened. Again, a lot of observations need to be made. Here are some possibilities:

> Did the narrator and the performing half of the group stay in contact with each other or did they get 'out of sync'?

> Did one 'entity' dominate the other, that is, did the group get the bit between their teeth and snatch the reins from the narrator; or did the narrator plough on with the narration, ignoring the contributions of the group and the possibilities they offered?

> Or did the narrator take anything that the group spontaneously created and make it part of the narrative?

> Did the narrator, while working with the group, still manage to keep contact with the audience?

> Did any members of the group make contact with the audience? And should they have done?

> Did the two entities work well spatially, i.e. did they move themselves into useful and suitable positions? [*Cross-refer Set 3, Workshops 9-10: Areas of the Stage and their Qualities, Narration from Different Areas*]

> Did the group act out literally what the narrator was describing? Or did they elaborate and create variations on what the narrator described? [*Cross-refer Section 8: Doubling the Information; Set 4, Workshop 19: Physical Life Accompanying Narration*]

> Did the group use dialogue or remain silent, letting the narrator do all the talking?

> Did the narrator give or deny members of the group cues to speak?

Did the group create images above and beyond playing characters in the story?

Was there any consistency to the imagery that was created?

Did the group create sound effects? Or music?

Were the individuals in the group sensitive to each other? Did they take advantage of any opportunities that their partners might have offered?

Did the group treat what they did as a joke?

Or did they commit themselves to the feelings and situations of the characters and the establishment of environments and atmospheres, however naive or simple the story?

Did the two 'entities' establish any consistent conventions?

Which of their choices were appropriate or suitable for the story?

Note: Again, most of these questions are probably way in advance of anything that might occur to the narrator or the group; or that they would be likely to achieve at this early stage. But they are worth asking.

3. Switch around the two halves of the group, so that the observers now participate and the participants observe. Use the same story and choose another first-time narrator. Instruct the participants to contribute in any way they can.

4. Make the observations as in 2 above. Possible additional questions:

How much had the second group benefited from observations made about the first group's rendition?

In what ways did the two versions differ from each other?

Did the versions of the two narrators create different worlds (styles) requiring different conventions?

5. Once all these questions have been discussed and shared between the observers and the performers, the time has come to point out that what they have just played, however chaotically, is third-person narration from outside the action. [*Cross-refer Set 3: Third-Person Narration from Outside the Action; Set 7, Subset 2, Workshops 39-40: Transitions for Narration*]

6. Time permitting, you could re-divide the group into new halves and repeat sequences 1–4.

There are many points to be made from the issues that have been brought up. The overriding one is for the company to understand that the 'rules' you are about to establish are for *a basic version of this mode, a starting point*, the model from which an infinite number of variations will eventually be created. Be judicious in establishing these 'rules' as the actors will be able to take in only so much information at any one time. At this stage, select those that are most relevant to what the actors have actually produced in the exercise.

Some Provisional Starting 'Rules' in this Mode

The narrator (or narrators, should there be a reason to have more than one) is the only person to have contact with the audience and the only one to tell the story.

The performing half of the group are inside the story and do not make contact with the half that is watching (their audience). They can only speak dialogue. They create the dramatised, physical, imagistic version of the story.

Narrator and group must stay in contact, if for no other reason than to ensure that the audience knows where to focus – and for the logic of the story. Together, they are of equal importance in sharing the telling of the story.

However, because narrators initiate the telling of a story and are providing a frame for it, they must always have the 'last word'. To this end, they must establish and sustain sensitive control of the storytelling.

The group may get genuinely carried away by their invention, but no matter how imaginative, ultimately it won't have any value if they lose contact with their narrator.

For their part, narrators must learn to give space to the invention of the group but take back the reins should they feel the story is getting lost in the invention. They, in turn, should offer opportunities (provocations) to the group.

Narrators must always maintain contact with the audience as it's to and for them, after all, that they're telling the story. They have to learn to share their focus sensitively between their colleagues in the group and the people in the audience.

Spatially, narrators have to consider where is the place best suited to talk to the audience while keeping contact with the group who are putting flesh on their words. They usually find that narrating from a downstage corner of the acting space is preferable. From here they can be in touch with both audience and actors without crowding, upstaging or masking the group. But there are other possibilities. [*Cross-refer Set 3, Workshops 9-10: Areas of the Stage and their Qualities; Narration from Different Areas*]

The group for their part have to decide whether they are going to be in the 'acting' area all the time or enter it for their specific contributions. This doesn't mean that they literally go offstage. In storytelling theatre, all the actors (storytellers) should be on stage, visible and available at all times. But they will need to differentiate between the area in which they perform and the area from where they watch while awaiting their cues. As it's obvious that the most useful acting area is usually down-stage centre, the most practical place from which to wait and watch is, on most occasions, upstage. From there, they can move strongly down into the acting area. But, again, there are other possibilities. [*Cross-refer Set 6, Workshop 36: Watching*]

If the group act out literally, free from embellishment, what the narrator is describ-ing, the result will tend to be an uninformative and obvious duplication for the audience of what they're hearing. On the positive side, the literal illustration of what is being said can establish a world of naivety or innocence; it can be used to comic effect; and it can create dramatic emphasis. However, in general, it's better that the performers find activities and actions that parallel – or elaborate without contra-dicting – what the narrator is establishing. This will provide a richer, more layered experience for the audience. [*Cross-refer Section 8: Doubling the Information; Set 4, Workshop 19: Physical Life Accompanying Narration*]

In the matter of dialogue and speech, the narrators can choose to do all the talking, or they may establish the dialogue and encourage the group to repeat it, a comic device that can wear thin with overuse. But for the basis we're establishing, it's preferable if they allow the group to speak their own dialogue, giving them clear cues and sufficient time to do so.

In the matter of the group establishing places and spaces, miming or turning them-selves into props and objects, the material should suggest what is appropriate. But again, for the sake of this basic set-up, it's useful if actors can become thrones, trees, doors, animals, and so forth, especially if the story being told is a fairytale, a leg-end, an adventure... This also applies to the creation of sounds: creaking doors, wind, rain, birdsong, horses' hooves...

The group must unquestioningly go with whatever is happening, neither rejecting nor contradicting it, nor wandering off on agendas of their own. The most impor-tant part of this work (in fact, the basis of all good acting) is the performers' abilities to play off their partners, giving and taking, collaborating and sharing on the instant the ideas that their individual imaginations have released, allowing each moment and event to develop and extend between them to its natural completion. This is not a recipe for anarchy. There is always the narrative itself as the controlling fac-tor. If an improvisation veers away from the story, everyone should make it their responsibility to get the narrative back on track.

The tendency with these early exercises is to treat them playfully, which is fine – but this can result in cheap gags and shallow work. At whatever level, however silly or unbelievable the story, the actors must play – and the narrators narrate – with total sincerity, total conviction, total commitment. Remember, the purpose of the exercise is not to show off how entertaining you can be, but *to tell the story*. If you focus on telling the story, giving the story all you've got, you *will* be entertaining.

The matter of conventions – the creation of a world – is probably a little too sophisticated to deal with at such an early stage, but it's worth mentioning to the actors that they should bear in mind for future development what sort of world they're trying to create. Every piece of theatre, every piece of storytelling, must have its own conventions, true to and right for the particular material. This may take a while to discover. As a simple example, the mention above of actors turning themselves into scenery may be a good option for one story but totally unsuitable for the next. [*Cross-refer Section 9: Worlds; Set 10 Workshops 48-49: Worlds*]

WORKSHOP 3: GROUP STORYTELLING MODE 2: MULTIPLE THIRD-PERSON NARRATION FROM INSIDE THE ACTION

Having established the ground rules for Third-Person Narration from Outside the Action, we can now apply those for Multiple Third-Person Narration from Inside the Action. In this mode, *all the actors* are narrators, narrating all the descriptions of their own character's actions, motives, thoughts, behaviour, background and appearance, as well as playing that character in scenes. As narrators, they employ the third person (*he* did such-and-such, *she* thought such-and such…), whereas in scenes they, of course, play in character using the first person (I) as they would naturally do in a conventional play. When narrating, they have a basic choice of (a) narrating as themselves – the actors – describing the character they're about to embody, or (b) narrating fully *in* character. However, I would suggest that, for the moment, they will find it easier if they choose the latter, both to narrate *and* play *in* character.

Note: Along the spectrum between these two choices, there are, in fact, many degrees of characterisation, requiring more advanced levels of skill. These will be dealt with later on. [*Cross-refer Set 4, Workshops 13-20: Third-Person Narration Inside the Action; Set 6, Workshop 36: Watching*]

Several Actors Tell a Story

1. Use the same story or stories that you've been working with in the previous workshops. Split the group in half so there will always be some observers.

2. Cast the main characters in the story, but suggest that anyone available should take responsibility for fulfilling smaller roles as and when they occur in the narration. Actors can, where necessary, play more than one character.

3. Explain very carefully that there's no longer a single outside narrator. The actors are now each responsible for their personal narration as well as playing in the events and scenes that involve their characters.

4. Since, in this workshop, they are improvising and might not always remember the exact sequence of events, they have to be alert as to when their character need enter the story. Warn them that since they're all functioning as narrators, they have to stay open and flexible as to when to take their turn and when to cede the narration to others.

They should only narrate when they are the doer, the initiator of the action, for example: 'Mary came to visit John' is Mary's narrative, although John is mentioned.

If, by any chance, you do happen to be working from a text and the actors are uncertain about identifying which part of the narrative is theirs, instruct them that any sentence, clause or phrase of which they are the subject belongs to them; for example, in this sentence from *Our Mutual Friend*:

> Mr Veneering is not at all complimented by being supposed to be Twemlow, who is dry and weazen and some thirty years older.

Veneering should take the first part of the sentence (the main clause) as he is the subject of it, whereas Twemlow should take the second part (the adjectival clause) as he is the subject of that, thus:

VENEERING　　Mr Veneering is not at all complimented by being supposed to be Twemlow,

TWEMLOW　　who is dry and weazen and some thirty years older.

5. Remind them that when they are not involved in either narrating or playing their character, they are available, as they were in the previous workshop, to contribute anything that helps to move the story forward: creating imagery, scenery, furniture, props, incidental characters, crowds, animals, sound effects, music…

6. They tell the story.

7. Discuss, always with the observers' contributions:

In what way did the effect of this mode differ from the previous one (narrator outside the action)?

Did they manage to keep the narration flowing between them?

Did the actors manage to make transitions from narration to scene and from scene to narration clearly and effectively? [*Cross-refer Set 7, Subset 2, Workshops 39-40: Transitions for Narration and Scenes*]

In what way did their work differ between narrating and playing in a scene?

Did they manage to narrate their own character's narrative or did they occasionally take over other characters' narratives?

Were the actors sensitive to each other?

When narrating, did they all make genuine contact with the observers?

Was there any noticeable difference in the way each of them did so?

How did they deal with the other elements of the story (environment, space, sound...)?

8. The observers now become the storytellers. They should tell the same story. They go through the same process. In the discussion, the same points as in 7 should be explored, but in addition they should make these observations:

In what way did this version differ from the previous one?

In what way was it similar?

Had the storytellers learnt from the observations made about the previous rendition?

Differences Between Narrating from Inside the Action and from Outside

All the actors, when narrating from within the action, have the opportunity to make contact with the audience.

The shared narrative can now be played with much more variety of identity, attitude and tone. The actors should be encouraged to exploit this.

The actors, now both narrating and playing scenes, require great flexibility in switching between third-person narrative mode and first-person scene-playing mode. They must make clear transitions between the two, which means changing their focus from the audience to their partners in the scene they're about to enter, and vice versa when they return from a scene to narration. [*Cross-refer Set 7, Subset 2, Workshops 39-40: Transitions for Narration and Scenes*]

The actors now have three areas of work: as narrators, as characters in scenes and as creators of environments.

The actors must make sure they maintain *between them* the logic and continuity of the story. They should already be able to understand how much alertness and flexibility they need to carry out this level of storytelling.

They can narrate either 'in character', 'straight' as themselves or in any nuanced shift along the continuum between the two. But I repeat my suggestion that, for the time being, they will find it more manageable if they both narrate and play in character. (The choice, for the moment, is probably best made by whoever is leading the session.)

Let me reiterate: this is an area of work which has tremendous variations and possibilities which will be developed in upcoming workshops. This is also a basic mode and from it innumerable more sophisticated variations can be developed.

An important point to make is that, now there is no longer one narrator holding the story together, everyone is responsible for the whole of the storytelling whether narrating, playing a character in a scene, creating environments, or even watching from the edge of the acting space. *In fact, this group responsibility is true for all storytelling modes*, but the point is made more vividly if mentioned now, when everyone has an identical function.

WORKSHOP 4: GROUP STORYTELLING MODE 3: FIRST-PERSON NARRATION

We now deal with stories told in the first person. [*Cross-refer Set 5; Workshops 21–23: First-Person Narration*]

One Actor Tell a Story

1. Use one of the same stories.

2. Ask an actor to choose any character from it and to tell the story through that character's eyes, narrating in the first person, from the viewpoint of 'I'. The actor works alone.

3. The group discuss how the story was told, applying many of the observation points and criteria from Workshop 1. Some additional points that might be made:

a.   In what way, if any, did the story being told in the first person differ from being told in the third person?

Did the narration seem more intimate, more personal?

Did the narration encourage stronger emotional expressiveness?

Did the narrator tell the story by reliving the experiences in the past or by looking back from the present with the benefit of distance? Or both?

Did the narrator act out literally what the narrative described?

b.   Did some events in the story seem very different, refreshed or reduced, by being told from a first-person point of view?

Did the story change radically in its attitude, mood, emphasis?

Did some events or details disappear totally?

Did new events occur?

4. Ask another actor to tell the story in the first person, but to choose *another* character from the story.

5. Discuss in what way the story was affected by being told through the viewpoint of another character and compare the impact of the two first-person versions.

6. Continue this process with actors choosing different characters to be first-person narrators, with the subsequent discussion of how the story was

affected. Do this as many times as seems useful. With sufficient time, the story could be told through the eyes of all its characters. Don't neglect to have the story told even by characters who put in brief appearances, only incidentally privy to the main narrative thrust.

Note: You will find that, depending on the choice of character, the narrative will probably start at different places in the story. A narrator could chose to start late in the story and then recall earlier experiences. With some character choices, certain events or facts may never be told, being beyond the knowledge of the narrator. So the story may acquire different emphases and structures. However, narrators might fill in such details of which they're personally ignorant by relating what they've been told by other characters.

Several Actors Tell a First-Person Narration

7. Return to the ensemble work, with the company or class divided into two groups. Ask another actor to tell a character's first-person account of the story and instruct the rest of the half-group to contribute, as in previous workshops, to the telling in any way they see fit, creating environments and playing characters. You may pre-cast the other characters if you wish, but I prefer at this stage, in this mode, to let the actors spontaneously take the initiative between them as new character appears within the first-person narrative. Another possibility is for first-person narrators to identify who should play each of the characters as they introduce them into the narrative. Make sure that both halves take their turn to perform.

8. As usual, discuss what happened, what the observers noticed, using many of the points from earlier workshops.

Some additional points to make:

> In what way, if any, did the contribution of the half-group differ from their involvement in the third-person modes?

> Was there full group responsibility?

> What was the quality of their listening?

> Did the first-person narrator move from narrative to scene (action) and scene (action) to narrative with fluency or remain stuck within the narration?

> Did the narrator set up a scene well enough that members of the group could realise it and engage in it easily?

> What happened to those playing in scenes when the narrator returned to narration?

If the narrator, while describing a scene or event, didn't attempt to inhabit it, did the group, nevertheless, try to create it or provide some image?

Did the narrator remain in the present, as it were, recalling past events, or did the narrator relive or re-experience the events as they had first happened?

Did the narrator move into a scene created by the group or did the group create the scene around the narrator?

9. Repeat this with as many characters becoming first-person narrators as you find useful, each time with a different actor as narrator and always following this up with a discussion.

Variations and Elaborations

These variations probably shouldn't be attempted in this introductory set of workshops. The actors need first to acquire some basic skills in narration and plot logic. [*Cross-refer Section 5: From Narrative to Narration: Plot Logic – Seven Questions; Set 2, Workshop 6: Text Logic; Set 14, Workshop 59: Plot*]

10. One actor tells a story already used by the group, choosing *two* characters from whose first-person viewpoint to tell the story. The actor can decide when to switch back and forth between the two characters' narratives; or you can call out the instructions to change whenever you feel the moment is appropriate.

11. A version of this is for several of the actors to choose a character through whose point of view they will tell the story in the first person. Select someone to start. Thereafter, any of the other actors can decide at any point to take over the narration with their character. So you have multiple first-person narrators telling the story.

Note: There should not be any other actors creating environments or acting out other characters in this exercise.

12. In both variations, the exercise should always end with a brief discussion about what was observed and what experienced. Some points to discuss:

Did the changes of narrator/character still maintain the logic and flow of the story?

Did the changes of narrator/character provide very different tones and attitudes to the story?

Note: In this first-person sequence you could, should you wish, use a story that's actually written in the first person. In which case you have the choice either of asking the actors to work with a text in their hands or to familiarise themselves with the story sufficiently to improvise on it. They shouldn't attempt to learn it verbatim. However, up to this point the actors will have been improvising, so working from a text this early in the process might be inhibiting. Once more, the judgement is yours as to whether you remain with improvised storytelling or try working from a text.

WORKSHOP 5: APPLYING THE THREE MODES OF NARRATION

Now that the three basic modes of narration have been established, however crudely, however basically, it's time to discuss with the company what qualities and advantages each of them has and for what sorts of stories each is most suitable. The following suggestions point out no more than rather obvious tendencies; *each mode is open to many possibilities.*

Third-person narration from outside the action is useful for didactic stories, for stories with a deliberate moral or a political or social agenda, stories that need an outsider's eye, stories that need a narrator to guide the audience or help them form a particular view of the material. The narrator will have a purpose and therefore do everything to ensure that the audience receives the story in a way that fulfils that purpose. The narrator's aim could be as simple as getting the audience to enjoy a story. The narrator can have any agenda or attitude towards the material, even if it appears to go against the material, for example, casting an ironic eye on the behaviour of the protagonists. At the most minimal level of contribution, the narrator might do no more than maintain the logical flow of the story, filling in the exposition where required. The narrator establishes the frame in which the story exists.

Multiple third-person narration from inside the action potentially creates the most energy because the whole cast is equally involved in the narration. It offers a variety of tones and attitudes and is therefore less helpful in making one specific point. Of course, there's no reason why all the narrators in this mode couldn't share an overall purpose (and in a production they would certainly do so), but because of the possible multiplicity of viewpoints, this would more likely be expressed in a variety of shades, contrasts and counterpoint. This mode is useful for stories with ambiguities of attitude, heavily plotted stories containing a large cast of characters and multilinear stories conceived on an epic scale to cover wide sweeps of history. It lends itself, almost too easily, to comedy. It's a democratic, egalitarian way of telling a story.

First-person narration is most appropriate for personal, deeply felt revelations, where the story is clearly seen through the eyes of one (usually main) character. The narrative is *ipso facto* subjective and more inclined to unreliability. It might contain memories, dreams, hallucinatory episodes, experiences of intense intimacy and emotion. Of the three modes, it's the least free for the group, who have to exist and behave exactly as perceived by the first-person narrator, since it is, rightly or wrongly, what that narrator believes to be so.

The first person can, of course, be someone not at the centre of the story, observing it from the sidelines, but with sufficient concern or interest in its content to create a need to relate it. In this case, the narrator's function might probably move somewhat closer to that of someone narrating in the third person from outside the action – the main difference, however, being that the narrator is still an actual character with relationships to the other characters.

Note: Always make clear that there's absolutely no definitive matching-up of a narrative mode with a particular genre or type of story. Every story needs its own analytical and imaginative response. Never trap any technique in a box. Remember that there may be many unforeseen, unpredictable possibilities awaiting your discovery.

Culminating Exercise

1. Having discussed these modes, divide the company preferably into no less than three groups. Then let them all take the *same* story from amongst those they've been working on in this sequence of workshops and go to separate spaces for, say, thirty or forty minutes to decide what each group believes is the preferable narrative mode to fulfil the story's potential.

2. They then prepare that version to present to the rest of the company. Allow them another twenty minutes or so. (As an alternative, you could assign a mode to each group, but that would deprive the actors of making their own analysis.)

3. Quietly monitor their progress, moving between the groups. Should they get bogged down in discussion for too long, you might gently point this out to them and urge them to explore choices on their feet. Beyond this, never interfere in what they are doing. Warn them when they have, say, only five or so minutes left.

4. The groups show each other what they've prepared.

5. Wait until all the versions have been shown. Then discuss the pros and cons of the choices and point out any fresh advantages that were thrown up by particular decisions.

Finally, from the work they've done through these five workshops, stress again what points you feel are worth repeating to your particular company, for example: the whole cast is responsible for the whole performance; narrators must always ensure they are in genuine contact with their audiences... and so forth.

This completes the first set of workshops. I've managed to carry through the entire set in a one-day class, easily during a weekend seminar. This does mean, of course, limiting the number of times a story is retold: not all the participants will necessarily have the opportunity to narrate in all the modes. But remember: these workshops are for the purpose of introducing the group or company to some basic principles and modes of telling stories, and not yet about their individual attainment of storytelling skills, workshops for which follow.

SET 2

WORKSHOPS FOR INDIVIDUAL STORYTELLING SKILLS

6–8

I mentioned practising scales before advancing to sonatas, let alone ensemble pieces. The previous set of workshops gave a general idea of the three basic modes of storytelling. By its nature, that set tends to a certain broadness or roughness of execution. This set of workshops is in effect about practising those scales – the development of skills for solo storytellers, focusing on individual narration. After the freedom of the earlier work, this work is precise and technical. But practice, I hope, makes perfect, technique leads to mastery and discipline to creative freedom. These exercises should be used when and where they seem most appropriate and spread throughout the development of a project. Actors can – and ought to – work on most of them for themselves.

WORKSHOP 6: LOGIC

In storytelling, two levels of logic apply: the common sense of words and grammar, and the coherent development of the story itself. Here, we're dealing with the first of these. Before making any attempts at interpretation, the actor has to learn how to deliver the narrative at its simplest level – the logic with which words and thoughts follow each other on the page. In *Different Every Night*, I described a process called Logic Text that I'd devised for working on the dialogue in plays. Here its use is extended to deal with all forms of prose and verse.

We might assume that most people are quite able to make sense of what they're saying. But many actors suffer from a delusional instinct – or even an ingrained belief – that if they just say the words, they (both performer and text) will make sense; the words will take care of themselves, leaving them free to get on with the more exciting aspects of acting and storytelling, which, of course, include making the text their interpretive own. With some actors, one can, at times, gets the impression that the text is actually a hindrance intruding between them and their acting. But if you decorate a house and move in before you've secured the foundations, it's likely to collapse.

Functions of spoken language that ought to be obvious turn out not to be obvious at all. For instance, there should be no ambiguity about the basic purpose of a sentence as to whether it's a statement, a command or a question; strings of adverbial or adjectival phrases should not become detached from what they're qualifying; antitheses should be clearly balanced; the give and take of conversations should sound as though the participants are actually replying to what's just been said to them... and so forth. The actor's role, for the time being, is as a medium for clear thinking through which the text is conveyed to its auditors, free from any attempts at interpretation. The actor is essentially delivering information, the basis upon which everything else can then be structured. And for this, the actor's main tools – besides a bit of nous – are clear intentions and those specific functions of voice and speech for describing and explaining: flexibility of pitch and accuracy of stress. Some knowledge of grammar wouldn't come amiss, either.

Let's look again at the excerpt from *Emma*.

> Mr Knightley and Harriet Smith! – Such an elevation on her side! Such a debasement on his! It was horrible to Emma to think how it must sink him in the general opinion... Could it be? No; it was impossible. And yet it was far, far from impossible. – Was it a new circumstance for a man of first-rate abilities to be captivated by very inferior powers? Was it new for one, perhaps too busy to seek, to be the prize of a girl who would seek him?... Oh! Had she never brought Harriet forward! Had she left her where she ought, and where he told her she ought! – Had she not, with a folly which no tongue could express, prevented her marrying the unexceptionable young man who would have made her happy and respectable in the line of life to which she ought to belong – all would have been safe; none of this dreadful sequence would have been.

> How Harriet could ever have had the presumption to raise her thoughts to Mr Knightley! – How could she have dared to fancy herself the chosen of such a man till actually assured of it!... Alas! Was not that her own doing, too! Who had been at pains to give Harriet notions of self-consequence but herself?

Emma is clearly in a state of considerable frustration, self-reproach, outrage, distress, agitation – well, you name whatever you think she's going through. Obviously, when fully performed, this text demands highly volatile expression. But that is precisely what is *not* wanted at the moment. The text, however passionate its implications, is a grammatically, semantically structured sequence of words that make logical sense and must do so to underpin the feelings that generate them. It's this underpinning that needs to be secured.

At the end of this workshop you'll find the Main Exercise for Logic Text. What follows in between is a suggested sequence of related material and techniques with their individual finger exercises to help towards that end.

Note: Exercising logic is not, nor should it ever become, an exercise in line-readings. It's an exercise in common sense. To avoid the danger of actors locking themselves into line-readings, this work should *never* be done at the start of a project, but only after the actors already have some familiarity with the text.

Sentence Function

In principle, the function of a sentence would seem clear enough to obviate any need for advice on how to convey it. But actors can become so absorbed by such aspects of their craft as characterisation or subtext or feeling that they lose contact with basic communication; they fail to see the sentence for the words. These words set between a capital letter and a full stop, do they express an agreement or a refutation, a wish or a belief? If they express a statement of fact, then state that fact. If it's a conjecture, let's hear it as that, don't give us another statement. If there's a question mark, ask a question. If it's an answer, reply. And if you set up a condition, as in this and the previous four sentences, then make sure you complete its terms (*If* such-and-such... *then* so-and-so; *When* so-and-so... *then* such-and-such). Of course, actors do sort of understand the sense of a sentence, but as is often the case in many areas of acting, only in a generalised way, rarely with precision (especially noticeable in performing classical texts). 'Sort of' is dramatic death. This work may seem pedantic or tedious, but I guarantee that, like preparing the soil for planting, the more care and nourishment you initially feed it with, the healthier the crop.

Note: Don't confuse the function of a sentence with a character's objective or a writer's subtext. Interpretation doesn't come into it (yet). It simply refers to the grammatical, semantic purpose of a sentence, to its simple, basic action, its bottom-line logic.

---

1. Select a few sentences at random from different texts.

2. With the actors, identify their function (their simple, non-interpretive action): to ask, reply, order, request, deny, agree and so on.

3. The actors then read them aloud, clearly expressing that function. Encourage them to emphasise the stress and inflection sufficiently to ensure that the logic is irrefutably conveyed.

4. Spend a little time analysing what distinguishes the difference in vocal expression between, say, a statement and a conjecture, an agreement and an offer...

5. The actors, while knowing exactly the meaning of what they're saying, speak in gibberish (nonsense syllables) to communicate sentences with different functions. From the sound alone (stress, pitch, rhythm, tone, etc.), the rest of the group should be able to recognise their function – statement, command, reply and so forth... They may even be able to grasp the actual content.

The Bare Bones of Sentences

> My Lady Dedlock (who is childless), looking out in the early twilight
> from her boudoir at a keeper's lodge, and seeing the light of a fire upon
> the latticed window panes, and smoke rising from the chimney, and a
> child, chased by a woman, running out into the rain to meet the shining
> figure of a wrapped-up man coming through the gate, has been quite
> been put out of temper.

When confronted by a long sentence, the actor needs to develop the ability to recognise which part of it is the basic structure that supports and makes sense of the rest.
The bare bones of a sentence is the essential idea stripped of all elaborations and
qualifications. The bare bones always contains at least one verb. This verb is the
motor by which the thought is driven through the full sentence. In this example
from *Bleak House* the stripped-down sentence is:

> My Lady Dedlock has been quite put out of temper.

If this statement doesn't receive its logical stress, the intervening accumulation of
images will derail the thought that's motivating it before it arrives at its destination.
It's not enough that Lady Dedlock has seen this sequence of images, but that she *has
been quite put out of temper* by seeing them. Imagery, such as a child running out into
the rain, can easily seduce an actor's imagination – and therefore emphasis – at the
expense of the sense in which it's employed. The actor has to judge the appropriate weight and proportion of any phrases and clauses in relationship to the bare
bones of the sentence. As a crude example:

> My Lady Dedlock (who is childless), looking out in the early twilight
> from her boudoir at a keeper's lodge, and seeing the light of a fire upon
> the latticed window panes, and smoke rising from the chimney, AND A
> CHILD, CHASED BY A WOMAN, RUNNING OUT INTO THE
> RAIN TO MEET THE SHINING FIGURE OF A WRAPPED-UP
> MAN COMING THROUGH THE GATE, has been quite been put
> out of temper.

– is not going to make sense of the sentence. But:

> MY LADY DEDLOCK (who is childless) looking out in the early
> twilight from her boudoir at a keeper's lodge, and seeing the light of a
> fire upon the latticed window panes, and smoke rising from the chimney,
> and a child, chased by a woman, running out into the rain to meet the
> shining figure of a wrapped-up man coming through the gate, HAS
> BEEN QUITE BEEN PUT OUT OF TEMPER.

– will make sense.

1. Select a piece of text with long sentences containing several clauses. Try to identify the bare bones within the complete sentences.

2. Speak the sentences, ensuring that the basic structure of the sentence is firmly established

3. Try to balance the additional clauses and phrases against the basic sentence.

Drooping, Dropped and Faded Endings

The point of a thought usually comes at its end, most frequently at the end of a sentence. When actors allow the ends to drop, droop or fade away, they aren't carrying through the intention of the thought. Which means they don't really know what they're talking about. They're certainly not communicating with each other or with the audience, pursuing neither action nor objective. This tendency to drop the end of a thought or a phrase often happens when, dealing with speeches of considerable length and complexity (like the one you're reading now), some actors, before they reach the intended point, either lose breath, energy and intention or anticipate and start to worry about what's coming next. The audience, in consequence, loses words, meaning and the will to go on listening. The purpose of a sentence must be carried through to its final syllable and beyond, onward to its auditors.

1. Select complex sentences from different texts. Ask the actors to read them, communicating them to a specific listener.

2. Ensure that the actors sustain their thoughts and intentions as they drive through the final syllable of the sentence to the person they're talking to.

False Endings

We've dealt with endings that aren't satisfactorily fulfilled. Now we're presented with the problem of non-endings treated as if they *were* endings.

A firm downward inflection (autonomically accompanied by an exhalation of breath) is usually a signal to the listener that a thought has been completed. If a sentence is constructed on an elaborate sequence of multiple and qualifying clauses, such as the speech we've just dealt with or the speech below from *Cymbeline*, the actor has to keep all those clauses, like juggled balls, up in the air until the thought is completed, at which time all the balls can be caught and brought to rest. Some actors, whenever they reach a comma, a dash or the end of a verse line, either fade or let their inflection droop (dropping the ball – see above) or – what we're dealing with *here* – make a firmly stressed downward inflection (bringing the ball to rest), causing a premature and false completion. The full thought will be fragmented into aurally disconnected phrases, each maybe intelligible in itself, but sequentially making little sense to an audience. The audience, hearing a firm downward inflection, will assume the thought is at an end and is likely to take a brief pause in their listening. But if the thought actually continues, they're caught by surprise and have to run to catch up with it. Possibly from sound-bite conditioning, we've become unused to sustaining extended thoughts either in our heads, in our hearing or in our speech. Actors have to re-learn a skill that's more or less atrophied from desuetude.

> IMOGEN   Ere I could tell him
> How I would think on him at certain hours
> Such thoughts and such, or I could make him swear
> The shes of Italy should not betray
> Mine interest and his honour, or have charged him
> At the sixth hour of morn, at noon, at midnight
> T'encounter me with orisons – for then
> I am in heaven for him – or ere I could
> Give him that parting kiss which I had set
> Betwixt two charming words, comes in my father
> And, like the tyrannous breathing of the north,
> Shakes all our buds from growing.

> *Cymbeline*, Act One, Scene Two

In Imogen's speech (which also happens to be one sentence) to a loyal servant, she laments her father's disruption of the leave-taking she'd been preparing for her husband, Posthumus, whom he has banished. The sentence's pay-off comes in the last two-and-a-half lines But the actor has first to get through all the details in the clauses and phrases of the six-and-a-half preceding verse lines before she can fulfil the thought that's motivating the sentence. The bare bones of this sentence is:

> Ere I could tell him how I would think on him, comes in my father and shakes all our buds from growing.

She has to sustain the thought through all of the speech's twelve lines. If the drive of the speech gets lost and breaks down into discrete fragments, this is what happens:

Ere I could tell him. [*drop the ball or bring it to rest*]
How I would think on him at certain hours. [*drop/rest*]
Such thoughts and such. [*drop/rest*]
Or I could make him swear the shes of Italy should not betray mine
interest and his honour. [*drop/rest*]
Or have charged him at the sixth hour of morn, at noon, at midnight
t'encounter me with orisons. [*drop/rest*]
For then I am in heaven for him. [*drop/rest*]
Or ere I could give him that parting kiss. [*drop/rest*]
Which I had set betwixt two charming words. [*drop/rest*]
Comes in my father. [*drop/rest*]
And like the tyrannous breathing of the north. [*drop/rest*]
Shakes all our buds from growing. [*drop/rest*]

Unbearable – in fact impossible – to listen to.

Because the point of this speech-sentence comes at the very end, the character
clearly knows what she wants to say ('Listen to how my father destroyed everything
I'd planned as a loving farewell'), so it's for the actor to commit to the character's
need to share her loss with a sympathetic ear. Then the prolixity of the speech
shouldn't present a problem. Some actors try to solve the problem of a long and
complex speech by rushing through it before (they fear) it flies out of their control.
That only compounds the problem. So long as the overall purpose of the sentence
is sustained, the actor can take her time, communicating calmly and specifically each
of the individual thoughts along the way.

Now, reverting to *Bleak House*, try this:

Lady Dedlock who is childless. Looking out in the early twilight from
her boudoir at a keeper's lodge. And seeing the light of a fire upon the
latticed window panes. And smoke rising from the chimney. And a child
chased by a woman running out into the rain. To meet the shining figure
of a wrapped-up man. Coming through the gate. Has quite been put out
of temper.

Once again, it's virtually unreadable, let alone comprehensible.

Note: Don't confuse a dropped or false ending with a pause. Filled pauses are justifiable and expressive. Just ensure that the pauses aren't accompanied by a drop in
energy and exhalation/lack of breath. Dropped energy usually results in empty
pauses. Empty pauses are momentary deaths in the life of a performance. Keeping
a pause alive is achieved by sustaining both (a) the intention together with its naturally generated energy, and (b) good breath support. You can take a breath and say
nothing but still sustain our interest for as long as you sustain your intention. Your
energy and body should feel lifted. [*Cross-refer this Set 2, Workshop 7, Voice: Breath*]

1. Select a series of extended and complex sentences, preferably from different sources so that the actors don't get too comfortable with one writer's particular style of structure. You can use the above examples to start off with.

2. Establish the bare bones of each sentence.

3. They read the whole sentence, sustaining the essential thought to the end and beyond.

4. They read the whole sentence, sustaining the essential thought to the end, but dealing clearly with each specific thought and clause along the way.

5. Challenge the actors to repeat a sentence, maybe more than once, slowing down, taking longer each time without losing the overall drive of the sentence. See how far they can slow down before losing the sense of the sentence.

Note: Slowing down does *not* mean taking huge pauses between words. There need be no pauses at all.

Lists and Repetitions

A sequence of repetitions or a list of items needs, for logic, some sort of movement in its delivery. A succession of words or phrases given equal value is hard to listen to and hard to take in. No narrative can remain static; there must be some sense of forward purpose. Lack of vocal variation isn't human. In a sentence such as 'He crept into the room on tiptoe, silently, restraining his breath, making himself as small as possible', these four qualifications require some sort of progression. How the progression is achieved will depend on the context. If, for example, the storyteller is trying simultaneously to convey secrecy and danger, it could be effected by increasing the intensity while decreasing the volume.

In the two excerpts we've been examining, the greater part of both sentences is taken up by what are essentially lists. In the Dickens sentence, the list is a series of pictures Lady Dedlock sees framed in her boudoir window. In the Shakespeare speech, the list is the planned details of the farewell to her husband that Imogen's father prevents her from carrying out. If all the items in these lists are delivered identically (in the same rhythm, volume, tone, and so on), the resultant drone will grind the narrative to a deathly halt.

Preceding the Lady Dedlock sentence, the text has established that 'The waters are out in Lincolnshire'. So a logical progression of sorts can be found from her looking out onto a damp and cheerless view that slowly transforms into something warm and homely. It's true that each thing she sees is a statement of fact, but logic insists that there must be some sort of reason for her to identify each of them. Were they all to be expressed in the same way, a single image would be more than sufficient to do the job. If, for the sake of example, all the images were meant to reveal the weariness of her life, there would nevertheless need to be an increasing sense of that weariness. The narration might grow heavier and slower as though it became almost too exhausting for the narrator to utter. If, as another instance, they were intended to convey her boredom, the narration might express increasing restlessness and irritation until the last phrase, 'has been quite put out of temper', is possibly snapped out.

Note: These examples assume that Lady Dedlock is subjectively narrating these third-person descriptions of herself (from inside the action) or that the text is being narrated on her behalf or with her attitude. If a narrator were describing her from either a detached or a critical stance (from outside the action), the progression might need to be dealt with quite differently – with surprise, with sympathy, sadness, irony, disapproval... The narrator has an interpretive *embarras de richesse*.

Imogen's speech is easier to handle as each of the things she wants to say to her husband expresses a different aspect of her feelings towards him, and therefore offers variations of tone: loyalty (promising to think on him), playfulness mixed with a certain anxiety (making him swear faithfulness), devotion by suggesting a means of being together though apart (praying at the same hours), intimacy (a kiss) and concern for his well-being (two charming words – charming in the sense of warding off evil). Clearly each of these reassurances of her love must be sufficiently needful for her to have thought them up in advance of his departure.

Here's part of another list, from the opening to *A Tale of Two Cities*.

> It was the best of times, it was the worst of times, it was the age of
> wisdom, it was the age of foolishness, it was the epoch of belief, it was
> the epoch of incredulity, it was the season of Light, it was the season of
> Darkness, it was the spring of hope, it was the winter of despair...

This excerpt – which is just the beginning of a much longer list – is not connected to any person with whom we can share some emotional or psychological connection. It presents an ironic view of the political uncertainty informing the nations facing each other across the English Channel towards the close of the eighteenth century. So how is this sequence of deliberately rhythmical and structurally repeated antitheses to be narrated? Perhaps with an increasing sense of exasperation or of mocking disbelief; possibly by an exaggeration of its innate metronomic beat. But in one way or another it has to be delivered with the sense that it's heading somewhere. To give every pair of opposites the same weight and shape would eventually reduce them to a sonic blur.

Note: Trying to convey the idea of progression in lists by giving examples of possibilities, I've been straying into areas of interpretation. My apologies. I want to confirm that at this early stage in the work we're trying to establish the bottom-line, common sense logic of a text, free of interpretation. If, as might be in the case above, you're confronted with a certain ambiguity or uncertain intention, you should, from a down-to-earth, sensible point of view, make whatever seems to you the most obvious – and logical – choice.

---

1. Get the actors either to read a piece of text or to improvise a speech or lecture that has repetitions or lists, attempting to give every phrase the identical expression (shape, inflection, volume and so on). It won't take long before it becomes unendurable to listen to and loses all meaning.

2. Choose material with lists or repetitions and explore different ways of narrating them, logically moving them forward in some sort of progression.

Note: A progression doesn't automatically mean speaking louder and faster. Remember you have the entire range of vocal expression at your disposal. [*Cross-refer Set 2, Workshop No 7: Vocal Variation*]

Antitheses

Antitheses are parallel but contrasting images or phrases that throw each other into stronger, often ironic, relief. ('When he came out, the sun went in. When he went in, the sun came out.') These are one of those literary devices that, more often than not, actors take for granted and allow to slip in under the radar. It's rare to hear one thing being fully compared or contrasted with another. The actor must commit to them. They are written for a purpose. The excerpt from *A Tale of Two Cities* is constructed totally on antitheses:

> It was the best of times, it was the worst of times, it was the age of wisdom, it was the age of foolishness, it was the epoch of belief, it was the epoch of incredulity, it was the season of Light, it was the season of Darkness, it was the spring of hope, it was the winter of despair...

Here are a couple of examples in the excerpt from *David Copperfield*:

> The light of my father's eyes had closed upon the light of this world six months, when mine opened on it.

> The first objects that assume a distinct presence for me... are my mother with her pretty hair and youthful shape, and Peggotty with no shape at all...

And three from *Emma*:

> Mr Knightley and Harriet Smith! – Such an elevation on her side! Such a debasement on his!

> Was it a new circumstance for a man of first-rate abilities to be captivated by very inferior powers? Was it new for one, perhaps too busy to seek, to be the prize of a girl who would seek him?...

---

1. Choose an appropriate piece of text and identify as many examples of antitheses as you can.

2. Ensure that the actors, stating them, really convey the contrasts embedded in them.

Imagery, Similes and Metaphors

These must never be treated as a cue for 'poetic' delivery prompted by the misguided belief that, for the moment, the writer, especially Shakespeare, has paused in the plot and action to show off some fine writing to decorate the text. Writers and their characters employ imagery deliberately because they feel the need to strengthen what they're trying to describe or to ensure they're expressing exactly the idea they need to communicate.

> comes in my father
> And, like the tyrannous breathing of the north,
> Shakes all our buds from growing.

Imogen chooses a most accurate and apposite image (containing a simile: 'like the tyrannous breathing of the north'; and a metaphor: 'shakes all our buds from growing') to combine two very different states: the violent, disruptive nature of her father's intrusion and its impact on the delicate, barely established expressions of farewell between her husband and herself. It's not in the least fanciful embroidery to the main idea. *It is the idea itself*, the essence of her experience and of the entire speech. And it has to be played with the intention to make the image vivid to at least three of a listener's five senses.

This is the opening sentence from *A Rose for Emily*:

> When Miss Emily Grierson died, our whole town went to her funeral: the men through a sort of respectful affection for a fallen monument, the women mostly out of curiosity to see the inside of her house...

The two words of this brilliantly economic metaphor give us considerable information about Miss Grierson, a somewhat remote but respected citizen of high status (a monument) in a small town. That decline (fall) in status has possibly been caused by a change in social values or personal fortunes, possibly by scandal or disgrace... It immediately whets our appetite to discover what actually happened to her. The image must be imbued with that significance. This sentence also contains an antithesis. (They're everywhere!)

From *Justine*:

> There is hardly time to think now: for teal and wigeon like flung darts
> whistle over me and I begin to shoot slowly and methodically.

This simile expresses an abrupt, violent start to the bird-shoot and contrasts with the stillness that had preceded it and the intention of the narrator to remain calm in the sudden panic.

Both these images express with imaginative precision what, to describe literally, would take much longer to less effect. Both are instrumental to the vitality of the writers' language.

The quality of the imagery and the way it's embedded in a writer's work is an important contribution to the particular world of a story.

---

1. Select some narratives from different sources with a good range of imagery.

2. Get the actors to express them, making them essential to the context in which they appear.

Note: When narrating or performing a text with such imagery, avoid the temptation of literal vocal illustration. Rather, try to express the attitude, the impact, the purpose behind the image. For example, 'for teal and widgeon like flung darts whistle over me' doesn't need the attempted mimicry of the sound of a missile speeding through the air (the words do that), but the sense of disorientation, excitement, abruptness caused by the event.

Conjunctions

One of our early Shared Experience discoveries was that conjunctions, words that we normally take totally for granted, took on a huge importance in the delivery of logical narrative. Their function is to connect one sentence to another, one phrase to another. They define the relationship of one thought to another.

> And... But... However... Nevertheless... So... Therefore...
> Consequently...Whereupon... If... Provided... Then... Or... For...
> Because... Although... That... When... Either/or... Neither/nor... Not
> only/but also... Before... After... As soon as... While... Until... Lest...
> As... Since... Thereupon...

In Imogen's speech, the three 'ors' sustain the list of what she has planned to say to her husband, and the 'for then' signals an interruption in that list to clarify why he should pray at specified hours. Try the speech without any or some of them and see what is lost. That succession of 'ors' seems to build up the pressure towards the explosion, 'comes in my father...' Conjunctions are not required to be heavily hammered home, but the thought behind a 'however' or an 'until' must be clearly conveyed. A conjunction warns us that there is about to be a change or adjustment to the thought that has preceded it.

Adverbial Phrases of Time and Place

Then we focused on words and phrases that established time. They too are often taken as read. These words help to orientate the listener to the chronology of events. It's imperative that we know exactly in which block of time we find ourselves, especially if the narrative frequently jumps between different periods. These are especially important when someone in the present might be remembering events in the past that referred to events even earlier (much as I have, in my section on Storytellers, remembered remembering Emlyn Williams).

> The next day... Some time later... The morning after the night before...
> The day before yesterday... Frequently... Annually... Soon... Ere... After
> a long while... Months went by... In the year 1421... Afterwards... The
> next second... At five p.m. precisely... In the spring... Every Monday...
> Quite early one morning... Round midnight... At twilight...

Words and phrases designating place also need the same attention.

> Here... There... Underneath... Inside... Outside... On the far side...
> Before... Behind... Above... In the distance... Nearby... Below...
> Downstairs... At the crossroads... A mile further on..... Around the
> corner... Close at hand.... In the shadows.... At the window..... On the
> top... At the bottom... In the country... At sea... On board... Ashore....
> Up river... Down the lane... Across the street... On the table... By the bus
> stop... One hundred metres back... To the left... Straight ahead... High
> up... On the road to Mandalay... Over the hills and far away... Next
> door... The back of beyond...

From *Bleak House* again:

> My Lady Dedlock has returned to her house in town for a few days
> previous to her departure for Paris, where her ladyship intends to stay
> some weeks; after which her movements are uncertain. My Lady
> Dedlock has been down at what she calls her 'place' in Lincolnshire. The
> waters are out in Lincolnshire. An arch of the bridge in the park has been
> sapped and sopped away. The adjacent low-lying ground, for half a mile
> in breadth, is a stagnant river, with melancholy trees for islands in it, and
> a surface punctured all over, all day long, with falling rain. My Lady
> Dedlock (who is childless), looking out in the early twilight from her
> boudoir... (And so on.)

This excerpt is filled with details of time and place. The profusion of details implies
a restlessness on her part, an inability to settle anywhere for long. Its narration
needs the most accurate stresses, otherwise we could easily become confused about
Lady Dedlock's actual whereabouts. Is she in Paris at the moment or in London or
in Lincolnshire?

These three sets of words provide the support for the main event, the bare bones of
a sentence, locating it in time, place and connection with the thoughts and events on
either side of it. Their sense is not necessarily achieved by heavy or loud stress but
by the genuine desire to communicate the logical thought, i.e. with the actor really
thinking.

Seven Questions

Not only the logic of a plot, but of individual sentences, depends on our receiving answers to the basic questions:

Who? Did What? To Whom? Where? When? And possibly How? And Why?

Of course, not every sentence or passage can or need contain all seven pieces of information. In the above extract from *Bleak House*, the first three sentences are essential. They provide primary information. Without them, the following two sentences have no purpose. These two offer an elaboration on what has preceded them, enriching but not vital, although they do make a convincing transition to the final sentence.

Conversation

Most speech is initiated as response to the speech of others. Conversation implies an exchange of thoughts. So it's imperative that, unless clearly an exception, a speech in any sequence of dialogue relates to what's preceded it. This is especially important in texts from a period in which the complexity and unfamiliarity of the language encourages actors to treat each speech as a self-contained, sealed unit exclusively for the examination of their character's feelings and psychology rather than the give and take and back and forth of conversation. However elaborate the dialogue, it is *always* conversation. Particular words respond precisely to particular words in a foregoing line of dialogue. If the audience doesn't hear these connections, it's inevitably lost. I've sat through too many productions of Shakespeare where I could hear and understand the words, but had no idea what the characters were talking about, simply because what they were saying seemed to bear no connection with what had just been said to them.

> IACHIMO. Believe me, sir, *I have seen him* in Britain. He was *then* of a
> crescent note, expected to prove so worthy as *since* he hath been
> allowed the name of. But I could *then* have *looked on* him without the
> help of admiration, though the catalogue of his endowments had
> been tabled by his side and I to *peruse* them by items.

> PHILARIO. You speak of him when he was less furnished than *now* he is
> with that which makes him both without and within.

> FRENCHMAN. *I have seen him* in France. We had very many there
> could *behold* the sun with as *firm eyes* as he.

In this sophisticated dialogue from *Cymbeline* (in which they are discussing the reputation of Imogen's husband, Posthumus, the banished Briton, who is now the guest of Philario in Rome), the Frenchman's first sentence echoes exactly that of Iachimo. Philario's line coming between their two speeches might cause the actor playing the Frenchman to lose contact with Iachimo's speech. However, Philario, by modifying Iachimo's opinion of Posthumus, provides the stimulation for the Frenchman to say what he does. These three speeches are interwoven conversation and have to be heard as such. The logically connected words and phrases I've italicised have to be vocally bounced off each other by the actors. Those commonplace words '*now*', '*since*' and '*then*' are the pivot of the whole exchange that the actors could easily fail to endow with their full value. The words '*seen*', *looked*', '*peruse*', '*behold*' and '*firm eyes*' reinforce the idea of Posthumus being put under intense scrutiny.

Intention

As I've briefly mentioned, a clear intention as to why I am saying these particular words to this particular person will go a long way to overcome lack of coherence. There will be almost no danger of dropped lines and fading thoughts; the intention will ensure that what is needed to be said reaches its intended hearer. In acting terms, every thought is an action that attempts to fulfil an intention. In the *Cymbeline* dialogue, Iachimo is trying to persuade Philario and his assembled guests that Posthumus's reputation is ill-founded. Every word is designed to achieve that purpose. Philario's intention is to defend Posthumus from this attack and the Frenchman's to support Iachimo's argument.

When audiences fail to understand what actors are saying, it often has nothing to do with lack of volume or poor articulation – in fact they can usually hear the words – it is caused by the actors' lack of intention. Any text not directed specifically towards someone (not that speakers have necessarily to be eyeballing their hearers) will dribble away into empty space. The words collapse like a ball that's lost its bounce, because they haven't chosen anyone to bounce them off.

I repeat: early in rehearsals or in a storytelling project, you are, rightly, not yet ready to interpret the deeper intentions or objectives of the characters. But you should be able to interpret the basic intention of the sentence-thought. A question is always a question, even if it's rhetorical; a statement is always a statement, even if it proves to be false. And that is precisely what is wanted in this work on logic. Actors can make perfect sense, logically, of a text well before they know or have even begun to consider what their characters' objectives or intentions are.

The Main Logic Exercise

1. If this work is done too early in the process, there's a risk – as I've already suggested – that the actors will mistake logic for imposed line-readings, which they will either obediently lock themselves into or resentfully, but rightfully, resist. The purpose, of course, is precisely the opposite. Once actors understand the fundamental logic of a text, they're in a position to do whatever they want with it, because now they know what they're dealing with. *You can only break the rules if you know what the rules are.* So it might be worth making this point before you start the first session.

2. The actors, seated and working from their texts, start to read through the text, applying many of the preceding disciplines, trying to the best of their understanding to express the logic, free of any interpretation, emotion or unnecessary colour. *They are trying to find the truth of the text that precedes interpretation.*

3. This is pedantic work, exact and exacting, usually slow work too, and, more often than not, irritating. I'd recommend doing no more than a half-hour at a time; concentration and patience only last so long...

4. This is the rare exercise that's likely to need considerable intervention, explanation, encouragement and insistence from you, the director, teacher or project leader. It often demands a far greater range of inflection or range of pitch than the actor feels comfortable with. At times, you may have to get the actor to repeat the text until it's accurately shaped. Unfortunately, the demand for (apparently mechanical) repetition can sometimes cause tension and with it the actors' loss of ability to 'hear' what they are, or should be, doing. So be cautious as to how hard you push each actor.

5. If it helps them to commit themselves to the level of logical expressiveness required, you might suggest the actors speak as if to someone whose command of English is not perfect. However, beware the danger of their either sounding patronising or as though talking to a very small child or a nincompoop.

6. All this work needs frequent practice, so that the narrator can eventually achieve absolute accuracy of logic. It's one thing to recognise the logic on the page, it's quite another to ensure it's clearly heard when expressed vocally.

Note: A by-product of this process is that it frequently solves the playing of a scene by clarifying for the participants what the scene is *actually about*!

WORKSHOP 7: VOICE AND SPEECH WORK

Stories offer particular challenges to the vocal and verbal skills of their tellers. Texts intended to be read rather than spoken often present a style of language – idiosyncratic to its author – that we're not in the habit of speaking. Narrators may have to relate stories dense with exposition and complicated syntax. They may need, within quick succession, to inhabit several different characters or switch narrative gears between, say, the coolly informative and the hotly engaged, the icily ironic and the warmly empathic. They may have to create vocally all manner of sound effects. These multiple functions demand vocal and verbal precision, flexibility and range to an unusually sophisticated degree.

Exploiting the numerous, if not innumerable, possibilities of the human voice and its relationship to language hasn't always been a priority for some actors. When I taught in drama schools, the voice classes were those the students most often tried to avoid. As speech is an actor's most frequent and obvious means of communication – certainly in theatre – I found this, at very least, surprising. I gathered they were bored by classes that didn't seem to connect with the rest of their training and frustrated by the restrictive, distractingly self-conscious methods often imposed on them. This was probably due to teaching then still based on artificial techniques that kept the voice in a closed system of its own, ignoring or denying its reality as part of – and dependent on – the rest of the human organism.

There was a time when excessive focus on how one sounded did create a very mannered form of acting in which voice took precedence over everything else – often to the exclusion of everything else. English actors were accused of acting from the neck up (the accusation, albeit a metaphor, itself revealing ignorance of how the voice functions). 'Say the words, laddie, just say the words!' or so old troupers are supposed to have boomed at neophyte actors. If you can track it down, listen to a recording of Sir Herbert Beerbohm Tree, a famous Edwardian actor, performing Othello. He more or less sings the text with huge swoops of sound that are supposed to express deep anguish, but now just make us giggle. In the social changes of the 1960s, the emphasis on working-class realism encouraged actors to revert from their professionally assumed, one-size-fits-all Queen's English to the accents they'd grown up with. Not to feel left out, quite a few actors whose original English actually *was* the Queen's suddenly acquired regional accents rather far from their places of birth. Now actors of the '60s sound almost as dated as Beerbohm Tree. Naturalism is always reinventing itself. Listen to pre-war recordings of the highly articulated, forward-placed voices of an imperially confident population – not as one might assume, a matter of class: both Cockneys and countesses spoke up, secure in their identities – and compare those ladies and gentlemen who attended rehearsals in suits and frocks, moving elegantly from French windows to drinks cabinet, with today's bejeaned and T-shirted actors: we find ourselves in a very different world...

...an uncertain world in which the pendulum seems to be swinging towards the inarticulate, both in what we say and how we say it. Times change, of course, and with it language. Throwing out the baby of good speech with the bath water of mannerism has many causes: possibly because of an ingrained reaction against that remote tradition of the voice beautiful; possibly because of our distrust in what we're told by press and politicians and therefore of words themselves; possibly because of the postmodernist dictum that everything is relative, which renders suspect any enthusiastically emphatic statement. Well-inflected, forward-placed speech suggests commitment. And commitment can catch you with your pants down; hence, for many, the preferred self-protection of inflection-lite, denasalised laid-backness.

Of course, the last thing actors need is to be preoccupied with what they sound like while they're performing. But what they do need is a fully developed natural voice that's capable of taking appropriate action when required ('natural' meaning their own voice at its full potential rather than some idea of a special voice developed exclusively for acting). But a functioning voice is a must. I, certainly, am pulled right out of a performance – and my disbelief reactivated – when I'm forced to listen to the strangulated voices and look at the accompanying physical tension of actors determined, it would seem, to encourage nodules on their vocal cords. Their strained attempts to scream or shout or weep or make whatever sounds they believe express deep emotion actually express nothing other than the strain. As an audience member, all I get from that sort of ineptitude is a sore throat.

Vocal quality seems no longer an important part of the performance. In reviews and other reports of theatre we get told a lot about what things look like, quite a lot about the music and, increasingly, about sound effects. But rarely, if ever, are we told what the actors sound like. Their challenge is somehow to wrench themselves free from the tyranny of any vocal fashion and to pursue what I can only describe as a classic norm, a perennial mean, which I would identify with what Patsy Rodenburg, in her very pertinent book, *Presence*, describes as the Second Circle of Presence. Neither the Third Circle (The School of Over-Articulated Voice), the circle of bluff in which one forces one's presence, nor the First Circle (The School of Inarticulate Voice), the circle of self-absorption in which one withdraws one's presence, is desirable. The Second Circle is where we're truly present with neither evasion nor exaggeration, but with the energy appropriate to the circumstance in which we find ourselves. This is precisely where the good storyteller needs to be – where we all need to be. This has nothing to do with accent but everything to do with clarity. What we listen to should be clear in audibility and sense. And more, it should be as exciting, as evocative, as witty and as attractive as anything we look at. We should be as captivated by the sound of people talking as we are by the sight of them moving. In storytelling, the text functions in so many different ways that storytellers really have to keep on their vocal toes.

Most of what I'm describing should, of course, happen quite naturally if the actor is playing truthfully. But the voice needs to be exercised so that, like the body, it's available to do whatever's required of it.

Note: In this workshop I'm merely pointing out, with some rather obvious exercises, a few of the possibilities that voice and speech have to offer. Development of the voice is a vast subject, well beyond the remit of this book or of my competence. So I'll preface these exercises by urging actors, for any serious training and for the well-being of their voices, to work, if they don't already do so, with a qualified voice coach. Voice work that's mishandled or, rather, mismouthed, can seriously damage your health.

Voice deals with the production of sound. Speech turns sounds into words.

Voice: Vocal Variation

The voice has a wide range of expressive elements, many of which are rarely exploited to the full:

VOLUME: Loud and soft and the range between their two possible extremes; one extreme could be silence.

PITCH: High and low and the range between their two possible extremes; inflection or intonation; moving up and down the scale. The specific range of an individual's pitch (or that of a piece of music) is called its tessitura: from how low to how high.

TEMPO: Fast and slow and the range between their two possible extremes; the rate and speed of delivery; how many syllables (beats) per second.

RHYTHM (not to be confused or conflated with tempo): The underlying pulse, regular or syncopated; in musical terms, how the pattern of the pulse is organised and where the stress (strong beat) falls within the structure of a bar.

LEGATO/STACCATO/PORTAMENTO: The types of transition from one note or word to the next. *Legato* (literally: bound) means a smooth, sustained delivery, flowing without a break. *Staccato* (literally: detached) is a percussive, punctuated delivery with clearly separated sounds. *Portamento* (literally: carrying) is a sliding or gliding through a sequence of several notes or pitches (such as the legendary downward-upward swoop of Edith Evans's 'Handbag')

RESONANCE: The vibration that carries the voice and gives it its penetration and – well – vibrancy. Different parts of the body, such as the cranium and the chest, act as resonators.

PLACEMENT: The position and mobility of such features as the tongue, jaws, lips that influence the individual character of a person's speech.

VOICED/UNVOICED SOUNDS: whether a sound, essentially a consonant, is accompanied by a full breath or a slight puff of air: the difference, for example, between 'd' (voiced) and 't' (unvoiced), 'b' and 'p', 'th' in 'this' and 'th' in 'thin', 'j' in 'James' and 'ch' in 'Charles', 'sh' and 'zh' (the French '*Je*')...

TONE: The quality of voice such as warm, cool, immediate, remote, caressing, hard, swooping, monotonic, denasalised, guttural...

TEXTURE: Another slightly more metaphoric way of thinking of vocal quality: gritty, oily, squeaky, creaking, rasping, hissing, chewed...

Volume

There's a tendency to push on the voice in order to talk more loudly. This usually results in a strained flattening out of the voice with a consequent loss of expression. When actors are told they can't be heard, their instinct – and objective – is, unsurprisingly, to speak louder, usually to the detriment of their performance as they substitute this objective for their objective in the scene, losing all contact with their partners as they belt out their lines at the audience. Rather than treating the voice as a projectile to hurl into the auditorium, they should think of widening, broadening and releasing it – opening it up sideways, as it were, in a wide embrace of the audience. Instead of forcing themselves on the audience, they should invite the audience to enfold itself within that vocal embrace.

At the other end of the spectrum, if there's a need to play quietly, it's unwise for actors to whisper. They'll be inaudible and damage their voices into the bargain. Whispering takes the voice off-centre, which limits the breath and strains the throat. They should talk normally but quietly. If the intention is clear and the articulation clean, they *will* be heard.

---

1. Choose a sentence or reasonably full phrase.

2. Starting quietly, focus about ten metres in front of you and repeat the sentence so that it will be heard adequately at that distance.

3. Gradually widen the release, as, little by little (maybe ten metres at a time), you increase the distance you wish your voice to reach. Always focus precisely on the exact point at which you wish to be heard, but make sure you remain physically on the same spot. Remember: release the words rather than push them.

4. The moment you experience any discomfort or pressure on the voice, go back and re-exercise the previous distance.

5. Then reverse the process, decreasing the volume.

6. Assuming your voice is in healthy working order, your commitment to the intention motivating the text will ensure you're heard.

Pitch

In our daily life, we inflect quite naturally, without giving a moment's thought to how we do so. It's one of the ways we make ourselves understood.[1] To my bewilderment, actors, when they get on stage, seem perversely to divest themselves of half their ability to inflect at just the moment you'd think that, in their profession of choice, they'd want to exploit as much of it as they had. A Canadian actor once lectured me on the fact that it was un-Canadian to inflect. She did so with quite a lot of inflection.

---

1. With a hum or solfège or any open-ended syllable (one ending in a vowel), sing an octave, first going up the scale and then back down.

2. The second time, start a tone higher.

3. Continue to work your way up the scale, tone by tone, until you reach a note that you cannot sing cleanly.

4. Reverse the direction. Sing an octave first going down the scale and then back up.

5. Continue to work your way down the scale until you reach a low note that you cannot sing cleanly.

6. Vary the vowels of your syllable. Different vowel sounds will help or hinder your ability to extend your range. An 'ah' sound is more helpful for upper notes, an 'er' sound for lower.

7. Instead of moving up and down scales one tone at a time, try singing over increasingly larger intervals to gain greater flexibility.

8. Applying portamento, try sliding up and down between two non-adjacent tones. Increase the space between the tones.

With committed exercise and practice in singing and speaking scales, you could extend both ends of your range by a couple of tones at least.

---

1. In Mandarin Chinese, intonation is critical. The understanding of words is based on a system of four tones which, if misapplied, completely changes the meaning of what's being said, as unsuspecting foreigners learn to their embarrassment.

Tempo

You can only talk as fast as the arrangement of words permits. Shakespeare, by his organisation of words, provides us with implicit stage directions as to whether a speech or line can be – and therefore should be – spoken slowly or fast. There's a limit to the speed with which you can get your tongue around certain sequences of words and it's pointless to fight against it. Too many hard consonants clashing against one another will inevitably slow you down.[2] Words that end or start with vowels help to move things along. A sentence containing monosyllabic words will take longer to say that one with polysyllabic words. Most monosyllabic words other than conjunctions or prepositions require a firm stress, whereas not all the syllables in a polysyllabic word need such emphasis. This is partially because the latter are usually constructed of qualifiers that have evolved as smooth additions to the stem word: thought, thoughtful, thoughtfully. The monosyllabic words make the muscles of the face, lips and tongue work harder, they have to move further more frequently and this slows things down. Try these two sentences:

This girl strolls with style, charm and grace.

This woman saunters gracefully, charmingly, stylishly.

Eight syllables against fourteen, yet the fourteen are easier to speak than the eight. They both have six stresses, but in the shorter sentence they have only two weak stresses between them to ease them along, whereas in the longer sentence, there are nine. Good writers, wanting to draw your attention to something of particular importance, will employ words that slow down your reading; or, wanting to move you swiftly though an exciting piece of action, will ensure that the sequence of words flows easily. The predominance of words ending in vowels is why Italian sounds so mellifluous and is spoken with such apparent easy rapidity.

Fast

If you want to go fast or are directed to speed things up, going fast for fast's sake will not achieve anything other than generalised gabble. But you can create the illusion of speed by treating the text with vigour in a slightly staccato manner, singling out those words or phrases you feel deserve slightly more attack. You'll find you have plenty of thinking time to colour what you're playing while moving the language with energy and apparent speed. Distinguish

---

2. China again! Mandarin speakers have great difficulty dealing with clusters of consonants (one of the reasons for their use of tones to extend their vocabulary). When I was directing *A Streetcar Named Desire*, the cast found it hard to reproduce the names of their characters without adding vowels to ease their verbal journey. Blanche became Bi-Lan-Chi, and Stanley became Si-Tan-Li, Stella Si-Te-La and Mitch, Mi-Chi.

between rush (bad) and attack (good). If you find you have sections in a text which are difficult to get your tongue around, keep repeating them, starting slowly, then building up the tempo as the muscles become more flexible, learning the necessary patterns required of them. Muscles have good memories and learn quickly. (Unfortunately, they forget quickly, too.)

Slow

On the other hand, though a cast can find it easy to fall into a collective, under-energised, slow mode of speech, actors rarely feel confident about deliberately dwelling on a single word or phrase for a sufficient length of time as a means of emphasis. They fear they'll sound false. But it's just one more way to make language expressive. Again, it's predominantly a matter of a sustaining the intention behind the point that's being made.[3]

1. Take a speech from Shakespeare and explore where the text allows you to go faster and where it slows you down.

2. From any source, take a small portion of a text that you find difficult to speak. Repeat it at a speed at which you can manage to enunciate it. As you get familiar with it, try speeding up. If you exercise the muscles often enough, they'll learn that particular pattern and you'll no longer find it a problem.

3. Take a piece of text and try to speak it as slowly as possible, making sure it's fully justified and makes complete sense. Employ different degrees of slowness. You should feel totally in command of what you're saying.

Resonance

Depending on which part of the body the sound is directed to for the production of resonance, different vocal qualities are created by what is essentially a range of echo chambers: the head comprising nose, mouth and skull, the throat and the chest all function as resonators. Each tends to express a particular area of experience: the head seems appropriate for the intellect (thought, reason, ideas), the throat for the senses (sensuousness, sensuality), the chest for delicacy of feeling (compassion, empathy), the gut (really low in the chest) for intensity of feeling (violence, rage, desire).

---

3. In his production of Oscar Wilde's *Salome*, Steven Berkoff slowed down the delivery of the entire text and at least doubled what might be its average playing time. The slow, deliberate delivery in which every word was sensuously explored was accompanied by a physical life of sustained slow motion. The result (for half the performance, at least) was to intensify the actors' performances and the audience's engagement, so that we experienced a totally unique world, sensual, decadent and menacing.

1. Experiment with different types of text or language, consciously shifting between resonators.

2. You may initially find that some resonators are difficult to locate or isolate. If so, work with a hum. To place the hum in the cranium, for example, try dropping down while humming and sustain the hum with the head hanging loose. Make sure your shoulders and neck are free. Sustaining the hum, slowly straighten up. As you return to the upright, open your mouth and release the sound fully as an 'Ah'.

If you are accurate, a hum will produce vibrations: a buzzing of the lips, a tickling sensation in the nose. When you release the hum as an open sound you may experience a light throbbing in the chest. Ideally, your whole body should feel a slight tingling, a sort of inner massage. Some people initially find these sensations disturbing. But it should actually give you a powerful sense of presence.

After humming, see if you are able to sustain the resonance using text.

Placement

Placement not only refers to resonators, but to the ways in which the position or manipulation of certain physical features affect vocal sound at or near its point of emission. Most of these are in the mouth or in the muscles that make up the mask of the face: jaws, tongue, lips, soft palate, cheek muscles, nasal passages. Lazy or nimble tongues, stiff or flexible upper lips, tense or released jaws, tight or soft cheek muscles, all have a bearing on the particular quality of an individual's way of speaking. You must first become familiar with how your own voice functions before you start to explore these possibilities. Used judiciously and with technical skill, their manipulation provides the means of changing the quality of voice to accommodate different states of feeling and contributes greatly to characterisation and aspects of dialect and accent.

There are certain physical states you should try to avoid: tensed shoulders, the head tilted back too far or the chin pressed too tightly forward onto your chest all affect the passage of the air through the throat and should rarely if ever be used as they can be damaging to the vocal cords. Bad posture such as a strongly curved (concave) lower back which pushes the stomach forward will automatically cause a compensatory shift to the neck, pushing back the head so that pressure tightens the throat.

If, by manipulating some physical feature to create a vocal change, you find that you're creating tension, gradually minimise the amount of effort you need to achieve the required vocal quality. As a warm down, always exercise the feature, say the upper lip or the jaw, to release the tension and restore it to its normal state.

The following are some basic exercises to wake up the muscles in the face and mouth:

1. To release facial muscles, stretch the face in as many directions as you can:

i.   Open the mouth as fully as you can and encourage the rest of the face, for instance the forehead, to extend in the same directions as the upper or lower jaws are moving. Then reverse this by scrunching the face into the smallest size possible, compressing everything towards the nostrils.

ii.   Stretch the face on diagonals.

iii. Smile as broadly as you can so that the corners of the lips are aiming for the ears.

iv.   Dilate your eyes and then close them tightly.

v.   Chew vigorously, allowing the rest of the face to participate.

2. To exercise the tongue:

i.   Extend the tongue straight ahead as far as you can, then retract it, trying to roll it up inside the mouth.

ii.   Stick out the tongue and rotate it in alternating directions, stretching it as far possible as you do so.

iii. Flap the tongue up and down and from side to side as freely and flexibly as possible.

3. With the mouth half-open and in a relaxed state, clench your fists together and shake them vigorously. Allow the rest of the body to respond to the shaking. If the jaw is free, you should hear and feel your back teeth clicking. Don't deliberately try to make this happen. It will occur naturally if the neck and jaw are free.

4. Blow out the lips with little puffs of breath.

5. Massage:

i.   Massage the face vigorously, especially those areas that tend to be tight, such as the forehead and the temples.

ii. Massage the cranium, trying to shift the skin.

iii. Massage gently just inside the bones forming the eye socket.

iv. Massage gently just under the cheekbones from the nose towards the jaw hinge.

v. Massage and pull on the ear lobes.

vi. Press on the upper lip just beneath the division of the nostrils and sustain the pressure for about a minute.

6. Explore talking through compressed lips, trying to make yourself as audible and comprehensible as possible.

7. Similarly, try the same process with a very loose jaw and the lips barely closing.

8. And with a floppy, heavy tongue; with a tense tongue; with a rigid upper lip; and so forth.

Breath

Breathing, for most of us, is something to which we give barely a thought. We breathe autonomically, if not always efficiently. We automatically take a new breath every time we express a new thought. So properly motivated by clear intentions to play specific actions (which require the expression of thoughts), an actor shouldn't need to think about when or where to breathe. In a good world, breath, thought and intention work together.

Actors are often encouraged to make decisions as to where to take a breath within a text, and to develop the ability to sustain a breath during a long speech. Some consider it sacrilege to take a breath in the middle of a verse line. Of course, there is absolutely nothing wrong in developing a fully expanded thorax; breath control is essential, one of an actor's necessary skills. But breathing by plan can become a mechanical matter that at times interferes with spontaneity and the flow of logic. Breathe when you need to! If the thought is correct, so will the breath be.

Breath keeps you alive; lack of breath kills you. This is metaphorically true when performing. The moment the air is depleted from your lungs it signals that you're empty of purpose. You are disempowered from holding the audience's attention. If your lungs are full, you are full – of life and purpose – and immensely watchable. Although breathing is a natural activity, in moments of tension or effort we may tend to lock our breath, and this can frequently occur from nervousness or unnecessary pressure. Distinguish between a pause when the lungs are empty and when they're full. [*Cross-refer this Set, Workshop 6, Logic: False Endings: Note*]

Breathing is not just a technical necessity, it can also be expressive in its own right. How a character breathes can be a revelation of what they're experiencing; for instance, someone trying to control their impatience or anger might take very full slow breaths, someone in fear or anxiety might take shallow breaths that make the chest rise and fall noticeably. This was a form of expression used to great effect in silent films. In *Don Juan*, a John Barrymore vehicle in which he casts Mary Astor aside, she falls prostrate on a staircase and exhibits the busiest and most expressive expanding and contracting ribcage I've ever seen.[4] In Von Stroheim's *Greed*, Jean Hersholt's chest heaves alarmingly as his drinking companion announces he's about to marry the woman that he himself is in love with, each heave creating a fuller and more threatening expansion.

The following are some very simple exercises for a five-minute voice warm-up:

1. Swing each arm in a full circle, up, forward, down and back. (Not in the reverse direction.) Do about six vigorous swings, one arm at a time. When you have swung one arm, if you can, look in a mirror and you'll see that this shoulder has dropped noticeably lower than the arm you're about to swing. When you have circled your other arm, you'll see that both shoulders are now balanced.

2. In a semi-crouch (i.e. with knees well bent and feet placed firmly wide apart), wrap your arms across your chest and grip the sides of your ribcage and take several deep breaths into your lower back. Feel your lower ribs expanding.

3. Get someone to stand behind you and place their first fingers and thumbs lightly on either side of your lower ribs. Try to widen their grasp by breathing into the back and side of your ribcage, opening it out as far as the breath allows. Breathing out, try to expel all the air, contracting your ribcage as you do so.

4. Yawn and stretch a few times.

5. Pant, exercising your diaphragm. Then turn the pant into a light unvoiced sound 'huh'. Take care not to hyperventilate.

---

4. For those who care about such matters, she played Brigid O'Shaughnessy in *The Maltese Falcon*.

Speech: Variety of Speech

Speech is about turning sounds into words: the crispness of articulation; the flexibility of the soft palate, tongue and lips in creating accurate consonants; the flexibility of the face muscles (the mask of the face) and jaw in creating accurate vowels. In dealing with accents and dialects, it concerns the technical skills in the placement of speech sounds that are unfamiliar to one's own way of speaking, for example Semitic glottal stops and Xhosa clicks.

However extreme an accent or vocal characterisation, it still has to be audible and articulate. Some of the areas to pay attention to: distinguishing between voiced and unvoiced consonants; ensuring final consonants are fully pronounced, such as words ending in 'nt'; being able to move nimbly between consonants that are not comfortable neighbours, such as 'th' and 's' and the combinations of sounds that tongue-twisters are based on: 'Unique New York', 'Red Leather, Yellow Leather', 'The Leith Police Dismisseth Us', 'She Sells Sea Shells' and the like.

Replacing final 't's with glottal stops gives us the likes of 'Fe-ge' aba' i'.' Lazy tongues provide 'f' when 'th' is needed: 'I can' fink of nuffin' – or more usually, 'I can' fink of nuffink' ('f' requires less effort or commitment than 'th', 'ink' requires less than 'ing'). Or perversely, the reverse: 'Thank You' becomes 'Thang Quiyooo' (a presidential candidate for The General Assembly?).

If you have any knowledge of languages, dialects or accents other than your own, you'll know how different they feel in your mouth. And in consequence how differently they make you think and feel in general. They change the way you move. They change your attitude. Learning an accent is not just a matter of getting the vowel sounds 'right'. Placement, rhythm, degree of inflection, volume, speed of attack, pitch and attitude all play their part. Many people are convinced they have no ability to 'do' accents, but this is not really the case. Potentially we all have the same body parts under our control. And we are instinctive imitators or at least parodists of other people's ways of speaking. Of course, the shape of our jaws, the length of our vocal cords, the size of our tongues differ and will produce qualities which make a voice instantly distinct. But what are vocal impressionists mainly doing other than shifting parts of their body into different positions.

Lost Consonants

One reason for audiences to think they can't hear is because consonants, usually at the ends of words, are often not fully articulated. So apart from the word itself losing full clarity, it can often elide with the next word into some alien verbal life form, totally unfamiliar to the ear ('I wen tout', 'I dough knee tam', 'the Ma Chair' – in *Alice...*). Loss of consonants is usually the result of unspecific thought or a weakening intention, usually because the actor is already anticipating the next phrase; and of lazy muscles that are moving as little as they can, just sufficient to get the sounds out at all.

---

1. Holding the tip of the tongue, try to say a piece of text as clearly and as communicably as possible. You will find that all those lazy muscles are forced to work hard. Now repeat the text with the tongue released (i.e. normally). You will that that the words are now fully and more easily articulated.

2. Select relevant tongue-twisters. Start by repeating them slowly, then, as the muscles of the mouth and face become used to the patterns, you can increase the speed.

3. Exercise the pairs of unvoiced and voiced consonants: 't d'; 'p b'; 'k g'; 's z'; 'sh zh'; 'ch j'; 'f v'; 'm n'. Pay special attention to accurate placement in order to avoid blurred or splashy sounds; for example, tapping the tongue on the back of the front teeth for 't' or 'd', do you use the tip or the blade of the tongue? And whereabouts on the teeth to you tap to achieve a clean sound?

4. Exercise words ending in 'nt': 'won't', 'can't', 'evident', 'plant'... Make sure the 't' is tapped. Exercise words ending in 'ing': 'ring', 'ringing', 'thinking'... Make sure the 'n' isn't neglected in 'dance', 'chance', 'glance'... Make sure that a consonant that finishes one word and starts the next is given its value both times: 'bad day' (not 'bad ay'), 'which cheese' (not 'which ease'), 'nice size' (not 'nice eyes'), 'big girl' (not 'big earl')...

Non-Verbal Vocalisation

There's an area of voice work that I never hear discussed, let alone encouraged. These are the expressive sounds we make on their own or as an accompaniment to what we're saying, presumably to reinforce the communication of our feelings on the subject we're discussing: a huge repertoire of sighs, groans, moans, gulps, gasps, grunts, tuts, clicks, raspberries, false laughs, sucked-in breath, yawns, stifled screams, nasal exhalations with the mouth firmly closed (a sort of sniff in reverse, sometimes paired with a buried grunt-cum-laugh), and so on and so forth. Many of them are culturally acquired (Israeli acquaintances make an 'oy' sound for instance, to convey annoyance or anxiety or sympathy for someone else's anxieties). They're usually involuntary and probably release our feelings more strongly than we intend, but they're very much part of human expression. You rarely hear them used in performance, they seem to be filtered out of an actor's vocal repertoire.

1. Take a section of first-person narrative.

2. Consciously try to apply whatever sounds you think might be appropriate as an accompaniment to, comment on or reinforcement of what you're saying.

3. Obviously this a self-conscious exercise. But its intention is to remind the unconscious that these sounds are totally permissible as part of our natural expressiveness. In time, they should feel they have permission to occur spontaneously.

WORKSHOP 8: PHYSICAL WORK

This workshop is to make the solo storyteller aware of some simple, rather basic physical matters. There are more and fuller movement workshops further on. [*Cross-refer to Set 6, Subset 1 & 2, Workshops for Physical and Spatial Awareness 24–31*]

Awareness

We've discussed in considerable detail what solo storytellers sound like. But although they may remain reasonably still as they narrate, we can't assume that they won't give us anything to look at. We can't ignore their physicality, what visual signals they're emitting, even when they appear still. We all tend to be on the involuntary move more than we realise, continually shifting, fidgeting, adjusting our bodies. If you've nothing better to do on a bus or tube ride, take a good look at people engaged in conversation; there's often a lot of movement involved that's apparently surplus to requirement with the listener at times not facing their interlocutor. However, when being told a story in the theatre, we focus exclusively on that single narrator and can't fail to register their movement, even the slightest shift. We may either be distracted by its irrelevance or endow it with unintended significance. So it's beholden on storytellers to be in command of their bodies, to make certain their movements are meant; not a matter of self-consciously watching themselves, self-consciousness often being the main cause of inadvertent movement, but the opposite: a full commitment to the objectives they're playing that automatically involves the whole person. What we observe should support what we're hearing.

A Responsive Body

Creating the way a character moves is not only a matter of external technique of the type that might be attributed, perhaps, to some dance training. Actors certainly have to go through technical exercise and practice to bring their bodies into an appropriately available condition, but how they move has to be connected with and motivated by the inner life of the character: feelings, values, thoughts, self-image, ways of relating to others… The tuning of their bodies must be so fine that they instinctively respond to their subtlest of thoughts and feelings with the most delicate expressiveness: an intake of breath or tilt of the head, flick of an eyelid or straightening of the spine.

However, they can also work the other way round, from the outside in, from soma to psyche. Our muscles are filled with memories; our bodies are repositories of our experiences. Every gesture we make contains some sort of feeling, however delicate. Moving the appropriate muscles will release the appropriate feelings. It is through their bodies that we 'read' other people's histories and interpret their thoughts and feeling. We recognise them by their behaviour. In order for the audience to recognise a character's behaviour, actors need to ensure their bodies behave recognisably.

Mime

Much of the movement when telling stories, particularly in an empty space, is essentially mime – the creation of what isn't there. As with voice work, this is a subject on which I'm not qualified to talk in any depth; there are many excellent practitioners who can teach you the techniques of different approaches and systems. The point I want to make here is that by working in an empty space, the storyteller, without any consciousness of doing so, is frequently employing some sort of mime. So it needs serious consideration.

Apart from working with an expert in mime, it's frequently a matter of trial and error until you find what seems right for the specific material you're involved with. If you do work with a teacher, avoid dependence on what you might call all-purpose mime as it can become formulaic and merely provide you with a series of visual clichés: this is how you mime walking, this is how you establish a flat surface and so on… This sort of work is excellent as a starting point. But you should be searching for what will contribute to the unique world you're creating. The interesting matter is deciding at what level the mime is to be executed: how realistic, how heightened, how selective…? For example: in naturalistic detail, as sometimes occurred in *Bleak House*, or, as I've described in *Section 9: Worlds* concerning some of the choices we came to for the *Arabian Nights* trilogy, sketched like a cartoon in *The Rogueries of Dalilah the Wily* and ornately exaggerated in *The Loves of Kamar and Budur*. Often, movement that looks convincing on stage is not at all how it's executed in actuality. Mime should never draw attention to itself; it should be totally absorbed into the reality of the world it's inhabiting. Its only justification is the way it helps to tell the story.

Gesture

When talking to others, most of our gestures occur spontaneously. They're rarely conscious or deliberate but the product of an instinctive belt-and-braces fear that, without them, our words might fall down before they reach their target and reveal the uncertainty behind them. Watch politicians at party conferences. They can't be aware of the distracting hand flapping that unnecessarily accompanies their speeches or, presumably, they'd stop it. Most of this involuntary movement is caused by an anxiety that what we're saying isn't really adequate or sufficiently forceful to affect its hearers. This virtually autonomic need for communication by gesture can be broken down into five categories, each of which, used appropriately, is immensely expressive and useful.

1. Illustrating
2. Contacting
3. Emphasising
4. Commenting
5. Responding

ILLUSTRATING is a literal acting-out of what is being described in words, expressing the same thing a second time. It's a way of saying 'I'm not sure that what I'm telling you is absolutely clear so I'm showing you, too.' Most of the time it's an unnecessary duplication. However, it can be effective as an expression of naivety or as a means of intensification. [*Cross-refer Section 8: Doubling the Information*]

CONTACTING is directed to audiences to ensure that they've got the point, that they're paying attention or, possibly, to encourage some sign of agreement or acknowledgement from them. [*Cross-refer Set 12, Workshops 54-56: To Develop Contact with the Audience*]

EMPHASISING underlines what the storyteller believes are details that the listeners should be sure to take notice of. Emphasis tends to shape the narrative.

COMMENTING is the need to make clear the storyteller's attitude to what they're narrating; to express approval, disapproval, surprise, pleasure; to lead the audience to understand the story in the way that the teller feels it should be received.

RESPONDING is a more spontaneous, subjective reaction to the material, as though, in the heat of the telling, the storyteller is suddenly hit by the implication of what he or she is saying, by an unanticipated access of personal feeling or attitude.

Of course, these categories are often combined within one gesture; maybe Commenting with Emphasising, Illustrating with Contacting. A storyteller's expressiveness will be intensified by the ability to become more particular and discriminating in the use of gestures; to be in charge of them, rather than to let them lead a life of their own. The dominant use of one type of gesture over another will give the story a particular quality. Remember: (i) gestures are not just the movement of arms and hands, but of the whole body, and (ii) since the face is part of the body, smiles, grimaces, frowns and the like *are* gestures.

1. The actor, seated, tells a story – or a part of one – five times, using just one type of gesture each time.

2. Discuss the difference between the five modes: what the observers received and what the actor thought and felt and whether there was any differences in the observers' responses.

3. The actor tells the story – or part of it – again, combining and/or alternating two types of gesture.

4. Build up the technique until the actor is using all five.

5. Repeat some of these exercises with the storyteller standing and able to move in the space. Discover how the five purposes are expressed spatially as well as gesturally.

6. Line up five actors, all of whom have learnt a small section of text. Have them narrate chorally. Assign a different one of the five types of gestures to each of them. You will then be able to see very clearly the particular impact of each gestural form.

Hands

If you've ever had the opportunity to watch Kathakali performers, you'll have probably been impressed by the virtuosity of their hand movements. They enact stories largely by means of the hands. These are a form of sign language[5] and to achieve it, they traditionally undergo intensive, decade-long training.

I'm certainly not recommending that path for us. Ten-year training! Hardly British! But the use of our hands and their potential expressiveness is almost never discussed, let alone developed in our own theatre – except, of course, by mime artists. But in storytelling, especially in an empty space, there's nothing to distract the audience from focusing on the actor with total concentration. Everything the actor does will be observed. With the greatest economy of execution, a hand gesture can convey whole worlds or the subtlest of meanings. Working on the hands will make the miming of props, the handling of props or transforming of hands *into* props that much more vivid. Because our hands are at the end of our arms, they are our main and most

5. Whenever I watch a signed performance, I'm almost always drawn to the signer. Most of the time they are so much more vivid than the actors they're interpreting that I have to tear my eyes away from them to watch the actual show. They are fine exemplars of playing objectives; theirs is to communicate with their particular audience and they do so in spades.

frequent means of contact with the outside world (think of the multitude of activities they're involved in: making food, art, objects, love, war; playing sports, instruments… acting!). Developing skills in their use tends to make everything the actor executes more finished, more precise, more refined, more aesthetically satisfying.

A. Warming Up Hands

1. Rub the hands together vigorously. Massage each finger and pull it gently to free the joints. Massage the back of the hands.

2. Clench the fists, then slowly extend the fingers as wide as they'll spread, then slowly re-clench them.

3. With fists clenched and then with palms open, rotate the wrists in both directions. Then rotate the forearms.

4. Rotate the thumbs in both directions.

5. Flick the fingers across the thumb and then the thumb across the fingers. Imagine you're trying to remove something sticky, first from the thumb and then from the fingers.

6. Very gently, hold the fingers and ease them backwards.

7. Gently, try to press the thumb towards the wrist.

8. Ripple the fingertips rapidly across a flat surface one by one, moving from the little finger to the thumb as if playing arpeggios. Try rippling them in the opposite direction.

9. Clap the hands in flamenco fashion, exploring different rhythms, trying to maintain a regular pattern of movement with each.

10. Snap your fingers. Try to create a sharp sound.

While exercising your hands, make sure that the rest of your body is relaxed and that you're not placing tension in your mouth or jaw, shoulders or neck. Make sure your wrists are always engaged.

B. Characterising Hands

The actors endow their hands with qualities and characteristics so that by looking at them, an observer would be able to understand that aspect of the whole person.

Clumsy hands
Hands that have never worked
Hard-working hands
Violent hands

Healing hands
Creative Hands (artists, technicians, craftspeople...)
Tired hands
Secretive hands
Nervous hands
Seductive hands

... and so forth.

1. The actors work by themselves. You can assign qualities, or a single quality for the whole company; or you can let the actors make their individual choices.

2. You can work in two directions: (i) from the inside out, that's to say from the 'character' to the manifestation of the character in the hands, you could also think of this as working from the whole to the part; or (ii) from the outside in, working from the hands to the 'character', from the part to the whole.

3. First explore from the inside out (i); in this approach, the state of the hands becomes the result of the exploration.

There are two ways of viewing the inner qualities and characteristics: (a) as an organic aspect of character (healing hands, creative hands...); or (b) circumstantial (nervous hands apprehensive about a forthcoming event, violent hands in a frustrating situation...).

Or think of it this way: why might someone be clumsy? Possibly because (a) that person is a dreamer, preoccupied with matters of the mind rather than the body; or maybe because (b) they're forced to make a quick decision after unexpected news...

4. Working (a) from character, it might help the actors first to find the appropriate characteristic by means of super-objectives and Laban efforts, so that the whole person is filled with this ability or condition. With healing hands, for example, the super-objective might be the overarching desire to make other people better, to cure the world of its ills; the Laban effort might be gliding (sustained, light and direct). Once they're engrossed in their characteristic qualities (healing, secretive, hard-working...), the actors should gradually concentrate the focus on their hands. Working from the whole to the part, they should allow the hands to become both the generator and expresser of how they're feeling and thinking. Hands become the physical centre of the person. *The person becomes a pair of hands.*

The sort of things you might look for: do the hands radiate their healing power in all directions or only towards those that need it? Is it directed through the fingers alone or through the palms or the entire hand? And so forth.

5. However, if the quality of the hands is (b) situational, the actors should imagine or recall a circumstance in which that quality might be engendered. This time they apply the equivalent of a scene objective (to control one's temper for example, if, say, violence is the characteristic) together with a Laban effort, maybe thrusting (strong, direct and broken). First, they work through the circumstances of the imagined situation that they hope may bring them into the right state of experience. Once that is secure, they proceed, similarly as in (a), to place that experience totally in their hands.

The sort of things to look for: do the violent hands prevent the release of energy or does the violence exude from the clenched knuckles or the back of the hand? Or does it turn in on itself? And how does this travel into the whole person?

6. Alternately, the actors work from the outside in (ii). In this exploration, the state of the hands leads to the whole person. Starting from the hands alone, they will need to choose a specific image of how the hands might be held or move with the particular characteristic in mind. They should then, quite technically, explore that physical choice. Be aware that every committed movement we make, no matter how small, is accompanied by some degree of feeling. Our muscle memories hold emotional patterns that are activated by their engagement. So, on the principle of working from the part to the whole, the actors, by continuing to repeat a movement or gesture that they've selected to their satisfaction, will evoke a specific feeling, however slight it might be.

For instance, if you keep making a flicking movement with your fingers and the back of your hand, it will almost automatically create the feeling of irritation and the need to be rid of something or someone. Try clasping your hands together; it creates a sensation of controlled suspension, a slightly anxious alertness, waiting to see how something will turn out; it's synonymous with, or can actually cause, a held breath. Keep shrugging your shoulders and it will elicit a state of indifference or unconcerned ignorance.

Working this way, the actors should allow sensations, thoughts, feelings to be aroused, rather than trying to anticipate them. Eventually, the whole person should be in action. What the actors end up with may well be considerably more complex than the quality of the hands that they began with.

Note: The use of props is optional. It's preferable to start with none and to introduce them only when the exercise is firmly established and the particular expression of the hands cannot be totally fulfilled without them. Ideally, props should be mimed. [*Cross-refer Set 9, Workshop 44: Working with Props*]

C. Working Hands

In these exercises, the actors put all their mental focus on the hands as though they're the essence of their physicality. They are vital to their livelihood and well-being. The actors should give them prime importance and treat them with care and respect, they should imagine them to be extremely strong, nimble and also very sensitive to the materials they work with; they read the material they work with (marble, wood, soil, etc.) as if it's Braille. It's preferable in these exercises for the actors to carry out activities that they are to some degree familiar with. Or they should at least think precisely and logically through the sequence of activity they've chosen to work on. Don't ever let an activity become generalised or approximate

1. They mime some activity, both strong and sensitive, in which they're working with wood: polishing it, carving it, sanding it, joining it, tongue-and-grooving it, sawing it...

2. They mime some activity in which they're working with soil: digging it, breaking it up, feeding it, tamping it down, planting in it, weeding it, removing stones from it, digging crops out of it...

3. They mime some activity in which they're working with a musical instrument – but only if they have some knowledge of playing an instrument. Or they can imagine they're technicians (a motor mechanic, a plumber) but, once again, they should only choose something of which they have sufficient technical knowledge.

4. They mime some activity dealing with food: washing it, chopping it, tearing it, kneading it, rolling it out, arranging it on platters, eating it...

5. They scrub a stone floor on their knees, using their hands vigorously.

6. They should imagine their hands as hard-working hands, much larger than their own, with thick wrists and muscular fingers, scarred and callused, but always sensitive to the job they practise. They should explore how they carry them around, how they rest them.

7. They should explore how the rest of the body supports the labouring of the hands or how the labouring hands affect the rest of the body.

Note: These sorts of exercises are essential if you are creating a physically arduous world where people's lives depend on labour. The audience needs to believe such characters have bodies and hands capable of the trades or crafts they follow.

Note: In working towards a production, these sorts of exercises should be done on a daily basis.

D. Social Hands

1. The actors imagine their hands are very fine, beautifully proportioned, the fingers slender, the skin smooth. They manicure them, oil them, moisturise them, paint or polish the nails.

2. The actors are smokers. They explore the variety of ways in which to handle a cigarette: taking it out of a packet, extricating it from a cigarette case, rolling it, tapping it, lighting it from matches, a lighter or someone else's stub, getting rid of the ash, inhaling, keeping it in the mouth, holding it in a variety of ways, stubbing it out and generally expressing themselves with it. (If you can, look for clips of Noël Coward in action; cigarettes became an extension of his arm, almost another limb.)

3. The actors explore their hands in relation to drinking everything from water to champagne, herbal tea to hot chocolate, in mugs, porcelain cups, tumblers, flutes, liqueur glasses, alone, with close friends, at formal functions. At the latter, what images of themselves might people wish to present.

4. In pairs, explore different sorts of social handshakes, hand-holding, hand-taking...

E. Revealing Hands

These exercises concern the ability of the hands to reveal or give away something about the character which might otherwise remain unknown or unseen, a form of subtext. The behaviour of the hands might be an habitual pattern that always occurs in certain situations (clutching, sweaty hands at awkward moments...), or it might be exclusive to an unusually stressful or emotional event (hiding hands under stretched sweater sleeves...).

1. Let the actors imagine themselves as people who are, unawares, always touching themselves for a variety of reasons:

Narcissism/Vanity
Sensuousness
Reassurance about one's muscle development
Concern for health
Self-consciousness about what one's wearing
Shyness

...and so forth.

2. They explore characters using hand gestures – without words – to express how they feel:

What can I do about it?
I'm not interested.

Leave me alone!
I don't know what to do.
I thought so!

...and so forth.

3. And then, situations in which a character might unconsciously manifest manual nervous tics:

Drumming fingers
Finger tapping
Clenching and unclenching fists
Hand-wiping or rubbing
Nail-biting
Pulling or clutching at clothing
Stroking hands
Wandering hands
Warming the hands
Punching a fist into a palm

...and so forth.

4. Improvise situations in which the characters wish to present themselves in a positive light while their hands are telling us something else. The actors may help themselves to achieve this by giving themselves one Laban effort which is consciously and socially applied, for instance dabbing (light, direct, broken) and another, which is unconscious, for their hands, such as wringing (strong, flexible, sustained) – in this case, the complete opposite.

F. Transforming Hands

1. We've talked about the ability of actors to transform themselves into elements of scenery. But there may be occasions when, by hands alone, a storyteller can convey an image or an object. Think of a hand as a glove puppet without the glove. Explore the possibilities of creating objects by the hands alone.

Butterflies
Books
Pens
Beating Hearts
Mirrors
Mice
Utensils

...and so forth.

G. Relating Hands

1. In the same way that the intention behind any speech should continue towards the person intended after the words themselves have been spoken, the intention behind any gesture should similarly continue to radiate its energy beyond the gesture and after the gesture has been physically fulfilled. If you point at someone, the fingertip should continue to send out its message. The actors, working in twos or even threes, should explore contacting each other by hand gestures, but not by touch. Once a gesture has been accomplished, the intention activating it should still be of sufficient importance for the actor to sustain the gesture for as long as the impulse remains. The actors must ensure that their intentions actually reach their partners. Make sure that the energy radiates from the appropriate part of the hand. There must be *no* talking and the actions with their intentions must be fulfilled exclusively by the expression of the hands. Naturally, other parts of the body will be involved in any hand movement, but the actors' focus must be on how they are using their hands to communicate. Some actions that might be tried:

Accusing
Admiring
Agreeing
Disagreeing
Apologising
Admonishing
Advising patience
Expressing impatience
Warning

…and so forth.

This isn't quite so easy as might first appear. In order to communicate with absolute clarity, actors have to dig quite deep to find the appropriate impulses.

H. Touching Hands

The actors work in pairs and can now talk. Improvise situations in which they explore ways in which characters might relate to each other by touch, such as stroking someone's lapels while conversing with them, or constantly jabbing them to make sure they're getting it! Start with casual acquaintances, gradually intensifying the nature of the relationships: work colleague, good friend, best friend, family member, lover, life partner… Periodically switch pairs. The need to touch is often the unconscious manifestation of a strength of feeling that the agent doesn't feel capable of expressing in words; it might also be to intensify or confirm what is being expressed by words; it might be to modify what has been said, for example, patting someone's hand while criticising them.

As these exercises are for the development of manual expressiveness, make sure that you don't let the actors become distracted by other concerns in the heat of improvising. And always be specific about the function of the hands that they're exploring (revealing, relating...). The hands should be their point of concentration. This should help to increase the imaginative range of their gestural repertoire and improve their actual handling of props when required. And most important: working on the hands develops an actor's concentration, precision, subtlety of communication and refinement of expression. A lot can be said by very little means.

Note: Think about the feet, too! [*Cross-refer Set 9, Workshop 47: Shoes*]

Cultural Physicality

It would be wonderful if we could retain the natural, expressive elasticity of baby-hood in that period before we're taught what is and isn't acceptable, what might or might not be dangerous. Of course, many physical responses are hard-wired within us, mostly associated with moments of intense experience. Fear, for instance: universally, above and beyond our specific time and place of existence, our bodies all react identically and unthinkingly to physical threat with two essential impulses: one to ward off the threat, the other to reduce our target area.

But cultures also encourage particular patterns of physical behaviour, partly influenced by environmental circumstances, partly in obedience to what has become socially agreed behaviour: what is acceptable to be shown and what should remain hidden. The physical expression of people's emotional life is very much shaped by the values of their society. Sulkiness, for instance, is not a particularly admired mode of conduct for adults in the UK. We identify petulance as the province of spoilt brats. Many British actors, especially men, find it quite unnatural to stamp their feet, toss their heads and pout. The instinct had been suppressed, if not entirely smothered; the body, of course, remains perfectly capable of executing such gestures. The closer we get to the Mediterranean, however, such wilful moodiness appears to be tolerated and expressed without inhibition.

1. Ask the company to move like Americans, or Chinese or Italians. Tell them not to worry about clichés.

2. Discuss what they come up with. They are certain to find that different cultures place their centres of gravity differently, use space differently, gesture differently, have a different relationship to the ground.

3. Explore physical gestures that are not instinctive to the actors, but are recognisable as belonging to other cultures (the French shrug, for example). Pool your collective knowledge of such gestures. If they feel unnatural, keep exercising them to find the impulse that creates them.

4. Similarly, explore variations of physical behaviour influenced by class. Who slouches? Who sits up straight, gesticulates, crosses their legs or doesn't, extends their little finger while drinking tea, scratches their crotch, keeps their elbows off the table while eating…?

Animals

Most actors will undoubtedly have done some work on animals during their training. But it's a resource that tends to be forgotten or patronised as 'one of those things we did at drama school!' But it's a rich source of material and stimulation to the physical imagination. Go to the zoo. Watch dogs in the park. After all, we are all interconnected and – even if at some distance – not as remotely as all that. Their use can range from a specific physicality, such as the way a dog cocks its head, to something more metaphoric: the way a seagull swoops for garbage might alert you to something scavenging in your character's nature.

1. Choose any creature from the animal kingdom that you have plenty of time to observe closely (Homo sapiens excluded).

2. Try to recreate that animal in as much physical detail as is humanly possible: shape, movement patterns, relationship to the ground. Do not intellectualise what you think you should experience (big cats are predatory, chickens are stupid, snakes are sneaky…); allow your actual physicalisation to affect the way you feel and think.

3. Gradually reduce the actual physicality of that animal, while retaining the energy, focus, tempo, pulse, quality of movement and any of the inner attitudes and feelings it might have generated. When you have finally eliminated all trace of the animal's external patterns, and resumed your own physicality, move about and carry out a few activities as normal. Observe how much you are influenced by all the animal's qualities you have retained.

Note: Between those two extremes of adaptation, there is a spectrum of degrees of characterisation which you might apply, depending on the particular reality of the world you're creating.

SET 3

WORKSHOPS FOR THIRD-PERSON NARRATOR FROM OUTSIDE THE ACTION

9–12

WORKSHOP 9: AREAS OF THE STAGE AND THEIR QUALITIES

This workshop, whose main concern is space, rightfully belongs in *Set 6, Subset 2: Spatial Awareness and Subset 3: Focal Awareness*. However, I'm placing it here as it provides a useful starting point to explore the range and vitality of third-person narration from outside the action.

Where storytellers place themselves – exploiting the unique qualities of different areas of the stage – will influence how an audience receives their story. Different spatial relationships between actors and audiences will affect the latter's response to what's being played: obviously, the closer, the more intimate; the further off, the more formal; above us, the actors are more likely to hold us in thrall; below to invite our appraisal... and so forth.

There is also a difference in impact between what is played from the left and the right sides of the stage (I'm giving left and right from the audience's point of view). This difference is caused entirely by the direction in which we read, an exclusively cultural phenomenon. When I worked in Israel, I had to reverse my natural predilection for one side over another precisely because Hebrew is read from right to left. Since we (in western cultures) read from left to right, we have a natural tendency to incline our heads to the left in readiness for the start of a new line. Looking to the left feels slightly easier than looking to the right. Action placed to the audience's left provides a more comfortable, intimate experience. Material which demands a warmer reception, when the desire for sympathy takes precedence over objectivity, benefits from being played in this area of the stage. Looking to the right requires a slight increase in effort. The head feels, just slightly, as if it's being held there by taut elastic, which releases totally when it reverses to the left. So, facing slightly to the right, audiences may well feel they have be more alert, to sit up and pay attention. Material in which reason takes precedence over feeling is better suited to this cooler side of the stage

Because we favour the left, of two (or more) actors standing on stage, the one (furthest) to our left will – all things being equal – appear stronger, warmer. [*There are many variables that can affect this, dealt with in Exercise B of this workshop*] That is because this actor is the first to gain and then hold our focus. There is a delicate illusion that this actor is standing on slightly higher ground than the actor to his right. This phenomenon is more pronounced when an actor, crossing the stage from left to right, appears to be walking slightly downhill and therefore moving with less effort than an actor crossing in the opposite direction, apparently clambering uphill.

The Six Basic Areas

Dynamic **UP-LEFT** Dominating/ Threatening	*Formal* **UP-CENTRE** Strong/Formal/ Authoritative	*Remote* **UP-RIGHT** Coldest/Most Remote/ Disturbing
DOWN-LEFT Warmer/Most Intimate/ Stronger *Warmer*	**DOWN-CENTRE** Strongest/Intimate *Hot*	**DOWN-RIGHT** Cooler/Less Intimate/ Weaker *Cooler*

A U D I E N C E

DOWNSTAGE-LEFT (actor's right) is the most sympathetic, intimate and warmest area. An actor on this side of the stage is stronger and evokes more sympathy than someone on the opposite side.

DOWNSTAGE-RIGHT (actor's left) is cooler, slightly less comfortable but is still intimate. It demands attention rather than sympathy.

DOWNSTAGE-CENTRE is the strongest area for the actor to be in good contact with all the audience, the best area from which to control them. But because of the proximity to the audience, it's also very personal. The actor sustains a sense of authority whilst remaining informal, familiar. Major scenes tend, conventionally, to get played in this area.

UPSTAGE-CENTRE has status and strength but lacks intimacy, suggesting formality, power, authority, dignity, distance, a certain coldness. Traditionally it's a place to establish authority figures: judges, enthroned royalty and the like...

UPSTAGE-LEFT (actor's right) has power, aggression, and is the most dynamic. Someone upstage-left will inevitably form the head of a diagonal. By breaking the flat, horizontal lines across the stage and disturbing its symmetry, a diagonal from up-left to down-right is the most kinetic line of action on stage. An actor not only has the strength of being stage left, but also of being above the other actors and therefore in a totally dominant position. This is strengthened by the likelihood that the other actors onstage are having to turn upstage to make contact and are therefore weakened by partially removing their faces from the audience.

Of course, if another actor were present down-centre and facing towards the audience, that person would take the greater focus, not only because of the characteristics of that area but also because the up-left actor at the top of the diagonal between them would be reinforcing that focus, if looking at the down-centre actor. But the up-left actor would still be implicitly strong because of the dominant, possibly threatening quality of that position. If the down-centre actor were to turn to face the up-left actor, the latter would immediately take total focus and power.

UPSTAGE-RIGHT (actor's left) is the most remote area, cold, disturbing, unforthright, mysterious, lonely, sly, good for ghosts and non-human manifestation.

Of course, these areas can be exploited to create complex and conflicting responses: a love scene between sympathetic characters, for example, may take on a disturbing tension for the audience if played, not down-left where it logically seems to belong, but in the chilly up-right. In a play where, unbeknownst to the characters (and the audience), a warm relationship is about to be destroyed, use of the down-right area instead of the more intimate down-left could endow the scene for the audience with a delicate undertone of unease. On the other hand, by placing the scene down-left where it more properly belongs, where it would be at its warmest, the poignancy might be that much greater when the relationship ultimately ends. The choice of where to place the action is a delicately expressive tool of the trade for actors and directors. Good use of areas has a subliminal influence on the audience's responses and perceptions. It's unlikely that the audience will be consciously aware of such effects and even less likely to understand what has caused them, whereas some other means of creating subtext or mood, such as lighting or music, often intrude too obviously on their awareness, taking the edge off their effectiveness.

Changing the position of a scene can seriously change its impact on the audience. I once placed down-centre what I thought was an important climactic scene, the confession of a murder. It was both the final revelation and the denouement of the show. The confession contained some excessively grotesque details, such as the murderer's habit of depositing dead cats on another character's doorstep as tokens of love, that caused a certain merriment in the audience rather than the shudders of revulsion I'd anticipated. My initial response was (of course) to blame the insensitivity of the audience. However, after the same response had occurred three previews running, I had to acknowledge that the misjudgement was mine alone and mine to rectify. I had the hunch to try the scene in the cold upstage-right area whereupon the laughs disappeared, never to return. Downstage, close to the audience, was somehow too normal a space in which to take its macabre details seriously. But by placing it in the space most remote from the audience, it found a more appropriate setting where the audience could accept it without reservation.

A. Area and Space

1. Place one actor, always facing in the same direction and with the same body shape (preferably standing face-front) in each of the six spaces. Observe in what way each area affects that actor's presence.

2. Play the same short scene (always with the same actors and, if necessary, the same arrangement of furniture) in each of the six areas of the stage. Evaluate and compare the effect of the scene in each space.

3. Ask an actor to walk across the stage from left to right and then from right to left and you will see immediately that with the first crossover, the actor appears to be walking downhill, free of effort. This is because it reinforces our natural movement of the head when we read. When returning, the actor appears to be walking uphill, the journey more effortful because it's going against the habitual directional flow of our reading.

A triumphal procession will probably be more effective moving from left to right, it will reinforce a sense of power and confidence. But success after a struggle will be more strongly reinforced by the eventual winner moving from right to left; the struggle is literally an uphill battle with the winner ending up on the 'stronger' side.

4. Try staging a debate or dispute in which the actor on the weaker (audience's right) side of the stage, gradually overcomes the other's arguments and ends up the winner on the stronger (audience's left) side of the stage.

B. Body Shapes and Positions

1. Two actors stand side by side centre stage. The one standing to the audience's left will, of course, take our focus and will appear the stronger of the two.

However, there are ways of counteracting the relative qualities of areas by several variables which can affect an actor's strength, warmth and ability to take focus.

a.   Variations in the direction actors are facing (specifically, how much of their face can be seen by the audience).

b.   Variations in body shape (sitting, standing, crouching, lying, kneeling, and so forth).

c.   Variations in level (standing on steps, platforms, etc.).

d.   Reinforcement (standing in a doorway or close to a chair or any element whose lines echo the lines of the body – in this case on the vertical).

e.   Direct focus (an actor looking at other actors who are facing away, or gesturing towards them in some way, will give them focus).

f.   Contrast/difference between two actors (one actor moving will be stronger than one who is still; one talking, than one silent; one wearing red than one wearing blue – the more dynamic attribute obviously gaining focus).

g.   Exception with three or more actors (if there are two or more actors moving and one still, two or more talking and one silent, two or more facing downstage and one upstage, two or more wearing red and one blue, the odd one out will always take our attention, even though the attribute is essentially less dynamic).

2. Explore the differences in strength achieved by different body shapes, e.g. sitting, leaning, crouching, kneeling, standing on tiptoe, lying down... To limit variables, ensure that for this exercise that the two actors are facing in the same direction, preferably out front.

3. Explore the differences in strength achieved by the body facing in eight different directions:

> Upstage-centre
> Upstage-left
> Upstage-right
> Right
> Left
> Downstage-left
> Downstage-right
> Downstage-centre

The more of the actors' faces we see, the more they will tend to take focus. However, actors facing upstage with their backs completely to the audience may well take focus in contrast to others whose faces are partially visible. To eliminate variables in this exercise, the two actors should adopt the same stance, preferably standing upright.

4. Explore, with as many variations as you can invent, the relative strength and warmth of two actors in different spatial relationships to one another and to the audience, in different areas, with different body shapes (crouching, sitting, etc.) and facing in different directions, as well as using contrast and direct focus.

5. With two actors positioned downstage-centre, try to find a way for the actor on the audience's right to appear stronger than the actor on the left.

6. Try to find ways for both these actors to achieve equal strength.

7. Gradually add more actors, one at a time. See if you can achieve equal, shared focus for the whole company deployed around the stage.

WORKSHOP 10: NARRATION FROM DIFFERENT AREAS OF THE STAGE

From this, we can see that where a narrator is placed on stage can radically affect the audience's appreciation of the story. Apart from the qualities emanating from the areas themselves, each choice will also cause a variation in the triangular relationship between narrator, characters and audience. Whether narrator or character is closer to the audience, whether the narrator stands between characters and audience or the characters between the narrator and audience, will make a different impact on our reception of the story.

Down-left and Down-right

In these positions, narrators are placing themselves on the visual edge of the frame – implying that they are less important than those acting out the actual story, their main role being to lead the audience's focus to where the action is being played out.

Stories which suggest a more personal and empathic regard for the characters, where subjective response comes before intellectual evaluation and the audience can listen most comfortably, more intimately, should be narrated from the down-left area (actor's right). The presence of a narrator here, because she inhabits a strong area, may at times tend to dominate the actor/characters to the right of her. But the narrator can counteract this, guiding our gaze to the characters by giving them her direct focus while they're in action. This, after all, is the narrator's purpose: to lead us to and through the story.

Whereas stories in which thought takes precedence over feeling are better suited to narration from the down-right area (actor's left). The presence of a narrator here will tend to be weaker than the actor/character's to the left of him who, because they're in the stronger position, will always be the first to draw our attention. So it is the narrator's information, rather than presence, that matters more here. Narrative with a cooler, even critical, attitude towards the material and the characters is probably more effective from here because of the slightly greater effort that's needed to watch a narrator in that area. Actors narrating from down-right will have to be more assertive to get our attention. And we will be forced to pay attention in a slightly less comfortable position. That sort of crispness might be good for more objective, somewhat didactic, texts.

Down-centre (seated on the floor)

This, on the face of it, seems a totally unsuitable place to narrate from, unless the narrator is the only one on stage. The narrator standing centre stage will totally dominate the proceedings, visually splitting the stage in half and forcing the action to be played out on either side of him, under almost all circumstances an unsatisfactory situation.

However, if the narrator tells a story from the floor, *seated* as far downstage as possible, the situation radically improves. This might conjure up images of a traditional storyteller telling stories in a marketplace or beneath a tree. Because he's seated or reclining, the actors can be seen behind him, able to use the entire central area of the stage, neither impeded nor obscured. The narrator, placed between the audience and the action, is, of course, dominant. The audience has to go through the narrator both visually as well as audibly to reach the actors, who give the impression of having emerged from his head. The effect is to endow them with a romantic distancing which works well for fairytales, dream-like or highly exotic stories in which bold, colourful plots and characters predominate over nuance and complexity. Technically, as long as the actors don't stray too far to the sides or corners of the stage, the two parties (narrator and actors) remain contained within a single audience focus. This offers the advantage of both the narrative and the action proceeding in unison. The actors must also take care not to move too far upstage; the laws of perspective will cause them gradually to disappear behind the narrator. On the other hand, this can be exploited to create the effect of characters magically rising from or subsiding into the narrator's head.

This position does not provide the most flexible or spontaneous form of storytelling because the narrator has little possibility of contact with the actors. He can, of course, turn around to look upstage. But this will destroy the image of the story emanating from his head. He will end up as an observer of a story rather than its creator.

Because both parties are visually combined, this is an occasion on which the actors should avoid acting out literally what the narrator is describing. This will only emphasise the implicit naivety of this form. However, by creating images which elaborate or counterpoint what is being described, they can enrich and deepen the world of the story and add a certain degree of sophistication to what is essentially a simple mode of storytelling.

To expand the possibilities and dynamics of this mode, it might be interesting for the narrator to be free to move sideways (always keeping low and well downstage). If so, the actors then have to move with him, rather like a still-attached soap-bubble, flowing with him wherever he goes.

Upstage Behind the Actors (raised for visibility)

Placing narrators behind the actors, necessarily raised at a higher level for visibility, turns them into puppeteers, deliberately in control and constant observers of their actions. This will tend to make them somewhat cold and manipulative. The sorts of stories applicable here might be satirical, harsher, the characters viewed critically, seen to be behaving foolishly or unworthily. The tone might well be brutal and mocking. Because the narrator is now behind the actors, he can observe everything that they do and so be in total control of the story, whereas the characters can only obey what they hear.

Behind the Audience (or possibly amongst them)

The narrator is amongst or preferably behind and close to the audience, so that they hear rather than see her while she metaphorically whispers into the audience's collective ear, establishing a sort of complicity between them, sharing secrets, encouraging, urging, prompting them to watch the story's enactment carefully. Her demeanour will tend to imply that she wants them to pay attention to her observations rather than to her, and is anxious not to disturb their attention to the fluency of the story being played out in front of them. An analogy might be of an ornithologist discreetly pointing out some very rare bird-life to a novice twitcher. She privileges them with information that only she possesses, powerfully suggestive of something mysterious, maybe slightly sinister, intimate or fraught with scurrilous gossip about celebrity misdemeanours and political improprieties... Accordingly, tales of intrigue, stories with an ambiguous moral, stories requiring discretion and sustained concentration by the audience work well in this manner of telling.

Moving Freely

Narrators feeling free to move wherever and whenever they choose in order to make the most appropriate contact with both audience and characters suggests a flexible relationship to a story that allows such spatially and physically dynamic narration. Material that is picaresque, shaggy-dog-like, rambling, comic, playful, surprising in its conventions, would lend itself to this freewheeling treatment. The narrator will, more likely than not, command a lot of the focus – though there's no reason why this freedom shouldn't be exercised with subtlety. This mode of narrative also opens up possibilities of interplay between narrator and characters.

---

1. To start with, take the same short piece of narration, which must include some descriptions of characters in action. The narrator tries out in turn each of the six stage areas (upstage-right, downstage-left, etc.). For this exercise, the narrator should always be standing on the floor. The characters must place themselves in a logical and suitable spatial relationship to the narrator. They should try to maintain the same manner of playing in each area to allow those watching to judge what effect or impact the narrator's position has on the material.

2. Discuss the qualities of each area and then, from your evaluations, try portions of different narratives that you think might be most suited to each of the areas.

3. Now the narrator explores the further variations described above (seated downstage, behind the audience, standing raised behind the actors, etc.). Discuss and evaluate.

4. Try any other spatial possibilities that occur to you.

Note: The options I've suggested are merely starting points. You may find that they have other and very different qualities and uses. This work is absolutely *not* formulaic and is a matter of constant trial and error. Try out possible ideas of your own. For instance, how would the story be affected if the narrator worked from the cold, remote up-right area of the stage? In order to assure the narrator's visibility, the characters might have to enact the story seated, lying and crouching or utilising the diagonally opposite down-left area. A choice like this might produce something especially apt for a ghost story. Explore!

WORKSHOP 11: NARRATION WITH ATTITUDES AND AGENDAS

I have suggested that, although third-person narrators from outside the action are usually reliable, that does not preclude their having attitude towards the story they're telling. Of course, the writing will most of the time make it clear how the tone of the narration might sound. But if you believe a particular attitude is likely to reinforce and enrich the material, you should allow yourself to pursue this. The narration might be delivered in impersonal, formal tones; possibly in the accent of the community in which the story takes place and with which the narrator would then presumably be identified; possibly in the tones of a culture different from that of the story; possibly an unschooled, demotic voice in contrast to that of its educated characters and vice versa... This is very much a matter of personal judgement. For example, the half of *Bleak House* that is narrated in the third-person present tense might benefit from a tone of satirical scepticism able to accommodate the expression of contempt and disgust, a voice very much from outside that world, observing it from a strong moral base. And this, of course, would contrast with Esther Summerson's warm, engaged and sympathetic first-person narration, that hesitates to criticise and apologetically modifies any disapproval that she does feel the need to express.

1. Ask each actor to make a decision to tell a story, either improvised or based on a text, with a very clear attitude to the material and the intention to convey that to the listener. The story must include some scenes of action for the group to fulfil. Initially, make strong and obvious choices. For example: just giving the facts without any attitude at all; then, completely sympathetic to the characters; then sharply critical of them. The actors playing the characters should fulfil their actions identically in each of the three narrative choices, that is to say, they should *not* be influenced by the tone of the narrative. Observers can then judge how much – or indeed whether – the narrator's attitude affected their feelings towards the characters. Or did that attitude merely rebound on the narrator?

2. Repeat the exercises, now allowing the characters to carry out their actions in accordance with the tone and attitude of the narrator, trying to embody the narrator's view of them. The narrators need not necessarily repeat the choices they made in the first exercise. The actors playing characters are told nothing in advance but must try to carry out what they believe to be the narrator's intention, that is to say, they must play in such a way as to justify the narrator's contempt, concern or admiration for them. The narrator might have different attitudes towards different characters.

3. The exercise can be repeated but with the narrators' attitudes becoming refined to increasingly subtle choices, such as a weary, rueful acceptance of the characters' fallibilities, an amused disbelief at their stupidity, or anxiety as to their welfare. The characters again try to fulfil what they believe their narrator is suggesting.

4. Discuss whether the storytellers in the previous exercises were successful in conveying a chosen attitude and tone, and how gesture and logic were utilised.

5. A narrator, without revealing it to the other actors, chooses a very specific manner or genre in which to tell a story, preferably one that's already been worked on or is reasonably familiar to the rest of the group. The actors who are playing the characters in the story try to perform their roles in the reality of the world they believe is suggested by the manner of the narration. If needs be, the narrator must try subtly to prompt the actors away from any misconceptions, but without stepping outside the story to do so. Obviously, nothing is discussed or explained before or during the exercise.

The exercise can be repeated as often as you want, either by the same narrator retelling the story in different styles or by new narrators telling the story in genres of their own choice. Initially, the narrator should not invent a style, but try to select a genre of which the other actors are likely to have some collective recognition (e.g. Chandler, Austen, Agatha Christie, Dickens, fairy stories for five-year-olds).

6. A narrator tells a story in such a way that the actors are encouraged to work in a particular way, this time not so much exploring a genre as carrying out a specific technique. For example, the narrator's agenda might be to encourage the actor/characters to use the space as dynamically as possible; or to play each scene with the maximum attack and rapidity; or possibly to play with intense thoughtfulness. Again, there is no discussion beforehand or specific instructions.

Note: These exercises demand a fair amount of sophistication and flexibility on the part of both the narrator and the group. Also, a reasonable knowledge of literary genres.

WORKSHOP 12: POSSIBLE RELATIONSHIPS BETWEEN NARRATORS AND CHARACTERS

A narrator remaining in one place to tell a story is always referring to the characters from a certain distance. But the possibility of moving around the stage opens up other forms of contact. Why would a narrator need to move? Presumably to assume a more intimate and involved relationship with the characters. Closer, the narrator can point out more nuances of their behaviour. By being in the same visual frame with the characters, the narrator, while remaining silent, can still reveal by gesture or expression an attitude to the characters while the latter are in action.

Now, if a narrator gets closer to the characters, there is the possibility of touching them or moving them around the space, even bringing them into contact with each other or moulding their bodies into positions that seem most appropriate at a particular moment. The narrator might possibly clothe them or place props in their hands (a technique used by the 'invisible' black-clad property men of the Kabuki Stage).

But a narrator can also touch and move a character in a very different way – a caring, supportive way. Let us imagine that a narrator, so affected by the plight of the characters, is moved to comfort them by holding them, embracing them, cradling them, supporting them physically. An exercise called Angels and Heroes deals with this idea:

Angels and Heroes

1. This is initially done in pairs, one actor assuming the function of Hero, the other that of Angel.

2. The Hero sets out on her mission. The actor should plan an initial scenario, for instance, to climb a mountain, to cross a swamp, losing resolve along the way, regaining confidence... and so forth. You might find it helpful to set up a range of objects around the rehearsal space, a sort of assault course, so that the Hero has some concrete obstacles to negotiate.

3. The Angel follows the Hero. Whenever he sees the opportunity, he takes care of the Hero by supporting her physically, holding her, soothing her, cooling her, warming her, calming her, encouraging her... whatever he feels that she needs at a particular moment. The Angel never speaks. The Hero can talk to herself or exclaim, if she feels the need.

4. The Hero does not solicit this support, in fact, she should be *totally unaware* of the Angel. The actor playing the Hero must accept whatever the Angel offers without comment and can enjoy what is given – the sense of comfort or support or warmth – but only for as long as it suits her.

5. For his part, the Angel must never make any decisions for the Hero, must never impose – only offer – and must allow the Hero to continue according to her own needs.

6. The two actors have to develop a sense of extreme delicacy and sensitivity towards each other: for example, the Hero should allow the Angel to hold her, but only for as long as she wants to be held; the Angel should allow the Hero to move on whenever she decides to do so.

Variations

7. This exercise can be played with an increasing number of Angels involved with one Hero.

8. Or with an Angel trying to take care of two Heroes.

9. Or with a band of Angels looking after a band of Heroes, without specific pairs being assigned.

10. A further variation could be the inclusion of a Villain or some sort of antagonist who would confront and challenge the Hero. Such conflicts can take the form of a scene rather than always remaining a purely physical confrontation. The Angel should be available to intervene, reassure, calm down, steady, prevent or support the Hero whenever necessary. Both Hero and

Villain should still be unaware of the Angel. You would need to establish conventions for the Villain; for example, should the Angel stand between the two, the Villain must accept the inability to get closer to the Hero. The Hero and Villain can speak, the Angel never.

11. Instead of developing scenarios in keeping with archetypes such as Heroes, Villains and Angels, the exercise could apply to contemporary, realistic situations. For instance, there could be a conflict between partners (business, marital or sexual) with each of the pair having an Angel of their own. But the rules would still pertain.

Note: Apart from its use to build the relationship between narrator and group, this is good work for the whole company to develop mutual sensitivity.

Character Awareness of Narrators

In this narrative mode, there's the assumption that the relationship is exclusively from the narrator to the characters and that the latter proceed with their lives unaware that their actions, behaviour and character are being described or commented upon. But there is also the possibility that the characters are aware of their narrator and react in various ways: possibly by contradicting the narrator's portrayal of them, by showing themselves in a different light or by seeking the narrator's advice as to what they should do next. If the narrator moves them physically, they could either acquiesce or resist. Again, I repeat, this work is always a matter of trial and error; there are few 'rules', but a lot of possibilities. The nature of the story and the text should keep the explorations within a relevant framework.

SET 4

WORKSHOPS FOR MULTIPLE THIRD-PERSON NARRATOR FROM INSIDE THE ACTION

13–20

With third-person narration from inside the action there is no outside narrator and all the actors are responsible for the narrative that concerns the characters they're playing. The characters narrate their own histories and talk about themselves as 'he' or 'she', while playing scenes as 'I'.

This is a purely theatrical conceit. The original text will give no indication of such an option; it will be written in the same convention as that dealt with in the previous set of workshops, from the point of view of an anonymous narrator telling the story from outside the action. It is only your – the adapter's – personal response to the form and content of a particular story that will decide on one mode of narration in preference to the other. Your choice may depend on whether you believe the story would benefit from a tight or spread focus, or on whether you want to hear one or several storytelling voices shaping the narrative.

Stories that might sway your decision in favour of multiple narration could be those that equally involve several main characters, or those that are multiplotted and heavily populated, or maybe stories written from several points of view, perhaps freewheeling comedies or picaresque adventures... The decision is yours.

Technically, third-person narration from within the action enables the entire company to make direct contact with the audience, offering the possibility of a variety of attitudes which could well be contradictory and, in consequence, interestingly unreliable. It is the most democratic form of narrative. And the most playful.

Note: To remind yourself of how to apply these two modes to a text (from inside or outside the action), *cross-refer to Section 6, Narrator to Narratee: the examples of both demonstrated in the excerpt from* Our Mutual Friend.

————

Having decided to use multiple third-person narration from within the action, you will next have to face a profusion of possibilities as to how the narrative should actually be performed. The initial and basic choice is whether actors narrate in character about their characters or as themselves about the characters they're about to embody. Until you become familiar with the principle, this may be somewhat confusing because of the innumerable degrees of characterisation possible along the spectrum between actors narrating as themselves and doing so totally in character.

So consider each option carefully.

1. The actors narrate as themselves, objectively, factually. This mode hardly varies from that of a third-person narrator from outside the action, except for the consciousness of the actors that they are talking about characters they'll eventually inhabit. They can narrate critically or empathically about their character, they can be amused by their character or remain non-committal...

2. They narrate as themselves *on behalf of their characters*, in the name of their characters, as it were, with a proprietary sense of the role that they're about to embody, which might suggest a stronger identification with the role than that in 1 above.

3. They narrate as themselves, but giving us glimpses, tasters, brief sketches of how they'll behave when fully in character and in action.

4. They narrate exclusively and fully in character.

5. They narrate simultaneously as actor *and* character, playing the character while at the same time critically commenting on the character. They present *and* represent the character, both objectively and subjectively, from outside and inside. This is not easily achieved. Actors need considerable practice to create this double effect, splitting the character in two, as it were, and then putting – and playing – the two halves together. Essentially, the actors perform with the physical and vocal properties of the character, showing you the character from the character's point of view, but the tone of the narration and manner of communication with the audience undercuts the self-evaluation to suggest that it may not be entirely reliable, if not downright inaccurate.[1]
    [*Cross-refer this Set 4, Workshop 14 below: Narrators Embodying their Characters while Commenting on Them*]

6. They narrate about their character, starting as themselves and ending as the character.

    a. They can make this transition imperceptibly, so for the audience there is no precise moment when the actor has taken over – or been taken over by – the character.

    b. They can make the transition abruptly, like a jump cut, at some appropriate point in the narrative.

---

1. This is not a million miles away from playing Chekhov, where the actor must represent the character from the character's point of view, honouring and expressing the character's genuine feelings of, say, unhappiness or unfulfilment, but at the same time playing in such a way that allows us to understand, more objectively, that many of the character's subjective feelings and choices of behaviour are foolish, insensitive and, at times, comic. The actor is creating a fully rounded, three-dimensional, contradictory and complex person.

They can, of course, reverse this process (from character to actor), most likely to occur when coming out of a scene back into narration. [*Cross-refer this Set 4, Workshop 13 below: Narrator Transforming into Character within Narration*]

7. When the text employs free indirect speech, the convention whereby the narrator becomes almost one with the character, taking on her thoughts, attitudes and feelings, even her speech, such as in the excerpt from *Emma*:

> Mr Knightley and Harriet Smith! – Such an elevation on her side! Such a debasement on his! It was horrible to Emma to think how it must sink him in the general opinion... Could it be? No; it was impossible. And yet it was far, far from impossible. – Was it a new circumstance for a man of first-rate abilities to be captivated by very inferior powers? Was it new for one, perhaps too busy to seek, to be the prize of a girl who would seek him?... Oh! Had she never brought Harriet forward!

– there is an interesting choice to be made as to which option to employ:

a. If the actor narrates as herself, she has the possibility of dealing with the text ironically or satirically, even parodying Emma;

b. or the opposite: empathising with her feelings of distress and confusion.

c. She can narrate the passage fully in character. This comes close to option 5 above by offering the best of both worlds; free indirect speech allows us into the character's head, whilst commenting on her.

d. Free indirect speech can also be converted into a first-person soliloquy to be played, of course, in character – another option!

Note: There is a difference between Free Indirect Speech and Indirect Speech. [*Cross-refer to Section 8: Converting Free Indirect Speech into Direct Speech & Set 4, Workshop 20: Indirect Speech Treated as Direct Speech*]

————

Each of these seven options creates a very different tone and attitude. You'll probably need to try out several of the choices before deciding which is the preferable approach for a particular story. It's possible that you could justify applying two or more of these options within the same story, but you'd have to ensure there was a consistency as to when each was applied.

The distinction between some of these options can be very delicate. Actors have to develop a sense of exactly to what point they're shifting along the continuum between their actual selves fully in the present and their characters fully in *their* reality.

Note: You should use texts for the workshops in this set. These exercises are not particularly easy; their demands are quite sophisticated and require accuracy of focus and execution. Give yourself time to absorb the instructions before you make use of them. Be sure you're clear about the purposes of whichever exercises you're trying. If you're applying these exercises in a workshop rather than a sustained project, you'll probably need time to ground yourself and the company in a little knowledge of your selected characters and situations before you embark. And the actors should learn their texts; working with scripts in their hands will be a hindrance. Take your time. And remember, you can always modify the instructions should this be more helpful for your own requirements.

WORKSHOP 13: NARRATORS TRANSFORMING FROM ACTOR TO CHARACTER WITHIN NARRATION

This transition from actor/narrator to character [*Number 6 in the list of options above*] is effected during a sustained piece of narration describing the character. How it's effected will make a particular impression on the audience. The choice should be in keeping with the nature of the story and its conventions as whole.

One way, demanding a lot of subtlety from the actor, is to make a gradual, imperceptible transition throughout the narration so that the audience is never quite sure exactly when the actor appears to have been replaced by some other person – the character. It can be disturbing, disorientating or seductive, luring the audience into the story almost without their awareness.

If, by contrast, the transition from actor to character is made abruptly, it can be comic, surprising, jarring. The narrator would need to decide at what point this would have its greatest effect. It might work well just at the completion of that piece of narration.

You might find that these techniques are most appropriate early in a story when the actors are likely to be describing their characters for the first time. This could be a useful way of introducing the audience to the storytelling convention. Or it might be a suitable technique for introducing each of the characters whenever they first appear in the story. All such choices depend on how you visualise the flow of the story and what you believe will enhance the particular impression you wish either to create or sustain whenever a character makes an entrance.

The process can, of course, be carried out in reverse, from character back to actor-narrator. Its emotional impact again depends on how and at what precise moment it's achieved. If the transition is abrupt, it can shake the audience out of their absorption in the story to a refreshed awareness that they are existing in the double reality of the theatre, a reminder of our complicity, our mutual agreement, to share in this act of imagination. Effected slowly and smoothly, the transition can provide a cooling-off period after a particularly intense episode. The smooth transition might work well as a character's final appearance in a story. If the writing allowed it, this might be a procedure for all the characters: a sort of character farewell/ensemble goodnight to the audience.

Here are two extracts describing the eponymous characters of *The First Arabian Night: The Loves of Kamar and Budur*:

> With every day that passed over him, Kamar al-Zeman increased in loveliness. All men were ravished by his charms; every breeze bore the tidings of his gracious favour. His eyelids were languorous as those of a gazelle; his eyebrows were arched like drawn bows. His back parts were bulkier than two sand heaps so that his waist complained of the weight it carried both behind – and before.

> Budur, than whom Allah hath made none fairer in her time, know that her hair is dark as the separation of friends; it falleth in rivers to her feet like a night without moon. Her complexion is as white as the day when lost friends meet; when she gazes towards the moon, two moons shine in one moment. Her breast, twin globes of ivory, is a seduction to all who see it. Her stomach hath gentle waves and creases like unto a folded scroll. Her navel is deep enough to hold one full ounce of ambergris. And all is based upon a hillock of blown sand which forces her to sit when she lief would stand. When she walketh away, her back parts are like unto mighty waves smiting one against another in a stormy sea. As for the centre and mystery of these delights, it is a petalled and vaulted haven for which words are inadequate.

1. Using these examples, or choosing some similarly sustained piece of narrative describing a character or a character's activities, instruct the actors, each in turn, to narrate to us, starting as themselves and ending fully in character. The transition should be seamless and imperceptible. [*For descriptions of other character to use, cross-refer in this Set, Workshop 14 just below:*

Sir Leicester Dedlock; and Section 9, Worlds, Character: Meg Bishop & John Beaver]

2. The actors, using the same material, now describe their character for us, but choosing what seems to them an appropriate moment in the narrative to shift sharply, in fact to jump, from narrating as themselves to narrating as their character.

3. Reverse the process. The actors start narrating in character and make a gradual transition back to narrating as themselves.

4. The actors start narrating in character but now make abrupt transitions back to themselves. They can choose at which point they wish to make the change.

5. Taking the same pieces of narration, allow the actors to move at will back and forth between their two personae during the narration.

6. The rest of the company describe and discuss what they have observed and the effect of the various processes. Consider the occasions on which each of them might be appropriate.

Note: Unless this exercise is used as part of a full rehearsal process in which a lot of other work has already been done, especially on character, I would recommend that, beforehand, some time is spent establishing a few simple choices for characterisation (inevitably superficial in the circumstances of a short workshop period), otherwise the actors will have no image to work towards, nothing specific into which they can transform themselves. I would suggest one basic physical and vocal change, a strong self-image, a specific energy and state of mind, all of which should be deliberately different from the actor's. Give the actors reasonable time to establish such choices. If practical, they could prepare them a day in advance. As this *is* an exercise, it's not critical for them to be too concerned with interpretive accuracy. However, the nature of the texts should suggest reasonably apposite choices. This note also applies to any exercise in which an actor/narrator is moving in and out of character, several of which are coming up.

WORKSHOP 14: NARRATORS EMBODYING THEIR CHARACTERS WHILE COMMENTING ON THEM

There are texts which both give an objective physical description of the character, at the same time delivering an implicit criticism. [*This is number 5 of the options listed at the beginning of this set for narrators describing their character*]

Here, slightly trimmed, is the portrait of a character from *Bleak House*, which not only describes his appearance but also expresses admiration for and criticism of his character in equal measure:

> Sir Leicester Dedlock is only a baronet, but there is no mightier baronet than he. His family is as old as the hills, and infinitely more respectable. He has a general opinion that the world might get on without hills, but would be done up without Dedlocks. He is a gentleman of strict conscience, disdainful of all littleness and meanness, and ready, on the shortest notice, to die any death you may please to mention rather than give occasion for the least impeachment of his integrity. He is an honourable, obstinate, truthful, high-minded, intensely prejudiced, perfectly unreasonable man.
>
> Sir Leicester is twenty years, full measure, older than my Lady. He will never see sixty-five again, nor perhaps sixty-six, nor yet sixty-seven. He has a twist of gout now and then, and walks a little stiffly. He is of a worthy presence, with his light grey hair and whiskers, his fine shirt-frill, his pure white waistcoat, and his blue coat with bright buttons always buttoned. He is ceremonious, stately, most polite on every occasion to my Lady. His gallantry, which has never changed since he courted her, is the one little touch of romantic fancy in him. Indeed, he married her for love. A whisper still goes about, that she had not even family; howbeit, Sir Leicester had so much family that perhaps he could dispense with any more.

Here, we want to try to embody the character physically and vocally, allowing the character to present himself in utter sincerity, while at the same time implying through the tone of the narration that he has his blind spots and is faintly ridiculous. This is something like pointing at yourself behind your own back! It means that the actor has to send out two messages at the same time – that the character must be taken seriously at his own self-evaluation and is indeed worthy of such consideration, but that he is quite blind to his less admirable traits. In this way you're giving the audience a rounded character of some complexity, rather than taking the easier option of turning him into a cliché or a caricature. The technique, like patting your head while rubbing your stomach, will probably take time to acquire.

The first two exercises below are designed to help you build up the material you need to fulfil Exercise 3.

1. Using the above text try narrating as *yourself*:

    i. with a very factual and balanced view of the character.

    ii. with a very warm attitude to the character whilst gently acknowledging his weaknesses.

    iii. with a very contemptuous, mocking attitude towards the character.

2. Now narrate in *character*, totally from the character's view of himself: formal, polite, authoritative, very sure of his status.

3. Narrate, as above, presenting him from his own point of view – which also means playing him vocally and physically in character, but *simultaneously* making it clear to us through the manner of the narration that he is very deluded about certain aspects of his character. *This variation is, of course, the focus of the workshop.*

4. Explore these variations using texts of your own choice.

WORKSHOP 15: ACTORS MOVING FROM NARRATION INTO SCENE

Equally important in giving meaning to a story is the *way* in which the actors move from narration into a scene. Usually, the purpose of the narrative is to lead the audience to the scene where a vital event will be enacted. Rarely will the narrative have more impact than the scene it precedes. This transition is often allowed to happen by default. But the journey from telling to doing is a major shift of energy, focus and reality and its manner of execution is part of the creation of a coherent and specific stage world. The most obvious change is of focus: from the audience to the other characters in the scene or, if moving from a scene back to narration, from the characters to the audience. This transition is, of course, affected by which option the performers have chosen for their narrative personae; whether they have to change from actor to character, character to actor or are always in character.

This is a slightly adapted excerpt from Thomas Hardy's *Jude the Obscure*. Jude has been tricked into marrying Arabella by her claim that she is pregnant.

JUDE	Jude felt their prospects as a newly married couple were not very brilliant. He, a stonemason's apprentice, nineteen years of age, was working for half-wages till he should be out of his time. His wife was absolutely useless in a town-lodging, where he had at first considered it would be necessary to live. But the urgent need of adding to income in ever so little a degree caused him to take a lonely roadside cottage that he might have the profit of a vegetable garden and utilise her past experiences by letting her keep a pig. But it was not the sort of life he had bargained for, and it was a long walk to and from Alfredston every day.
	So to the cottage he took her on the evening of the marriage. A little chill overspread him at her first unrobing. A long tail of her hair was deliberately unfastened, stroked out and hung upon the looking-glass which he had bought her.
	What – that wasn't your own?
ARABELLA	O no – it never is nowadays with the better class.
JUDE	Nonsense! Perhaps not in towns. But in the country it is supposed to be different. Besides, you've enough of your own, surely?
ARABELLA	Yes, enough as country notions go. But in towns the men expect more, and when I was barmaid in Aldbrickham –
JUDE	Barmaid at Aldbrickham?
ARABELLA	Well, not exactly barmaid – I used to draw the drink at a public-house there – just for a little time; that was all. Some people put me up to getting this, and I bought it just for a fancy. The more you have the better in Aldbrickham. Every lady of position

	wears false hair – the barber's assistant told me so.
JUDE	I don't like to see it.
ARABELLA	Lord, how countrified you are. Most men think otherwise.
JUDE	I don't care what most men think – if they do. How do you know?
ARABELLA	I was told when I was serving in the tap-room.
JUDE	I thought you always lived in your father's house.
ARABELLA	You ought to have seen I was a little more finished than that.
JUDE	Jude thought with a feeling of sickness that though this might be true to some extent, for all he knew, many unsophisticated girls would and did go to towns and remain there for years without losing their simplicity of life and embellishments. Others, alas, had an instinct towards artificiality in their very blood, and became adept in counterfeiting at the first glimpse of it. What had he done that he deserved to be caught in a trap that would cripple them both for the rest of a lifetime?

Use the above excerpt or take a text of your own choice containing narrative followed by a scene and further narrative, that involves the narrator/character with other characters. Assign roles accordingly. In each exercise, the scene should be played fully. The other actor(s) in the scene – in this case, the actor playing Arabella – should already be active in the scene ready for the narrator/character to enter it and should remain in it during the final section of narrative.

1. The narrator starts the narration out of character, objectively, very much in the here and now, but slowly makes a subtle and seamless journey into the there and then of the character. By the start of the scene the actor will have achieved a full transformation. The audience shouldn't be aware of the actual transition until it has been completed. At the end of the scene, he should reverse the process with the final section of narrative, slowly making the transition from character back to himself as actor.

2. The actor plays all the narrative out of character with as much objectivity as possible (as above), but changes sharply into character just before he enters the scene with total subjectivity. At the end of the scene, the actor should reverse the process, changing sharply from character to actor as he embarks on the final section of narrative.

Note: These first two exercises are extensions of *Exercises 1 & 2 respectively in Workshop 13 above.*

3. The actor plays the whole sequence totally in character, i.e. subjectively.

4. The actor plays the opening and closing pieces of narrative in character while simultaneously commenting on the character, sympathetic and critical at the same time. In the case of Jude, for example, the actor should sincerely express Jude's sense of betrayal and disillusionment but at the same time make sure we see his naivety. But he plays the scene fully in character without any 'comment'.

Note: This exercise is an extension *of Exercise 3 in Workshop 14, above.*

5. Evaluate the different impact of the four options. Focus particularly on the change of energy, rhythm, focus and intensity in moving into and out of a scene.

WORKSHOP 16: TRAMPOLINE WORDS

'Trampoline Words' is a technique to facilitate an actor's transition from narration into a scene (or back again). This is especially important if, during the narration, the action is building to a crescendo or if there is need for a clear change of dynamic between the two.

One of the ways for actors to build the required intensity as they move from one form to the other – storytellers are often required to leap into a scene at the peak of its action – is to use the final phrases of the narrative as an emotional run-up towards the scene with the last word or two acting as a trampoline or springboard to launch them into the dialogue at the necessary pitch.

The King was exceeding wrath with his son and in a voice towering with rage cried out,

> Woe to thee, thou son of adultery! How durst thou disobey me in this wise before my court! Hitherto none hath chastised thee,

and he commanded that he be imprisoned in an old tower wherein there was a dilapidated saloon and in its middle a ruined well.

In the first half of the above sentence from *The First Arabian Night: The Loves of Kamar and Budur*, the storyteller can, for example, start relatively calmly and build into the required degree of rage so that by the time he reaches 'cried out' he uses those words as a trampoline to hurtle into the scene.

The King was exceeding wrath with his son and in a
VOICE TOWERING WITH RAGE *CRIED OUT*:

> **WOE TO THEE, THOU SON OF ADULTERY! HOW DURST THOU DISOBEY ME ON THIS WISE BEFORE MY COURT! HITHERTO NONE HATH CHASTISED THEE...**

The principle can be applied to any form or direction of a transition between the two states. If there's a need to put the brakes on the narration, say, after an intense exchange of dialogue, the trampoline can accommodate that as well, with a gentle knee-flexing rather than a bounce. The run-up or run-down can be extended or shortened to accommodate all sorts of situations: comedy, surprise, shock... So in the second half of the above sentence a diminuendo can be achieved by the same principle, using 'and he commanded' as the trampoline.

> **HITHERTO, NONE HATH CHASTISED THEE'**

> ***AND HE COMMANDED* THAT HE BE IMPRISONED IN AN OLD TOWER** wherein there was a dilapidated saloon and in its middle a ruined well.

The trampoline words can also define the exact moment that the narrator's focus shifts from the audience to the other actors in the scene, or from the actors to the audience. That moment can also be taken by the those actors as their cue to start or end a scene, create a new image or change a locale. The precision this achieves effects the equivalent of a clean cinematic cut. [*Cross-refer Set 7, Subset 2, Workshops 39-40: Narrative Transitions for Flow and Continuity*] You could also think of Trampoline Words as a pivot between two states.

1. Use the above text and other passages of your own choice with different moods and energies and in which the narrative builds to a scene of dialogue.

2. Instruct the actors to explore building to the Trampoline Words that will launch them appropriately into a particular scene. It may be a violent take-off or a lively bounce or an easy lift… Explore the variety of emotional and attitudinal possibilities suggested by the material.

3. Choose passages of text that move from a scene back to narrative. Reverse the journey, allowing the Trampoline Words to accommodate the mood and tone of the transition. If the scene has been intense, the Trampoline Words may need to be no more than a mild bend of the knees to move into calmer narrative.

4. Make sure that the other actors in a scene are specific in shifting their energies appropriately in or out of a scene, in unison with the narrator whose tone and energy should affect their execution.

WORKSHOP 17: NARRATIVE AS DIALOGUE

If one of the main endeavours when adapting an existing story is to retain as much of its original language as possible, you will have to use your ingenuity in looking for ways to bring dramatically and theatrically alive a great deal of descriptive and observational narrative. One technique is to treat narrative as dialogue, exactly as it is written.

The audience is still hearing the narrative but they are simultaneously seeing it employed as dialogue in action. It's a very useful device for maintaining both the writer's words and the dramatic drive of a scene without interruption from any narrative comments that may be scattered throughout a scene. Too much flicking back and forth between narration and dialogue can be distracting and tedious, *unless* it's appropriately comic, or because the situation is erratic and the characters on edge. The contact is now, of course, between the actors rather than between actors and audience. It allows the partners in a scene to sustain their interaction.

To make the idea clearer, here is a variation and more extended version of the above exchange from *The First Arabian Night: The Loves of Kamar and Budur*. This first layout distinguishes between narrative and speech: the actors would conventionally narrate the former to the audience and play the latter to their partners in the scene:

KING   On a day of High Festival, when the audience hall was filled with the Grandees of his court, King Shahriman summoned his son and said

O son, I have sent for thee that I may lay a commandment upon thee that thou marry; for I am mindful to wed thee to a certain king's daughter...

PRINCE   When the prince heard this much from his royal sire, he was moved by youthful folly to reply,

For myself, I will never marry; as for thee, thou art great in age and small in wit! Hast though not already questioned me on this matter and heard my refusal? Indeed, thou dotest and are not fit to govern a flock of sheep.

So saying, Kamar-al-Zeman rolled up his sleeves, being in a fit of frenzy.

KING   The King was confounded before this great Assembly; but presently the majesty of Kingship took him and he cried out in a great rage,

PRINCE   so that his son trembled and his brow was spangled with sweat,

KING   Woe to thee, thou son of adultery! How durst thou answer me on this wise before my court! Hitherto none hath chastised thee,

and he commanded that he be imprisoned in an old tower wherein there was a dilapidated saloon and in its middle a ruined well...

The following layout treats both narrative and speech as dialogue and the actors play the entire text *to each other* as if it were one sustained scene:

KING   On a day of High Festival, when the audience hall was filled with the Grandees of his court, King Shahriman summoned his son and said, 'O son, I have send for thee that I may lay a commandment upon thee that thou marry; for I am mindful to wed thee to a certain king's daughter.'

PRINCE   When the prince heard this much from his royal sire, he was moved by youthful folly to reply, 'For

	myself, I will never marry; as for thee, thou art great in age and small in wit! Hast though not already questioned me on this matter and heard my refusal? Indeed, thou dotest and are not fit to govern a flock of sheep.' So saying, Kamar-al-Zeman rolled up his sleeves, being in a fit of frenzy.
KING	The King was confounded before this great Assembly, but presently the majesty of Kingship took him and he cried out in a great rage,
PRINCE	so that his son trembled and his brow was spangled with sweat,
KING	'Woe to thee, thou son of adultery! How durst thou answer me on this wise before my court! Hitherto none hath chastised thee', and he commanded that he be imprisoned in an old tower
PRINCE	wherein there was a dilapidated saloon and in its middle a ruined well.

To recapitulate: With this material, which contains descriptions of characters in action, direct speech and one line of indirect speech ('and he commanded that he be imprisoned in an old tower'), you have these four possible choices of how to perform it:

1. The two characters can narrate it *in its entirety* (including the direct speech) exclusively to the audience.

2. They can narrate the descriptions of the action to the audience and play the direct speech to each other. *This is the basic convention in this mode* (as in the first layout above).

    Note: This choice is dealt with in greater detail in *this Set 4: Workshop 18 following.*

3. A slight variation on 2: They can narrate the descriptions of action to the audience and play to each other the direct speech *and the one line of indirect speech now rewritten as dialogue*: 'And he commanded that he be imprisoned in an old tower' becomes 'Imprison him in the old tower!'

4. They can treat the whole sequence as dialogue, *exactly the way it was originally written* (as in the second layout above) and play all of it to each other as a complete and uninterrupted scene.

1. Using this scene or any other of your choice which has a combination of interwoven narrative, direct and indirect speech (preferably more than the one sample I've offered in the scene above), ask the requisite number of actors to carry out each of the four possibilities listed above.

2. After you've completed all four, discuss the different values and qualities that each option offers.

Note: Your focus in this workshop should finally be on *Variation 4: Treating the Text as Dialogue*.

Whether you choose to play text as narrative or dialogue will always be a matter of personal judgement: which choice best tells the story or makes a particular point at that moment. It's one way of dramatising narrative passages and, if appropriate, balancing the ratio between narrative and dialogue in a performance. There's no reason why both choices shouldn't be used within the same scene.

WORKSHOP 18: JUSTIFYING NARRATIVE INTERRUPTIONS DURING A SCENE

Occasionally a sequence of dialogue, a scene, is interspersed with narrative comments, usually quite brief, rather as in the scene above. Most often, the adaptation will have already removed some of these interruptions to the flow of the scene. Or, as described in the previous workshop, they might have been subsumed as dialogue. That, however, may not always be suitable. On the other hand, you may wish to retain such narrative interpolations for their possible irony, additional information, comic effect, or as a vital part of the plot. Or they may fulfil a private need of the narrator's... and so forth. In which case, you are using the basic convention for this narrative mode [*Choice 2 from the previous Workshop 17*].

The use of these narrative interpolations presents two technical problems:

A   How the other character/actors justify the 'disappearance' of the narrator/character from the scene and the pause in the flow of the action.

B   How narrator/characters negotiate their exits from and re-entrances into the scene.

A. Actors in a Scene Justifying Their Partner's Narration

When an actor/character turns to the audience with some narrative in the middle of a scene, there is a problem for the actors who remain in the scene: how are they to behave? What reality do they find themselves in? What they must *not* do is freeze or go dead while they wait for the 'narrator' to turn back into the scene. They must sustain some sort of stage life, depending on what conventions have been established. Here are some possible solutions.

1. These first options can be applied *whether the actor is narrating in or out of character*. The actors in the scene can sustain and develop the action they were playing while their partner turns to the audience so that they stay in the reality of the scene, ready to continue as soon as the narration has been completed and the narrator returns to the scene.

For example: if one of them was the last to speak before the interruption, they are probably awaiting a response to what they just said, in which case they can build their inner expectation of the narrator's eventual response.

If the last to speak was the actor about to narrate, the group can develop their reaction, ready to respond as soon as the narrator turns back into the scene.

In either case, they must realistically justify the length of the time it takes before they can resume the scene, usually by intensifying their inner state, by needing, maybe, to recover from the impact of what has happened up to that point, or to gather their thoughts, or to search for the right words, or to control their emotions...

In addition, they must always give themselves a reason why they think their partner has turned away from them. They might, for instance, interpret this behaviour as embarrassment or anger or grief or any emotion appropriate to the situation.

2. There's a second option that might be employed *when the actor narrates in character*. If a convention has been established that, even within scenes, all the characters are aware of the audience and are free to talk to them at any time during the performance, then it's perfectly acceptable for the partners left in the scene to listen quite openly to what their colleague is telling the audience and to react to it as part of the flow of their scene together.

If what is being narrated to the audience is something they mustn't or shouldn't know, then they must find some justifiable action to distract them until the narrator is back in the scene, such as the options in 1 above. Or they could try to eavesdrop on what that narrator is telling the audience, presumably as unobtrusively as possible!

3. There's a third option that might be employed *when the narrator narrates out of character, i.e. as the actor*. If an appropriate convention has been established, they can all come out of character, too and listen to the narrative as themselves, then,

together with the narrator, resume their characters when the narration ends and the scene is continued.

To cut to the chase: the group has either (1) to sustain the life of the scene as though it is not being interrupted, or (2 & 3) to make a transition into a reality that justifies their acknowledged awareness of the interruption.

B. Narrator/Characters Negotiating Their Exits from and Re-entrances into a Scene

Now we're looking at the other side of the coin: examining how the actors who shift between scene and narration make *their* transitions.

There are two basic requirements: their movement in and out of narration should never impede the flow of the story; and they must always make sure that they're in a space where they can make clear contact with the audience, which does not mean, however, always rushing down-centre.

If they're playing an extended scene periodically interrupted by brief comments to the audience, they need usually do no more than turn out to the audience while remaining in their current physical position in the scene; the less distance they travel, the better. If the cast happens to be physically intertwined, the narrator must, if necessary, find a way of thrusting a head through the tangle of bodies to contact the audience. (It's conceivable that narrators could narrate hanging upside down if that was where they happened to be at the critical moment.) If the narrators wish to confide information to the audience that the other characters must not hear [*see option A2 above*], they will, of course, want to get as far away from the others as is practical and deliver it as unobtrusively as possible. A lot will depend on the length of the narrative and its relative importance.

They will also need to effect their turning away from the scene in such a manner that makes dramatic, psychological sense for the actors remaining in the reality of the scene: they need a moment to regain their poise, for instance, or to control their annoyance or wipe their tears or restrain their laughter... Ideally, they should make a choice that's an aspect of their need to talk to the audience so that they don't lose logical and dramatic flow.

However, because of their instinctive concern not to hold up their partners in the scene any longer than necessary, narrators, when they do have short comments to make to the audience, have a tendency to rush what they're saying, snatching themselves away from their audience before the thought's been completed. Rather than fulfilling what they're meant to be doing at that moment, they're anticipating what they're about to do, which causes an unsatisfyingly blurred effect for the audience. Whatever the situation, however brief the comment – maybe no more than a single word – the narrator has to stay calm and, as it were, catch the audience's eye, state whatever has to be stated, allow another beat to ensure the audience has received it

– and only then turn back into the scene. This sequences need take no more than a matter of seconds. The responsibility lies with the actors in the scene to keep the pause alive, as suggested in A above.

Note: In fact, any narration, whatever its length, should have these three components:

1. Narrators first make sure they have the audience's full attention.

2. They then deliver their narration.

3. When the narration ends, they remain with the audience for a brief beat sufficient to cement what they've said, to make it clear they've finished, even to share a possible response. Only then can the next part of the story take place.

Note: There may be more than one character narrating during a scene.

The following extract is from *The Nibelungenlied*. You'll need a bit of back-story.

Gunther, King of Burgundy, is married to Brunhild, an Icelandic princess. His sister Kriemhild has married Siegfried, King of the Netherlands. Siegfried has been instrumental in Gunther's successful wooing of Brunhild. She had been renowned for her great strength and had made a condition that she would only marry the man who could beat her in throwing a javelin and hurling a rock. Siegfried, by means of a cloak of invisibility and his legendary strength (greater than hers – and Gunther's), substituted himself for Gunther (don't ask how!) and subdued Brunhild, both on the field of sport and in the bridal chamber. In a fit of exuberance he unwisely stole a gold ring from her finger and a girdle from her waist as trophies of his secret triumph. He has even more unwisely given them to his wife, Kriemhild, who has put two and two together. Some years later, this couple makes a state visit to Burgundy. Queen Brunhild is disturbed by the familiarity between the two men as she believes Siegfried should behave as befits a vassal towards her husband, King Gunther. Between the two Queens there is intense rivalry concerning status.

> BOTH   The two mighty Queens met at the doors of the
>   cathedral. And their thoughts were on two
>   splendid knights.
>
> KRIEMHILD   Said fair Kriemhild,
>
>   My husband, mighty Siegfried, is of such
>   merit that he might rule over all the
>   kingdoms of this region.

BRUNHILD   Answered Queen Brunhild,

What can you mean? That hardly seems
likely while my lord, King Gunther, is
alive.

KRIEMHILD   See with what splendour he stands out
from the other knights, like a moon against
the stars. It is not for nothing that I am so
happy.

BRUNHILD   However splendid your husband may be,
you must nevertheless rate him lower than
your noble brother, my lord Gunther. He
takes precedent over all other kings.

KRIEMHILD   Believe me, Brunhild, my husband is of
such worth, he is fully Gunther's equal.

BRUNHILD   I did not speak without cause, Kriemhild.
When I saw them together for the first
time, I heard Siegfried himself say that he
was Gunther's vassal, and so I consider
him to be my liegeman.

KRIEMHILD   How could my noble brother have married
me off to a liegeman? It would be a sad
thing for me if that were so. If you care for
me, do not repeat such things.

BRUNHILD   Why should I renounce my claim to a
liegeman who owes us service?

KRIEMHILD   At this lovely Kriemhild lost her temper.

You will have to renounce your claim to
him. He ranks above my noble brother,
Gunther.

BRUNHILD   You are getting above yourself. I should
like to see whether you are held in such
esteem as I.

Brunhild was growing very angry.

KRIEMHILD   We shall very soon see! Witness whether I
dare enter the cathedral before the Queen
of the land. You will have visible proof this

day that I am a free noblewoman and that my husband is a better man than yours. I claim to be of higher station than was ever heard of any queen that wore a crown. You will see how your 'liegewoman' will walk in state in Burgundy.

BOTH And now indeed fierce hate grew up between these ladies.

BRUNHILD If you deny you are a vassal, you and your ladies must withdraw from my suit when I enter the cathedral.

KRIEMHILD We certainly shall. Now, my maidens, we shall make Brunhild eat her words.

Thereupon, Queen Kriemhild made to enter the cathedral.

BRUNHILD The Lady of the Land, prompted by great malice, harshly ordered Kriemhild to halt.

A vassal may not enter before a Queen!

KRIEMHILD It would have been better for you had you held your tongue. You have brought dishonour on your own pretty head. How could a vassal's whore ever wed a king?

BRUNHILD Whom are you calling whore?

KRIEMHILD I call you one. My dear husband, Siegfried, was the first to enjoy your lovely body, since it was not my brother that took your maidenhead.

BRUNHILD I shall tell Gunther of this.

KRIEMHILD What is that to me? Your arrogance has got the better of you. I can no longer keep your secrets.

BRUNHILD Brunhild began to weep

KRIEMHILD and Kriemhild delayed no more but once more made to enter the cathedral before Gunther's Queen.

BRUNHILD | Halt, liegewoman! Halt! Your remarks have offended me deeply.

KRIEMHILD | You would do better not to stand in my way.

BRUNHILD | You declared me to be a whore – now prove it!

KRIEMHILD | I prove it with this gold ring on my finger which my sweetheart brought me when he first slept with you.

BRUNHILD | Never had Brunhild known a day so fraught with pain.

This noble ring was stolen from me! But now I shall get to the bottom of this affair and discover who took it.

BOTH | The two ladies were now very agitated.

KRIEMHILD | You shall not make me the thief! If you cared for your honour it would have been wise for you to hold your tongue. As a proof that I am not lying, see this girdle which I have round me – you shared Siegfried's bed!

BRUNHILD | Brunhild burst into tears when she saw it. She was resolved that Gunter should hear of this.

Call the Lord of Burgundy here instantly. I want him to know how his sister has insulted me; for she openly declares me to be Siegfried's whore.

GUNTHER | The King found his wife in tears. He said, very tenderly,

Dear lady, has anyone distressed you?

BRUNHILD | I have cause to be distressed. Your sister means to rob me of my honour. She has said for all to hear that her husband made me his whore.

GUNTHER | She would have acted very ill if she had.

BRUNHILD   She is wearing the girdle that I lost and my ring of red gold. I shall regret the day I was born unless you clear me of this monstrous infamy.

GUNTHER   Ask Siegfried to appear. He must either admit that he made this boast or deny it.

SIEGFRIED   And Kriemhild's husband was summoned at once. He had no idea what was amiss.

               Why are these ladies weeping? Why has the king sent for me?

GUNTHER   I deeply regret this necessity, but my lady Brunhild tells me some tale of your having boasted you were the first to enjoy her lovely person – so my sister, your wife, lady Kriemhild, avers.

SIEGFRIED   Then Siegfried the Strong spoke,

               If she said this, she will regret it before I have finished with her. I am willing in the presence of all your vassals to rebut with my most solemn oath that I ever said this to her.

GUNTHER   If the oath you offer is duly sworn here I shall clear you of all treason.

SIEGFRIED   Brave Siegfried raised his hand to swear.

GUNTHER   But the mighty King said

               Your great innocence is so well known to me that I acquit you of my sister's allegations and accept that you are not guilty of the deed.

SIEGFRIED   If my wife were to go unpunished for having distressed Brunhild, I should be extremely sorry, I assure you.

BOTH KINGS The two mighty knights exchanged glances.

SIEGFRIED   Women should be trained to avoid irresponsible chatter. Forbid your wife to indulge in it, and I shall do the same with mine. I am truly ashamed of her unseemly behaviour.

KRIEMHILD   The comely Kriemhild departed in silence.

BRUNHILD   Brunhild was so dejected that all could not but pity her.

In this sequence, there should be crowds of liegemen and maidens belonging to both camps. So use as many actors as you have to create the scene. I would suggest that the two Kings are also present throughout the scene. (They could, for their own very good reasons, be keeping low profiles, not wishing to be embroiled in their wives' quarrel until summoned to do so.) This way, everyone will be dealing with the same problems.

1. Use this text or a scene of your own choosing, one that's liberally sprinkled with narrative. Cast the roles.

2. The acting group try out, in turn, the three options in A above; and the narrators try out the technicalities detailed in B for handling narration during a scene. Obviously, it is necessary for the choices of both to be coordinated. For example: if the narrator drops character to narrate as the actor, then the group can apply option 3.

3. Whoever is running the session should decide the order in which the options are explored. And should also decide whether the same actors should play the main roles in all the variations or whether to recast each new version.

4. For the purposes of this workshop, all the narration must be played directly to the audience.

5. Make sure the actors are very specific about exploring and experiencing the differences in their execution of each variation.

6. Although all the actors will probably have been involved in the exercises, it's worth discussing the quality and impact of each option. Possibly there will be other people watching who can describe what effect each variation had on them.

Note: It's important that the actors know *exactly* what reality they're in at every moment of performance. You cannot be too detailed or precise enough in the choices you make. If you allow sloppy thinking and insufficient rigour in establishing conventions, actors and audience end up with a dissatisfying sequence of endless stops and starts, the actors, out of sync with one another, applying arbitrary and inconsistent transitions with the consequent loss of flow, clarity and reality for the audience.

Note: These *Workshops 15-18* offer starting points and basic techniques for making transitions from narration into scene and scene to narration. These transitions are dealt with in additional details further on [*Cross-refer Set 7, Subset 2, Workshop 39: Narrative Transitions for Flow and Continuity; & Workshop 40: Pitch and Tone for Third-Person Narrator Outside the Action Setting up Scenes*]

WORKSHOP 19: PHYSICAL LIFE ACCOMPANYING NARRATION

This deals with various options for the sort of physical expression that might accompany narration describing the behaviour or activity of a character. It applies to first-person narrators as well as third-person narrators within the action [*Cross-refer Section 8: Doubling the Information; and Set 2, Workshop 8: Gesture*]:

1.   Narrating an activity without executing the activity.

2.   Narrating the activity and at the same time literally carrying out that activity – in effect, illustrating or in effect doubling what they are narrating.

3.   Narrating the activity while performing some other – possibly analogous – activity, i.e. layering the experience.

4.   Narrating the activity and in some way physicalising their attitude to it or feelings about it, without actually enacting it.

5.   Carrying out the activity whilst narrating something else.

In the following extract from *Bleak House* in the third person from inside the action, Lady Dedlock has just learned that a shameful secret concerning her has been uncovered and that she is also falsely implicated in a murder.

So! All is broken down. Her name is in these many mouths, her husband knows his wrongs, her shame will be published – may be spreading while she thinks about it – and in addition to the thunderbolt so long foreseen by her, so unforeseen by him, she is denounced by an invisible accuser as the murderess of her enemy.

Her enemy he was, and she has often, often, often, wished him dead. Her enemy he is, even in his grave. This dreadful accusation comes upon her, like a new torment in his lifeless hand. She has thrown herself upon the floor, and lies with her hair all wildly scattered, and her face buried in the cushions of a couch. She rises up, hurries to and fro, flings herself down again, and rocks and moans. The horror that is upon her is unutterable. The complication of her shame, her dread, remorse, and misery, overwhelms her, and even her self-reliance is whirled away like a leaf before a mighty storm.

She veils and dresses quickly, leaves all her jewels and money, listens, goes downstairs at a moment when the hall is empty, opens and shuts the great door, flutters away, in the shrill frosty wind.

The following, in the first person, is also an extract from *Bleak House*, in which Esther Summerson, after a serious illness – presumably smallpox – looks in the mirror for the first time since her recovery.

My hair had not been cut off, though it had been in danger more than once. It was long and thick. I let it down, and shook it out, and went up to the glass upon the dressing-table. There was a little muslin curtain drawn across it. I drew it back; and stood for a moment looking through such a veil of my own hair, that I could see nothing else. Then I put my hair aside, and looked at the reflection in the mirror, encouraged by seeing how placidly it looked at me. I was very much changed – O very, very much. At first, my face was so strange to me, that I put my hands before it and started back. Very soon it became more familiar, and then I knew the extent of the alteration in it better than I had done at first. I had never been a beauty, and had never thought myself one; but I had been very different from this. It was all gone now. Heaven was so good to me, that I could let it go with a few not bitter tears, and I could stand there arranging my hair for the night.

1. The actor narrates, using either of these excerpts, sitting or standing, but without any physicalisation or use of gesture.

2. She narrates, illustrating for us – acting out precisely, literally – all the actions that she describes.

3. She narrates, carrying out any activity other than what she is describing: in the first piece possibly putting on outer clothing – a cloak, hat and scarf – or sipping a glass of water; in the second, maybe preparing herself for bed or carrying out some domestic chore such as folding clothes or doing some embroidery.

4. She narrates but this time physicalising her emotional response to what she is experiencing, especially by commenting or responding, but not by illustrating. [*Cross-refer Set 2, Workshop 8: Gesture*]

5. She narrates these compressed versions of the extracts while fulfilling *all* the actions described in the full extracts, but which have now been omitted (but are gathered in parentheses below the compressed extracts for reference):

i. So! All is broken down. Her name is in these many mouths, her husband knows his wrongs, her shame will be published – may be spreading while she thinks about it – and in addition to the thunderbolt so long foreseen by her, so unforeseen by him, she is denounced by an invisible accuser as the murderess of her enemy. Her enemy he was, and she has often, often, often, wished him dead. Her enemy he is, even in his grave. This dreadful accusation comes upon her, like a new torment in his lifeless hand.

    The complication of her shame, her dread, remorse, and misery, overwhelms her, and even her self-reliance is whirled away like a leaf before a mighty storm. She leaves all her jewels and money, goes downstairs at a moment when the hall is empty, flutters away, in the shrill frosty wind.

The actions omitted from the above compressed excerpt:

   'She has thrown herself upon the floor, and lies with her hair all wildly scattered, and her face buried in the cushions of a couch. She rises up, hurries to and fro, flings herself down again, and rocks and moans.' 'She veils and dresses quickly', 'listens', 'opens and shuts the great door'.

ii. My hair had not been cut off, though it had been in danger more than once. It was long and thick.

    I went up to the glass upon the dressing-table. There was a little muslin curtain drawn across it. I was very much changed – O very, very much. At first my face was strange to me. Very soon it became more familiar, and then I knew the extent of the alteration in it better than I had done at first. I had never been a beauty, and had never thought myself one; but I had been very different from this. It was all gone now.

The actions omitted from the above compressed excerpt:

   'I let it down, and shook it out', 'I drew it back; and stood for a moment looking through such a veil of my own hair, that I could see nothing else. Then I put my hair aside, and looked at the reflection in the mirror, encouraged by seeing how placidly it looked at me', 'I put my hands before it and started back', 'with a few not bitter tears, I could stand there arranging my hair for the night'.

6. Discuss these five different possibilities and what advantages or particular qualities they offer.

7. Try the same sequence of exercises with similar narrative material of your own choice.

Note: *Exercise 5* is a way of compressing the text without losing its details: that is, replacing descriptions of action by the action itself while narrating other parts of the text. [*Cross-refer Section 8: Doubling the Information*]

WORKSHOP 20: INDIRECT SPEECH AS DIRECT SPEECH

There are occasions when a character's speech is indirect, as for instance 'he said *that* he thought such-and-such…', rather than 'I think such-and-such…', and the implied dialogue remains in the third person rather than changing to the first person. In this example from *Emma*, Mr Weston and his wife have been entertaining a party of several friends for the evening, including Emma, her father, her sister, brother-in-law and Mr Elton. When it becomes time for them to leave, they discover it's snowing.

a. MR WESTON   Mr Weston, with a triumph of a different sort, was confessing that he had known it to be snowing some time, but had not said a word, lest it should make Mr Woodhouse uncomfortable and be an excuse for his hurrying away. As to there being any quantity of snow fallen or likely to fall to impede their return, that was a mere joke; he was afraid they would find no difficulty. He himself wished the road might be impassable that he might be able to keep them all at Randalls and with the utmost goodwill was sure that accommodation might be found for everybody, calling on his wife to agree with him that, with a little contrivance, everybody might be lodged,

MRS WESTON which she hardly knew how to do from the
            consciousness of there being but two spare rooms in the
            house.

If you decided that it would be preferable to reduce the amount of narrative at this
moment in the story, most of this can be converted into direct speech:

bi.   MR WESTON   Mr Weston, with a triumph of a different sort, was
            confessing,

            I've known it to be snowing some time but I said
            not a word lest it should make Mr Woodhouse
            uncomfortable and be an excuse for his hurrying
            away. As to there being any quantity of snow
            fallen or likely to fall to impede your return, that's
            a mere joke; I'm afraid you'll find no difficulty. I
            myself wish the road might be impassable that I
            might be able to keep you all at Randalls and with
            the utmost goodwill am sure that accommodation
            may be found for everybody,

            calling on his wife to agree with him.

            With a little contrivance, everybody might be
            lodged,

MRS WESTON Which she hardly knew how to do from the
            consciousness of there being but two spare rooms.

Or, more colloquially:

bii.   MR WESTON   Mr Weston, with a triumph of a different sort,
            confessed,

            It's been snowing for some time, but I didn't say
            a word lest it make Mr Woodhouse
            uncomfortable and be an excuse for his hurrying
            away. As to there being any quantity of snow or
            likely to be, that's a mere joke; I'm afraid you'll
            find no difficulty. Myself, I wish the road were
            impassable so that I might keep you all at
            Randalls. With the utmost goodwill I'm sure that
            accommodation can be found for everybody. (To
            his wife) You agree with me, don't you? With a
            little contrivance everybody can be lodged,

MRS WESTON Which she hardly knew how to do from the
            consciousness of there being but two spare rooms.

With this excerpt, which contains description of character, action and indirect speech, you have various options:

1. You can narrate it in its entirety, as in the original: (a) totally to the audience; or spoken to the audience while physically relating to the other characters; or sharing the narrative between the audience and the characters.

2. You can narrate to the audience those phrases of the passage which contain narrative and adjust the indirect speech to become direct speech (bi and ii), i.e. conversation with the other characters.

3. You can treat the narrative as if all of it, narrative and indirect speech, were dialogue. In this case, it would all be played, exactly as it is written (a), entirely to the other characters and none of it to the audience. [*Cross-refer This Set, Workshop 17: Narrative as Dialogue*]

The choice you make will, in part, be dictated by how important the need is to be in direct contact with the audience at that juncture; whether it's useful to be in greater complicity with them concerning parts of the text; whether there has been too long a gap since someone last talked to them. Other considerations might be the preference to keep a scene playing unbroken for as long as is practical to sustain the psychology and logic of the situation; or to avoid making the other characters sustain the reality of a scene longer than might be convincing during chunks of narration. The overall tone of a story, whether it is treated playfully or with more weight, will also influence your decisions about these conventions.

Take this excerpt or one with a similar block of indirect speech. Assign the text to an actor (in this case, to two: Mr and Mrs Weston – although she only has one line of narrative) and let the group represent the non-speaking characters involved in the situation. The same two actors can play the text for all four versions. Or, should you prefer, a different pair can take each one.

1. The two actors play the text in its original version (a), almost entirely to the audience, though remaining amongst the other characters and relating to them socially, spatially and physically. Occasionally, the Westons might nod or send a word or two in their direction. In this version, while Mr and Mrs Weston talk to the audience, the other characters' justify there unawareness of this fact. [*Cross-refer this Set 4, Workshop 18 above*]

2. Two actors again play the full text (a), but totally to the audience, away from and without any sort of spatial or physical relationship to the rest of the characters who, again, have to find their way of justifying their ignorance of the fact and – this time around – the physical absence of the Westons from their

midst. The two narrators can refer to the other characters (e.g. point them out from a distance, as it were) for the audience's benefit, if they find that helpful.

As a suggestion, the group in versions 1 and 2 can occupy themselves with fetching coats, cloaks, scarves, gloves, bonnets and hats, wrapping themselves up, surveying the snow and considering whether or not they should travel home. In version 1 they could move around the Westons and involve them in their activities, such as handing them garments while they're engaged in narrating to the audience. In version 2, their activities would act as a background to the narration of the Westons. A possibility: Mrs Weston could be totally involved with her guests until called upon by her husband for her opinion about accommodating their guests. [*Cross-refer this Set 4, Workshop 18 above*]

3. Two actors play the text a third time, using version (bi) or (bii). This time they give only the narrative to the audience and the rest, the indirect speech now converted to direct speech, to the other characters.

4. Two actors, again using the original version (a), play it *entirely* to the other characters as though the narrative and the indirect speech were dialogue, directing none of it to the audience. [*Cross-refer this Set 4, Workshop 17 above*]

Discuss what differences, what qualities and advantages these four versions revealed, and how they might affect the impact of the story.

Note: These exercises incorporate, as noted, some of the earlier workshop techniques in this set.

SET 5

WORKSHOPS FOR FIRST-PERSON NARRATION

21–23

Stories written from the perspective of a first-person narrator, from 'I', present a much less complicated starting point than those in the two previous modes. There is no ambiguity about the narrator's identity. Whether narrating or playing in a scene, 'I' am always fully in character. Where this form of narration does offer options is in the stance from which narrators tell their stories.

They may recall their stories with the benefit of time and distance, possibly able to look back on what happened with more objectivity or with the irony of hindsight, certainly in a different emotional state from the one in which they first experienced it. Or they might relive it, indeed experience it, as if for the first time. Between the extremes of 'objective' recall and 'subjective' reliving there is a broad spectrum of states to explore. The text itself will not necessarily indicate what state that might be. This is more likely to be a dramatic rather than a literary choice. The narrator may be unreliable, remembering inaccurately or slanting events to put them in a more favourable light.

The challenge of first-person transitions between narration and scene is to find out what sort and degree of emotional shift is required. This will include an adjustment of objectives away from the audience to the other characters in the scene. Trampoline Words can certainly be applied in this mode. [*Cross-refer Set 4, Workshop 16*]

First-person narrators may not necessarily be telling their own story but relating the story of someone they know or knew, have observed or only heard of, in which case they may also function as a commentator or as someone trying to piece together the evidence to try to make sense of the story. But, whatever the circumstance, there must always be a strong reason for wanting to tell the story.

Note: Preferably, you should use texts for this set of workshops.

WORKSHOP 21: RECALLING

This is to explore the experience of the characters looking back on events from some distance of time, possibly re-evaluating themselves and the people they were involved with at the time.

Here is another excerpt from *Bleak House*. It is Esther's birthday. She has just been told by her godmother that her mother was her disgrace and she is her mother's, that she is different from other children and set apart.

> I went up to my room, and crept to bed, and laid my doll's cheek against mine wet with tears; and holding that solitary friend upon my bosom, cried myself to sleep. I knew that I had brought no joy, at any time, to anybody's heart, and that I was to no one upon earth what Dolly was to me.

1. The actor relates the above excerpt very much remaining in the present recalling the past in several ways:

i. Wanting to share with her hearers the bitterness she feels towards her godmother's treatment of a very young, naive girl.

ii. Wanting to express a sympathetic humour towards her former naive and vulnerable self.

iii. Wanting to remain as factual and as objective as possible, despite being touched by this childhood memory.

2. The actor tries as many other ways of recalling this excerpt as you find useful.

3. Take some suitable material of your own explore, asking the actors to recall the memories in as many ways as you find useful.

WORKSHOP 22: RELIVING

This is to explore the experience of being plunged back into the past and living an event again – as if it were happening to you for the first time.

1. Using the same excerpt from *Bleak House*, the actor relates the episode, reliving it exactly as she experienced it, trying out several different possibilities:

   i. the utter panic and confusion she experienced.

   ii. how totally alone she felt, without anyone to comfort or support her.

   iii. her perception of herself as unloved and unlovable.

2. Try as many other ways of reliving this excerpt as you find useful.

3. Take some material of your own and explore the reliving of that in as many ways as you wish.

4. Using whatever material you've chosen or the excerpt above, the actor explores *both* reliving and recalling the experience, moving to and fro within the same piece of narration as and when one of the options seems more apt.

WORKSHOP 23: THE GROUP IN RELATION TO THE FIRST-PERSON NARRATOR

Because, in first-person narration, the story is the personal (often secret, private) property of the storyteller, the group of actors who support its telling are very much constrained by the subjective viewpoint of the narrator. The story is being told exclusively through the perception of the first-person storyteller, therefore the group, especially in improvised pieces, cannot elaborate beyond what the narrator has established, though, of course, they *can* embellish what the narrator *has* established.

The movement from narration to scene will probably require somewhat different methods of transition from those for third-person narratives. There are two fundamental shifts: one in which the narrator moves to the scene, the other in which the scene moves to the narrator. That is, either the group physically sets up the characters and environment of a scene into which the narrator is drawn; or the narrator stays *in situ* while the group forms the scene around the storyteller. The choice very much depends on whether the incident or scene is recalled or relived and on the intensity or tone of the narration.

In the case of reliving an experience, either the emotional strength of the telling can draw the other characters in the scene to surround the narrator; or the power of the scenic image, embodied by the group, can pull the narrator back into the scene. If trying to resist an unhappy memory, the narrator might appear to be dragged or sucked back into it by force or the scene might descend remorselessly to trap her; if the re-experiencing is of a happy circumstance, the narrator may run to join it or be joyfully surrounded by it.

In the case of an incident recalled with irony, curiosity or possibly amazement that this actually did happen, a narrator might move in and around the scene, simultaneously an active participant and a sceptical observer surveying this memory. It's possible, that if the role were split between one person actually experiencing events and another recounting them, narrators could watch themselves in action.[1]

Unless some other convention has been established, the default 'rule' for the group should be that their characters are actually bought into existence by the power or nature of the narration. They materialise from the narrated memories of the first-person storyteller.

The reverse transitions, from scene back to narrative, require exactly the same considerations. Does the narrator flee from the scene or leave it regretfully, or thoughtfully, or with relief? Or does the group creating the scene dissolve, leaving the narrator where she is? Or do they stay where they are, retaining the final image of the scene while the narrator moves on to another part of the story. But, unless otherwise stipulated, the group should dematerialise as soon as they no longer linger in the storyteller's consciousness.

---

1. In Shared Experience's production of *The Mill on the Floss*, directed by Nancy Meckler and Polly Teale, the role of Maggie Tulliver was shared between three actresses playing her at different stages of her life, and able both to observe and relate to one another.

Here is an edited excerpt from *Bleak House*. It precedes and leads into the
previous excerpt:

ESTHER   It was my birthday. Dinner was over, and my
                godmother and I were sitting at the table before
                the fire. The clock ticked, the fire clicked; not
                another sound had been heard in the room, or in
                the house, for I don't know how long. I happened
                to look up from my stitching at my godmother,
                and I saw in her face, looking gloomily at me, 'It
                would have been far better, little Esther, that you
                had had no birthday, that you had never been
                born!' I broke out crying and sobbing, and I said:

                          O, dear godmother, tell me, pray do tell
                          me, did Mama die on my birthday?

GODMOTHER   No. Ask me no more, child.

ESTHER   O, pray do tell me something of her. Do
                now, at last, dear godmother, if you please!
                What did I do to her? How did I lose her?
                Why am I so different from other children,
                and why is it my fault, dear godmother?
                No, no, no, don't go away. O, speak to me!

GODMOTHER   Let me go! Your mother, Esther, is your
                disgrace, and you were hers. The time will
                come – and soon enough – when you will
                understand this better, and will feel it too,
                as no one save a woman can. Unfortunate
                girl, orphaned and degraded from the first
                of these evil anniversaries, pray daily that
                the sins of others be not visited upon your
                head. Forget your mother and leave all
                other people to forget her. You are
                different from other children, Esther,
                because you were not born, like them, in
                common sinfulness and wrath. You are set
                apart. Submission, self-denial, diligent
                work, are the preparations for a life begun
                with such a shadow on it. Now, go!

ESTHER   I went up to my room, and crept to bed, and laid
                my doll's cheek against mine wet with tears; and

> holding that solitary friend upon my bosom, cried
> myself to sleep. I knew that I had brought no joy,
> at any time, to anybody's heart, and that I was to
> no one upon earth what Dolly was to me.

Using the above excerpt, the two actors involved try different approaches to moving from narration into a scene and back to narration. Ensure that there is a flow between the two states. The point of the exercise is to effect an appropriate transition. This demands a commitment on the part of the actor playing Esther to establish a clear tone and attitude, and a sensitivity on the part of the actor playing her godmother in establishing the scene in a way appropriate to the narration, sensing how and when to break the image of the scene when Esther returns to her narration.

Start with the simplest, most available choices and then, developing confidence, try more nuanced or challenging options. Don't, when using these excerpts, constrain yourself by the way you think they ought to be played. Remember, you are using this material in order to discover techniques. (Obviously, the choices you make should have some emotional logic with the scene. But that still leaves plenty of room for interpretive freedom.)

1. Explore the transitions in 'recalling' mode. Do this several times, each one with Esther looking back on the scene with a different attitude. [*Cross-refer Set 4, Workshop 21*]

2. Explore the transitions in 'reliving' mode. Do this several times, each one with the narrator playing Esther imagining different ways in which she might have originally experienced this scene. [*Cross-refer Set 4, Workshop 22 for suggestions*]

3. Repeat the same exercises with the two actors exchanging roles.

Note: You may need to consider the deployment of furniture (e.g. two chairs, possibly, in the excerpt above), whether it is already in position or needs to be moved during a transition. This means clear decisions as to how and where Esther begins her narration. Is she already seated or does her godmother set up the scene for her? And so forth.

4. Explore the same processes, using material of your own choice, possibly with more characters in the scene. [*Cross-refer Set 6, Subset 1, Workshop 25 Give & Take: D. Leader & Chorus, particularly, may prove useful for the exercises in this Workshop*]

Note: I stress again: all these suggestions in Sets 3, 4 and 5 are just examples of many possibilities waiting to be discovered. They are indications of *ways of thinking* about moving between sections of narrative and scenes.

SET 6

WORKSHOPS FOR BUILDING AN ENSEMBLE

24–36

As I write this, the ensemble as a theatrical ideal doesn't quite have the currency it once did. We still pay lip service to its virtues *in absentia*, and on the rare visit of a company, such as the Maly Drama Theatre from St Petersburg, we're quick to attribute the rich fruits of its work to an ensemble ethos. Reviewers often make loose with the word to describe productions with large casts, though their only discernible ensemble skill is managing not to bump into each other. We talk about a group of actors working together. But that would be true of almost any theatre production. (They *have* been known to exist, but it's the rare production in which the actors deliberately set out to work *against* each other.) So what do we really mean or anticipate when we talk about an ensemble?

Somebody starting a relatively simple job, say in an office, will need several days to learn the basic ropes – exactly what their specific job entails, office routines and etiquette, company policy, hierarchy, functions and personalities of co-workers – and will be taught much of this by the others already there. This is a routine rite of passage that most people cope with. But imagine the situation if most or all of the people in an office were starting their jobs on the same day. There'd undoubtedly be considerable confusion, time wasted and mistakes made. Inevitably they'd come up against procedures that hadn't been sorted out, continuously running to catch up only to find they were going backwards.

This is the reality for the majority of theatre productions. A collection of individuals, most of whom don't know each other or have never worked together, varying in experience and skill and sharing no common language or training, have somehow, within a month or so, to come together in a coherent production. It's dependent on the bonhomie of the actors, their willingness to muck in, and the ability of the director as to how many of these obstacles are overcome. They usually get by on series of prescribed rituals like the first readthrough, some sort of process of staging, discussions of how a scene should be played, maybe the occasional theatre anecdote, even some sessions of physical warm-ups as well as some sociable warm-downs ('Coming for a...?' accompanied by a twist of the wrist and a nod of the head in the direction of the nearest pub). But most of the time they're desperately trying to understand each other's values, processes, words and frames of references, as well as sensing where the power lies and working out the rules of interpersonal conduct required of them this time around. By the first performance, they've somehow managed to pull together something acceptable but are probably far from performing at the peak of their powers. In consequence, the average production seems constructed of single ply, proceeding along a thin and narrow linear surface. The

veneer may be glossy, but underneath there's little of the texture, depth and resonance that come from multi-plied exploration. The difference is like that between
a solo melodic line, played more or less in key, and a melodic line supported by layers of harmonic and contrapuntal orchestration with all its rich complexity of
rhythms, instrumental colours and thematic variations.

When I watch such performances I'm aware of how I, for a good many years, would
start the first day of rehearsals with an enthusiastic announcement to the company
of all the wonderful things we were going to explore over the next three or four
weeks, only to realise, as I sat watching the dress rehearsal, that I'd touched not one
of them. It had taken us all our time and effort to achieve even the first basic level
of communication. And of course, in show after show, with different casts but the
same limit of time, the identical pattern occurred – always going back to square one,
unable to break out of this Groundhog Day nightmare-cum-farce. I only wrenched
free of this when I managed to work with the same actors over much longer periods.

The simplest aim of an ensemble is to do just that: with each successive project, to
move on from where it left off, so that there is less and less need to repeat what's
already been established and the performers are liberated to advance with what they
currently know into areas of increasing challenge, elusive, complex and rarely
touched on within the usual conditions of work. The building of an ensemble
requires time, continuity, the willingness to explore and the acceptance of failure
as part of the search. Then the performers can gradually open themselves up to
deeper, less familiar areas of experience and expression. A growing common language means less need to talk – we don't have to keep translating each other – and
that's always a good thing.

An ensemble consists of talented individuals transformed into a creative body with
shared values, skills and a vision enriched by ever-growing experience. The ulti-
mate goal is not at all, as some actors suspect, the subjugation of the individual to
the collective will (or the director's ego); quite the contrary. The group should be
enhancing and promoting the skills of the individuals within it. The performers are
developing an understanding of each other, a rapport that raises both their group
and individual game: mutual talents stimulating each other to greater achievement,
a generosity that opens up possibilities that each alone might never have discovered. The energy of a group focused on a shared goal generates an instinctive urge,
singly and en masse, to reach further, higher, deeper... In a true ensemble, actors
assert their talent and individuality neither at the expense of – nor in spite of – the
others, but *because* of the others.

The fruits of true ensemble work are seen in its fluidity, coherence, detail and
complexity; the space vibrates simultaneously at many levels of experience so that it's
hard to absorb them all at one viewing. You feel taken over by the performance, not
in the way that, say, a great musical can excite an audience, exhilarating as that may
be, but by the way it releases experiences broader and deeper than those of sensation

and sensationalism. The performers have accumulated – and continue to accumulate – layers of skill and understanding so that, just by their presence, each one conveys a depth and texture far removed from the thinness of the single ply I've mentioned. These skills should inspire a recognition in the audience of our shared empathy, our human potential to communicate at all levels of body, thought and feeling. I believe these high claims are justified for a medium whose raw material (live actors, live audiences, live characters) makes it the most human of all the art forms.

SUBSET 1: PHYSICAL AWARENESS

The first of this set of workshops is to encourage physical work with particular stress on group imagination. The way to ensemble playing seems best approached through the body. The body, after all, is what contains all our experience. Our thoughts and memories and feelings are not disembodied abstractions wafting about in the ether. They are deeply enmeshed in our tissue. Working physically with others also has the incidental but not insignificant benefit of helping to overcome inhibitions about personal contact. Being in close contact with others is one of the conditions of being an actor. But at times it can cause difficulties, particularly early in an actor's career when there may still be areas of reserve, with the misinterpretation, at times, of intimacy as an invasion of privacy. Touch covers most aspects of human experience: comfort, support, protection, friendship, guidance, affection, empathy, play, work, reassurance, confrontation, competition, forgiveness, love… as well as sex and violence. And as theatre rarely deals with casual acquaintanceships, physical contact with other people is hardly avoidable. There have been periods of theatre governed by rules of decorum and restraint, but that's hardly our reality now. In order for actors to develop ensemble skills, they have to develop mutual trust and respect. And then they have to leave their inhibitions behind.

Working together physically, actors learn the possibilities and limitations of each individual colleague, such as weight, flexibility, stamina and strength, and can accordingly adjust how they relate technically on a one-to-one basis. Also, by recognising and then letting go of those formerly unconscious areas of resistance that they, like all of us, have been accruing over the years, they become more available to respond creatively to the imaginative choices of their partners. This awareness of others and concern for what they're doing eliminates actors' preoccupation with self, that tendency which, intentional or not, results in a sort of performance self-ishness at the furthest point of the spectrum from good ensemble practice. An actor has to learn that generously sharing one's energy, focus and imagination with others and generously accepting theirs in return doesn't destroy one's identity or one's creativity: it only strengthens them.

Collective physical work yields surprises. The group finds itself executing work with unexpected dexterity and imagination. Each of these exercises is to develop sensitivity towards others and to learn the pleasures of really working together.

WORKSHOP 24: MIRROR EXERCISES

Most actors are familiar with some sort of mirror exercise, but it's an excellent starting point in the development of mutual awareness, as well as a quite a lot of self-knowledge. This sequence starts with pairs and eventually involves the whole company.

A. Two Actors

1. The company pairs off. Each of the pair face one another.

2. The first stage: in advance, they decide who of the pair will initiate movement and who will reflect it.

3. Initiators must never try to trick their reflector, but to move in a logical and sequential way that can be followed. It won't be helpful to move your right hand, for example, and then without any connection, suddenly wiggle your left foot. Consequently the movement, to start with, tends to be slow and sustained rather than sudden and quick. Eventually, increased subtlety and awareness should allow for something sharper – just so long as it comes out of a physically logical sequence of impulses.

4. Reflectors must try to recreate exactly what is initiated and never to elaborate or do their version of what they see. Instead of merely trying to copy the external movements of their partners, *they should try to become one with them* by also reproducing their energy and mood.

5. Reflectors should take care not to get focused exclusively on that part of the body that is obviously in motion. They must take in the whole person. Every movement, however slight, causes repercussive adjustments in the rest of the body.

6. Initiators should know exactly what they are doing with their body, how they are moving. However, an accurately observed reflection may reveal something about their body that they're unaware of. So dealt with seriously, this sequence of exercises can be self-correcting.

7. The second stage: after a reasonable time, say seven minutes, the pair should reverse roles.

8. The third stage: neither takes the initiative. Both participants are responsible for allowing movement to happen. This requires a great deal of patience, generosity and sensitivity. Eventually, it should be difficult – virtually impossible – to tell which of them was the initiator. We are gently entering a stage where we start to 'read' others more deeply, beyond their obvious actions. *The aim of the exercise is for two to become one.*

Note. There can be a tendency for some actors to work from their heads rather than their eyes, so that if the initiator moves a right arm, the reflector will move a right arm too. Remind them they are looking into a mirror and the initiator's left is the reflector's right and vice versa. Directors may have to do some side coaching: Remember, it's a mirror!

B. Four Actors

1. Two actors, side by side, face two other actors, also (obviously) side by side. They are looking in the same mirror which can be as wide as they wish.

2. The actors side by side must always be in some sort of physical contact. Have them go through the same three stages again. Each actor now has two people to be aware of: the one they are mirroring and the other with whom they are in some actual connection.

3. If they haven't eventually taken the initiative themselves, you can point out that there is no reason for them to stay on the same spot but to move sideways within the mirror, whose width can be unlimited.

4. You can also point out – if necessary – that they can see what the partner on their side of the mirror is doing by watching that partner's reflection.

C. The Whole Company

1. You can build this exercise, adding another pair of actors at a time. But the final session is to have all the actors, divided into two, on opposite sides of a very wide mirror than contains them all.

2. You proceed through the three stages asking them to be in physical contact, first with one, then with two, then three, four, five others on their side of the mirror.

3. If they still aren't being enterprising, encourage them to move sideways along the width of the mirror. They can also move closer to or further away from the mirror.

4. Continue to build the number in physical contact until every actor is in some sort of physical contact with as many people as possible on their side of the mirror. As the numbers mount, the actors will have to use their ingenuity as to how they connect. It's just about possible for eight people to be in physical contact.

6. They are likely to – in fact, they will – get into inextricable tangles. By now they should have begun to sense the limits of what they can impose on their partners in terms of physical positions. If someone is clearly trapped in an uncomfortable position or likely to be pulled off-balance, the others must find a way to adjust. Because they have their reflection to look at, they can more easily see what they need to do to extricate themselves from possible knots.

7. By the end of this exercise, the company will have come into very close contact with most of the others in the group. But concentration on making the exercise work usually eliminates any self-consciousness. The company at times end up laughing at the ridiculous knots they've tied themselves into. More often, they create something surprisingly beautiful and ingenious. With time, the actors should become more fluent and accurate in their mirroring. When the exercise is working well, a sense of well-being often manifests itself as a whole company moves as one. An ensemble!

8. If you repeat this sequence, it would be sensible to make sure that people are working in different pairings.

Note: Initially, you should pair actors who are roughly the same height and shape. Later, you should pair people with totally different body shapes. Then there has to be a sensitivity and awareness by initiators that what is possible for their bodies may not be appropriate for their reflections. By the same token, the reflectors have to judge how literal they can be in mirroring their partners and analysing what part of the movement is its essence and what is its intention.

WORKSHOP 25: GIVE AND TAKE EXERCISES

These exercises are a development of the previous sequence and could be called Moving Mirror Exercises. I was shown them by a former member of The Open Theater, an American group highly influential in the 1960s and '70s, who originally devised them. Over time I've developed them for my own use so that they may no longer correspond exactly to what I was first taught. *This sequence is conducted with absolutely no talking.*

A. Moving Mirrors

1. The company stands in a circle, evenly spaced and accurately circular!

2. An actor comes into the centre of the circle, moving in a *repeated* rhythmical pattern. Instruct them that any actor can start the sequence. (Directors, don't ever make the selection – allow time for someone in the group to take the initiative.) Initiators must decide exactly how they are going to move before they actually start to do so. This ensures that what they present to the others is absolutely clear.

3. They move around the inside of the circle, always executing exactly the repeated pattern of movement – maybe using some of this time to refine what they are doing – until they choose someone to whom they decide to give it.

4. They approach that person and place themselves in front of them as in the mirror exercise, but always moving in their pattern.

5. The chosen person, the taker, begins to mirror the offered movement.

6. The purpose of the taker is not merely to copy or mirror or imitate, *but to become one with the giver.* So, should the giver's choices express some level of feeling, that must be mirrored too. It's never just a matter of reflecting the external movement of the giver, but also matching the level of energy and intensity in its execution. Recognising the inner state can often simplify the physical mirroring.

7. Takers don't have to copy the whole pattern and rhythm at one go. They should absorb it, detail by detail, maybe just starting with the rhythm, then the larger shifts of the body, gradually adding the increasingly smaller details until they achieve the whole pattern. This exchange should take as long as is necessary. Initially, actors, out of nervousness and embarrassment, have a tendency to rush to get it over with. On the other hand, it should never be allowed to drag on indulgently.

8. The exchange lasts until the taker is mirroring the giver to the latter's satisfaction. If the taker is inaccurate, the giver must find a way to indicate the inaccuracy while continuing to execute the movement pattern. Similarly, should the giver appear satisfied with the taker's mirroring and prepare to end the exchange, not noticing that the taker does not yet feel ready to do so, the latter must communicate this to the giver while continuing to acquire the movement.

9. Once they are working together, the two participants should spend some time in this state. Even more profoundly than in the simpler mirror exercises, they can arrive at a sense of complete harmony in which they both feel and appear to be functioning as one. When this happens, a sensation of wholeness, a sort of vibration or hum, seems to permeate the entire space and affect everyone present. *This is the purpose and ideal of the whole exchange.*

10. When the exchange has been completed to the satisfaction of both parties, they then change places. The giver moves into the taker's space in the circumference of the circle, continuing the movement for the time it takes to arrive in the vacated place, while the taker moves out into the middle of the circle, still executing the *same* movement.

11. The taker continues the movement in the middle of the circle until ready to create an entirely new personal pattern of movement and rhythm. This transition must be done in 'one'. That means, the taker cannot slowly let it evolve from the previous movement or work it out while developing it. The taker has to visualise it while still moving in the old pattern. And only when the taker feels ready, should the transition be instantly effected. The new pattern of movement should have no connection whatever with the previous one. The taker now becomes a giver, presenting a totally new energy and experience.

12. Once takers have made the transition to giver, they move around the inside of the circle giving themselves time to ensure they know what they are about to offer.

13. Then the new giver approaches another actor on the circumference of the circle and the exchange begins again.

14. This process continues until everyone in the circle has experienced it at least once.

Note: It's important that the others in the circle not involved in an exchange should try to mirror what is being done; not physicalising it fully, but marking it lightly, sensing its inner impulses, rhythm and the degree of energy. This will increase their own flexibility when they eventually do the exercise. It also keeps the company fully involved in the exercise.

B. Moving Mirror with Sound

The giver creates a rhythmically patterned sound to accompany the movement. The sound should be created vocally, but percussive use of the body can be added. And of course, this sound becomes part of the exchange. The exercise follows precisely the sequence described above (in A).

Note: If you feel the company is capable of this, you could make this the start of the whole sequence, eliminating the need for A.

C. Moving Mirror and Sound with a Theme

The session can next be conducted with a theme, so that, in some manner, each person's pattern of sound and movement will express that theme. The theme, of course, is stated before the sequence begins. The theme can range from the abstract (joy, thoughtfulness, the threat of war) to the concrete (bubbles, mud, shoes, a tree) and something inbetween (the end of the day, autumn, waking up). The response to the theme (and therefore the execution) can range from the literal to the metaphorical. This is a useful way to begin exploring any subject matter connected with the material you are working on (with *Bleak House*, for instance, I might start with the very broad topic of neglect). At this stage, you're not yet likely to derive anything of practical application, but it does get the company's bodies, thoughts and feelings beginning to focus on themes and subjects that you will eventually be embodying in the production.

Note: If you're devising, it's a very healthy approach towards the development of material.

D. Leader and Chorus

This sequence should, ideally, follow on immediately after C. It also works with a theme – in fact, it needs a theme.

1. The circle disbands. The whole space is now available.

2. Either select the leader (or giver) or let someone volunteer.

3. Taking a theme or topic (possibly one of those you have already used in the previous sequence C), instruct the leader to explore it.

4. Leaders no longer have to create a rhythmical and patterned movement, but can move freely and expressively in the space in any way appropriate to their feelings about the theme. Leaders should allow physical expression to emerge logically, allowing themselves to experience a natural flow of thoughts and feelings on the subject. They move through a range of experiences that

are totally fulfilled and absolutely *not* intellectually calculated. They do not have to relate to the rest of the group. The leaders' only obligations are to ensure that they're visible and audible to the others and to behave with clarity and the aforesaid physical, mental and emotional logic. Their behaviour and exploration can be realistic or heightened.

5. The rest of the group no longer have to mirror exactly what the leader is doing. Their mission is to try *to become one with the leader*, trying to identify with what the leader is experiencing, and moving *similarly* to the leader but in their *own* way. So, for example, if the leader happens to keep close to the walls, it would clearly be inappropriate for any of the group to remain in the middle of the space, but how they related to the walls would be open to personal variation. Or if the leader were working on the floor, it would be inappropriate to remain standing.

6. If the leader's behaviour is externally clear and internally logical, it is not unusual for the group almost to anticipate how it will develop. At times, the collective flow is seamless as the entire company literally moves as a single unit in the space, still maintaining their individuality within their experience of the leader's choices. (Should the leader, while exploring a theme, feel the need to relate to one or more of the others, that would mean that the rest of the group should and could relate similarly to one another.)

7. Leaders explore a theme for as long as they sustain the impulse to do so. They should allow the theme to move wherever it seems to want to go and to flow with it rather than trying to control or dominate it.

8. When leaders feel they have exhausted the theme (or themselves), they pass the leadership on to another person in the group. This is accomplished by gently placing a hand on that person's shoulder. It doesn't need to be seen by the rest of the group. In fact, it is quite revealing to observe how the group senses that there's a new focus even if they don't literally see the changeover.

9. New leaders don't drop what they're currently doing, but allow their own exploration of the theme to emerge slowly from what they're currently experiencing of the previous leader's explorations at the moment of changeover. This ensures there's a smooth transition from one leader to the next.

10. The exercise continues as before. Everyone should have the opportunity to become the leader.

11. In this sequence, the exploration of theme becomes much more specific, detailed and useful in its eventual contribution to the development of material, either to support an existing text or to a devised piece.

12. This is an effective way of the forming a group into a chorus within a relatively brief period. The simple instruction, *to become one with the leader*, ensures this. They all retain their individuality while being part of a whole.

Note: This Give and Take sequence of exercises needs time.

Note: Twelve actors in a circle is probably a comfortable maximum.

Note: When introducing Give and Take, try to work through all the sequences within two sessions. If you have limited time, you can, as I've already indicated, start the process with B.

These two Mirror sequences have many purposes:

As a warm-up or part of a warm-up session.

As a means of the company getting to know each other on a one-to-one basis: learning each other's natural energy levels, physical tendencies, cultural influences, areas of confidence, areas of avoidance and particular skills, such as coordination, sense of rhythm or imaginative use of the body...

As an opportunity for the director or whoever is guiding the session to observe the way in which each actor functions.

As a way of learning what it really means to give and take; a generous desire to share and a willingness to accept.

As a means of learning when it's appropriate to lead, to initiate, to take over; and when to follow, to give in, to let go of one's ego, to support. Because of the structure of the exercise, everyone has to experience both states. So there is no chance either of exploiting or avoiding the challenge.

As a means of recognising individual habits and patterns and therefore of breaking them. Some people always apply the same sort of movement, the same rhythm, the same sort of vocal qualities. These may be merely a matter of thoughtlessly staying in their own comfort zone; they may be indications of certain areas of inhibition (not releasing the voice loudly for fear of losing control). Once the actors grow more familiar with one another, they can offer a movement to partners for whom they know its particular pattern will challenge them to break out of the mould in which they seem trapped; not just physical patterns, but of energy, tempo, rhythm and mood.

As a means, therefore, of each person extending their physical, rhythmic and vocal repertoire.

As a means of gradually learning to feel or understand what it is like to be somebody else.

As a means of discovering their own playfulness, imagination and inventiveness.

As a means of developing coordination. As the company become confident within the exercises, they can execute increasingly complex patterns of movement and sound.

As a means of developing material if devising and of exploring material if working from a text.

As a means of creating imagery.

As a means of building an ensemble, imperceptibly, naturally and organically, without any need to draw attention to the fact or self-consciously imposing the concept on the company.

WORKSHOP 26: CONTACT EXERCISES

These exercises are also about actors moving and working together physically, but they focus on the use of space as well, and can develop improvised choreography.

1. The actors move around the space, initially without interaction. Give the actors the following sorts of instructions, varying the order:

> Turn (stipulate whether this is 90° or 180°)
> Stop (freeze but sustain the intention to move forward)
> Continue (start walking again)
> Floor (lie fully supine)
> Up (stand up)
> Kneel (stipulate whether on one or both knees)
> Backwards (walk)
> Run, etc.

…Invent instructions of your own…

2. You no longer give the instructions. Let the actors move in the space using the above movements on their own, i.e. each individually deciding when and what to execute.

3. Give instructions again, this time adding some that require interaction such as:

> Touch (in any way with any part of the body; the touch should be soft, pliable and giving).
> Resist (touch again but this time as resistance, i.e. pushing against each other).
> Lift (part or all of a colleague's body; lift no more than you are safely able to).
> Lay down (lay someone on the floor).
> Raise (raise someone off the floor).

Don't neglect the original instructions in 1. This sequence is accumulative.

4. Allow the actors to execute the same processes on their own, without your instructions, but deciding individually when and what they choose to do. They will soon be executing complicated group interactions.

5. Add instructions concerning the use of space and patterns of movement:

> Curves (only move on curves)
> Straight Lines (only move in straight lines)
> Corners (only move within corners)
> Periphery (keep to the edges of the space)

6. You could also add instructions concerning props and portable objects such as chairs:

> Sit
> Straddle
> Move (the chair)
> Seat (someone)
> Raise (someone from the chair)
> Pass (the book)
> Read (the book while walking)

7. Add music. The actors move freely, making their own choices at will. This will create a framework in which the physical work is influenced by personal response to the music.

Things to consider:

Create any other shared physicality that suits your needs. You can stipulate very specific instructions such as touch without hands.

Mix the instructions from all the lists.

The actors may find that at times they are working in clusters, rather than pairs. This is excellent.

Make sure actors do not reject or refuse other actors offers or approaches.

Note: Do not allow these sequences to become hand-dominated. Keep encouraging the actors to use every part of their body, especially with instructions like touch and resist.

Contact work encourages:

An ease in physical contact between performers.
The realisation that there an infinitude of unforeseen ways in
     which bodies can be creatively joined.
Physical imagination.
The use of the whole body, especially those parts that tend to get
     neglected or ignored in routine work.
The use of space.

WORKSHOP 27: BALL GAMES

This sequence of games played well is an analogy for good acting practice.

A. The Basic Game

1. The company stands in a circle. Let's say there are fifteen actors. They number off in sequence, one to fifteen. The actors should check who are the actors on either side of them with the higher and lower number than theirs. Fifteen is between fourteen and one.

2. Hand a (tennis) ball to the actor who is One. Instruct the actors to run freely in the space. While running, they are to throw the ball to each other in sequence (One, Two, Three) calling out the next number just before they throw it: One calling 'Two!' Two calling 'Three!' onwards to Fifteen calling 'One!', One calling 'Two!' again and on through Fourteen calling 'Fifteen!' and Fifteen calling 'One!'…

3. The actors run in any direction at a comfortable speed and throw the ball as instructed. When you decide they've done enough well enough (not dropping the ball too often), bring them to a halt.

4. Ask them what the exercise is for.

These are some points you might make, should they not have exhibited their awareness of them while playing, nor included them in answers to your question:

The purpose of the exercise is collaboration, cooperation.

Throwers should not try to fool or trick or in any way make it difficult for their catchers to get the ball.

They should throw the ball intending it to be caught.

Both thrower and catcher are responsible for the ball being caught.

They should not call the number and throw at the same time; they should call to make sure they have their catcher's attention, then throw. *This should take no more than an additional half-second!*

The thrower should not have to waste time looking around the space to find the catcher.

The catchers should anticipate and arrive in their throwers' view just before they call.

The rest of the company should make sure they keep out of the way when they're not engaged in an exchange.

Everyone must keep running all the time, but running easily, not forcing their energy or stamina.

They should not get into patterns, but run freely in all directions, using the whole available space.

They must ensure they don't collide with anyone else.

Their aim should be to keep the ball constantly in the air; no dropping allowed!

They should call and throw in a regular rhythm.

They should aspire to become an absolutely smooth, rhythmical ball-throwing 'machine', without gaps or pauses or slowing down.

Inevitably there will be one or two people who are convinced they're no good at catching and will panic every time a ball comes in their direction, inevitably letting it drop. Be patient and encouraging. You should, from time to time, make the general point that throwers must always throw to the ability of their catchers. Later on, as they develop their skills in this sequence of games, encourage them all to feel good about themselves and the way they are moving in the space (love yourselves in the space!).

B. Variations

1. They carry out the game exactly as before, but with one exception: this time they can count downwards as well as up, but still always in sequence: 'One', 'Two', 'Three', 'Two', 'One', 'Fifteen', 'Fourteen', 'Thirteen', 'Fourteen', 'Fifteen', 'One', 'Two'…

After they've played for a while, the point to draw to their attention this time, if they haven't caught on to it, is that as soon as they've thrown the ball, they should not rush away (as they've probably been doing in the previous session) but should stay put; the ball might be thrown directly back to them. For every throw there are now two potential catchers – one of them the previous thrower – who should be ready and in view of the thrower in case their number is called.

2. They play the game exactly as in B1, but this time, they don't call by numbers; they keep the same sequences, but now they *call each other by name*.

3. They play, as before, but this time, *there is no calling at all*, neither of number or name. In fact, they play in silence. But always in sequence, upwards and downwards.

At the end of this sequence, ask them what changed with the three approaches. They *should* reply that each variation made the playing easier: calling by name was more personal, intimate, so their reaction was that much quicker; the silent version was the smoothest because, without words, they *had to* make real contact. They could no longer assume, as with calling a number or name, they would get a response. This made them more present, more immediate and that much more connected to their partners.

4. They play again, as in B1, calling numbers again, in sequence in both directions. As they run around the room, hand additional tennis balls to free-handed actors as they pass by you. Introduce maybe four extra balls the first time you do this. So now there will be several sequences of calling carrying on simultaneously.

The points to make this time:

> First of all, to stay calm.
>
> Throwers and catchers will have to adjust their rhythms; some numbers are likely to be called twice or more at the same time.
>
> They have to find their way to keep the game moving and still get the balls caught and thrown appropriately.

You can gradually increase the number of balls in play. There could be fifteen balls in action; you might even try to have more balls in play than there are players. The actors become very skilful at catching and throwing two balls at a time.

5. Play as B4 with several balls, but you can now use the options of calling by name or silence.

6. At some point, you can instruct them – in the middle of a game – to forget about sequences. They are free to throw to anyone. So depending on what sort of calling has been set up, they might call numbers at random, names at random, or throw in silence, which mean they all have to be literally and metaphorically on their toes.

7. Play any variation you wish. But this time, instruct them to challenge their partners by throwing the ball harder or from a greater distance or that much faster. The intention must still be to ensure that between them they keep the balls in the air. The actors will still have to judge the catching capability of anyone they're about to throw to and adjust their throwing accordingly.

A company of actors can, in a short space of time, become amazingly skilful at handling several balls.

C. More Elaborate Variations

1. Instruct the actors to pass the ball to their partners, not only by throwing directly but by any means they can invent. They can move between different partners; there is no sequence and no calling.

Give them time to discover some of the possibilities for themselves (it's a good way to observe how imaginative and daring each actor can be). But you might need to offer some suggestions: bouncing the ball off the wall or off the floor, rolling it – maybe with the nose, passing it from mouth to mouth, or neck to neck, kicking it, heading it…

In this variation, running may not always be possible but it should remain the default state. And there'll be no longer any sense of a company working together with a collective objective. Each pair will be playing at a different rhythm and speed depending on their particular means of getting the ball to their partner.

Note: This variation has a completely different structure from any of the others.

2. Return to the previous structure. They now play the game in any of the combinations or variations you choose (except C1 above), but this time, you provide them with a given circumstance or preoccupation. For example:

They're fed up to the teeth with working together and find each other irritating.

They adore working together.

They're tired after a heavy week.

They've had wonderful offers of acting work.

They're worried about their futures.

They're bored stiff playing ball games.

They've just fallen in love with someone not part of the group.

They know that they're playing the game beautifully and feel good about themselves, individually and collectively.

…and so forth; invent whatever you think useful.

Give them a moment to absorb the given circumstance; then instruct them to start playing.

They must maintain the given circumstance through the game. They must also allow it to affect their behaviour. *But* make it clear that, whatever their reaction to the circumstance, they must still stick to the rules of the game: that is, they *must* collaborate in ensuring the balls stay in the air (even if their given circumstance is that they all loathe each other!). This will require a lot of concentration and imagination on their parts.

When you feel they have really explored the given circumstance within the 'rules' of the game, bring them to a halt. You can now point out to them that they have been 'acting':

Throwing and catching the ball is their *action*.

Collaborating to keep the balls in the air and to maintain this perfect ball-throwing machine is their *objective*.

The given circumstances are their *points of concentration*.

Pairs are developing *relationships*.

Note: Working in silence instead of words emphasises the point that, when they use text, they should never assume that simply by speaking they are automatically making contact with their partners, that the words will do the work for them.

This sequence of ball games seems open to endless variations, so don't hesitate to create any of your own that might support the needs of your own projects or productions.

I've never known a company of actors not to become enthusiastic about these ball games. If you carry out some versions of them daily – as part of a warm-up – their skills in coordination, cooperation and initiative develop rapidly, often to an impressive degree. They build up stamina and physical dexterity and learn to deploy themselves well in space. You could, should you have the time, every so often keep a session going for a good hour. Most important, these games are another powerful but totally unhectoring contribution to the transformation of a company into an ensemble.

WORKSHOP 28: MASSAGE

Often on a Saturday morning, at the end of a hard week's work, I would suggest that the company pair off and give each other a massage. This proved immensely popular, a sort of warm-down for the weekend. The rehearsal room would take on a soothingly peaceful atmosphere. After a while, I started to see that this had considerable possibilities of development and could be connected with the previous exercises (Mirror, Give and Take, Contact).

A. Massage Plus

1. The company divides into pairs. If there is an odd number in the group, create a threesome.

2. One of the pair relaxes supine on the floor. The other, the giver, works firmly but sensitively through the taker's body, preferably starting at the head by releasing the neck. At some point, should both wish, the taker can turn over and let the masseur work on the back.

3. There should be no conversation, but takers can certainly indicate any part of their bodies that requires special attention. Also, if a giver in any way causes discomfort, the taker can signal that fact to their masseur.

4. Once the massage has been completed (say, after fifteen minutes) the giver explores moving the taker in any way that is possible, taking into account the use of weight, balance, strength and flexibility. Takers make themselves totally available, never resisting, initiating or deliberately helping, apart from keeping

---

themselves as light as possible. (This is achieved quite literally, by thinking 'light', imagining oneself airborne and freed from gravity.) It is often a revelation to observe the ingenuity with which a giver finds way to move a taker. Any part of the giver's body (not just the hands and arms) can be used to effect movement. Givers should never use force or strain either on themselves or their partners. They should only work within what is possible for them. They should be discouraged from feeling the need to show off their strength.

5. When the giver has explored as much as seems possible or desirable, half the sequence is over and both relax side by side for a couple of minutes. Whoever is running the session may have to time the various changeovers.

6. Then the roles are reversed, giver becomes taker and vice versa. The taker, when ready to move into giver mode, should get up very slowly. After having remained totally relaxed for a half-hour, it's necessary for the body to take time to adjust to initiating movement.

7. They complete the sequence in their reversed roles.

B. Moving Together

1. At the end of the above sequence, the pair should again be lying side by side. As a development, their objective now is to find any way they can of moving together. Neither takes the initiative. The roles of giver and taker no longer apply. (This is not dissimilar to the third stage of the basic Mirror Exercise.)

2. One way of starting is for them to breathe in unison so that they become rhythmically in tune.

3. Slowly, the pair find ways of moving together, gently and lightly to start with. Eventually, they can find themselves executing the most sophisticated and beautiful movement. As with the give-and-take exercises, they begin to function as one organism. They must never force an idea or impose one, but allow the movement to evolve. *Of course, there is no talking.*

C. Group Massage and Moving Together

1. These sequences can be carried out in threes, fours and fives until the whole company is involved together.

2. In the massage sequence, there is one taker and the rest givers. Each giver tends to concentrate on a specific part of the taker's body.

3. In the next stage, when takers make themselves totally available to be moved around, each giver must pay attention to what the other givers are doing or

intending to do, so there is no conflict caused by individuals literally pulling in different directions. Again, there should be no discussion. Communication must be solved by other means. Eventually, the givers function as a harmonious whole, improvising ways of moving and carrying their taker with ease and imagination.

4. Finally, there is no longer the categories of givers and taker, but three, four, five or, indeed, the whole company working and moving together without discussion. With a growing understanding of each other's bodies and the discovery that there's no end to the possible ways in which bodies can combine, a group of actors can take off on unexpected flights of physical imagination.

Note: These sequences do need time – so they should be staggered throughout the rehearsal period. It would be ideal if, when working in pairs, each member of the company gets the opportunity to work with every one of the others. This can take a while to achieve. There should be no gender provisos: men should work with men, women with women, and women with men.

The mutual knowledge and trust developed within the company goes very deep into each actor's psyche and soma. The purpose, clearly, is to make them all fully available and accessible to each other and able to respond to whatever the storytelling may require.

SUBSET 2: SPATIAL AWARENESS

WORKSHOP 29: DEFINING THE SPACE AND SELF-BLOCKING

These exercises are to develop the group's collective awareness of the space they inhabit and the most dynamic ways of exploiting its potential, free of fixed blocking. [*Cross-refer Set 3, Workshop 9: Areas of the Stage and Their Qualities; Previous Workshop 26: Contact Work*]

A

1. The actors move in the space. If you wish, you can specify how they move, applying some of the instructions used in Contact Work: running or walking, possibly crawling, skipping, marching or bounding, just so long as they are constantly covering ground. You can specify whether their movement should be fast, slow, leisurely, cautious, erratic, alert, whether they should move only on curves or on straight lines, using sharp angles to change direction. If you feel this overcomplicates the essential exercise, leave these elaborations for a later date. At this stage, there is no physical contact.

2. They deploy themselves so that they keep the entire space covered and balanced at all times. If necessary, draw their attention to pockets of space that may have become either unused or overcrowded.

3. Ensure that they each maintain an area of comfortable space around themselves at all times.

4. After a reasonable time, start to limit or define what space they can use. For example, instruct them to move only around the perimeter of the space and to leave the centre empty.

5. Next, instruct them to move only within corners – and to find the least obtrusive way of getting from one to another, should they wish to change corners.

6. Instruct them all to move only using one side of the space; then the other; then only the upstage plane, then only the downstage.

7. Have them move in the whole space but only on diagonals. Then only in curves.

8. Repeat any of the above, but now moving in pairs.

9. Then divide the company into groups and have them moving in the space in their divisions.

10. Invent whatever patterns of movement you would like to explore or consider useful for the work as a whole.

11. Discuss what kinds of atmospheres, relationships or events have been evoked or suggested by any of the spatial formations they've been exploring; where they feel strongest, weakest, most safe, most exposed and so forth.

B

This next sequence of exercises is probably more useful later in the rehearsal period when, should you be working from a text, the characters and their relationships are already well in development. If you are devising a piece, then you will have to decide at what point its use becomes most practical.

1. All the actors are in character. Either select an actor or let someone volunteer to begin.

2. The rest of the company, also in character, group themselves together facing the selected actor. Ensure they each allow enough space to be able to move out of the cluster individually.

3. The chosen actor takes any line of text and plays it with a strong choice of intention. It will, of course, be outside its context in the story.

4. The actor plays it to one or all of the group, depending on its content. It need not necessarily be to the character for whom it's meant in the story.

5. The actor must move and use the space appropriately as part of fulfilling the line, its action and its objective.

6. The rest of the group must react physically and spatially. All the actors, every one of them, has to make some choice of reaction, even if the line has little or no meaning for them in the context of the play. They can react individually or share their reactions with others.

7. They should sustain, as much as they can, their relationships within the story. This is an opportunity for them to explore those relationships outside the confines of the events in the story.

8. They should be encouraged to be daring in their physicality, especially in relationship to each other. The collective result of a group's reaction can become surprisingly complex and imaginative, both in the different physical relationships between them and in their use of the space.

9. This next instruction may sound a little mechanical – at the start certainly – but reactions have to executed in *two* beats: the first in absorbing the impact of the line, the second in taking action, i.e. moving. It's a matter of two seconds.

8. Once they have all reacted and moved, they remain in their new positions.

9. The same actor then plays a second line (which need have no logical or sequential connection to the first) with a strong intention, and the group react again.

10. After the actor initiating the lines has done this six times or so and the group has just moved to new positions, call out the name of another actor who will, from the current position, start playing a sequence from his or her character's lines.

11. This continues until all the actors have had the chance to play some of their text.

C

You apply the same sequence as in B. But this time, with an added component: you specify how the group should react spatially. For example, they can only move on curves; they can only move in and out of corners; you might specify that they must work on the floor, or – should there be furniture – sit and stand on it and so forth. This forces the actors to use areas of a performing space they might usually neglect.

A choice might contain them within a very tight area which would force them to intertwine, support, lift, hold or climb on each other. For this last choice, make sure that they are sufficiently warmed up and have been exercising their abilities to support or lift each other during earlier rehearsals.

Note: These exercises help to develop the actors' skill and instinct in self-blocking.

WORKSHOP 30: CONSISTENCY OF PLACEMENT

When establishing the position of an imaginary object, say a door, in an empty space, it's imperative that it doesn't keep shifting. Audiences are quick to notice discrepancies or imprecise placing. As an example, yet again from *Bleak House*, one of that company laid a mimed baby on a chair. Some time later, an actor who hadn't been paying attention sat in the chair – and on the baby! It got a very loud gasp from the audience whose total acceptance of this reality had been rudely disrupted. This consistency of where something is placed demands discipline. It can usually be helped by lining up the imagined object with some fixed feature in the theatre. This is similar to the use of the fixed point in mime where the performer establishes such a point from which all other movements emanate. It becomes a sort of centre of energy.

> Set up several locations in the space where particular features are supposed to be: for instance, a door, a window, a hearth, a hole in the ground. Establish the dimensions of these features and any relevant details, such as the height and position and type of door handle, the way in which the window opens. Then have the company, one after another, until they are all participating, go into the space and make use of these imagined features. Keep them at it until you find their accuracy has reached an acceptable level. Periodically revive this exercise.

WORKSHOP 31: FLOOR WORK

Working in an empty space, the floor takes on an increased importance for both performers and audience. It is the one scenic element that an audience can't avoid seeing if they are looking down on the actors. (The surrounds of a space can be lit in such a way that they disappear into darkness.) The floor becomes a background against which the actors perform. For them, a floor is the sole scenic element they can use. A bare floor invites the expressive possibilities of less habitual ways of moving: kneeling, squatting, crouching, lying, reclining, various sitting positions, rolling, crawling, dragging oneself along… And it opens up the possibility of a fresh range of physical relationships. Culturally, we don't have much relationship to the floor, apart from standing on it – and we pretty much take that for granted. Our feet are seldom in conscious contact with the earth; we rarely ground ourselves and exploit the support and energy it offers. So if the world of the story you're working on suggests the floor as a critical part of its cultural reality, it's worthwhile developing a physical language and relationship with it and increasing your physical language.

---

1. Practise getting down on the floor and standing up again in the most efficient, economic and effortless ways possible. Reduce the number of different movements required to achieve getting from one position to another.

2. Try standing up from as many floor-based positions as possible, such as getting in and out of a supine position, a prostrate position, a lotus position, a crouch, and so forth.

3. Explore moving from one floor position to another, such as from a lotus position to lying prostrate. Execute these shifts at various speeds – fast, slow, with sudden bursts of energy, speeding up, slowing down… Execute them all with the least amount of effort or strain and in the fewest moves.

It may be necessary for the company to do specific exercises to strengthen the stomach and thigh muscles and to avoid putting strain on the lower back. Actors on the floor should look as natural as on their feet.

4. Practise moving in pairs on the floor.

5. And then in larger groups.

6. You can apply the contact work, specifying use of the floor.

SUBSET 3: FOCAL AWARENESS

To be fully freed from the constraints of blocking, actors need to develop spatial skills as instinctive as those they've acquired for acting. In addition, adaptations of big stories may demand the simultaneous acting-out of several events, but these mustn't present the audience with problems of focus – unless, of course, a production, such as certain promenade performances, is deliberately designed to let the spectators choose where to look and what to watch. The disciplined concentration of the actors on the reality of the story they're telling usually solves this issue. But some embedded techniques for controlling focus can reinforce this.

WORKSHOP 32: SPATIAL FOCUS

As a reminder, the following elements are involved [*Cross-refer Set 3, Workshop 9: Areas and Their Qualities, Exercises 5–8*]:

1. Area: Down-centre, up-right, etc.

2. Relative position: For example, an actor standing on the (audience's) left will tend to take focus from an actor to their (audience's) right.

3. Direct focus: For example, an actor looking or gesturing towards another actor will give the latter focus.

4. Body direction: For example, facing out front, i.e. a full face is stronger than a partial view of the face.

5. Body position/level: For example, standing is stronger than kneeling, crouching, lying, etc.

6. Reinforcement: For example, someone standing in a doorway will be reinforced by the uprights of the door.

7. Contrast/difference: For example, someone moving fast will take focus over someone moving slowly.

8. Exception: For example, one person facing upstage when everyone else is facing in a direction that shows some part of their face; someone moving slowly when everyone else is fast.

---

1. Instruct an actor to enter the empty space and choose a place that takes the strongest focus. He'll probably aim for down-centre.

2. Then instruct the rest of the actors to enter, one at a time, and choose a place and physicality that give them equal focus with those already present.

3. Once they are all in the space and presumably in a balanced focus, ask each in turn to make the smallest adjustment possible that brings the focus to them. This can often be achieved by the most delicate of means, maybe the raising of an arm or opening of a hand.

WORKSHOP 33: INDIVIDUAL GIVING AND TAKING FOCUS

1. Set up a space in which several individuals could have a reason to be, with some simple, non-dramatic activity to occupy them, e.g. sunbathing in a park, reading in a library, eating in a coffee shop…

2. The actors enter, one at a time, each allowed enough time to establish themselves and take focus. They do not relate to the others, unless they have some function that requires them to do so; for example, if someone in a café has decided to be a waiter, that function should be fulfilled in the simplest way.

3. There should be no talking beyond what is functionally necessary (e.g. that waiter taking an order, a librarian checking out a book). They should not try to create any dramatic situation. They are all simply getting on with their own activities.

4. Each person, quite naturally, will attract focus by the fact of making an entrance into the space. If the last people to enter find that there is too much action going on, they will need to do so in such a way that draws the focus to them, but it must always remain within the reality of what's been set up.

5. Once all the actors are in the space and their activities have more or less balanced out, instruct the actors periodically to try to *take* natural focus, i.e. without resorting to any drastic and unjustifiable methods.

6. When someone has taken focus, the others should allow a certain time for that to be established, before another actor takes focus. There should never be two people fighting for focus at the same time, there should be no sense of competition. When the exercise has established itself, there should be an easy flow of focus from one actor to another. Encourage the actors to find the subtlest and most imaginative ways of accomplishing this.

7. When everyone has satisfactorily achieved this exercise, instruct the actors now to *give* each other focus. Again, this should happen as naturally as possible. As soon as the group feel that someone's activity seems to justify being given focus, they should communicate to that person that they are offering focus and that actor should respond by firmly taking it.

8. Finally, they should all be prepared to take and give focus as the improvisation dictates.

Ways of giving focus are mainly by a slight withdrawal of intensity. Whatever people are doing, they should slightly lower their energy. But everyone must *justify* these 'drops' and at all times maintain their reality, i.e. they never stop acting. Actors giving focus should never feel they have to shift down into a lower acting gear.

WORKSHOP 34: GROUP GIVING AND TAKING FOCUS

Now apply the above exercise to groups rather than individuals.

1. Set up the company into two groups, each with an improvisational situation of their own, logical within the same space, such as two tables of people in a coffee shop. Or two families in a park. Now, of course, they can and will be talking. Their choices of situation should ensure that they remain comfortably in the improvisation for a reasonable length of time.

2. Allow them time to establish themselves. They should both be played at the same time.

3. Then instruct both groups to *take* focus. It's a matter of developing a level of sensitivity so that, as the improvisations progress and their situations periodically become more dynamic, each group can recognise such moments as their opportunity to take focus. Again, there should be no sense of competition or fighting. The focus should flow back and forth naturally within the situation. The group not in focus should never drop their energy artificially. They should be as alive as the group with focus and sustain their improvisation, though possibly with a justified lessening of intensity.

4. Next instruct them to *give* focus. A group should sense the moment when the other group has, within its improvisation, quite naturally become more dynamic as the opportunity to do so.

5. Then let them both groups give and take focus at appropriate moments in the flow of their improvisations.

6. Then divide them into four or more groups if possible, and repeat the sequence.

7. After each of these sequences, it is sensible to discuss which techniques worked, which were acceptable, what were too obtrusively executed, which were the most imaginative choices made.

Note: The characters in their groups can, of course, be aware of the other groups, but they should never let their improvisations bleed into each other. However, it might be acceptable for an individual to move from one group to the other, either temporarily or permanently.

WORKSHOP 35: ENTRANCES AND EXITS

These exercises combine work on both focus and transitions.

Whenever someone has to enter the space, anyone else on stage – unless there is a narrative or dramatic reason why they should not do so – must find a way to give them focus, not merely as a technical matter but as a reality. We are always affected to some degree by anyone who enters our space or environment. What frequently happens in performance is that actors (as opposed to their characters), knowing that the actor/character will appear, take it for granted and simply fail to register that appearance, unless the text demands a clearly defined reaction. This work helps to rectify this dramatic sin of omission. The form the focus takes will depend on the situation and the relationship of each person on stage to the one who is entering. That person can be expected or unexpected, late or early, expressing alarm or anxiety, threat or relief – well, anything, really. People already on stage might find the new presence annoying or pleasing, the bearer of eagerly awaited news or an object of curiosity and so forth.

The focus does not have to be achieved by the rather obvious means of simply looking at the person entering. One can be aware of someone's arrival without doing so. The body can take on a tension or a relaxation, a deliberate decision to ignore or avoid them. These reactions can be effected by a range of means such as clearly changing one's place in the space, shifting one's body position, and even subtler 'gestures' like gritting one's teeth (remember, the face is a part of the body and can gesture, too), as well as inner changes of energy, alertness or breathing with the least perceptible ghost of a movement.

This equally applies when someone leaves a space.

---

1. Set up a situation and space into which one of the actors will enter for a particular purpose. The rest of the company should already establish themselves in the space and give themselves a particular purpose for being where they are. That purpose or intention could either be connected with the imminent arrival or in total ignorance of it.

The group should share a decided attitude towards that person who is about to enter, along the lines of these various suggestions:

    i. The company knows why the person is entering.

    ii. The company doesn't know the reason.

    iii. Each of the company can decide individually whether or not they know the reason.

iv. All the company have positive feelings towards the enterer.

v. They all dislike the enterer.

vi. The company expects news from the enterer, not knowing if it will be good or bad.

vii. The company are waiting for an order to take some sort of critical action, and (a) knows the person who will bring the order or (b) does not know who will bring it, and (c) maybe will not know the person who actually arrives.

viii. The company neither knows nor expects the enterer.

ix. The company knows but does not expect the enterer.

The person who is entering needs to have a reason for coming; and also an attitude to the situation, such as:

ix. The enterer is confident about the reason for coming.

x. The enterer is insecure about coming.

xi. The enterer knows everyone present.

xii. The enterer knows none of the group.

xiii. The enterer knows some and not others.

xiv. The enterer is the bearer of good news.

xv. The enterer is the bearer of bad news.

xvi. The enterer doesn't expect to find anyone there.

Combine as many as logically possible of the above circumstances, plus any others of your own invention.

Obviously, the choices of the two lists must match up coherently.

Both parties need to flesh out their choices with specific and relevant given circumstances.

The purpose of the exercise is on focus. However, the person entering must allow sufficient time for the group firmly to establish their circumstances, and then choose a suitable moment to appear. The strength of the improvisation depends on what precedes the entrance. *The arrival should effect a change in the group.* The improvisation need not continue too long after the actual entrance once its impact has been fully achieved.

2. Devise situations in which someone has to make a departure. The departer is, of course, already with or part of the group. The group may already know

that the departer will be leaving, the departer may inform them, or leave without informing them. Apply similar attitudes from the previous exercise of someone arriving. You will need time to establish the group and the situation before the departer departs. Leave enough time after the departure for the reactions of the group to be expressed. *The departure should effect a change in the group.*

3. Devise situations in which several people will arrive and/or depart. Now each member of the group should have their own intention and an individual attitude towards the arrivals or departures. This, of course, will be a much more extended and complicated improvisation. Make sure the given circumstances are sufficient to accommodate a lot of activity. Even though some of the people in the improvisation might not have any contact or relationship with some of the others, every entrance or exit must cause some sort of reaction from each person present.

Note: The main purpose of these exercises is to give focus to arrivals and departures. But these arrivals and departures are also transitions which transform the situation. *Make sure the actors allow themselves to be changed by every arrival and departure.*

WORKSHOP 36: WATCHING

When actors, not for the moment in the action, are watching the performance of their colleagues from the periphery of the stage, the way in which they watch is vital to the well-being of the show. This is a critical aspect of focus when a company is in the process of telling a story. They must learn to give their partners full and generous concentration in as relaxed and as natural a manner as possible. They should never feel any obligation to fake reactions, but should allow themselves to respond spontaneously to whatever in their colleagues' performance amuses or in any way affects them. They need to realise that even while watching they have a powerful presence, and that to some degree they will always exist within the audience's awareness. In fact, their watching presence contributes a positive additional layer to the audience's total experience of the performance. Remember that, in telling stories, the double reality of theatre is reinforced for the audience; they are involved both with the story *and* the storytellers – the what of the story *and* the how of its telling.

This concentrated watching has important purposes: by focusing on those in action, the watchers are sending their own positive energy to contribute to the energy of their performing partners; they are subliminally supplementing the audience's powers of concentration and by so doing reinforcing their focus on the action. And at the simplest level of justification, they are only behaving with the same consideration that they will expect from their partners when they are performing.

It's important to realise that the moment any one of the actors watching allows their focus to drift, even for a short period, this will distract the audience and dilute the impact of the performance. By placing their concentration elsewhere than on the action – simply by looking at their hands, say – they are removing their energy from their partners and inadvertently stealing part of the audience's attention. But, I reiterate, the watching must be conducted totally free of strain or apparent compulsion, but in the most relaxed and honest way possible.

You should spend time making this clear to the actors and, during rehearsals and performances, observe and monitor its execution. It's not something that you can actually rehearse; but one way in which you might work on this practically, during a rehearsal, is by asking actors who are not involved in a scene or an exercise to watch the action from a space *within* the acting area, rather than from their usual place 'out front'. In this way, they effectively become part of the action.

One reason for keeping the actors onstage throughout the performance is that, together with the audience, they create a cohesive, undistracted sharing of the complete experience.

SET 7

WORKSHOPS FOR TRANSITIONS AND TRANSFORMATIONS

37–40

Theatre is contained within a single space and a single timespan, to be experienced by the audience at the very moment of its performance. So the challenge for theatre has always been: how do we get from here to there, from one time and place to another time and place within the same time and place? Classic and neoclassic theatre avoided the problem by defining a play as obeying the unities of time, place and action: a single action taking place in one space for the same duration that the audience spent watching it. One of the solutions in medieval theatre was to set up scaffolds in a round and promenade the audience from one structure to the next: Heaven over here, Hell over there. Another was to build their structures on wagons and bring Heaven and Hell *to* the audience. But the open-air theatre of the Elizabethan solved the problem by means of the imagination: on the fixed architecture of what was an open and essentially empty, if highly decorated, stage it eschewed both scenery and the unities and found unlimited freedom of time and space by the evocative powers of actors and language. Shakespeare frequently moves from one location to another within a single scene by verbal suggestion. For him, time is flexible; within the same passage of text events with both short and long timespans can occur concurrently. But such agility became lost once the theatre moved indoors. Light sources of increasing sophistication provided the tempting possibility of replicating actuality, and with this growing desire for scenery came the growing need for machinery to shift it. And in this respect, things have been going downhill ever since. Imagination, light on its feet, has been replaced by a cumbersome literalness. True, over the centuries the labour-intensive ropes and pulleys of Serlio and Inigo Jones have been replaced by the touch of a screen, but swamping the stage with digital effects has a cumbersomeness all of its own.

The human mind functions with amazing rapidity; memories, plans, conjectures, ideas are unconsciously negotiated with speed probably well beyond the capacity of any current computer. Our thoughts can move through time and place within what feels like a considerably longer period than the actual seconds we've been daydreaming. Once – rather like playing Ladder Words, a game in which you try to move in a set number of changes from a starting word to a closing word, altering one letter at a time – I managed to chart how my thoughts had led me from contemplating a photo to seek out a song I hadn't heard since I was a child, song and photo having no apparent connection. I moved through a sequence of memories from different periods of my life, through reminders of chores I had to do, to considerations of where I was at the present moment, relationships, ideas from books I'd just read… and so on. And this seemingly random riffling through my mind had taken a mere fifteen seconds to accommodate at least thirty distinct stages. Of course, digitally generated images can change fast. But imagine a performance in which thirty such images were (faster than in a pop video) projected in fifteen seconds. You would barely register one image meaningfully before another had superseded it. So what's the difference between such images and those flashing through our synapses? Simply that the digital images are imposed on us from without, whereas the pictures created by our minds – and not just pictures, but thoughts about them, too – come from within us and, presumably, have already been processed by our unconscious before being delivered to our awareness. They are ours, of our making, so we have no difficulty in registering them. And, of course, they're in personal harmony with what's happening on the stage because that's what brought them into being.

As I said when discussing the empty space, the more frequent and abundant the scenic images that confront an audience, the fewer they'll absorb and the fewer of their own they'll create. But liberated from such visual overload, each person can make instantaneous, instinctive associations of their own. Given the right cues, an audience can make rapid imaginative transitions. And, of course, so can the performers.

By a word, by a gesture, an actor can provide the audience with such cues. Merely the business of donning or doffing a hat or shifting a piece of furniture can slow things down. The actor, the unencumbered human being, is the most efficient, supple and speedy maker of transitions. This flexibility allows an actor to be in two or even more periods and places at once: somewhere within the past (there and then) reliving a previous event elsewhere (there-er and then-er), while talking about it to the audience, seated in this theatre (here and now). It's even possible that an actor or a character could be simultaneously participating in two concurrent scenes.

One of the main characteristics of stories and storytelling – uninhibited movement with the utmost frequency and rapidity from place to place, time to time and character to character – demands the freedom to effect fast and frequent transitions without number. For actors to work unassisted by any means other than what they can create themselves, it's been necessary to devise a repertoire of techniques for moving from one state to another. Transitions mean transformations of space, time, environment, mood, character, costume, objects, events, situations... The Elizabethan model is the one that best answers many of a storyteller's needs.

SUBSET I: ACTIVITIES AND ENVIRONMENTS (WITHOUT TEXT)

WORKSHOP 37: TRANSFORMATION EXERCISES

A. Individual Transformations of Activities

1. An actor, A, mimes a recognisable activity (maybe brushing one's teeth).

2. Another actor, B, who can see a possibility, comes into the space copying A's activity and gradually, *with the least amount of physical change*, transforms it into another activity (maybe playing a flute).

3. A transforms the original activity to conform to the new one. A and B, briefly, continue this activity together (playing the flute); then A leaves, and B continues the new activity (flute-playing) alone.

4. A third actor, C, enters the space, copying the flute-playing and then transforming it into something else (say doing chin-ups on a bar). B briefly copies this transformation and then leaves the space. C continues with the chin-ups.

5. Continue in this pattern until each of the company has had at least one opportunity to create a transformation, but do keep going beyond that until all possibilities seem to have been exhausted and the invention dries up.

6. The original activity will have gone through several transformations so that, like Chinese Whispers, the final activity will bear little resemblance to the original.

B. Accumulative Transformations of Activities

1. Set up as above: one actor, X, miming an activity.

2. The next actor, Y, transforms not just the activity itself, but also the whole shape and movement of actor X, who remains in the exercise. *In this version, no actor leaves the exercise.*

3. The difference from Exercise A is this: actor Y does not copy and then transform the existing activity, but by making a particular physical relationship

with actor X creates a new activity in which they are both involved, though not necessarily behaving identically. We don't want a whole line-up of people doing the same thing, say, five teeth-brushers or ten flute-players. Imagine, for instance, that actor X mimes pruning a potted plant. It might be possible for actor Y to place his head where the pot is supposed to be so that X is now cutting Y's hair.

4. A third actor, Z, has to see the possibility of adding to the combined shape and movement of X and Y (the haircutting) in such a way as to transform their activity into another – different – shared event. For example, by bowing on one knee before Y, actor Z might suggest that X is no longer cutting Y's hair but placing a crown on Y's head. The actors already in the situation must judge how much they need adjust to accommodate the new activity. *Their adjustment should be as minimal as possible.* The slightest physical adjustment or shift of attitude may be sufficient.

5. Continue until the whole group is involved. The transformations should *not* be made through intellectual associations, but purely from physical, spatial and visual suggestion. As the group gets larger, it's sometimes helpful for the actor who is searching for an idea to look at the active group through half-closed eyes. The loss of detail often makes the overall shape and movement more evocative. The final image in this exercise is often something quite broad to accommodate increasingly varied types of movement. The last actor might, by conducting them, transform the entire group into an orchestra.

Note: Make sure that each actor *transforms* the group activity rather than elaborating or adding to it. [*Elaboration exercises are taken care of by Workshop 38 below*]

C. Group Transformations of Situations (Places and Events)

If characters are required by a story to move from one location to another, there tends to be some unspoken convention that they should move from one area of the stage to another. However, by an actor's power of suggestion, such transitions can be made *in situ* by a slight shift of attitude and the least physical adjustment. In the performance of *Bleak House*, the heroine, Esther Summerson, narrates how she travels to London by coach, her destination being the offices of a lawyer where, on arrival, she's seated by a hearth to warm herself after her long journey. The transition and transformation was achieved instantly – as fast as a cinematic cut – by the actor who, while remaining seated, adjusted her jogging motion in a carriage to warming her hands before a fire, while simultaneously other actor/characters gathered round her.

The principle is to achieve a change *with the utmost economy*. Even when several actors appear in two successive scenes, either as the same or different characters, there's the possibility of changing instantly from one to the next with a similar minimum of text or fuss.

1. You, the director or project leader, make all the suggestions throughout this exercise. Instruct the group (immediately without discussion or dialogue) to create a specific crowd of people (e.g. a bus queue). The group creates an image and continues to keep it alive, but should not develop a story. There should be no conversations. But they can say a few words or vocalise if appropriate.

2. Instruct the group to transform with the minimum of change or effort into another group (e.g. football fans watching their team's opponents score). And this they do *instantly*. Continue to give them fresh images, e.g. anti-war demonstrators, mourners at a state funeral, and so on…

3. The criterion for this exercise is *to change radically by the subtlest of means, with the least possible amount of movement or effort*. It might be no more than a change of focus. A change of attitude is often sufficient to effect a transition. The nature of the images will almost certainly alter the relationships within the group.

4. Keep this exercise going with frequent transformations. Once the group has created an image, they have solved that challenge and you can move on. The sequence should have the effect of rapidly projected slides, one following on the other.

D. Transitions of Time

Imagine characters remaining in the same scene but with a time jump, e.g. 'Two hours later, they'd still not come to an agreement.' On the Trampoline Word 'agreement', the actors would adjust their physicality and attitudes to convey that passage of time and suggest what had transpired within it. A sequence of several time changes under the same circumstance – waiting for someone to arrive, say – might be achieved without intervening narrative.

1. Establish a situation which could possibly last for a long while. It does not need to be dramatic. As examples, one or more people are waiting for another person to arrive or to receive some news via their smartphone, or a group of people are involved in some physical activity such as painting a room, learning a script… Make sure they have sufficient given circumstances to support them.

2. The less conversation the better. They should only speak when absolutely necessary, usually about practical matters. *What the actors must never do is to refer to the time!*

3. Periodically, you – whoever is leading the session – will announce a time lapse: 'One hour later she hadn't arrived' or 'Three hours later they had got behind with the work...' The time gaps should be appropriate to the situation.

4. On cue – your final word ('arrived', 'work') – the actors make a transition that suggests the passage of time and conveys what might have happened in the interim and how they now feel.

5. The transition should be achieved, as in C above, with the minimum of effort and as much delicacy and subtlety as possible.

Variation D I

1. The same set-up, but this time, whoever is leading the session will not announce the time gap. So beforehand, the actors must decide what their sequence of time gaps will be, taking into consideration the nature of the situation. They might occur every hour, or every twelve hours, every day or every week or even every five minutes... You might want to put a limit on the number of hours or days for which the situation could conceivably continue.

2. The actors themselves effect the transitions. They do this without discussion. With no verbal cue to mark the changes of time, the actors will have to develop the sensitivity to each other described in the mirror exercises when there are no longer leaders and followers, so they have to sense between them the moment of change. [*Cross-refer Set 6, Subset 1, Workshop 24: Mirror Exercise A8; Workshop 28, Massage, Exercise B: Moving Together*]

Variation D2

1. There is no reason why you shouldn't put time into reverse, starting at the end of a situation and then working backwards towards its beginning. The coaching would then be on the lines of: 'Three hours earlier they were starting to paint the ceiling...'

E. Transformations by Clapping

1. Call on two actors, without any preparation whatsoever, to go into the acting space and *instantly* start improvising a situation, the first situation that leaps into their minds. They can, of course, talk.

2. Any time after it's established, clap loudly once. The two, again *instantly* and without any discussion, change to a *totally new* situation.

3. Continue to clap after any duration you feel is appropriate; it could be ten seconds or five minutes...

4. The two actors keep transforming to a new and totally unconnected situation.

5. When you feel they have done enough, call on another two actors to go through the same process.

6. And continue, mixing the pairs.

7. Make sure the clapping is sharp and clear.

There are several 'rules' the actors have to learn in order to fulfil this exercise. First, observe how many they discover for themselves in action. Then feed the rest gradually, so the actors have time to absorb them:

> The transformations should be effected by the actors taking advantage of the physical positions and shapes they happen to be in at the moment of clapping. *Their physicality should be the stimulation to their imaginations to create a new situation*, never intellectual connections such as the situation or subject matter of the current improvisation.

> Neither of the pair should wait for the other to establish a situation. Both should take that responsibility (as in the much referred-to Mirror Exercise). Otherwise, there's the likelihood that one of the pair will fall into the role of leader and the other into that of follower.

> They must never try to plan ahead, but trust to the physical inspiration of the moment when the clapping occurs. Spontaneity is the absolute law here.

> As soon as one of them has established a situation, the other must instantly accept it, never reject it. They must never fight over whose idea to use, should both set up a situation simultaneously. One of them must concede.

> Every situation must contain a *conflict*, however subtle – and therefore *objectives* – otherwise they'll ramble on or drift, talking too much because there's nowhere for them to go dramatically.

> The actors must not let the exercise become a talking shop, but should make the event as physical and active as possible. The improvisation should never be about inventing clever dialogue.

> The actors should create characters and relationships.

> They should be prepared to change gender, age and ethnicity.

> They should establish as quickly as possible enough given circumstances to support the improvisation (relationship, place,

time, reasons for being where they are...) so that if you decided not to clap for twenty minutes, they could continue without running out of steam.

They can, if they have the ability, play in different styles and genres, or create fantasy realities.

However, all situations should have their own logic and consistency.

They must always play with the utmost truth and seriousness. They should commit totally to whatever they're playing, however ludicrous the situation.

Most of the time, the actors will instinctively go for comedy, but there's absolutely no reason why situations shouldn't be moving, frightening, dramatic – all human life can be there.

The actors should conduct this exercise with as much relaxation as possible. They may initially tense up in anticipation of the claps and the anxiety of coming up with a new idea. This, of course, will block any hope of spontaneity. They should stay in the moment and forget about the possibility of clapping. It will happen when it happens.

There is absolutely no possibility of planning. This exercise is based totally on allowing their instinct to be creative. Encourage them to hang loose. Staying in their bodies and not in their heads is the key.

The more the actors experience this exercise, the more skilful they become in developing their generosity, initiative, imagination and character range. The exercise should eventually operate on the level where the actors flow from one situation to the next.

Variation E1

You no longer clap. The actors have the autonomy to allow transitions to occur whenever it seems right to them. Again, this must occur though an instinctive communication between them.

Variation E2

Try the exercise with more than two actors. The height of the company's skill will have been achieved when the whole ensemble together can execute the exercise.

Variation E3

Set up the exercise with themes or subjects: partnerships, the economy, evolution, or anything connected with material you happen to be working on at the time. Even though there now will be the overall connection of a theme, each situation should be totally different from the previous one, and always transformed through the actors' physicality and not through the subject matter, which remains as a leitmotif.

Note: When devising, this is also a useful way to develop material.

WORKSHOP 38: ELABORATION EXERCISES

A. Elaborating an Activity

1. An actor mimes a recognisable activity. The choice of activity should allow for the possibility of others joining in (e.g. decorating a Christmas tree).

2. One by one, the other actors enter and *add* to the activity being created. They do *not* change it. They do *not* double up on what anyone else is doing. While not changing the established group activity, the elaborations should each effect a sort of transformation in mood, attitude, energy.

3. The others already in the activity should adjust or respond to each additional contribution as appropriate. For example, if the latest addition is executed with great delicacy it might encourage them individually to carry out their activities with greater refinement and precision or to be deliberately brusque.

4. This exercise tends to remain realistic. No conversations; speech is only permissible when justified for purely practical purposes ('Pass the scissors!').

B. Creating an Environment

1. An actor goes into the space and creates an activity or uses the space in a way that suggests a particular place or environment (a bar, a laundrette, a garden, a beach, a volcano…). There is no talking.

2. As soon as they have an idea what sort of environment is being suggested, the other actors, one at a time, enter the space in order to *add to* and

substantiate the environment (never merely duplicating what has already been established).

3. Continue until the whole group is in the environment. With each addition, not only is there a firmer establishment of the place with increasing, specific details, but also a sort of transformation of the mood or energy.

4. This exercise does not require a shared activity. Each actor should be carrying out a different activity, whether on their own, in pairs or in groups. [*It is not the same as Exercise A in which an activity is shared*]

5. This exercise does not have to remain in a realistic world. It could be a fairy-story world or a science-fiction world. But in this case, actors setting up such a world will have to be very specific and clear in communicating its reality to the rest.

6. It's possible that some actors may misread the initial provocation and unwittingly take it in a direction never intended by its initiator. In this case, those people already in the exercise have to decide whether to adjust to this new direction or determinedly stay with what was first established, hoping that the mistaken actor will eventually comply.

Note: It's preferable to conduct these exercises without props, but if you feel it will be more germane to your purposes, by all means include them; in which case you might limit their type or quantity or specify whether they should be taken literally or be transformable. [*Cross-refer Set 9, Workshop 44, Exercise E: Transforming Objects*]

Note: There should be no conversation during this exercise, but if a non-realistic environment is established, the actors could, vocally or percussively, create sounds and music.

SUBSET 2: NARRATION AND SCENES (WITH TEXT)

WORKSHOP 39: TRANSITIONS FOR FLOW AND CONTINUITY IN STORYTELLING

In storytelling, the operative word is telling; in theatrical storytelling, telling is also achieved by playing. Narration and scenes interlock in a variety of ways. Their relationship, how and why they pass from one form to the other, depends on the particular intentions of writers and their texts, and has many facets to consider: the ratio of scenes to narrative, the frequency of the alternations, the viewpoint of the narrator, the sort of events that are narrated as opposed to those that are rendered as scenes and so on…

…also the purpose of the narrative. Scenes have one basic function: to show the characters in action. Narrative has many: to provide exposition, to describe events, to analyse situations, to interpret the characters' behaviour, to enter their thoughts, to establish atmosphere, to moralise, to comment on the action, to set events in a wider social or historical context, to encourage the audience to think about the story in a particular way…

So the manner in which the narration is conveyed and in which transitions from narration to scene and scene to narration are effected must be as varied as its functions. Changes of focus, tone, time, place, energy, tempo, reality and characterisation all come into play. The nature of these shifts is as much a part of the world of the story as the story itself; their specific execution is one of the conventions by which the particular life of the story is defined.

While we're about it, we should also take account of transitions from one narrator to another if a narrative sequence is shared between two or more storytellers; transitions from one scene to another, too, if they occur without intermediate narration or with nothing more than a brief linking phrase. So we have the following seven basic types of transition:

1. From Outside Narrator to Outside Narrator

2. From Outside Narrator to Scene

3. From Scene to Outside Narrator

4. From Inside Narrator to Inside Narrator

5. From Inside Narrator to Scene

6. From Scene to Inside Narrator

7. From Scene to Scene

One common denominator that applies to all these transitions, irrespective of type, is the technique I call 'Passing the Baton'.

Passing the Baton

For the purposes of story-theatre, I'm assuming that stories need words and telling them needs speech. Consequently, one of my tenets is that the narrative should have continuity; if the audience were to close its collective eyes, it would, at least, hear an *entire* and fluent story. Of course, the verbal always takes place within a visual context; physical action and imagery will always accompany the language, but they should never be a substitute for it, exceptions being those rare occasions on which characters in a scene are, for whatever dramatic reason, not talking to one another or on which narrators stay silent during some non-verbal action that they've instructed us, the audience, to watch with them.

This continuity of language must be smoothly sustained through a story's many transitions. Using the analogy of a relay race, whoever currently holds the baton, that is, the person speaking, must ensure that it – the story – is passed safely and smoothly to their successor, who should be equally primed to receive it. If a clean transition is not made, one of two things can occur:

1. If the actors in a new piece of narration or a new scene start to speak before receiving the audience's focus, the audience will have to wrench their attention abruptly from the actor or actors they are currently focused on in order to find out who's suddenly doing the talking. They're likely to miss the first few words, and this may leave them temporarily disorientated or lacking important information. Audiences, initially, have to *see* who is talking in order to *hear* them.

2. If the actors ending a piece of narration or a scene withdraw themselves from the audience's focus before the new scene or narration has been established – effectively leaving a moment without text or action – the audience will not know where to look and be momentarily lost in the gap between the two events.

———

The seven types of transition I've enumerated are very much basic approaches, initial techniques for dealing with the possible structures you'll come across in your work. But – a word of warning – you won't always find those structures conveniently deployed in the discrete and organised manner in which I'm presenting them in the following two workshops. Every story you approach will have its structural idiosyncrasies regarding dialogue, exposition, description and the like. You may find several of the transitions I've identified jumbled together, in which case you'll have to extrapolate the techniques you feel best serve your purposes, adjusting and modifying them according to your material. It's important therefore to understand their underlying principles. They're set down to help you learn skills that you can develop and explore further for your own uses.

As I've suggested, you should collect a supply of stories that interest you to apply to some of the exercises. But for these two workshops 39 and 40, I've set out, at the end of this set, texts from *Riders of the Purple Sage* and *Bleak House* for your optional use. I've identified which texts should be used with which types of transition.

This subset requires fairly developed skills and will benefit from earlier workshops. [*Cross-refer Sets 3, 4, & 5: Outside & Inside Third-Person and First-Person Narrators; Set 6, Subset 3, Workshops 32–36: Focus*]

1. From Outside Narrator to Outside Narrator

1. This type of transition is probably the easiest to effect as the actors involved are all fulfilling the same function. So its execution is literally baton-passing. Use the first text at the end of this set, *Riders of the Purple Sage*, or choose material of your own with a sustained section of narrative. Divide it between an appropriate number of narrators.

2. To simplify this first exercise, instruct them to stand in a row in the sequence of their narration and let the first narrator begin. This time around, the actors should concentrate on carrying through the logical flow of the story without interpretive embellishments.

3. Narrator A, coming to the end of his section of narrative, should indicate, through his delivery of the text, that the story is to be continued by someone else. He should textually 'hand over' with the knowledge of what is to follow. Narrators should never allow the audience to think the story has come to a full stop. There are two exceptions to this: (i) if the narration happens to be the completion of a discrete section when both storytellers and audiences need a brief breathing space; (ii) if what follows is intended to be totally unexpected: a surprise, a shock. Otherwise, narrators should lead the audience to whatever's coming next.

4. The narrator B, about to take over, should, just as the current narrator has reached his final word, effect a delicate but deliberate preparatory move or gesture to bring the audience's attention to herself. When she's sure that she's drawn the focus from her predecessor to herself (a matter of a second), she should begin her own narration.

5. Narrator A should sustain the audience's focus on himself until he is certain that narrator B has started the succeeding piece of narration. Then he should switch his own focus from the audience towards her.

6. All the narrators should give their focus to the current narrator. By doing this, they contribute their energy to the support of that narrator and reinforce the audience's concentration. [*Cross-refer Set 6, Subset 3, Workshop 36: Watching*]

7. Proceed along the line of narrators in this way until the sequence is completed.

Note: The narrators remain in their line-up positions.

Variation 1A

8. Allow the narrators, in any order, to stand, sit, squat or take up whatever physical position in whatever area of the stage they wish. This time, they can narrate with as much colour and attitude as they wish.

9. Now, when it becomes their turn to narrate, they will have to decide whether they're going to move towards the audience or whether they're going to stay put and draw the audience's focus to their current position. Depending on where they are, this is likely to require more movement than in the first exercise, so they'll have to readjust their timing.

10. Those narrators not involved in a transition may also have to move to ensure the new narrator is not masked. They should at all times be focused on whoever is narrating. If they wish, they can move to whatever position they find most conducive to supporting and listening to whoever is narrating. They can also respond freely to the story.

Variation 1B

11. Transitions will be affected by different conventions, for example:

    a. If the performance has established that narrators can acknowledge each other during their handover, decide whether their relationship is formal, casual or familiar.

b. If they have each been assigned different aspects of the narrative to relate (description, commentary, exposition, action, dialogue – in this case even dialogue is narrated...) or different feelings towards characters and events, there may be some implicit attitude conveyed between them regarding their relative opinions of the story as they effect the changeover and while listening.

c. If the story is being narrated in a heightened or dramatised manner, with the narrators giving full rein to vocal and physical expression, make sure everyone is inhabiting the same heightened world.

In these cases, the baton-passing will have to take into account variations in speed and energy according to the impact of what has just gone before. This may encourage the narrators to move in the space. They may have to allow slight pauses during a transition for the intensity of a moment to calm down or, if their narrative justifies it, to take advantage and build on it. If the previous narration has been low-key, they may have to raise the level of energy. They will have to develop a sensitivity to the variations that are sure to occur from performance to performance.

12. Whatever options are taken, the handover has to be clean and clear for the audience. When the 'baton handover' has not been smooth, rework it until it becomes seamless. The criterion for this is the comfort and ease with which an audience is able to follow the story.

2. From Outside Narrator to Scene

1. Use the second text at the end of this set, *Bleak House*, or your own choice of narrative, which needs to be followed by dialogue, possibly interspersed with further narrative. Assign the narrators and share out the characters between the group.

2. You need to decide whether the actors in the scene are going to start in their 'watching' space or whether they will already be *in situ* within the scene. If the latter, they should be in character.

3. The narrator or narrators follow the procedures established in the previous exercise: coming to the end of their section of narrative they must indicate, through their delivery of the text, that the story is to be continued by someone

else. They should textually 'hand over' with the knowledge that a scene or some dialogue is about to follow.

4. The actors in the scene have collectively to use the *same cue*, the narrator's final word, to start taking focus as they ready themselves for the start of their scene. If they've been in their 'watching' space, they will probably do this by simultaneously transforming into character and moving into the area designated for the scene. If they are already there and in character, they can take focus by an activity connected with the scene or by a small gesture. Like the narrators above in Exercise 1, they have to make sure they've gained the audience's attention – and not until then – before they start to speak. All this should take no more than a couple of seconds.

5. Then the narrator, as before, transfers his own focus from the audience to the scene, whether he's remaining where he is or retiring to a watching place. This choice will depend on how active he's likely to be: if the scene is long and sustained, he may well withdraw; if he has frequent interventions during the scene, he should probably stay put. [*Cross-refer Set 4, Workshop 18: Justifying Narration Interruptions During a Scene*]

6. Anyone withdrawing to a watching space should do so with the utmost economy of movement, with their focus always on the scene. They sustain their focus on the scene until they're again in action. [*Cross-refer Set 6, Subset 3, Workshop 35: Watching*]

3. From Scene to Outside Narrator

1. Wherever possible, the actors at the end of a scene should try to do much the same for the narrator as the narrator has done for them before the start of a scene: that is to say, playing the last moment with a sense of the story's continuity and sustaining the audience's focus on themselves until the narrator has taken the focus again. However, the dramatic situation may not allow a clinching exchange of dialogue or an emphatic final speech. It might end with a character still pondering a situation, uncertain of what to do, or rambling erratically; sometimes the end of a scene is intentionally inconclusive.

2. In such cases, narrators must take responsibility for the changeover and find the appropriate means to bring the focus back to the narration, either as they move forward from their watching space or activate themselves from

where they've remained during the scene. A simple gesture or step towards the audience should regain their attention.

3. In every performance, the situations and their intensity will vary, so narrators have to develop a feeling for such nuances, allowing the particular rhythm and energy to guide the right moment to regather the reins. The final beats of a scene may need a moment to breathe, a period of stillness, of quiet, allowing its impact to resonate – a recovery time for both actors and audience. At times, it may be appropriate for narrators to snatch back the baton sharply, at others to creep up on it and coax it back gently into their hand. The criterion, always, is what choice will most enhance that moment in the story.

4. You might feel that the image or physical action of a scene should be sustained for a while under the new narration. With the same sensitivity that's required of the narrator, the actors in the scene will have to find the right moment and appropriate energy to dissolve the scene before they once more give all their focus to the narrator as they retire to their watching space. If the narration is only briefly interrupting a scene before it's resumed, the actors can probably stay in place until they once more pick it up. [*Cross-refer Set 4. Workshop 18: Justifying Narrative Interruptions During a Scene*]

5. Use the same *Bleak House* text at the end of this set or chose a piece of text which accommodates movement out of a scene into narration and try out some of the variations described above.

4. From Inside Narrator to Inside Narrator

1. Technically, transitions between characters sharing or alternating narrative, which is often the case when all the characters are functioning in multiple third-person narrative mode, are identical to those between actors narrating from outside the action, as in Exercise 1 above. Choose a piece of narrative which allows two or more characters to talk about themselves and the events around them (in the third person, of course). Or use the second text, *Bleak House*, at the end of this set in which all the characters share the narration.

2. Their relationship to each other in the story should inform the way they pass the baton between them in terms of attitude and emotion, and will

depend on what conventions have been established [*Cross-refer Set 4. Workshop 18: Justifying Narrative Interruptions During a Scene*]:

> The characters are all aware that they are able to communicate with the audience, in which case they can acknowledge that fact and listen in, even indicating to the audience their agreement, disapproval, surprise or any other response they might have to what the current narrator/character is telling them.

> They each believe that their contact with the audience is something exclusive to themselves, in which case they will be unaware of any narration other than their own.

> As a corollary to this, you might decide that they are surprised or shocked to hear and see someone else communicating with the audience.

> Narrators may want the other character/narrators to hear what they are telling the audience; they might even encourage them to listen to what they have to say.

> Narrators may wish their narration to be a private matter between them and the audience, in which case they'll find a way to make it so, attracting as little attention to themselves as possible.

> The characters in a scene may be too busy with their own activities to take much interest in what someone else is narrating.

> If the actors are narrating as themselves (that is, out of character), they will be functioning almost identically with the outside narrators in Exercise 1. Here you have the option of letting the other characters sustain their lives unaware of the narration or, also, dropping out of character to listen as themselves, the actors.

3. Explore narrating the chosen text with as many of these conventions as you find useful. Only apply one at a time. Be rigorous about this, otherwise you won't be able to judge the full impact of any one option.

5. From Inside Narrator to Scene

1. Use the same *Bleak House* text at the end of this set or choose you own section of narrative followed by dialogue, possibly interspersed with further narrative. Assign the narrators for this exercise; there may be more than one needed, depending on the text. It's possible – as will be the case in the excerpt from *Bleak House* – that all the characters in the scene have narration. Otherwise, share the roles in the scene between the rest of the group.

2. If the narration has been made in character, the main element of the transformation is the actor's change of focus from the audience to the other characters in the scene. Usually the narrative will provide sufficient and appropriate impetus for actor/characters to launch themselves into the scene at the right level of energy. They, of course, can help this with the gear shift of Trampoline Words. [*Cross- refer Set 4: Third-Person Narrators inside the Action, Workshops:13-20. especially 16: Trampoline Words*]

3. The other important element to change is that of intention. The intentions of storytellers when narrating in character is usually to gain the audience's understanding, approval, complicity, sympathy and such regarding their involvement in the story. When they enter a scene – just as in a play – their immediate intentions become what they want from the other characters in the scene. Nevertheless their intention to gain the audience's understanding still remains as an overarching super-objective: now, instead of telling the audience about themselves, they are showing themselves in action. Therefore, when completing the narration to enter a scene, there should never be the sense that the narrator has abandoned the audience or put them on hold. Narrators should be inviting the audience to join their character as it rejoins the scene; drawing them into the scene with it.

4. If they're narrating out of character – that is, as themselves – they must use one of the techniques for changing into character to enter a scene. [*Cross-refer Set 4, Workshop 13: Narrators Transforming from Actor to Character During Narration*] Their narrative intention may well be in a more critical mode than if narrating in character, now perhaps wanting the audience to understand how foolish or destructive, how flawed their character might be; in this mode, as themselves, they have an overview of the whole story. Once they're in character in the scene, their intention will almost surely be subjective, self-justifying and sympathy-seeking. But the overarching objective still applies. So the playing of the scene will require a little more sophistication. This is somewhat similar to the narrative mode in which the actor reveals the character simultaneously from two points of view. [*Cross-refer Set 4, Workshop 14: Narrators Embodying their Characters While Commenting on them*]

5. The difference between this transition and the transition from outside narration into a scene [*Exercise 2 above*] is that the group in the forthcoming scene does not have to attract the audience's focus. Narrator/characters bring that focus with them as they enter a scene. Any preparation that's needed for the scene, such as shifting chairs, have discreetly to be carried out by the rest of the group behind the narration as it nears its completion. [*Cross-refer Set 9, Workshop 46: Moving Objects during Transitions*]

6. If, by unlikely chance, the character narrating is not actually involved in the forthcoming scene, then the other characters will have to claim the audience's attention in the normal way, taking the baton, before they start to play their scene. In this case, the narrator will function technically just like an outside narrator, keeping the audience's focus until the scene is established and then giving that focus to the actors in it.

6. From Scene to Inside Narrator

1. The character coming out of a scene to narrate is simply reversing the previous transition. The focus naturally accompanies the narrator making that reversal. The narrator will need to supply a fresh input of energy appropriate to the new narration, establishing the level at which the audience must now accept the story; in a sense, reminding them that their active presence there is vital to the proceedings and that the quality of their attention will have an effect on the performance. Whatever tone the narrator wishes to establish – whether tranquil, aggressive, ironic, detached… – the delivery must, in every case, be more expansive. Inevitably, the narrator is now relating directly to a much larger group of people than there were in the preceding scene. You could think in terms of focusing *in* to play in a scene and focusing *out* to narrate to the audience.

2. The actors in the scene keep it alive until the narrator has taken the focus and has started talking. The narrator having done so firmly, the actors dissolve or break the scene and retire to their watching area. Or, should the scene be soon to resume, they stay put and keep the scene alive until such time. [*Cross-refer Set 4. Workshop 18: Justifying Narrative Interruptions During a Scene*]

3. If, however, the other actors have to reorganise stage furniture and set up a new scene – behind the narrator, as it were – they must do so without

distracting the audience. They achieve this by giving focus as much as possible to the narrator while carrying out their chores and accomplishing whatever is needed calmly, quietly and naturally (no tiptoeing or any equivalent heavy signalling that they're meant to be discreet!). They *will* be discreet by letting the audience understand from their low-profile demeanour that they are currently of no interest whatsoever. But usually, just so long as the narrator has its firm attention, the audience will barely register anything else happening, even if quite elaborate changes are being carried out. [*Cross-refer Set 6, Subset 3, Workshops 32-36: Focus; and Set 9, Workshop 46: Moving Objects during Transitions*]

4. Choose a relevant piece of text or the second of the texts below to explore this process.

7. From Scene to Scene

1. This sort of transition from one scene to another (which is the case in many plays) may have individual, technical matters that have to be taken into account. For instance, if all the actor/characters are in both scenes, they can make use of the Group Transformation techniques [*Cross-refer this Set 7, Workshop 37 C*]; at an agreed moment – presumably the final word or beat of the first scene – they all transform from one time and place to another. To explore this transition, either use both the second and third texts at the end of this set or choose material of your own that has two scenes in succession.

2. If the same actors are in both scenes, but playing different characters, the same technique applies; but this time the transition is enriched by the additional transformation of character which must happens simultaneously. (This will be the case if you use the two *Bleak House* texts at the end of this set for the exercise as they involve different characters.)

3. We are visualising these as transitions in an empty space, but if, for instance, chairs were part of the reality and needed to be redeployed, then, should all the actors be involved in both scenes, they might have to shift them as part of the transition. However, actors who are not involved in the new scene can start to rearrange them from the moment the transition begins, discreetly placing them around and behind the actors who are already starting to play the scene. [*Set 9, Workshop 46: Moving Objects during Transitions*]

4. Successive scenes can sometimes be lightly bridged by brief narrative, establishing, say, a location, e.g. That evening, they walked in the woods. And such a phrase would, of course, be the pivot for the change of scene. If, however, you move from one scene to the next with no intervening narration, the world of the story might suggest effecting transitions in a totally different way. If so, you may want to borrow from cinematic techniques, such as cross-fades and dissolves… [*Cross-refer Set 10, Workshop 49: Film Language*]

These suggestions are for basic modes of making transitions, sustaining the flow of the story without clumsy breaks or interruptions. *The common denominator is that everyone involved works from the same cues, making use of Trampoline Words and Passing the Baton.*

No doubt much of this sounds pedantically obvious and/or unnecessarily complicated, but it is not something that actors carry out instinctively. These techniques have to be exercised to high levels of both sensitivity and accuracy. They should not draw attention to themselves; the actors should deal with them so naturally that they are virtually unperceived – the art that conceals art. Of course, underpinning these technical skills must be the actors' instincts, both individually and collectively, to keep a story moving fluently forward. Otherwise, they'll crash on the trampoline, fumble the baton and lose, if not the race, the audience.

WORKSHOP 40: PITCH AND TONE FOR THIRD-PERSON NARRATOR OUTSIDE THE ACTION SETTING UP SCENES

There seem to be two basic approaches by which a narrator outside the action can tonally set up transitions into scenes. One is by supportively building up the narration to the equivalent emotional head of steam that the characters need as their level to start playing; that is to say, being strongly involved with their experiences, identifying with them and helping to launch them into their action; the other is by remaining factual and level-headed, functioning as a counterpoint to whatever emotional heat the scene might require. Of course, there are many degrees between these two pairs of extremes and the choice of attitude will depend precisely where along the Subjective-Objective and the Sympathetic-Critical spectra the narrator takes a stand. [*Cross-refer Set 4, Workshop 16: Trampoline Words*]

Depending on where narrators are located on the stage and on the amount of freedom of movement the convention of the story-world has given them, they can also double as stage managers. While still narrating, they might designate the space for the action, pacing out the perimeter and pointing out whatever might be helpful to the audience's understanding of the forthcoming events. Should scenic elements be used, narrators might also function as prop masters, placing objects and chairs within the acting area. They might lead or beckon the characters into the space and arrange them in their starting positions. At the end of the scene they could reverse the process, moving the characters away from the space and clearing away any props as they resume the narration. In this case, the scene participants would make themselves totally available to the narrator, who would be very much in control of how such transitions were effected.

A

1. Either use the *Bleak House* text at the end of this set or take a sustained piece of narrative that is setting up or leading into a scene, possibly containing narrative interventions. Assign the narrator and characters in the scene.

2. The narrator builds the narration to the appropriate emotional pitch to help launch the actors into their scene. The narrator plays this narration twice: first sympathetic to the characters, then critical of them.

3. The characters play their scene, taking the level of their playing from the narrator.

B

Repeat as above, but on this occasion, the narrator maintains a calm, factual, possibly cool tone. In this case, the actors have to assume responsibility for the pitch at which the scene begins. The narrator plays this objective narration twice: first sympathetic to the characters, then highly critical of them.

C

1. In this exercise the narrator also functions as a stage manager. Again, use the second text below, or find a section of narrative that's suitable in content and length. It will also need some narrative to follow the end of the scene. You will have to prepare whatever the narrator needs to handle: furniture, props, possibly pieces of clothing. Assign the narrator and characters as usual.

2. While narrating, the narrator sets up the physical space and brings or beck-ons the characters into it. The text will suggest what details need to be dealt with.

3. The characters begin the scene. The narrator stays ready in the role of stage manager to provide anything else they might need *during* the playing, which may include (as in the *Bleak House* excerpt) further narrative.

4. When the scene is over, the narrator, while continuing to narrate, removes the actors from the space in any way that seems fit, from a nod of the head to actually leading them away, and restores the space to its former condition.

5. For this exercise, the narrators can chose whatever attitude they wish towards the characters and story.

Texts for Use with
Narrative Workshops 39 and 40

Text 1: *Riders of the Purple Sage*

The following extract is from Zane Grey's *Riders of the Purple Sage* to use with *Exercises for Transition Type 1 in Workshop 39: From Outside Narrator to Outside Narrator*:

> In searching around in the little hollows, Venters, much to his relief, found water. He composed himself to rest and eat some bread and meat, while he waited for sufficient time to elapse so that he could safely give the horses a drink… The longer they rested the better…
>
> The sorrel wandered off down the sage between the trail and the cañon. Once or twice he disappeared in little swales. Finally, Venters concluded Wrangle had grazed far enough, and, taking his lasso, he went to fetch him back. In crossing from one ridge to another he saw where the horse had made a muddy pool of water. It occurred to Venters that Wrangle had drunk his fill, and didn't seem the worse for it, and might be anything but easy to catch. And, true enough, he could not come within roping reach of the sorrel. He tried for an hour and gave up in disgust. Wrangle did not seem so wild as simply perverse. In a quandary Venters returned to the other horses, hoping much, yet doubting more, that when Wrangle had grazed to suit himself he might be caught.

As the afternoon wore away, Venters's concern diminished, yet he kept close watch on the blacks and the trail and the sage. There was no telling of what Jerry Card might be capable. Venters sullenly acquiesced to the idea that the rustler had been too quick and too shrewd for him. Strangely and doggedly, however, Venters clung to the foreboding of Card's downfall.

The wind had died away, the red sun topped the distant western rise of the slope, and the long purple shadows lengthened. The rims of the cañons gleamed crimson and the deep clefts appeared to belch forth blue smoke. Silence enfolded the scene.

It was broken by a horrid long-drawn scream of a horse and the thudding of heavy hoofs. Venters sprang erect and wheeled south. Along the cañon rim, near the ridge, came Wrangle, once more in thunderous flight.

Venters gasped in amazement. Had the wild sorrel gone mad? His head was high and twisted in a most singular position for a running horse. Suddenly Venters descried a frog-like shape clinging to Wrangler's neck. Jerry Card! Somehow he had straddled Wrangle and now stuck like a huge burr. But it was his strange position and the sorrel's wild scream that shook Venters's nerves. Wrangle was pounding towards the turn where the trail went down. He plunged onward like a blind horse. More than one of his leaps took him to the very edge of the precipice.

Jerry Card was bent forward with his teeth fast in the front of Wrangle's nose! Venters saw it, and there flashed over him a memory of this trick of a few desperate riders. He even thought of one rider who had worn off his teeth in this terrible hold to break or control a desperate horse. Wrangle had indeed gone mad. The marvel was what guided him. Was it the half-brute, the more than half-horse instinct of Jerry Card? Whatever the mystery it was true. And in a few more rods, Jerry would have the sorrel turning into the trail leading down to the cañon.

'No – Jerry!' whispered Venters, stepping forward and throwing up his rifle. He tried to catch the little humped, frog-like shape over his sights. It was moving too fast; it was too small. Yet Venters shot once... twice... the third time... four times... five! All wasted shots and precious seconds.

With a deep-muttered curse Venters caught Wrangle through the sights and pulled the trigger. Plainly he heard the bullet thud. Wrangle uttered a horrible strangling sound. In swift death action he whirled and with one last splendid leap he cleared the cañon rim. And he whirled downward with the little frog-like shape clinging to his neck.

There was a pause which seemed never ending, a shock, and an instant's silence.

Then up rolled a heavy crash, a long roar of sliding rocks dying away in the distant echo, then silence unbroken.

Wrangle's race was run.

Text 2: *Bleak House*

I've reorganised and edited this excerpt from *Bleak House* for possible use in Workshop 39 with the Exercises for Transitions from 2 to 6 inclusive, and for the exercise in Workshop 40. The whole narrative can be delivered by a single external third-person narrator with other actors playing the characters within the scene. Or, divided up, the narrative can be shared by several third-person narrators within the action (in fact, all the characters have narrative in this extract), either as themselves or in character. To facilitate the latter option, I've started a new paragraph in the narrative whenever a different character might take over the narration. When characters are mentioned collectively, you will have to decide to whom you assign that section of narrative.

In setting up the scene with multiple third-person narratives, you will have to decide whether you establish the characters in their places in the scene before they start so that they narrate from within the scenic space; or they start their narration outside it and move into the designated area during or after their initial narrative.

The characters are Grandfather and Grandmother Smallweed, their grandson, Bartholomew (Bart), his sister, Judy, Charley, an orphan who drudges for them and Mr George, an ex-trooper.

> In an ill-favoured and ill-savoured neighbourhood, bearing the name Mount Pleasant, the Elfin Smallweed, christened Bartholomew, dwells with his family in a narrow street where there yet lingers the stump of an old forest tree whose flavour is about as fresh and natural as the Smallweed smack of youth.
>
> The house of Smallweed has discarded all amusements, discountenanced all story-books and banished all levities whatever. Hence the gratifying fact that it has had no child born to it and that the complete little men and women whom it has produced bear a likeness to old monkeys with something depressing on their minds; no child until, for the first time,
>
> Bart's grandmother became weak in her intellect and fell into a childish state. With a disposition to fall asleep over the fire and into it, she has undoubtedly brightened the family.

Mr Smallweed's grandfather is likewise of the party. He is in a helpless condition as to his lower limbs, but his mind, unimpaired, holds the first four rules of arithmetic. His God is Compound Interest.

Judy, Bart's twin, happily exemplifies the family's likeness to the monkey tribe. Attired in a spangled robe, she might walk about the top of a barrel-organ without exciting much remark. Judy never owned a doll. It is very doubtful if Judy knows how to laugh. If she were to try, she would find her teeth in the way.

At present, in the grim parlour certain feet below the street, Grandfather

and Grandmother Smallweed,

seated on two black horse-hair chairs on either side of the fire-place, while away the rosy hours.

Judy sets a sheet-iron tray with tea-cups on the table; the bread she puts in an iron basket; the butter – and not much of it – in a small pewter plate.

Thereupon the four old faces hover over the teacups like a company of ghastly cherubim.

GRANDFATHER	Where's the girl?
JUDY	Charley, do you mean?
GRANDFATHER	Eh?
JUDY	Charley, do you mean?
GRANDMOTHER	Charley over the water, Charley over the water, over the water to Charley, Charley over the water…
GRANDFATHER	Drat you, be quiet! You're a chattering, clattering broomstick witch, that ought to be burnt. You're a brimstone idiot! You're a sweltering toad!

And the good old man throws a cushion at her.

It not only doubles up Mrs Smallweed's head against the side of the chair, causing a highly unbecoming state of cap,

but the necessary exertion recoils on Smallweed himself, throwing him back into his chair like a broken puppet,

until, in the hands of his grand-daughter, he has been shaken up and poked and punched like a great bolster.

When there is silence, he says

GRANDFATHER   If that's her name. She eats a deal. It would be better to allow her for her keep.

Judy purses up her mouth into No without saying it.

GRANDFATHER   No? Why not?

JUDY   She'd want sixpence a day, and we can do it for less. You, Charley, where are you?

A little girl in a rough apron and a large bonnet appears, her hands covered in soap and a scrubbing brush in one of them.

JUDY   What work are you about now?

CHARLEY   I'm a-cleaning the upstairs back room, miss.

JUDY   Mind you do it thoroughly. Shirking won't do for me. Make haste. You girls are more trouble than you're worth, by half.

GRANDFATHER   Been along with your friend again, Bart?

Bart nods.

GRANDFATHER   Dining at his expense, Bart?

Bart nods.

GRANDFATHER   That's right. Live at his expense as much as you can, and take warning by his foolish example. That's the only use you can put such a friend to. That's advice your father would have given you, Bart. He was a good accountant and died fifteen years ago.

GRANDMOTHER   Fifteen hundred pound. Fifteen hundred pound in a black box, fifteen hundred pound put away and hid.

Her worthy husband discharges the cushion again, crushes her head against the side of the chair and falls back in his own.

Judy shakes up his internal feathers, restores the cushion to his side and plants the old lady upright in her chair,

ready once again to be bowled down like a nine-pin.

GRANDFATHER   I should like to throw a cat at you instead of a cushion. You are an old pig, You are a brimstone pig, You're a herd of swine. But your father and me were partners, Bart. When I am gone, you

> and Judy will have all there is. But you won't
> want to spend it. You'll get your living – Judy to
> the flower shop and you in the law.

One might infer that Judy's business rather lay with the thorns than the flowers.

GRANDFATHER   Yes, you'll get your living without it – and add
                more to it.

A close observer might perhaps detect both in Bart's and Judy's eyes some little impatience to know when he may be going.

JUDY   If everyone is done, I'll have that girl in to her
                tea. She would never leave off if she took it by
                herself in the kitchen.

Charley is accordingly introduced and under a heavy fire of eyes,

sits down to her basin and a Druidical ruin of bread and butter.

JUDY   Now don't stare about you all the afternoon, but
                take your victuals and get back to your work.

CHARLEY   Yes, miss.

JUDY   Don't say yes. Do it without saying it and then I
                may begin to believe you. Oh! see who it is and
                don't chew when you open the door.

Judy takes the opportunity of jumbling the remainder of the bread and butter together as a hint she considers the eating and drinking terminated.

JUDY   Now! Who is it, and what's wanted?

MR GEORGE   Whew! You are hot here. Always a fire, eh? Well,
                perhaps you do right to get used to one

GRANDFATHER   Ho! It's you, Mr George! How de do? How de do?

MR GEORGE   Middling. Your granddaughter I have the honour
                of seeing before; my services to you, miss.

GRANDFATHER   This is my grandson. You ha'n't seen him before.
                He is in the law and not much at home.

MR GEORGE   My services to him, too. He is very like his sister.
                He is devilish like his sister.

GRANDFATHER   Judy, see to the pipe and the glass of cold
                brandy-and-water for Mr George.

The sportive twins, disdainful of the visitor, retire together, leaving him to the old man, as two young cubs might leave a traveller to the parental bear.

Mr George is a swarthy man of fifty, well-made and good-looking; with crisp dark hair, bright eyes and a broad chest. His powerful hands, as sunburnt as his face, have evidently been used to a pretty rough life. He sits forward in his chair as if he were, from long habit, allowing space for some accoutrements that he has laid aside. His step, too, is measured and heavy and would go well with a weighty clash of spurs. One might guess Mr George to have been a trooper.

GRANDFATHER   And how does the world use you, Mr George?

MR GEORGE   Pretty much as usual. Like a football.

GRANDFATHER   Don't be down-hearted, sir. You may rise again.

MR GEORGE   You'll sell me up at once, when I am a day in arrear.

GRANDFATHER   Never, never, my dear friend! But my friend in the city that I got to lend you the money – he might!

MR GEORGE   You can't answer for him? You lying old rascal!

GRANDFATHER   I wouldn't trust him. He will have his bond, my dear friend.

MR GEORGE   So you think your friend in the city will be hard on me, if I fail in a payment?

GRANDFATHER   My dear friend, I am afraid he will. Ha'n't you no relations, now, who would pay off this little principal or lend you a good name that I could persuade my friend in the city to make you a further advance upon?

MR GEORGE   If I had, I shouldn't trouble them.

Mr George laughs, and with a glance at Mr Smallweed, strides out of the parlour, clashing imaginary sabres and other metallic appurtenances as he goes.

The old gentleman makes a hideous grimace at the closing door.

GRANDFATHER   You're a damned rogue. But I'll lime you, you dog, I'll lime you.

Mr George strides through the streets with a massive kind of swagger and a grave-enough face, It is eight o'clock now and the day is fast drawing in. He stops hard by Waterloo Bridge and reads a playbill; decides to go to Astley's Theatre. Being there, is much delighted with the horses and the feats of strength; looks at the weapons with a critical eye; disapproves of the combats, as giving evidence of unskilful swordsmanship; but is touched home by the sentiments. In the last scene, when the Emperor of Tartary gets up into a cart and condescends to bless the united lovers by hovering over them with a Union Jack, his eyelashes are moistened with emotion. The theatre over, Mr George comes across the water again and makes his way home.

Text 3: *Bleak House*

The following scene between two different characters, also from *Bleak House*, is to provide material when working on Exercises for Transition 7, moving from one scene straight into another. I would suggest that the actor playing Grandfather Smallweed transform into Tulkinghorn (an eminent and manipulative lawyer) and the actor playing Mr George transform into Mr Snagsby (a mild and insecure law-stationer).

You can explore the transition in two ways: either using the optional opening line of narrative or doing without it.

Below the scene, I have laid out text covering the transition to suggest how it might best work. But, first, here is the scene:

Mr Tulkinghorn is not alone tonight. [*Optional*]

TULKINGHORN	Now, Snagsby, to go over this odd story again.
SNAGSBY	If you please, Mr Tulkinghorn, sir.
TULKINGHORN	You told me, when you were so good as to step round here, last night –
SNAGSBY	For which I must ask you to excuse me if it was a liberty sir; but I remember you had taken a sort of interest in that person, and I thought it possible that you might – just – wish – to –… I must ask you to excuse the liberty, sir, I am sure.
TULKINGHORN	Not at all. You told me, Snagsby, that you put on your hat and came round without mentioning your intention to your wife. That was prudent, I think, because it's not a matter of such importance that it requires to be mentioned.
SNAGSBY	Well, sir, you see my little woman is – not to put too fine a point on it – inquisitive. She's

inquisitive. Poor little thing, she's liable to spasms, and it's good for her to have her mind employed. In consequence of which, she employs it – I should say upon every individual thing she can lay hold of, whether it concerns her or not – especially not. My little woman has a very active mind, sir. Dear me, very fine wine.

TULKINGHORN   Therefore you kept your visit to yourself, last night? And tonight, too?

SNAGSBY   Yes, sir, and tonight, too.

TULKINGHORN   Fill your glass, Snagsby.

SNAGSBY   Thank you, sir, I am sure. This is a wonderfully fine wine, sir.

TULKINGHORN   It is a rare wine now. It is fifty years old.

SNAGSBY   Is it indeed, sir? I am not surprised to hear it, I am sure. It might be – any age almost.

TULKINGHORN   Will you run over, once again, what they boy said?

Mr Tulkinghorn leans quietly back in his chair.

Then, with fidelity, though with some prolixity, the law-stationer repeats Jo's statement.

Transition between the Two Scenes/Text 2 and Text 3

For this particular exercise I recommend ending the preceding scene with Mr George's last line of dialogue and laugh. In that way, both actors will still be in the scene for the transformation. The texts would go as follows:

MR GEORGE   If I had, I shouldn't trouble them.

Mr George laughs.*

(*) Mr Tulkinghorn is not alone tonight. [*Optional*]

TULKINGHORN   *Now Snagsby, to go over this odd story again.

* The baton is passed by the actor playing Mr George on the word 'laughs' – the cue for the transition – and received by the actor playing Mr Tulkinghorn on the word 'Now'. (If you use that optional line of narration, Tulkinghorn's first words would, of course, be 'Mr Tulkinghorn'.) As Tulkinghorn speaks, they have both to

transform into their new characters while whoever is playing Grandmother Small-weed leaves the scene. This should be done as unobtrusively as possible. If the first pair are still seated at the end of their scene, the second pair could possibly start seated with the slightest shifting of body positions to accommodate both their changed characters and relationship and, possibly, to suggest a desk between them.

SET 8

WORKSHOPS FOR CREATING SOMETHING OUT OF NOTHING

41–42

WORKSHOP 41: BRINGING THE SPACE ALIVE

One of the great pleasures and challenges of telling stories in an entirely empty space is finding ways in which the actors can convey or conjure up environments by their imaginative use of body and voice. The work is inevitably – and properly – suggestive rather than literal, applying a sort of visual synecdoche. The audience joins up the dots.

In our early Shared Experience efforts to create locations, we had to experiment until we came up with what seemed to answer our specific needs; there were no rules, no blueprints to follow. Every story throws up its individual demands of time, place and manner, and you have to find your own solutions to those demands.

For example, in *Bleak House* (in which our sole element was six black folding chairs), the subject of poverty and wealth was underpinned by how the actors were deployed in the space. Scenes in stately homes were suggested by chairs placed far apart from which characters communicated as if across greatest distances; those in hovels piled characters together on the floor in a cramped space, a sort of no-man's-land that uncomfortably straddled the borders of two or three least sympathetic stage areas. [*Cross-refer Set 3, Workshop 9: Areas of the Stage and Their Qualities*] The aristocracy seated by their grand fireplaces kept slightly away from the extreme heat created by generous amounts of fuel, the women, on occasion, protecting themselves by the mimed use of hand screens; wretched families huddled around a meagre, improvised hearth.

Frequently, the most convincing images were not the ones that were realistically accurate. To create the illusion (*Bleak House* again) of a character ascending a dark winding staircase, the actor, without the help of actual stairs, kept his body twisted in the direction that the staircase presumed to curve, an imagined candlestick held well above his head, which was slightly tilted back so that his eyes were raised upwards towards his destination, while his free hand slid up a mimed handrail and he lifted his feet higher and with more effort than he would have done on even ground. This image was reinforced by another character standing at the bottom of the imaginary stairs, craning to watch him vanish up into the gloom, twisting her body as though trying to see beyond his disappearance round a bend. As the distance between them appeared to lengthen, they slightly raised their voices. By quite unrealistically angling their heads and corkscrewing their torsos, and by the way they adjusted their raised candles, the two actors were able convincingly to create the image that one of them was eventually standing at the top of the stairs conversing with the other who remained at the bottom. In actuality they were standing only a few feet apart on a flat floor.

Another possibility we discovered, this time during work on *A Handful of Dust*, was of creating an illusion of greater space and more people than we actually had. The acting area for this production was a floor made of reflective metal with a back wall in grey velvet constructed along the width of its upstage edge. This floor and wall were set well within the full width of the actual proscenium stage so that their edges created a sort of inner proscenium arch, or the equivalent of a movie screen frame. The actors were only in character and action when they worked within this frame. When not involved in the action, they sat in chairs placed off the metal floor to the sides, outside the frame. As they stepped off the metal floor, exiting from the action, they cleanly dropped character. In this way, they defined very clearly for the audience the space within which they acted from the surrounding space from where, out of the action, they watched. When working on episodes demanding large numbers of people in large spaces, we were able to take advantage of this spatial arrangement by placing such scenes very close to the edges of the acting area with the characters appearing to relate to other imagined characters off-screen, as it were, beyond this inner proscenium. For a scene in a nightclub, we crowded the chairs together in a cramped corner of the up-left acting area (audience view) with the cast of ten moving tightly from imaginary table to table, perching or sitting or standing, gossiping and greeting each other, as well as imagined people offstage, out of the frame. The chatter, the hand-waving, the blowing of kisses the incessant movement, the crammed space and the sense of other party-goers extending beyond the acting area gave the illusion of a large supper club crowded with guests.

[*Cross-refer Set 6, Subset 1: Physical Awareness, Workshops 24-26 and Set 7, Subset 1: Transformations for Environments: Workshop 37, Exercises C & D & Workshop 38, Exercises A & B – all technical exercises to prepare for this work*]

A

As well as through the literal miming of objects or surfaces, environments can be evoked by the way in which the actors move in the space and relate to it. These initial exercises are to explore and develop some techniques:

> EYES: The depth of the actors' focus can suggest open spaces with distant horizons or enclosed spaces with defined boundaries. Darkness can be conveyed by dilated eyes; well-lit spaces by relaxed eyes, extremely bright spaces by slightly closed eyes.

> BODY: An expanded chest, a lifted spine, shoulders opened wide, arms hanging freely can convey an open space; a reduced or relaxed ribcage can suggest a comfortable and undemanding

interior. A very contracted torso, a collapsed ribcage and arms close the sides can suggest an extremely restricted space.

SMELL: Whether there is a particular odour or scent, pleasant or disagreeable, in an environment can be conveyed by the way the actors breathe, by the dilation of the nostrils

HEARING: Environments contain sounds that they enjoy, that irritate them, that may make them want to listen more carefully to identify them, that connect you with the environment... The type of sound and their attitude to it can be conveyed by the degrees of alertness in the body and the angle of the head.

1. Each actor finds a space in the room and works alone. Remaining in the same place, they should try to create suggestions of simple environments by the above means, one element at a time. They don't need to stay with any one environment, but explore several. For instance, by inhaling they should be able to convey sharp, fresh, ozone-laden sea air, the cloying smell of heavily scented flowers, the dusty smell of a room that's been shut up for a long time... Their focus should be able to distinguish between looking from a high point over an immense valley and looking at library stacks or trying to iden-tify someone in a crowd... Their bodies should be able to convey temperature, weather conditions, familiar or unfamiliar places, and whether there is a source of music in their environment or rare birdsong...

2. The actors, still staying on the spot, each then try to establish a single, more detailed environment by applying as many of those means as possible to cre-ate one image.

3. Let the actors, without travelling in the space, shift between imagining themselves in and out of doors, continuously alternating until, with the min-imum of effort, they achieve a very clear distinction between the two.

4. The actors each choose two slightly more complex contrasting spaces and, again, without moving, try to establish them by frequently changing from one to the other until they achieve – by all or any of the above means – a distinc-tion between the two.

5. The actors then add two further elements to their creations:

POSITION: Where they might place themselves in an environment, such as keeping firmly to the edges or moving into the centre of the space...

MOVEMENT: Whether they move with small steps or large strides, firm steps or cautious steps, use their arms in some way...

6. The actors should try, first for themselves individually, then collectively, to suggest the lobby of a very swank, five-star hotel; a large hospital ward (as visitors); a crowded club; or whatever environments you choose. They should not mime objects or act out any situations. And they shouldn't talk, except briefly and then only logically in terms of the location. When they are working together, they will obviously have to include the presence of the others as part of the environment. Their aim should be to convey these places purely by use of their stage position, physical stance, movement, eyeline, hearing and breathing. Find out how little they need to do in order to communicate specific and adequate information. [*Cross-refer Set 7, Workshop 37C: Group Transformations of Place and Event*]

7. A character could have a feeling about an environment that is contrary to received opinion. Whereas conventionally we tend to feel more open, expansive and take up more volume, breathe deeply and extend our gaze in a wide open space with a beautiful view, it's conceivable that someone might feel threatened or depressed or in some way uncomfortable in such surroundings, whereas they might feel secure indoors in a very cramped space, in which most of us tend to feel restricted, inhibited, even claustrophobic.

Now let the actors collectively choose an environment. They should each, privately, decide on a very definite attitude towards it. See whether they can still convey the environment in spite of their feelings about it. For example, they might feel very disapproving of the five-star hotel suggested earlier, they might be bored by scenery...

B

The purpose of the exercises in A was to explore some of the techniques helpful to create the idea of a place. Now you can explore in much greater detail and with much more freedom many different possibilities of creating an environment. The previous work should provide a good grounding.

How you set up this work will very much depend on your circumstances: whether you're working from the text of an existing story or devising a project or exploring technique in a workshop. So your instructions to the actors need to be specific to your needs. Let's assume, for the sake of setting up this exercise, you're trying to create a dense forest. These are some of the points you might consider:

How much of the acting space do you want/need to use?

Are your explorations with a specific image in view? Or are they open-ended?

What is the atmosphere you wish to achieve? Or are you waiting to see what atmosphere is created by the actors' explorations?

What sort of forest do you want: a vast rainforest with exotic, dangerous plants and intense scents; a milder, domestic version; or the archetypal forest of fairytales?

Does the material suggest that the actors transform themselves into objects like trees and foliage?

If so, what sorts and conditions of trees might they be: gnarled, twisted and stunted, or with dense canopies and mighty trunks, or traditional Russian birches?

Could the trees have personalities and attitudes?

How literal, how selective or how heightened should such embodiments be?

And does a degree of stylisation belong within the overall world of the story that you're creating; is it within its conventions, its reality?

Or should the actors create the idea of a forest by the way they react to and deal with a totally imagined (unrepresented) environment around them (as they've been doing in the A exercises above)?

What means might they try to this end: negotiating uneven ground littered with the debris of fallen foliage; straining to peer through the permanent dusk; contracting their bodies to avoid collisions with branches…?

What sort of people would be in this environment? And why?

Does this environment need people in it at all?

Could the actors simultaneously be people and objects, for example, treating each other's arms as branches to be pushed out of the way?

Would the sounds, made by the actors, of scurrying in the undergrowth and fluttering in the treetops suffice to create the illusion of a forest?

Would the contrast of a small clearing reinforce the idea of a forest?

Would the forest be in spring or winter mode (or summer or autumn)?

Is there the threat of dangerous plants, insects, reptiles...?

How much or how little needs to be done in order to create the illusion of such an environment?

Some of these questions might be discussed before starting on the actual explorations; others might be more appropriate later on. It depends on how much is already clear to you.

1. Set up the actors to explore, in an empty space, different ways of bringing to life environments such as the above forest, a public square, a restaurant, an auditorium, a beach... or any place of relevance to you. They all explore the same environment.

2. Let the actors first work on their own for twenty minutes or so. They can do anything except talk. Then have each of them show the company any of the ideas they may have come up with.

3. Then let them work in twos or threes, possibly developing some of the preceding suggestions. The actors should work without discussion, communicating physically by the way they contribute creatively to each other's 'offers'. At the end of the session they show the others what they have found.

4. Select two or three of the ideas or images that seem most suitable for your purposes, divide the company into two or three groups and let them develop and refine these ideas.

It's not at all unusual – in fact it's rewarding – to have to work through immense amounts of material before you find an image that suits your purposes. By then, what you do find is pretty certain to have some depth and resonance. You'll have rid yourself of considerable dross. Don't be impatient and grab at quick results; they rarely survive for more than twenty-four hours before their novelty wears thin.

Note: The reason the actors shouldn't talk is that by discussing the environment they'll weaken the other means they have at their disposal to create it.

WORKSHOP 42: INDIVIDUAL IMAGES

As well as establishing environments, the company will have to create individual images within them. Often, the recreation of actual behaviour can look false when mimed; then it's necessary to find something that reads more convincingly than a literal replica. But, for an illusion to work, above and beyond any spatial and corporeal solutions, actors have totally to believe in what they're evoking. This was one of Ruth Draper's great talents.

Here are two examples from our work on *The First Arabian Night*. We wanted to create a raft on which an exhausted and fainting princess floats out to sea. After endless experimentation we came up with a simple idea (the best solutions are most often the simplest, the ones you only arrive at after jettisoning a lot of other stuff): three of the cast lay flat on their backs with the actor playing the heroine lying across their thighs. Then in unison the three rotated their hips from side to side which created the rocking movement of a tide.

Later in the proceedings, the same heroine (prone to being in the wrong place at the wrong time) had to be carried off in a fainting condition across the pommel of a bandit's saddle. We eventually found this image by means of the actor who played the bandit standing, one knee bent, across which the heroine collapsed, head down and hair flowing. He then supported her waist with one hand and, with the other held above his head, mimed whipping his steed, whilst rocking backwards and forwards on the spot. Someone else created the sound of horse's hoofs galloping through sand by slapping his hands against his chest in the rhythm of a canter. *Et voilà!* One princess abducted on horseback.

The actors don't always have to use their entire body to create an image. If a dish or platter were needed, it might suffice for the actor to transform a hand, palm upwards and fingers spread, while the other hand held the wrist; or possibly letting another actor 'carry' it. A clenched fist could become a doorknob… [*Cross-refer Section 2, Workshop 8 Physical Work: Hands*]

This work more or less conforms to the sorts of thinking and questioning detailed in the previous workshop on environments.

1. The actors create objects and animals such as thrones, canoes, horses, doors, tables… first individually, then in pairs and, possibly, depending on the subject, in larger groups. You'll find that actors, left alone to explore a challenge, will come up with highly imaginative offerings. They should work physically without discussion.

2. Always allow the actors to see each other's work and, if appropriate, to talk about what they've seen.

3. If you've already established an environment, make sure that the images you've found conform to its world and conventions.

My advice is to work patiently until you discover what you're searching for. I'm certain that wonderful solutions are always lurking in our imaginations, waiting to be released by anyone with sufficient perseverance to coax them into existence. When they do finally appear, solutions can be both surprisingly counterintuitive and absolutely right. The examples I've mentioned only arrived after we'd wandered up several culs-de-sac.

SET 9

WORKSHOPS FOR
USING ELEMENTS

43–47

WORKSHOP 43: NECESSARY ACCESSORIES

I've stressed that the actor can create everything necessary for a full experience of theatre. But on occasion, a story may be helped by some visual, aural or physical element, especially if it seems to require a particular 'look' or 'sound' to place it within a recognisable tradition or genre.

The storytelling should always start from the principle of actors in an empty space. If this fails to provide all that's absolutely vital – and only after having been deemed *absolutely* vital by rigorous questioning (Do we need a door? Why do we need a door? What would happen if we didn't have a door?) – then it's the time for you to introduce appropriate accessories into the work; appropriate may even mean a set designed to fill every inch of the stage from wing to wing and floor to flies. Anything's possible! Never think of the empty space as a form of limitation, a ceiling on what is permissible or possible. Quite the contrary. It's perfectly possible to start with nothing and end with a stage crowded with costumes, awash with lighting, resonating with music – *as long as that is what the story truly demands.*

But whatever you introduce must always stay within the expressive control of the actors; never something imposed on them, above and beyond their reach, or to which they cannot relate. Ideally, any items of design or technology should emanate from the needs of the characters who, in a sense, conjure them into being.

Questions of convention will define what sort and quality of items should be used: literal and realistic; transformational; selective (in terms of colour, material and the like); metaphoric or thematic…; where they're to be placed in the performance space, how they're to be used: whether lifted, carried, pushed or pulled…

While I was preparing the adaptation of *The Black Dahlia* (the fictionalised account of a notorious, unsolved murder in 1940s Hollywood), I had a fortuitous dream in which very large men in double-breasted suits and fedoras violently kicked away any objects obstructing their path. I awoke to a possible and thrilling way of rapidly changing the novel's numerous scenes in which tables, desks and chairs were necessary. Once the technical problems had been solved – items of furniture on castors that could indeed be kicked, shoved and pushed so that they slid, flew and skidded across a smooth aluminium floor almost of their own volition – scene-changes were swift and unexpected, often over before the audience had time to register them. Equally important, they underscored the endemic violence of the novel. So the practical solution to moving furniture also became a metaphor for one aspect of the production.

Often, the subject matter of the story might suggest the use of thematically appropriate generic objects or materials, such as cardboard boxes, rope, newspapers, balls, coat hangers, luggage, scarves... which can be used and transformed by the actors to suggest whatever is needed. I've seen two dance pieces which utilised this technique brilliantly. In one, the dancers paraded onto and around the stage with a length of rolled canvas tucked under their collective arm, which they proceeded to unroll and use in a variety of ways through a sequence of dances: suspended above them, placed beneath them with the corners raised, hung diagonally, wrapped around them... The other piece used piles of newspapers in which the dancers swam or which they stuffed into their leotards to change their body shapes or tore into confetti – or actually read! Both were exhilaratingly witty and inventive. And deeply satisfying: the choice of material allowed the individual dances within both pieces to be surprisingly varied within a gratifying coherence.[1]

The Method & Madness production, *Demons and Dybbuks,* that we constructed from several Isaac Bashevis Singer short stories, constantly referred to books. Appropriate enough: Jews have always defined themselves, amongst other things, as People of the Book (the *Torah*). Because the main character in each story is a writer, we decided that, apart from chairs, books should be the sole element in the show. The set was piled with books. The actors explored many ways in which they might be handled, consulting them, dipping into them, searching through them, losing themselves in them, riffling their pages, turning down their corners, cracking their spines, carrying them, admiring them, arranging them... We tried balancing them on our heads, turning the pages with our feet, expressing our love, awe, reverence, excitement towards them and so forth. They became expressive extensions of what the characters were experiencing. The show became storytelling about storyreading.

This workshop is not so much about the actual handling of objects as searching for those appropriate to specific texts. The following are suggested ways of pursuing the search:

1. Choose a text that interests you.

2. List the possible objects, material, items of clothing or furniture that might be applicable for it. I've suggested generic items such as balls, cartons, rope...

3. As an example, we'll assume you thought that the last of these, rope, might be a relevant or thematic choice. Fill the rehearsal room with coils in different strengths, sizes, textures; you may feel that, in the specific context, twine is also acceptable, possibly balls of string, balls of knitting wool, ribbons even...

---

1. The first piece was by the American choreographer, Alwin Nicolais; the second by an Israeli, Ruth Ziv-Ayal.

4. Invite the actors to explore their possibilities in three ways.

i. As they actually are, for their prime use. Essentially, this means tying and untying, binding and unbinding people and objects. Might knots become a relevant source of expression? Would the company benefit from learning to tie fancy knots?

ii. Explore using the various ropes and strings – without transforming them – for purposes other than their original intention. Coils of rope can be sat on, areas can be roped off, string can be used to measure off distances, and so on…

iii. Explore transforming them into objects, animals, people even, that have no actual connection with their normal or possible use.

5. Do they satisfyingly reinforce the nature of the story, its theme, environment and details of plot? Do they reinforce the nature of the world you're creating? Evaluate their practical possibilities. They should always be functional as well as metaphorical, otherwise they won't become integrated into the performance, merely a comment on it.

WORKSHOP 44: WORKING WITH PROPS

Actors like props. Unfortunately, if they get their hands on them too early, props can become distractions, a means of avoidance or denial, taking focus at the expense of text and action. Actors can hide behind props. Their right to use props has to be earned. Actors shouldn't be allowed near them until they profoundly, achingly, need them. The relief when they finally get hold of them will ensure they use them expressively, and through them convey all manner of subtleties and subtext.

The following exercises are designed to develop the actors' ability to handle props expressively and accurately.

A. Creating a Mimed Activity

1. It's probably a good idea, as with some other exercises, to split the group into two, so that the actors can observe each other.

2. Instruct the actors to carry out, *in mime*, a mundane, repetitious and continuous activity involving props, such as drying dishes, shelling peas, ironing, scrubbing a floor, giving themselves a manicure, sawing logs…

3. Instruct them not to create any particular circumstance and in no way to dramatise the action or make a story. They quite simply carry out the activity. They should be prepared to execute it indefinitely (until you stop the exercise).

4. Coach them to be specific in the handling of their imaginary objects:

> Feel the texture – rough, smooth, damp, dry, hot, cold, abrasive…

> Create the nature of the material – rigid, rubbery, flexible, jointed, floppy, fryable, fragile…

> Establish the weight.

> Define the size and shape.

> Allow enough space when you move them, especially in relation to your body or the floor.

> Remind yourself which muscles are most activated by their use.

5. Point out that this activity is an action: to sew on the buttons, to knit the sweater, to wash the windows…

6. Once the activity is well established, ask the actors to give themselves a reason (an objective) for doing this activity; preferably one which involves another (absent) person, such as to fulfil a promise, to give a surprise, to prove a point… Instruct them to make the purpose and the person very specific. Don't stop the exercise for these instructions; give them while they continue to work on the activity.

7. Observe how the purpose makes the mimed object more concrete and informs the activity with greater expressiveness. This is because their concentration on the technical accuracy of their execution has been replaced by their concentration on the imaginary circumstances. The activity is now serving the objective.

8. To enrich the exercise, you can, if you so wish, give them points of concentration or preoccupations; given circumstances such as where they are carrying out the activity, at what time of day or night, whether it's hot or cold, etc.…

9. Encourage them to keep their purpose alive and, in fact, to intensify and elaborate it. Urge them to commit as much as they can both to the action and the objective. And to keep the given circumstances alive.

10. Finally, when you feel that they have sufficiently embodied the activity and inhabited the situation, bring the exercise to a conclusion.

11. Point out that, just as the activity was their action, their purpose in carrying out the activity was their objective. The given circumstances in which they were doing it were points of concentration. In other words, they were acting.

12. Have a brief discussion in which those watching can state what they observed. Frequently, the imaginary props become increasingly 'real'. The way the actors handle them usually reveals their states of mind.

13. If they're the sort of props that are reasonably available in a rehearsal room or workshop, you might ask them to repeat the exercise, now using the real objects. Observe how alive and expressive the props and their handling become. The actors will have developed a need for these props and in consequence will handle them with great specificity.

14. You can apply this exercise to rehearsals. If there is a scene in which, for example, the characters prepare and sit down to a meal, first have them play the entire scene miming the props (and food), then provide them with the props (and food) and let them repeat it.

B. Props as an Extension of the Actor's Expressiveness

1. As in A, let each actor chose an activity which needs objects.

2. This time, they start *with the props in their hands*. Let them exercise the activity technically until they feel comfortable with them and know what they're doing.

3. Coach them through a serious of imagined circumstances (They're about to go on a first date; they've just been fired; they've had a row with a close friend, etc....) Watch to see if the handling of the props conveys or expresses some aspects of the state the actor might be experiencing. Coach them from one circumstance to another without feeling any need to make logical connection between them. But allow the actors enough time to absorb each new circumstance before you move on to the next. Occasionally give the actors a brief interval in which they put their concentration back on the actual activity without any imagined condition.

In this exercise, the props should become an extension of the actor/character. The handling of the object should reveal to the audience something about the character they didn't necessarily know before. Don't advise the actors of this beforehand, otherwise they may deliberately try to give you the result they think you want. Let them discover it in action, allowing the circumstances to have their effect on them.

C. Endowing Props with a Life of Their Own

1. Use actual props. Let the actors have a problem with an object; it won't do what they want it to, for example, a shirt refuses to be buttoned or a chair doesn't want to be sat on.

2. Let the actor try to give the object a life of its own so that it develops a personality with attitude. Let the actor have a quarrel or fight with the object. In this exercise, the object becomes another character, most of the time in conflict with the actor. Of course, the object can also collaborate with the performer. Effectively, each actor is playing a scene with a prop as partner.

D. Developing the Handling of Mimed Objects

1. Divide a flat surface, such as a table, into eight imaginary spaces. Leaving one empty, place in each of the remaining seven an imaginary object, such as an overripe peach, a mug brim-full of boiling hot tea, a rose with a very prickly stem, a sharp double-edged razor blade, a heavy weight for old-fashioned kitchen scales, and so forth.

2. The participants in the workshop must first memorise where the imaginary objects are placed.

3. In turn, they move, in mime, one of the objects into the empty space currently available.

4. The actors have to handle the imaginary item with care and accuracy and to remember, when their turn comes, in which space each object currently resides and which is now the vacated space.

5. This is obviously useful for precision in handling mimed objects and accuracy in placing them. It's also good for concentration.

6. You can develop this exercise into moving larger mimed objects to different areas in the rehearsal space.

E. Transforming Objects

1. The group stand in a circle.

2. Hand one of the actors any object or prop that is to hand – a chair, broom etc....

3. The actor transforms the object by the way he or she handles and relates to it.

4. That actor then hands the object in its transformed state to a neighbour.

5. The neighbour receives it as such and then transforms it into something else and passes this to the next actor.

6. Continue until everyone in the circle has taken a turn; or if the group imagination is really flourishing, let the exercise continue around the circle a second time.

7. Repeat the process with another object.

Note: The Exercises for Hands [*Cross-refer Set 2, Workshop 8: Hands*] will, of course, enhance and refine your work on handling props.

WORKSHOP 45: SOMETHING TO SIT ON

An empty space should mean a space with nothing in it apart from the actors. This works totally well as long as the world being created is one in which people need only stand or in which constant and varied contact with the ground is part of the culture. However, of necessity, purity has to be sullied and emptiness encroached upon if a world requires the actors to sit or to lie on something raised. To enact sitting without support, certainly for any length of time, would be an unreasonable demand on even the most skilfully athletic of mimes; to mime lying on a bed would need a sadhu's powers of levitation.

What sort of seating you choose – stools, benches, chairs with all their variations of size, shape, material, as well as objects like luggage – will very much depend on the world you're trying to create. [*Cross-refer this Set 9, Workshop 43 above*]

Chairs

Chairs, I think, merit a section to themselves. There have been times, I must admit, when the challenge – the stimulation – to the imagination caused by the restraints of budget began to fade, and I never again wanted to look at a stageful of chairs! But those were momentary lapses in the faith of a believer, from which I recovered with redoubled commitment. Chairs in an empty space become surprisingly beautiful and take on a significance far beyond their actual appearance or purpose. They are, of all objects, the ones that seem most able to lend themselves to all manner of possibilities. Their use can range from literally providing something to sit on to defining spaces, from structuring architectural forms to being transformed into whatever else in the way of props might be needed. Their shape also evokes the presence of human beings.

One might consider beds of greater resonance, being the site of key moments in life: 'birth, and copulation, and death' – and sickness, too, as well as Sunday morning lie-ins. But they're cumbersome, not particularly supportive, only fit for lying on, which tends to incapacitate actors and remove them from a good relationship with the audience. A chair gives firm support, is easy to move and use at all angles. It can be sat on conventionally or straddled à la Dietrich, leaned on, stood on, perched on, have one foot raised on. The back can be sat on with feet on the seat, laps can be sat on in it. It can be tilted back on one or two legs. You might, seated on it, even be held aloft by a Chinese acrobat on a unicycle. Chairs can be made of wood, moulded plastic, straw, wicker, cane, rush, leather, aluminium, they can be upholstered and padded; they have a multiplicity of backs, narrow and high, spindled, slatted, solid, carved, curved, with armrests or without, they can fold or collapse like deckchairs, they can tilt into sunbeds or recliners with built-in footrests. There are wheelchairs and chairs on castors, swivel chairs and rocking chairs, wing-back chairs, and carvers and Morris chairs and office chairs and ergonomic chairs and stacking chairs. A chair has an interesting shape – a double L; you can lay it on the floor on its back or its side and 'sit' on it in those positions. They can provide barriers. They can be built into structures. They can be transformed into other objects. They can even be worn.

1. Explore with the actors the effect of working with different sorts and sizes of chairs, stools and small benches.

2. Find the best way of deploying them in the space, picking them up, carrying them and placing them with the greatest ease and the minimum of movement and effort. What is the effect of dragging them, carrying them cradled in one's arms or held aloft over one's head?

3. Explore physical relationships with them, not necessarily realistic. See in how many ways the actors can sit on them. Endow them with life as in *Workshop 44, Exercise C.*

4. Two actors explore working with one chair.

5. Investigate the possibilities of luggage, cartons, coils of rope or other likely objects as substitutes for seating.

WORKSHOP 46: MOVING OBJECTS DURING TRANSITIONS

If you're going to use props and furniture, they're unlikely to remain in the same position throughout the performance. The problem then becomes how to move or adjust them without delaying or breaking the flow of the storytelling or drawing unnecessary attention to their redeployment. Ideally, the audience should barely be aware that this is happening. Again, you need to establish the rules by which each production deals with this matter.

If you're pursuing the convention that all the storytellers remain on stage for the duration of the performance, that automatically implies the objects they're using do the same. But rarely will all of them be in continuous use. So you need to establish an area or areas where they're to be placed when not required for action. It might be convenient – especially if chairs are a major item – that they belong in the same area from where the actors watch the performance when they, too, are not in the action. If the world of the performance is more casual or rougher, there might be a convention of shoving anything unwanted somewhere out of the way. Unless there is a particular reason to the contrary, they should be set up in their 'waiting' position at the top of the show.

You will probably find that most movement of objects will have to occur in the transition between scenes, which is more than likely to be covered by narration. Once the narrator has firmly gained the audience's attention, the rest of the company can calmly rearrange the furniture from one set-up to the next behind the narrator's back. Just so long as the audience is totally engaged with what the narrator is telling them, they will be unaware – or only subliminally aware – that any activity is taking place at all. It is, of course, the narrator's responsibility to keep the audience totally engaged with the narration. As an exception, the narrator might possibly wish to point out the 'scene change' to the audience.

If a transition occurs without any covering narration – that is, directly from one scene to the next – the actors will have to make the physical changes in the open, as it were. Again, it's unlikely that all the actors will be involved in the new scene; in which case, once the actors who start the scene have brought the audience's focus to them by the means described in *Set 7, Subset 2*, the others can move the required furniture and props around them.

If, by chance, all the actors are involved in the upcoming scene, then, as the one who starts the scene gets the audience's attention, the rest will arrange the objects in the most efficient and unobtrusive way as they 'enter' the scene. It's possible that whoever has the initiating dialogue could first get the audience's attention by moving a chair or prop.

Occasionally, a section of narrative will contain a lot of brief changes of time or place that are not full scenes, but nevertheless require a shifting of furniture or props. The technical exercises below are for the actors to develop the pertinent techniques and agility to accommodate such situations.

Every story will present its own problems and solutions. Using the above suggestions as a basis, you will have to adjust them to the particular needs of your material.

1. Spend some time with the company finding the best way of lifting, carrying and placing a chair with the minimum of effort. Obviously the design of the chair will affect how they achieve this. The most practical chairs should, of course, not be too heavy and should have a sufficiently open back so that the actors, assuming they were already seated, could, while rising, place one hand behind them to grip the rear of the seat and then carry it with them to another part of the stage, set it down beneath them and sit in it again almost in one action. Again, I recommend letting the actors explore the problem; they're usually the ones to come up with the best solutions. And they're the ones who will be dealing with the matter in performance. They should practise getting up from a chair, moving it and sitting down on it again with the minimum of effort and the fewest movements.

2. The company pairs off. One of the pair carries a chair and follows their partner. The partner moves at will around the space and can decide to sit and then get up again at any time. The chair-bearers should be ready to seat their partners at any moment without the latter needing to indicate this to them. With practice, they can develop such a rapport and such a smooth transaction that the audience barely notices. Of course, there is no talking during this exercise.

3. You can elaborate the exercise by dividing the company, half of them carrying chairs and with the responsibility to seat *any* of the other half who wishes to sit down.

4. Cover the space with piles of objects so that it resembles an obstacle course. The whole company should now be prepared to accommodate each other in any way they can as they move around the space: shifting things out of the way, helping partners to climb over objects, seating them if required. You can elaborate this exercise by adding instructions used in Contact Exercises. [*Cross-refer Set 6, Subset 1, Workshop 26: Contact Exercises, especially No 6*]

5. You can either improvise the following exercise or use text. You need two scenes with an intervening portion of narrative. Pre-set the furniture and props for the first scene. Cast the narrator and the characters in both scenes. The actors play the scene. As the scene ends, the actors 'pass the baton' to the

narrator who takes the audience's focus and delivers the narration while the others rearrange the furniture and props for the next scene. (They should, of course, have already worked out and practised this change.) The narrator completes the narration and passes the baton to the actors who play the next scene.

Note: All these exercises should be conducted with an increasing economy and efficiency of means. This encompasses learning how best to handle a particular object and to read each other's body language.

WORKSHOP 47: SOMETHING TO PUT ON

When we began telling stories, we'd already decided against the use of any elements of design or technology, and this implicitly included costume. But it would have been distracting and, indeed, false – let alone chilly – for the actors to perform naked. They had to wear something. We wanted to make clear to the audience that what they did wear was their own 'everyday' clothing, and not something to represent their characters. Accordingly, they performed in whatever they were wearing. This produced two problems: aesthetic mess and unintended significance; since clothes were the only element in the acting space apart from the actors themselves, the audience tried to derive some sort of interpretation from them. So that convention had to be rethought.

The outcome of our rethinking was that the actors should indeed wear contemporary clothes, something that was currently available and what they personally might wear. But this would be decided by four criteria: the clothes should be within the same generic type or style (e.g. evening dress, denims, leotards, tracksuits, overalls...); they should in some way enhance or suggest, by colour, cut, material and a point along the spectrum between formal and casual, something of the world we were creating; they should be comfortable both physically and aesthetically; and, finally, should not impede any stage action. So, when we were performing the exotic stories of *The First Arabian Night*, serendipity offered us what was then the fashion of tie-dyed muslin shirts, harem pants, scarves and accessories that had been made, for the most part, in India, all of which were in bright variegated patterns and colours. They were light, loose and easy to move in, and didn't inhibit the considerable physicality in the show, nor snag and tangle when the actors intertwined in intricate images. They also showed off the body which suited the erotic motif of the show. When we did *The Second Arabian Night*, a rough, urban piece of stand-up comedy, the company wore denims, jeans and T-shirts which looked and helped them feel streetwise, up-front and limber. We chose beiges and creams as these colours suggested a warm climate, athleticism and light-spiritedness. If, during the narration, there was a specific mention of clothing, the donning of a cloak, for instance, or the dropping of a veil, such references were mimed. What the actors wore was *not* what the characters were wearing.

Of course, if you release yourself from the – pure to me, austere to you, perhaps – principle of wearing clothes rather than costumes, that is, not wearing anything for scenic or dramatic effect, then you'll be confronted with endless possibilities and the need to make hard choices consistent within the world of a story and true to its conventions. The greater the rigour of the decision-making, the greater the likelihood of a satisfying choice.

As examples of possible conventions, clothes might be chosen for their ease in making quick adjustments, such as collars being worn open or buttoned, up or down. The company might wear clothes in layers that were added, one by one, to suit the development of a story or, by a reverse procedure, easily removed layer by layer as the story progressed. Maybe the actors could each have a length of material to drape or tie in anyway they saw fit. Maybe a selected kit of, say, one hat, one glove, one scarf, one cloak, and so forth, could be available for each actor; or maybe a pile of random clothing, items from which were to be grabbed by whichever actor got to the pile first. And so on. The constant questions should be: do the chosen clothes and the manner of their use enhance the flow of the performance; do they and how they're worn, put on and taken off reinforce and belong within the world of the performance?

Sometimes costume changes within the performance supports the world being depicted or strengthens its themes. In *The Black Dahlia*, changing clothes became part of the action. During scenes in locker rooms, the characters got in and out of boxing gear and police uniforms or, elsewhere, stripped off for sex and then redressed. Their rough, highly energised execution echoed the novel's stress on 'sex and violence'. The changes, effected in front of the audience, were always justified by the action. In a Shared Experience production of Arthur Schnitzler's play, *La Ronde*, ten characters, representing the entire range of *fin de siècle* Viennese society, engage in a daisy chain of ten encounters, showing them before and after sex. Two actors, elaborately dressed and accessorised in period detail down to their undergarments, played five characters apiece. The world of the play is both realistic and satirically observant of social and sexual hypocrisies. The actors needed to wear authentic clothes because so much of the action was focused on the minutiae of their being removed and re-donned. This was technically challenging enough for the actors. But the real problem came between scenes in which one or other of the two had totally to change costume for a new character. For them to have vanished into the wings to do so would have made tiresome delays in the flow of the what is written as a relentless round of sex. The practical solution to a difficult problem became a positive contribution to the performance. We decided that their elaborate costume changes should become scenes in themselves. Focusing on the act of changing clothes – and hairstyles – reinforced the themes of class distinctions and class similarities, sexual desire and sexual dishonesty, and informed the actors' transitions from one character to the next, while displaying their virtuosity in getting elegantly in and out of authentic clothes without resort to rigged costumes – or the dreaded sound of Velcro.

But let me stress again: whatever solutions you come up with, they should conform rigorously to the chosen convention. They should not hold up or slow down the flow of a story. Nor should they, by sending the actors offstage to change, destroy the presence of a group of storytellers holding between them the structure of the tale they're telling. The issue of what actors wear is surprisingly difficult to resolve: not only does it involve matters of image, truth to convention and flow of action, but, unavoidably, the sheer practical, technical and, finally, unpredictable process of human beings actually getting in and out of clothes that seem determined to sabotage them.

Clothes are a profound part of how we see ourselves or wish to present ourselves. They can tell a whole cultural and psychological story about a character. So whatever convention you decide upon, the particular significance of clothes in a story has to be very much absorbed into the actors' performances.

---

1. Get the company or class to do a bit of dressing up. If you have access to them, bring into the rehearsal or workshop some racks of old clothes or costumes, hats, shoe, gloves. Let them work with just one basic item: a hat, a pair of shoes, a pair of gloves, a scarf. Let that item become an extension and an expression of a character, suggested by what they have chosen. Be sure to discourage anyone who immediately dons a cliché. Find different ways of wearing or using each item. Search for its expressive possibilities. The actors should imagine and then indicate (by mime) what other items of clothing that one piece suggested.

2. Eventually, let them put together a complete outfit. See if the actors can gradually, item by item of clothing, and maybe jewellery, bring a character to life. The donning of each piece should suggest a particular element of the character. Make sure they explore the weight, the movement, the texture, the size and shape of the clothes. Explore how they move in the clothes, standing, sitting and so forth; find out how particular clothes affect their relationship to the space; and the relationship of one wearer to another.

Shoes

Working in an empty space, shoes, like chairs, need a special consideration of their own. Of everything we wear, they have the greatest influence on our physicality: they define our relationship to the ground, they support our entire body, they effect our balance and how we move through space. Many actors announce to the world (from the next world in the cases of Beryl Reed and Alec Guinness) that they haven't fully achieved their characterisation until they've 'put on the shoes'. On the one hand, this is an irritatingly trivial account of creating another person. On the other, there is a certain amount of truth, given the difference we experience in ourselves from going barefoot to wearing well-structured trainers or cowboy boots or four-inch stilettos or flip-flops. There's a total change in the way we feel and think as well as move. Think of Japanese women shuffling on geta or dancers turned out in ballet pumps. But there's a stereotypical image that accompanies some footwear which is hard to shake off – and can, to a certain degree, prove too easily suggestive. Trainers do make you feel sporty. And no doubt having to thrust the pelvis forward to maintain balance on very high heels must contribute to a sense of erotic provocation. Of course, clichés are tired truths and at times may be just what's required. But the far more interesting way of working with footwear is to banish all preconceptions and allow what's on your feet to have its actual effect on you. Walk around in the shoes, let your body experience the physical sensations they stimulate and allow these to affect your attitudes and feelings, in short, to 'tell' you who you might be and in what frame of mind. You'll achieve an aspect of character more authentic, more individually yours. So even if you *do* end up feeling athletic in trainers or sexy in heels, it will be *your* sense of athleticism, *your* sense of sexiness, rather than some generalised imitation.

SET 10

WORKSHOPS FOR WORLDS
48–49

Every new production is, or should be, a new world. There are no rules for creating a world, only some principles, one being that a world should be true to itself, that its components should be consistent; another is that the physical world of a performance should derive from the text, the story and its language, rather than being imposed upon it. This, for me, is the most creative, the most open-ended aspect of evolving a production. Its realisation is the purpose of rehearsals: the discovery and embodiment of the rules of the particular game that the actors are going to play on this occasion, ideally a game that has never been played before.

To exercise your understanding of the concept of worlds, here are a couple of suggestions. But, really, you'll need to invent exercises of your own to accommodate the specific material you're working with. Every story is and demands a unique world of its own.

WORKSHOP 48: DEVELOPING WORLDS FROM OTHER DISCIPLINES

Worlds from Portraits

A

Gather several portraits, each of which is in the uniquely identifiable style of its artist, such as Modigliani, Kokoschka, Gainsborough, Freud… Or cartoonists such as Gerald Scarfe and Saul Steinberg. Have the actors study them and deconstruct the elements that have gone into their creation. From these, make reasonable conjectures as to the sort of reality in which the sitters exist. Looking as they do, how do they move, talk and sound? How might they think? What sort of language might they use, what sort of environment might they live in, how might they use space, what might be the dominant energy, rhythm and tempo of their world, which elements from our actuality are dominant in theirs and which absent, at what level are these elements portrayed (realistic, heightened, lightly sketched, and so forth)? How much of our own understanding, intelligence and knowledge must we filter out to inhabit their psyches? How much of theirs should we (try to) acquire?

1. Taking one portrait at a time, say one by Modigliani, let the actors work individually: first, responding spontaneously to the portrait physically, then maybe making lists of its attributes with their possible implications and then embodying these.

2. Pool the group's findings. Discover what, if any, are the areas of agreement.

3. When these are established, continue, now as a group, to develop a Modigliani world in action and behaviour. What sort of objectives might these people have? What subjects might they discuss? What sort of music might they listen to? Use any means you think helpful to stimulate the creation of a unique world.

4. When you have gathered sufficient information and material, set up some improvisations for the people who exist in this world.

5. Check whether the various elements are consistent; is the world becoming self-confirming?

B

Take a text with a distinctive language and try to match it with the people who inhabit the world of an artist's vision. (You may, if you wish, use what you've been working on in Exercise A above.) Or, the reverse, try to match a painting *to* a text. You are unlikely to find perfect one-to-one equivalents. Although there may be similarities and correspondences, there's unlikely to be a total correlation between one artist's vision of life and a writer's. Of course, the choices are ultimately subjective. Can you, for instance, neatly pair up any German Expressionist artists with any German Expressionist writers? You may find that the images of several artists contribute to the realisation of one author's texts. You may find you have to adapt both visions until you feel they blend into one.

Don't take the easy route of adapting someone else's interpretation – Tenniel's illustrations for *Alice in Wonderland* or the Phiz illustrations for some of Dickens's novels – without rigorously convincing yourself of its validity.

Worlds from Music

The use of music can lead actors to launch themselves into very subjective and generalised moods. It can, by contrast, be used as an ironic counterpoint to what is happening. Neither, for the moment, is what we want. For the purposes of this work, make sure that you are analytic about what you're listening to. Music, however atmospheric, moody and evocative it may be, is constructed of specific elements. These are what you should be considering.

Is it loud or soft? Slow or fast? Is it syncopated or regularly stressed? Does it constantly modulate? Does it ripple with arpeggios or slide with glissandos? Is it in major or minor key? Staccato or legato? Does it have wide leaps between notes or stay within a very contained range? What is the underlying rhythmical structure? How many beats to the bar? Is it tonal? What is the instrumentation? Is it struck, plucked, drawn or blown? Is it blown through wood or brass? Is it a cappella? Is it dissonant or discordant? Is it resolved? Is it rhythmically danceable? Does it have complex harmonics and counterpoint? Be careful you aren't lured into simplified clichés; a lot of music will inevitably have strong cultural or national references and identities. Don't be seduced into adopting ready-made results.

Having analysed the music, try to find the physical correlations for its component parts. If, for example, the music is created by woodwinds, does that mean that the world it inhabits is constantly caught in warm little breezes, where everything flutters and ripples or gets caught in little gusts? If the wind comes through brass, does that make it a much windier world? Try to build up, as objectively as possible, physical and spatial equivalents of what the music is doing. If the music is legato, should movement be smooth, sustained, gliding? Who are the people that inhabit such a world? Are they calm? Or are they untouchable? Serene or remote? Will they move in straight lines or curves or both? Are they warm rather than cool, cool rather than warm, neither, either or both?

Some music conforms to particular genres which instantly conjure up stereotypical images? Dixieland, punk, tango... Try to transcend such images – not by denying them, but by building through them to the essence of the music. What exactly is it within some of the music, say, of early twentieth-century British composers (Vaughan Williams, Elgar...) that identifies it as pastoral and almost instantly dumps us in idyllic English landscapes; what in the music makes us visualise green fields, meadows and dells, grazing cattle, gentle streams and the like? Is it simply a cultural association that we have laid on the music? Maybe that music might suggest different worlds.

Choose a piece of music: a song, a harp sonata, a string quartet, a steel band, a consort of guitars... The instruments can be acoustical or electronic. Try to create from it a world with inhabitants who echo or parallel what the music is doing. Create the environment in which they flourish. Because music is so seductively evocative, try to be as rigorous as possible. If, say, the music moves slowly, then so must you. If it moves regularly and steadily, then so must you.

Don't, at first, be afraid to be literal. Once you are slow and steady, then you can find out where that might lead you. How does it make you think, feel, look at the world? You'll find creative freedom through initial discipline.

WORKSHOP 49: FILM LANGUAGE

This exercise is not so much to devise a particular world, as to look for devices that will help you in the devising. The components that go to make up a world should include technical matters, such as the way in which you move between different sections of a story. The techniques of film can offer some ideas worth exploring in theatrical terms.

How can one best recreate on the stage the movement of events described in fiction? Literary fiction is justifiably thought to be closer to film than to theatre, in that film and fiction both share the same flexibility of movement in time and space and possibility of changing viewpoints. There may well be, from the vast range of cinematic techniques, some that can help to transfer fiction to the stage. Without resorting to the literal use of screens or lighting (or any other technology), the actors, relying totally on themselves in the space, should explore what might be the theatrical equivalents of long-shots and close-ups, zooms, dolly and tracking shots, wipes and fades, dissolves and irises, jump-cuts, multiple soundtracks, split-screens, slow-motion and speeded action? In your experiments, you may come up with a technique that exactly suits your purposes. The aim of this workshop is to build up a repertoire, a language, of possibilities for future use.

1. Take a sequence of two scenes and try to move from one to the other via a dissolve. This means that the second scene is beginning before the first scene has completely ended; the duration in which they both exist can be of whatever length seems appropriate. Explore dissolves of different durations.

2. Then, by a fade-out and fade-in. Here one scene has to fade completely before the new scene emerges. What might the actors do in the brief interval between the two scenes?

3. Next, by an iris-out and iris-in. The iris is a closing in, usually in the shape of a circle, on a particular and relevant part of a full scene, which is then held briefly before a fast fade-out. In the reverse procedure, a very tight image is gradually expanded to reveal a full scene around it.

4. Now by a jump-cut. That is, as it says, snapping from one scene to another abruptly with no transition at all.

5. Play a sequence (narration or scene) moving between slow and speeded motion.

6. Explore any other cinematic techniques that appeal to you. For instance, moving from long-shot to close-up is really a matter of controlling space. If you fill the stage with your entire cast or group, ensuring you use the full depth, the audience's gaze will spread, as it were, to take in the whole picture – the equivalent of a long-shot. If two of the actors then move into a down-stage area (with the rest of the company giving them focus), the audience's eye will automatically shutter down to the smaller space nearer to them to watch the two in close-up. If one of those actors then moves to the other side of the stage, the audience's eye will again spread to take in both – a change of lens.

Are any of these options even possible to achieve in a technology-free space?

Frequently you will find, throughout many of these different storytelling exercises, that you have to work through clichés to arrive at something imaginative: a world both inevitable and unexpected.

These are fairly sophisticated exercises and are helped by some knowledge of art and film, and familiarity with a wide range of play or novels. I suggest them as stimulations to create techniques of your own for developing an understanding and eventual realisation of specific worlds.

SET II

WORKSHOPS TO DEVELOP MUSIC AND SOUND SCORES

50–53

These are a some of the exercises we devised while working on early storytelling projects to develop group sensitivity and to generate musical effects that could be applied improvisationally in performance. You might even generate sustained pieces of music from them.

WORKSHOP 50: JAMMING

1. The actors lie on their backs in a circle on the floor with their heads towards the centre of the circle.

2. Ideally, each performer's head should be in contact with two or more other heads. If the group is large, this may not be possible. But everyone should be physically in contact with others. The reason for skulls to touch is so that they can feel the vibrations produced by their vocal work. They can also hear more accurately the variety of sounds their partners are creating.

3. They start to generate a drone and gradually allow it to develop in any way that seems to flow from the ensemble. Different textures, tunes and rhythms will emerge.

4. No one should try to dominate the procedure or in any way impose their ideas on the rest. The sounds should emerge from an unspoken, felt agreement in the group, rather like with the mirror exercise in which neither side of the mirror leads or follows, but both allow things to occur. [*Cross-refer Set 6, Subset 1, Workshop 24: Mirror Exercise A8*]

5. When you feel that the group has learned to accomplish this with a certain amount of finesse, you can give them a particular theme as a framework within which to improvise, such as a musical genre: Dixieland, bee-bop, heavy metal, eighteenth-century chamber music, polyphonic church music... Or the style of a particular composer: Bach organ music, Debussy orchestral music... Or using a particular technique or form: humming, syncopating, clicking the tongue... Or the interpretation of an image: a storm at sea, an

Amazonian jungle at night, waking with a hangover, the pleasure of slowly drifting into sleep…

6. You should include sessions in which to listen to music.

WORKSHOP 51: PASSING MUSIC AROUND A CIRCLE

1. The group sits on the floor in a circle. Decide in which direction of travel the music is to move.

2. Someone, A, starts to create a short and *repeated* musical phrase with a melody and rhythm. She can hum, sing, whistle, drone, use the floor or her body percussively or use a combination of means to achieve the phrase.

3. When A feels secure with her phrase, she passes it to a neighbour, B. They continue repeating this phrase together.

4. When B feels ready, he stops repeating this initial phrase and *immediately* establishes a phrase of his own. This should not be derived or developed from A's phrase. Each new phrase has, musically, to harmonise with or be in counterpoint to whatever's been established while remaining unique in itself.

5. A continues to sustain her original phrase and does so until the music comes round to her a second time.

6. When B is secure with his new phrase, he passes it to neighbour C; B and C sing this phrase together. (A, of course, keeps her original phrase going.)

7. When C feels ready, she switches from B's phrase to another phrase. B continues to sustain his phrase. As does A.

8. When C feels ready, she passes it on to neighbour D and they perform it together briefly. So now A, B and C are each performing their original phrases while D creates a new phrase.

9. And so on around the circle until the last person, say J, passes a new phrase back to A, who creates a new phrase which can continue around the circle again, if you so wish. Before J passes on a new phrase, there will be ten phrases being performed simultaneously.

10. Make sure each person keeps their own repeated phrase going after they have passed it on. If it's a large circle and the exchanges slow, it can be an effort to sustain the repetition. If someone's tongue or jaw is getting tired or tense, they can, briefly, relax, ensuring they still retain their beat, and allow themselves some recovery time before resuming their phrase.

11. This exercise can be developed with themes as in *Stage 5 of Jamming, above*.

WORKSHOP 52: BECOMING INSTRUMENTS

You may require the company to create musical sounds specific to a particular culture. When we were working on *The Arabian Nights*, we listened to a collection of recordings specialising in Middle Eastern and North African music, categorised by country and instrument. We slowly learned the subtleties and complexities of unfamiliar rhythmic patterns. We learned to recognise the sounds of unfamiliar instruments. As we'd decided that our empty space would be truly empty (apart from the human beings who inhabited it), this automatically excluded the use of musical instruments. So the actors taught themselves to imitate them vocally or by percussive use of their bodies and the floor.

WORKSHOP 53: CREATING SOUND EFFECTS

We discovered that, apart from what it could do musically, the voice contains a potential treasury of sound effects and, further, that the rest of the body is an amazingly efficient sounding board for all sorts of aural effects. Rhythmically patting, rubbing or slapping different parts of the body, bare or clothed in different materials, can create a gallery of sounds, such as types of rainfall, horses travelling at various speeds over changing terrain, and so forth. Individual actors can create complex sounds by the simultaneous use of voice and body. As with the creation of images, the sounds that evoked the right response were not always accurate replicas of those we were trying to reproduce, but created the convincing illusion of them.

In a production of *The Seagull*, we created sounds by not creating any sounds at all, but by the actors imagining what they needed to hear (music played on the far side of a lake, departing carriages), which allowed the audience to hear in their mind's ear their own sound score.

Again, you have to decide what conventions are most apposite for the world of the story.

———

Occasionally, you do find an actor in your cast who actually is a talented musician. Years later, when Method & Madness was performing Noël Coward's *Private Lives*, we were blessed with an Elyot (the role created by Coward himself) who was a superb pianist. This allowed the performer a huge freedom in dealing with that section of the second act in which the character is required to play the piano. Instead of having to mime to a recording with all the artificiality and lack of spontaneity that this imposes, he could very much respond to the moment, playing his choice of music from a repertoire of prepared possibilities for as long or as briefly as seemed appropriate at any one performance, even in parts of the text which did not specify its use – just so long as it was justified by the action and didn't draw attention to the actor's pianistic skills for their own sake. In this way, music became an integral part of the action and an additional texture to the world of the play. A fine musician in the company can be a gift to be taken advantage of in the nicest way possible.

SET 12

WORKSHOPS TO DEVELOP
CONTACT WITH THE AUDIENCE

54–57

It's very easy for storytellers to appear to talk to their audiences, sending the story in their direction without actually making contact with them. When this happens, it's a clear indication that the actors in question are not really playing their objectives. Which, in turn, means that they're not telling a story but just declaiming a lot of lines. If I tell you a story, I do so with the hope of getting some sort of response from you – of pleasure, of concern, of amazement... If I fail to contact you, there's no possibility of receiving your reaction. The whole edifice of a piece of story-theatre collapses without its foundation: the essential requirement to talk genuinely to the audience and to interact with them, incorporating their responses into the texture of the storytelling.

WORKSHOP 54: PERSONAL STORIES

1. Each actor tells a personal story. The story should be about an event or circumstance that has had some impact on them. It's up to each actor to decide how self-revelatory they're prepared to be. They should in no way be coerced to tell anything that they don't wish to.

2. They must make very specific contact with all of their listeners. Observe the variety of ways in which they actually do contact the audience, the occasions on which the contact is clear and those on which the storyteller retreats from the audience.

3. Observe how they deal with the more personal or difficult parts of their story, what happens to their focus when they attempt to remember more painful details.

4. They must respond to the reactions of their listeners; that is to say, allow these to influence the way they continue to tell their story.

5. When they have finished the story, find out from the rest of the group whether or not they felt they were contacted, specifying the moments and the quality of the contact and the moments when they felt avoided or ignored.

6. Ask the storytellers to say when they felt they had made contact and when they had not.

7. Discuss any discrepancies between the two sets of responses.

The reason for asking actors to use stories from their own lives is to supply them with material in which they have an investment. If the story matters to them, they'll be more than likely to make a strong commitment to the telling, an intensity which makes the story that much more vivid, that much more personal. This may throw into relief any less commitment in previous attempts at narration and help to improve their future contact with an audience.

WORKSHOP 55: OBJECTIVES TOWARDS THE AUDIENCE

1. The actors, in turn, tell the same story, preferably one they all know well.

2. They each choose a very specific objective of their own, that is, a clear reason for wanting to tell the story to their listeners, e.g. to make their hair stand on end, to make them laugh, to offer them something to think about, something that perhaps had never occurred to them...

3. The actors must respond to the reactions of the audience. If they are truly playing their objectives, this should happen automatically. Getting or not getting the sort of response they're aiming for should make them continuously adjust the way they're telling their story. This spontaneity should be no different from that when playing a scene. The audience is the equivalent of their partners in a scene.

4. Observe how different the telling is on each occasion. Observe how the form of contact with their listeners varies with different intentions. Observe the difference in the audience's response to the story told with different objectives.

5. Discuss with the whole group. Did the audience ever feel moved, or even manipulated, to respond beyond just listening and absorbing the story? From their audiences' responses, did the storytellers feel that they had achieved their objectives?

WORKSHOP 56: ENDOWING THE AUDIENCE WITH AN IDENTITY

1. An actor tells a story or part of one, endowing the audience with a particular identity. Preferably make use of a first-person narrative, though this isn't essential. Use a text for this.

2. The same actor tells the same story a second and possibly third time, giving the audience a completely different identity on each occasion.

3. The other actors, in turn, tell their own stories two or three times each, changing the identity of the audience at each telling.

4. Having endowed the audience with a collective identity, the storyteller must, of course, have an objective that is specific to that identity.

Storytellers could identify the audience as enthusiasts of the story's author, with whom they want to indulge their own enthusiasm. Depending on the content of the material, they could treat the audience as students they were intending to instruct, or as people opposed to the sentiments in the story whose opinions they wished to shift. To refer again to *Bleak House*, storytellers playing members of the legal profession could treat the audience complicitly as professional colleagues from whom they seek approval or admiration; or, as characters who are victims of the law, they could try to shame the audience as incompetent and corrupt purveyors of justice. A storyteller playing Jo, the wretched crossing-sweeper, might treat the audience as other waifs who would understand his plight, or as charitable folk who would offer him succour.

5. Discuss. Did the audience understand or sense that they were being endowed with a particular identity? Did this endowment of the audience help or hinder the storytellers in their narration?

Note: None of this needs to be spelt out or hammered home for the audience. The audience doesn't necessarily have to know or recognise that they've been endowed with an identity. The endowment should be used as a leitmotif that sharpens the narration and gives it a more precise purpose; it's likely to heighten the story's theme.

[*Cross-refer Section 6, Attitudes to Audiences: What is the Relationship between Storytellers and Audience*]

WORKSHOP 57: SPATIAL RELATIONSHIPS BETWEEN STORYTELLERS AND AUDIENCE

These are ideas for exploring your physical relationship to the audience. These will require a flexible space. And enough people to form audiences.

1. Storytellers tell a story in such a way that the audience finds it has to move; for example, whispering so that they need to come closer to hear; or taking over more and more space so that the audience has to move into tighter groups.

2. Storytellers narrate from a position that creates the maximum impact (appropriate to the story) on the audience: from above, looking down on the audience, who have to look up at them; in a circle surrounding the audience; with the audience in a circle surrounding them…

3. Storytellers move freely amongst the audience, eliminating any established separation of space between them.

4. Storytellers divide up a story into different sections from which they take one section apiece. The audience is similarly divided into the same number of groups as there are storytellers. Each storyteller tells their part of the story to each of the audience groups in whatever sequence they can. Obviously, most or all of the audience will hear the story out of order. Find out what impact hearing the story in this way has on the different groups. Did it make sense? Did hearing the end before the beginning totally spoil the story? Might there be advantages?

———

Note: Throughout any storytelling project, whether it's a day class or a long rehearsal period, make sure that there is always a sufficient number of people available as audience. In this way, the desire and ability to make real contact will become second nature for the storyteller.

Note: It's important to ensure that actors do not develop a protective storytelling persona that allows them to hide or avoid. Storytelling should always start clean and transparent and only be coloured by the demands of character, situation, function – and, of course, the story.

Note: Storytellers should always draw the audience to them, rather than thrusting themselves at the audience. You're trying to bring the audience to where the story is happening, which is in your imagination and your presence.

Note: Storytelling is a form of conversation.

SET 13

WORKSHOP TO
DRAMATISE NARRATIVE

58

I've found that one of the most stimulating aspects of using non-theatrical material is finding ways of rendering passages of narrative active and dramatic. This has often meant coming up with solutions that, as far as I knew, had not been used before. Once more, there are no formulae. Every piece of text has to be explored for its unique dramatic possibilities.

WORKSHOP 58: EXAMPLES OF POSSIBLE APPROACHES

> My Lady Dedlock has returned to her house in town for a few days previous to her departure for Paris, where her ladyship intends to stay some weeks; after which her movements are uncertain. My Lady Dedlock has been down at what she calls her 'place' in Lincolnshire. The waters are out in Lincolnshire. An arch of the bridge in the park has been sapped and sopped away. The adjacent low-lying ground, for half a mile in breadth, is a stagnant river, with melancholy trees for islands in it, and a surface punctured all over, all day long, with falling rain. My Lady Dedlock (who is childless), looking out in the early twilight from her boudoir at a keeper's lodge, and seeing the light of a fire upon the latticed window panes, and smoke rising from the chimney, and a child, chased by a woman, running out into the rain to meet the shining figure of a wrapped-up man coming through the gate, has been quite been put out of temper.

This text from *Bleak House* has as much to do with Lady Dedlock's psychology as it has to do with place and atmosphere. The description of her Lincolnshire estate and what she can see from her window reflects her inner state. So as a piece of narration, this can serve a double purpose: while telling us about the landscape, she can reveal her isolation, her restlessness, her lack of fulfilment, her emptiness, her loneliness. Watching a happy labouring family reveals everything that she is missing. An actor who is playing the character and narrating in the third person can use this as a means of making every detail personal and intimate. It becomes almost an inner monologue spoken aloud. (And of course, Dickens being Dickens and *Bleak House* being in part a mystery, he is offering the alert reader some early clues.)

———

It was one of those delightfully irregular houses where you go up and down steps out of one room into another, and where you come upon more rooms when you think you have seen all there are, and where there is a beautiful provision of little halls and passages, and where you find still older cottage-rooms in unexpected places, with lattice windows and green growth pressing through them. Mine, which we entered first, was of this kind, with an up-and-down roof, that had more corners in it than I ever counted afterwards, and a chimney (there was a wood fire on the hearth) paved all around with pure white tiles, in every one of which a bright miniature of the fire was blazing. Out of this room you went down two steps, into a charming little sitting-room, looking down upon a flower garden, which room was henceforth to belong to Ada and me. Out of this you went up three steps, into Ada's bedroom, which had a fine broad window, commanding a beautiful view, to which there was a hollow window-seat, in which, with a spring-lock, three dear Ada's might have been lost at once. Out of this room, you passed into a little gallery, with which the other best rooms (only two) communicated, and so, by a little staircase of shallow steps, with a number of corner stairs in it, considering its length, down into a hall. But if, instead of going out of Ada's door, you came back into my room, and went out at the door by which you had entered it, and turned up a few crooked steps that branched off at an unexpected manner from the stairs, you came on Richard's room, which was part-library, part sitting-room, part bedroom, and seemed indeed a comfortable compound of many rooms.

We've already described occasions in which narrative can be used as if it were dia-logue. [*Cross-refer Set 4, Workshop 17: Narrative as Dialogue*] Something similar might be applied to the above passage, which describes how the three orphans, Esther, Ada and Richard, discover their new home at *Bleak House*. The manner in which this passage is written expresses the excitement and happiness of their being welcomed into a caring home. Although it is written in the first person for Esther, it is, I think, justifiable to share this description between the three of them, so that it almost becomes dialogue as they dart from room to room. So again, the descrip-tion, more importantly, conveys the joy, high spirits and sense of belonging they're experiencing, rather than the architectural layout of the house. It suggests a lot of movement, not necessarily carrying out the actions described – the text already does that – but by finding additional ways to express their shared surprised delight by, for example, running in odd directions, bumping into each other, occasionally throw-ing themselves into chairs, by the two girls hugging each other, or even by standing dreamily as they narrate: by blending theatrical images with the literary images. [*Cross-refer Section 8: Why Not? Doubling the Information*]

RICHARD	It was one of those delightfully irregular houses where you go up and down steps out of one room into another and –
ADA	and where you come upon more rooms when you think you have seen all there are and where -
ESTHER	and where there is a beautiful provision of little halls and passages
ADA	and where you find still older cottage rooms in unexpected places with –
RICHARD	with lattice windows and green growth pressing through them.
ESTHER	Mine, which we entered first, was of this kind
ADA *and* ESTHER	with an up-and-down roof
ESTHER	that had more corners in it than I ever counted afterwards, and a chimney
RICHARD	– there was a wood fire on the hearth –
ESTHER	paved all around with pure white tiles in every one of which a bright miniature of the fire was blazing.
ADA	Out of this room you went down two steps, into a charming little sitting-room, looking down upon a flower garden,
RICHARD	which room was henceforth to belong to
ESTHER	Ada and me!
ADA	Out of this you went up three steps,
RICHARD *and* ESTHER	into Ada's bedroom,
ADA	which had a fine broad window, commanding a beautiful view, to which there was a hollow window-seat,
RICHARD	in which, with a spring-lock, three dear Ada's might have been lost at once.

And so on...

You could divide this excerpt between them in many ways and combinations, but whenever the original narrator (Esther) is clearly expressing what sounds personal to her, the actor playing Esther might need to retain such lines for herself. There would have to be decisions as to which lines, if any at all, were preferable for Esther to narrate to the audience and as to whether Richard and Ada could ever address the audience or should treat their text entirely as dialogue (probably the latter). It's possible that the three actors could learn the entire section and be free to interrupt or overlap each other or all talk at once. Once again, there is a myriad of small decisions to be made. But the overriding intention, of course, is to find the manner that best expresses their shared delight, their sense of security, of being cared for, and their growing intimacy (all three met for the first time only the day before).

———

The opening sequence from *A Tale of Two Cities* might be transformed into an after-dinner conversation between port-drinking club members alternating with a debate between working-class ale-drinkers in a tavern. The past tense is changed to the present.

CLUB DRINKER A   It is the best of times.

TAVERN DRINKER B   It's the worst of times.

CLUB DRINKER C   It is the age of wisdom.

TAVERN DRINKER D   It's the age of foolishness.

CLUB DRINKER A   It is the epoch of belief.

TAVERN DRINKER B   It's the epoch of incredulity

CLUB DRINKER C   It is the season of Light.

TAVERN DRINKER D   It's the season of Darkness.

CLUB DRINKER A   It is the spring of hope.

TAVERN DRINKER B   It's the winter of despair.

CLUB DRINKER C   There is a king with a large jaw and a queen with a plain face on the throne of England.

TAVERN DRINKER D   There is a king with a large jaw and a queen with a fair face on the throne of France.

CLUB DRINKER A   In both countries it's clearer than crystal to the lords of the State preserves of loaves and fishes, that things in general are settled for ever.

TAVERN DRINKER B   It's likely that in the woods of France and Norway, there are growing trees, already marked to

> come down and make a certain movable framework with
> a sack and a knife in it...

This passage could also be treated as a history lecture. Or a debate between two professors of history with opposing views.

———

These examples are merely indications of possibilities you might find in the narrative. But every story should stimulate your imagination to make discoveries of your own.

Note: A reminder: the point of this exploration of narrative is to find viable, dramatic ways of *retaining the original language* of the writer. [*Cross-refer Set 4, Workshop 17: Narrative as Dialogue; Section 8: Converting Free Indirect Discourse into Direct Speech*]

SET 14

WORKSHOP FOR PLOT

59

WORKSHOP 59: LOGIC AND DEXTERITY IN HANDLING PLOTS

These exercises are not about interpretation. They're concerned with the clarity and logic of a story, the common sense of it, constantly applying the seven basic questions. They are quite advanced and require considerable skill and dexterity in narration. [*Cross-refer Section 5: Plot; Set 2, Workshop 6: Logic, especially Seven Questions*]

1. The group familiarises itself with the plot of an existing story in reasonable detail, chronologically and with sufficient knowledge of the characters' motivations to make sense of the events.

2. One person begins to tell the story from the beginning.

3. At any convenient point, another actor can, unplanned, take over the story; and then any of the others, including the original narrator.

4. Each narrator has to ensure that they continue the logic set up by the previous narrator. If they're aware that their predecessors have omitted something of relevance, they must find a way to insert it within their own narration in the most convincing way possible (not as if correcting a lapse). They must also try to justify and make use of all the details of their predecessors, even if they seem arbitrary.

A. An Alternative

1a. As an option, the group leader, director or teacher can decide to call out who should take over the story – and at which point. This, too, must not be decided in advance.

B. A Variation

1b. The actor who starts the sequence can decide to open the story, not at its natural beginning, but from some further point in its plot, even at its denouement.

2b. The subsequent narrators now need to adjust their narratives to accommodate this departure and ensure the entire plot is eventually covered.

Improvised Elaborations

C. One Plot

1c. Now try the exercise without learning the plot of an existing story. This time, whoever starts the exercise, improvises a story.

2c. Those who follow will have to be dexterous about sustaining a logic while juggling facts and characters that may at times appear to be arbitrary or unmotivated. They may also need to find justifiable ways of eliminating or qualifying facts that can in no way make sense in terms of plot logic. Including the initiator, they can participate in any order and as frequently as they wish if they see a way to clarify or improve the story's progress.

D. Multiple Plots

1d. Another improvised telling. I would use no more than three or four actors at a time for this. The actors each prepare an improvised story of their own. They do not share their stories with the others beforehand. The only things they need to agree on is the genre (folk tale, fairy story, a piece of realism), and where and when their stories take place. Other than that, they learn about them as they hear them narrated.

2d. Actor A begins a story but doesn't complete it. Whoever is leading this session will probably have to decide at which point to stop each storyteller.

3d. The other actors in turn, begin their own stories. They can, if they wish, imply or make some light connection to that first story of A, should they see the possibility.

4d. The second time around (not necessarily in the same sequence), anyone can develop either their own story or someone else's, and make further connections to the initial story of A. A, however, must always stay with their original story, incorporating where and if possible, additions from the other stories.

5d. They continue until Story A reaches some sort of conclusion. Ideally, most of the contents of the other stories should have found their way into A's narrative.

6d. What you're trying to achieve is the equivalent of a multistranded novel with its central plot (that of A) and several tributary plots flowing into it. You're also trying to develop the actors' ingenuity in sustaining logical and coherent plotting. This is not an easy exercise and needs a lot of skill. You should probably come to it by way of a lot of work on the earlier exercises.

For Two Actors

E. Collaborating

1e. Two actors share the telling of a story that they both know well. Apart from deciding on the story, there must be no planning.

2e. They have very different attitudes to the nature and qualities of the story, and slight variations of minor details, which each wants to persuade the audience is the correct version.

3e. Without appearing to contradict or disagree with their partner, they must share the narration as harmoniously as possible while attempting to absorb or refute each other's variations and attitudes to the material as convincingly as they can.

4e. In the pursuit of their individual takes on the story, some events and facts may get confused; it is their shared duty not to lose the logic of the plot.

F. Supportively Interfering

1f. A tells a story.

2f. B is totally positive towards A and the story and tries to be supportive: agreeing with whatever A says, filling in details that A might have missed (or so B thinks) and repeating details that should be emphasised for the audience (or so B thinks).

3. A tries to continue the story as smoothly as possible, handling B's contributions in the least disruptive way possible.

G. Critically Interfering

1g. A tells a story.

2g. B is negative towards the story and in total disagreement with A, constantly critical, and trying to put the audience straight about A's inaccuracies.

3g. Once again, A tries to sustain the narration as smoothly as possible, handling B in a way that A hopes will allow the story to be completed.

SET 15

WORKSHOP FOR
SHORT-STORY STRUCTURES

60

WORKSHOP 60: FRAMING AND LINKING STORIES

If you decide to create a performance from several short stories, the reason you made this particular selection should no doubt influence the way in which you put them together. What is the connection between the stories? Do they have a chronological progression or does each travel further back in time than its predecessor? Are stories encased, one within another, like Russian dolls? Are the stories totally discrete, apart from characters who may appear more than once? Do all the stories explore the same themes? Do they form an argument? Do characters tell each other stories as a form of advice or consolation? How stories are linked, both internally and externally, will be as important as the stories themselves, and strongly influence the nature of the world of the performance. I've already described the way in which we assembled stories in some of our own storytelling projects. [*Cross-refer Section 8: Short Stories*]

Here are a few ideas for structures to link stories:

I. Discrete Stories

I suppose it would be perfectly reasonable to chose a group of stories with nothing in common but your pleasure in them.

A	B	C	D

Some other connections might be:

A unifying character or a whole community participating in all of them: Sholem Aleichem's Tevye stories; folk tales of tricksters and fools such as, respectively, the French Reynard the Fox and the Polish-Jewish villagers of Chelm; the Compson, Sartoris and Snopes families who inhabit William Faulkner's invented Yoknapatawpha County in Mississippi and reappear in many of his novels and stories...

Authorship: stories by Hans Anderson, Guy de Maupassant, Sigmund Freud, M. R. James, Raymond Carver...

Themed authorship: Kipling's *Just So Stories*, Ovid's *Metamorphosis*, Aesop's *Fables*...

Genres: creation myths, ghost stories, anthropomorphic animal stories, historical romances, dystopias...

Myths and legends: the Bible, Greek myths, Arthurian legends...

Subject or theme: the disasters of war, parents and children, the *Titanic*...

Variations on a single story: *The Sacrifice of Isaac, Rumpelstiltskin*...

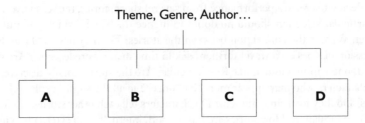

Theme, Genre, Author...

2. Linked Stories

The end of one story causes the start of another. Links could be made by character, memory, theme, location...

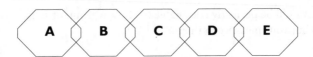

3. A Long Story

Interspersed with stories not connected by plot but by themes intended to reinforce those of the main story.

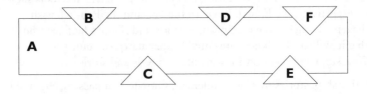

4. A Frame Story

Embracing stories within stories within stories. This will tend to be stories in which one of the characters is told a story by another character, in which that second character is told a story by another character, in which yet another character... but frequently returning to the frame story.

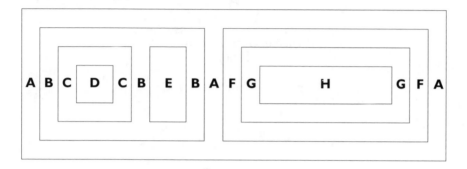

5. One Story Leads to Another Story

Which leads to another, all incomplete... until the final story resolves them all.

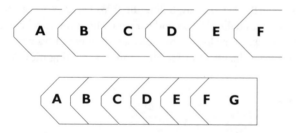

6. Stories Told Within the Context of a Trial or Debate

In which each side brings a new story to refute the arguments of their opponents and to strengthen their own.

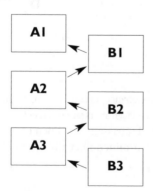

7. A Group of Storytellers Compete

(a) to tell the best story, (b) to tell the same story most effectively, (c) to illustrate a common theme by the most appropriate story...

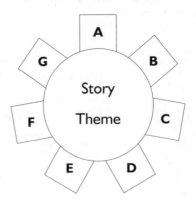

8. Multiple Concurrent Frame Stories

In which the first narrator tells us a story which frames a second narrator telling the first narrator a story which frames a third narrator telling the second narrator a story which frames a fourth narrator, say, telling the third narrator a story from which the third narrator resumes telling the second narrator who resumes telling the first narrator who completes the story for us: an increasing number of frames with a sequence of narrators, creating the effect of receding mirrors yielding multiple reflections...

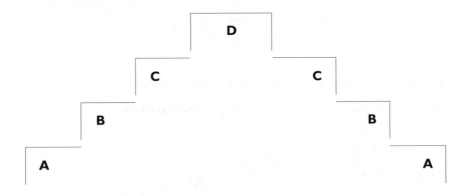

As a somewhat academic exercise, create groups of stories, randomly selected from totally different sources (for instance, Greek myths, Grimm's fairytales, stories from Chelm, De Maupassant...). Then try to find structures that will shape them into cohesive productions with strong identities.

HAPPILY EVER AFTER

Summing Up

Storytelling in theatre starts with an actor, a story, an empty space and an audience.

Storytelling activates the imagination of both the teller and the listener/watcher.

In storytelling, the actor's super-objective is to tell the story to the audience. That means that every activity carried out by the actor during the performance, from moving a chair to watching the other actors, contributes to the flow, the logic and the development of the story.

Storytellers contain the entire story within themselves. The storyteller is implicitly present within the actor at all times, whatever other roles and functions that actor might be fulfilling.

All storytellers should ideally be onstage throughout the performance.

Every storyteller is responsible for every part of the performance.

The purest space from which to tell a story is an empty one.

The incorporation of any element of technology or design should only occur after rigorous questioning proves its necessity.

Any technology or design that *is* decided upon must be within the storyteller's creative and expressive control.

When narrating, storytellers must be in genuine contact with their audience, open to respond spontaneously to *their* responses and to incorporate this interaction into the manner in which the narrative proceeds.

Every story should live within the rules and conventions of a world which is uniquely its own.

Nothing should be pre-set or fixed. The only unchanging elements are the text and the conventions and rules of the world that's been created. If the performance is improvised, then, of course, even the text is free.

In adaptation, the closer you stay to the word and the spirit of the original, the more you'll find yourself in creative harmony with the story and its author.

———

I hope this book will encourage you to make discoveries of your own. Much of the work I've described will lead you to additional ways of adapting and telling stories. I have the feeling that beyond any one technique lies another and, beyond that, yet another waiting to carry you deeper into more and more fertile territory. The really exciting discoveries occur when you force yourself to struggle with the unique ingredients of each and every story. Rather than trying to make them conform to what you already know and do – or worse, removing whatever it is that's giving you a hard time – allow those problematic aspects of the story to reveal ways of doing things that are appropriate to that story alone. Ideally, with every story you tell, you should be creating a world that only this particular group of people at this particular time could have brought into existence.